# HISTORICAL ARCHAEOLOGY

# HISTORICAL ARCHAEOLOGY

*Second Edition*

## Charles E. Orser, Jr.

*University Distinguished Professor of Anthropology*
*Illinois State University*

Upper Saddle River, New Jersey 07458

Library of Congress Cataloging-in-Publication Data

Orser, Charles E.
  Historical archaeology/Charles E. Orser, Jr.—2nd ed.
    p. cm.
Includes bibliographical references.
  ISBN 0-13-111561-8
1. Archaeology and history.    I. Title.

CC77.H5077 2004
930.1'09—dc22

2003022461

**Publisher:** Nancy Roberts
**Editorial Assistant:** Lee Peterson
**Senior Marketing Manager:** Marissa Feliberty
**Marketing Assistant:** Adam Laitman
**Production Liaison:** Joanne Hakim
**Manufacturing Buyer:** Ben Smith
**Permissions Specialist:** Michael Farmer
**Cover Art Director:** Jayne Conte
**Cover Design:** Bruce Kenselaar

**Cover Image Specialist:** Karen Sanatar
**Cover Illustration/Photos:** *Helmets*—Ira Block/NGS
  Image Collection; *Island*—Getty Images Inc.—
  Hulton Archive Photos
**Photo Researcher:** Linda Sykes
**Image Permission Coordinator:** Michelina Viscusi
**Composition/Full-Service Project Management:** John
  Shannon/Pine Tree Composition, Inc.

Credits and acknowledgments borrowed from other sources and reproduced, with permission, in this textbook appear on pages 351–354.

Pearson Education LTD., London
Pearson Education Singapore, Pte. Ltd
Pearson Education Canada, Ltd.
Pearson Education -- Japan
Pearson Education Australia PTY, Limited

Pearson Education North Asia Ltd
Pearson Educación de Mexico, S.A. de C.V.
Pearson Education Malaysia, Pte. Ltd
Pearson Education, Upper Saddle River, New Jersey

ISBN 0-13-111561-8

*To Janice*

# CONTENTS

# PREFACE

Archaeology is an odd discipline. Most people have heard of it and think they know what it is, but the same people actually know very little about it. Archaeology is perhaps the most famous and yet least understood academic pursuit in existence! Movies depict us archaeologists either as bold adventurers or as absent-minded scholars digging in the shadow of lofty pyramids. We are seen cutting through dense jungles and poring over clay tablets. We get excited about ancient stone tools and faint drawings on cave walls. These images, though often quite fanciful, are not totally incorrect. Archaeologists do get excited about what we do; we love the past and we want to share our passion for it with all who will listen. Archaeology is an adventure, but it is also a sophisticated discipline that studies the entire spectrum of human history. We archaeologists investigate the full range of human life, from our origins to our modern-day urban landfills.

Archaeology, like most of today's complex areas of study, has a number of specializations. None of us can be expected to know everything about the entire sweep of human history. Some of us study ancient ways of life, while others of us concentrate on more recent history. This book explores the archaeology that focuses on modern history in all its fascinating regional, cultural, and ethnic diversity.

Historical archaeology, the archaeological study of recent history, has expanded dramatically in recent years. This book provides an introduction to this exciting field by covering its basic methods and concepts. The first three chapters describe fundamental principles, the history of the field, and basic definitions.

From there we move to consider the methods of historical archeology, and explore such topics as time and space, historical artifacts, survey, and excavation. I present some basic archaeological theories and discuss some of the archaeological research that is being conducted across the globe. My focus is on the Dutch global empire. I also briefly examine the changing face of historical archaeology, by explaining cultural resource management. We end our trip through historical archaeology with a look at career prospects in the field and at ways students like you can help save the past from senseless destruction. Major references for further study are provided at the end of the book. A glossary is also presented as an easy guide to some of the archaeologists' more technical terms.

This second edition has been significantly revised and expanded. I have corrected the mistakes from the first edition and updated many of the examples. I have also expanded the references to include works of importance published since the first edition. One new addition is the inclusion of short vignettes, I call them "time travels," at the end of each chapter. These are entirely based on archeological and historical research conducted by professional historical archaeologists. They are intended to indicate the richness of today's historical archaeology. I have included those sites that I think are interesting or which have something especially enlightening to say. I could easily have chosen thirteen other sites, because the field today is so vast and varied. My hope is that these brief examples will encourage you to explore historical archaeology further.

No one book can hope to offer an exhaustive overview of today's historical archaeology. The field is simply expanding far too rapidly for that. My goal, therefore, is to offer this brief volume to give you insights into the fascinating world of historical archaeology. An exciting field of study awaits you and you are very welcome to join us!

Charles E. Orser, Jr.
*Illinois State University*

# ACKNOWLEDGMENTS

I would like to express my thanks to Brian Fagan for guiding me through the first edition and for all his wisdom gained from years of successful writing for educational purposes. I am extremely fortunate to count Brian as a mentor.

I am also deeply grateful to all my colleagues who assisted me during the arduous task of writing this book. Many individuals graciously answered questions, supplied information, and provided illustrations, including: Douglas Armstrong, Uzi Baram, Kevin Barton, Mary Beaudry, Stephen Brighton, Eleanor Casella, David Colin Crass, James Delle, Charles Ewen, Richard A. Fox, Pedro Funari, John Halsey, Scott Hamilton, Donald Hardesty, Edward C. Harris, Robert Hoover, Katherine Hull, Gerald Kelso, Susan Kepecs, Adria La Violette, Susan Lawrence, Kenneth Lewis, Donald Linebaugh, Barbara Little, Randall McGuire, Rochelle A. Marrinan, Stephen Mrozowski, Robert Paynter, David Ryder, Prudence Rice, Elizabeth Scott, Paul Shackel, Peter Schmidt, Suzanne Spencer-Wood, W. Haio Zimmermann, and Rebecca Yamin. Please forgive me if I have inadvertently left someone out; my oversight was not intentional.

Much of the work for this second edition was completed while I was on sabbatical from Illinois State University. During this time I held a Faculty Arts Fellowship at the National University of Ireland, Galway. The sabbatical and the fellowship allowed me to work on this text relatively uninterrupted. I wish to acknowledge the Provost's Office at Illinois State University and my departmental colleagues for awarding the sabbatical. I also wish to express my sincere gratitude to John Waddell, William O'Brien, and all the members of the Department of

Archaeology, NUI Galway, for making my stay both intellectually rewarding and personally enjoyable.

I also appreciate the guidance and assistance of Nancy Roberts and all the wonderful people at Prentice Hall. Nancy's patience and the staff's professionalism have been an inspiration. I also wish to note the dedicated assistance of Linda Sykes and John Shannon. It has been a joy working with them. As well, I wish to thank the following reviewers: Beyy A. Smith, Kennesaw State University; Laurie A Wilkie, University of California–Berkeley; and Mark S. Warner, University of Idaho.

I also wish to extend my most heartfelt thanks to Janice L. Orser, who assisted with editing, reading, and many other much-appreciated tasks. I also appreciate the assistance of Jeanne M. Schultz, who helped with the illustrations.

# HISTORICAL ARCHAEOLOGY

# Chapter 1

# WHAT IS HISTORICAL ARCHAEOLOGY?

*"Archaeology has revolutionized history."*

V. Gordon Childe, 1944

In the year 1781, Thomas Jefferson, the future president of the United States, retired to the peace of his country estate at Monticello, Virginia, where he indulged a passion for academic research (Figure 1.1). Surrounded by "his family, his farm, and his books," Jefferson sat down to compile a lengthy discourse, which he entitled *Notes on the State of Virginia*. He wrote of laws and money and of products "animal, vegetable, and mineral." He was especially interested in the native peoples of his beloved state, and like many learned men of the time, he wondered about their origins. European settlers in America asked about the builders of the silent earthen mounds that dotted the landscape of the eastern United States. In some places, the mounds were majestic and flat-topped, in others small and rounded. Were the Mound Builders a vanished race who had migrated to the New World, perhaps from as far away as the Holy Land, and then constructed the great mounds after battling and subjugating the Native Americans around them? Or were the mysterious earthworks built by the forebears of the Native Americans who still lived in eastern North America? Were the mounds built by someone else entirely?

Jefferson was cautious and initially decided not to take a stand on the Mound Builders' origins. The debate raged for years among his friends, in the coffee shops of Philadelphia and Boston, and with antiquarians around the world. But unlike his contemporaries, Jefferson decided to use excavation to find conclusive information about the mysterious people.

**Figure 1.1**  Thomas Jefferson, early American archaeologist.

Jefferson chose an earthwork near the Rivanna River, a small mound that was a "repository of the dead" (Figure 1.2). In 1784, his slaves dug a perpendicular trench through the tumulus, "so that I might examine its internal structure." He recorded layers of human bones at different depths, many lying in complete confusion, "so as, on the whole, to give the idea of bones emptied promiscuously from a bag or basket."

The story of America's first scientific archaeological excavation, one of the earliest in the world, is well known. Jefferson was the first scientist to identify the Mound Builders as Native Americans. He stands as the first person in the history of archaeology to make a careful and, for his day, scientific, excavation of a Native American burial mound.

But even Jefferson, the great thinker that he was, would never have guessed that he and his contemporaries—the slaves who performed the digging, the carriage driver who drove him to the earthwork, and the merchant who sold him the

**Figure 1.2** Earthen mound in the eastern United States.

paper on which to make his pioneering notes—would one day themselves become the subject of archaeological study. Little would Jefferson suspect that two centuries later, archaeologists would comb through the soils of his estate searching for archaeological information. Perhaps he would be surprised to learn that the many common, and to him, uninteresting, objects that he and his contemporaries used in their daily lives would be unearthed with the same care and wonder that he felt toward the smoking pipes and copper ornaments of the ancient North American Mound Builders. Jefferson might even be delighted to discover that archaeology is now as much a part of the study of history as are historic buildings, faded documents, and governmental archives.

## ARCHAEOLOGY OF THE RECENT PAST

Eccentric pith-helmeted professors, ragged adventurers overcoming all odds to retrieve a priceless relic, and excavations in the shadow of great pyramids are all popular images of archaeology. Most people know that archaeology deals with ancient history and with old things, but beyond that, they may know nothing concrete about the discipline. Agatha Christie, the famed mystery writer and wife of well-known British archaeologist, Sir Max Mallowan, once remarked that she liked being married to an archaeologist because the older she became, the more he liked her! Many people assume that archaeology focuses only on the old and the venerated, and the older the better.

Nothing could be further from the truth. Today's archaeologists study the entire range of human history, from our origins in East Africa more than 2.5 million years ago to Victorian railroad stations and nineteenth-century mining towns. Some archaeologists even spend their careers researching modern garbage dumps and landfills as a way of interpreting ancient rubbish heaps, and as a dispassionate means of studying contemporary waste management. Modern archaeology is not treasure hunting, nor is it the search for mysterious lost worlds; *archaeology is simply the systematic study of humans in the past.* This general definition covers not only prehistoric technology and ancient human behavior, but also social organization, religious belief, material culture, and all aspects of human culture throughout history.

Archaeologists and historians often divide the enormous span of human existence into *prehistoric* and *historical* times. This division is merely a convenience because time creates an unbroken flow of history. In general terms, however, *prehistory* is *that portion of human history that extends before written documents and archives.* Prehistoric archaeologists deal with a very long time scale, for prehistoric archaeology is the primary source of information on 99 percent of human history. Prehistoric archaeologists investigate how early societies all over the world came into being, how they differed from one another, and how they changed through time. Their research constitutes the primary source of information on the development of native cultures the world over.

"Historical times" is a generic term that refers to *that portion of human history that begins with the appearance of written records and continues until today.* History is the story of literate societies, those that first appeared in Mesopotamia and in the Nile Valley in about 3250 B.C. But we must not be mislead by this date. Writing did not appear simultaneously in all parts of the world, and in those places we may say that prehistory continued much later. Literate civilization developed in northwest India in about 2000 B.C., in northern China by about the same time, and among the Maya of Central America about the time of Christ. Many parts of the world entered written history with the arrival of European explorers after the fifteenth century A.D. Some parts of Central Africa, New Guinea, and the Amazon Basin remained effectively in prehistoric times until this century.

Many of the world's most spectacular discoveries come from the archaeological record of the earliest civilizations. The royal library of Assyrian King Assurbanipal from Nineveh, the gold-rich tomb of Egyptian pharaoh Tutankhamun, the terra-cotta regiment buried by the tomb of Chinese emperor Xuang Ti in the second century B.C.—all properly come from historical times. The investigation of these sites can be characterized as *text-aided archaeology, archaeology carried out with the aid of historical documentation that sheds light on human life at the time.*

Many specialties exist within text-aided archaeology. Assyriologists, Egyptologists, Mayanists, and Sinologists (specialists in Chinese civilization) are just a few of the highly trained archaeologists who focus on single societies, or even minute details of a single period. In addition, classical archaeologists study the civilizations of Greece and Rome, and European medieval archaeologists investigate the abbeys, ruined churches, and residential settlements of people throughout the continent. Scholars in these text-aided realms of research concentrate on architecture and changing art styles as well as on the economic and social circumstances of past life. Finally, is *historical archaeology, the archaeological study of people documented in recent history*—like Jefferson and his contemporaries—the subject of this book.

Historical archaeology is the archaeology of a more recent past. It is a past that includes both the colonial and early modern history that most people learn in school, as well as the well-remembered history that has unfolded in living people's lifetimes. The latter is of vital importance. For historical archaeologists, the history that people carry around in their heads, their own personal experiences, is often as important, and sometimes more so, than the "official" histories in books. Historical archaeology breathes life into the arid history composed of innumerable dates and dusty personages; it animates the people who lived in the past. It treats not only kings and queens, and the rich and famous, but the common folk, the anonymous makers of history. Historical archaeologists study European colonists, African American slaves, Native American fur traders, Chinese railroad laborers, German immigrant farm wives, early Australian convicts, and all those people who built the "modern" world. These often-anonymous millions are too frequently left out of documented history. Historical archaeology offers exciting opportunities to study changing social roles in the past and the ways in which our world today was shaped by the actions and attitudes of the past.

A clear overlap exists between text-aided archaeology and historical archaeology. Historical archaeologists are text-aided archaeologists, but not all text-aided archaeologists are historical archaeologists. Both groups of historical detectives use the same techniques to locate historical records and the same critical methods to evaluate them. The difference is that historical archaeologists are interested in the most recent past. For this reason, we may also term historical archaeologists as *modern-world archaeologists*.

Historical archaeology is important not only because it is a means of studying the past, but because it has the potential to teach us about our world. We may not be able to relate to the circumstances faced by people who lived many centuries ago, except on the most basic, human level, but we can certainly achieve an understanding of the long-forgotten and often-compelling histories of once-anonymous folk. We are the descendants of these men and women.

British archaeologist Stuart Piggott once described archaeology as the "science of rubbish." He is partially right. Archaeologists do spend much of their time delving into old garbage heaps and abandoned dwellings. But it is their interest in the mundane things of the past that allows historical archaeologists to direct their eyes to the prosaic details of day-to-day history. These are the minute elements of daily life that never appear in government reports and census rolls.

In recent years, excavations at Red Bay, Labrador, have revealed astoundingly comprehensive information on sixteenth-century Basque whaling in the Strait of Belle Isle off northeastern Canada. This chapter of European history is virtually absent from the history books. The enslavement of Africans centuries ago has direct relevance to many present-day problems faced by people of African descent in the United States, many parts of Africa, South America, and the Caribbean. Historical archaeologists study African enslavement from the humble artifacts and discarded food remains found in slave quarters and plantations. One can even trace the survival of traditional African beliefs through telltale artifacts found in such sites, beliefs never mentioned in the documents kept by the slaves' masters. The trowels of archaeologists add an engrossing dimension to African American history. It reveals facts not accessible by other means. Similarly, the archaeology of early modern consumerism sheds light on current patterns of purchasing, and helps demonstrate in tangible ways how so many people in the world came to depend so profoundly on the mass, global market of today.

Prehistoric archaeology documents the emerging biologic and cultural diversity of humankind. It shows us how our earliest ancestors faced and solved the challenges of daily existence. Many of these problems, except for their antiquity, are not all that different from the dilemmas of survival faced by much of humanity today. In contrast, historical archaeology, because of its more recent focus, holds a mirror directly before the face of the contemporary world and reflects the complex roots of our own increasingly diverse society. This unique reflection of our recent past is a vital tool for achieving a better understanding of ourselves. Small wonder, then, that the rapidly growing field of historical archaeology is becoming a useful tool for social scientists and historians alike. This book describes this exciting field of modern archaeology.

## THREE PAST DEFINITIONS OF HISTORICAL ARCHAEOLOGY

Historical archaeology has strong roots in the historical preservation movement. In its earliest days, historical archaeology was a full partner in the often-herculean efforts to interpret sites of national importance to an eager public. In the United States, archaeology at places like Jamestown and Colonial Williamsburg provided many of the architectural details that made historic homes and their yards come alive for modern visitors. These preservation efforts made it clear that the lives of real men and women, once-living individuals, had to be inserted into the reconstructed buildings and landscapes. Modern historical archaeology grew out of this realization.

The new discipline borrowed much from all the other kinds of archaeology practiced before it, including many of the same excavation techniques and analytical approaches. But throughout its development, historical archaeology has also invented its own rich perspectives. As the number of archaeologists engaged in the study of the most recent centuries increased, so, too, did the definition of the discipline change. The varied interests of its rapidly growing number of practitioners has meant that the field presents an engrossing array of research opportunities and different ways of approaching history. Three definitions of historical archaeology have appeared.

### Historical Archaeology as the Study of a Period

When the Conference on Historic Sites Archaeology—the first professional historical archaeology organization founded in the United States—was organized in 1960 at the University of Florida, its expressed purpose was to focus on the "historical" period, a period that was then being defined as "post-prehistoric." Soon afterward, archaeologist Robert Schuyler defined historical archaeology simply as "the study of the material remains from any historic period." This viewpoint envisages human history as a layer cake, with the bottommost, thickest layer being prehistoric times and the thin top layer being the historical period. In between prehistory and history is a somewhat blurred era, one that is neither prehistory nor history (Figure 1.3). For example, the region of New England colonized by English settlers flourished within historical times, but the surrounding Native American peoples were technically still in prehistory. Many experts refer to the transition period, that frontier between history and prehistory, as "protohistory," or literally as pre-literate history. The noted British prehistorian Grahame Clark mentioned three archaeological periods: "autonomous prehistory," "secondary prehistory," and "history." Secondary prehistory is his term for the transition period.

The broadly defined historical archaeology envisioned by Schuyler includes numerous subfields: classical archaeology, medieval archaeology, post-medieval archaeology, historic sites archaeology, industrial archaeology, and "a series of mainly unnamed areas of research such as the study of literate civilizations in India and the Islamic world." These subfields are firmly rooted in different periods of history. Classical archaeologists study a period beginning with the Minoans around 3000 B.C. and ending with the Later Roman Empire at about A.D. 527; medieval archaeologists concentrate roughly on the A.D. 400 to 1400 period; post-medieval archaeologists focus on the period from A.D. 1450 to 1750; historic sites archaeology considers the period from A.D. 1415 to industrialization; and industrial archaeology studies the world's complex technologies after about A.D. 1750. These subfields are also linked with various parts of the world: Classical archaeology is associated with the Mediterranean and Europe, medieval and post-medieval archaeology with Europe, historic sites archaeology with the world colonized by the European superpowers, and industrial archaeology with Europe and the European post-colonial world. These periods of emphasis for the subfields of historical archaeology are somewhat arbitrary—for example, the post-medieval period in Scotland is considered to extend from 1488 to 1609—but their usage demonstrates how historical archaeology can be seen to focus on a broadly conceived historical period. Schuyler's "historic sites archaeology" approximately corresponds to our historical archaeology or modern-world archaeology.

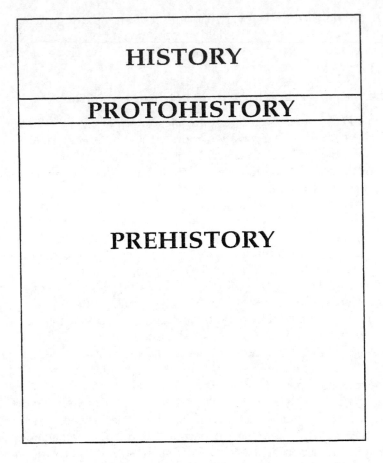

**Figure 1.3**    Representation of history, protohistory, and prehistory.

The situation in Great Britain, as suggested by Schuyler's use of the term "post-medieval archaeology" was different from that in the United States. The archaeology practiced throughout Europe was not institutionally linked with anthropology, and as a result, post-medieval archaeology developed as an extension of medieval archaeology, a subject matter than was clearly text-aided. Early post-medieval archaeologists, like many of their contemporaries in the United States and Canada, were interested in learning more about the artifacts they were uncovering at sites occupied in recent history. In 1963, K. J. Barton and John Hurst launched the Post-Medieval Ceramic Research Group in Bristol to serve as a forum for the detailed examination of glazed ceramics, a most important source for archaeologists. Barton and Hurst established 1450 as their initial date of interest and their end date as 1750. After only three years, the interest in the group's work had grown so large that they disbanded the ceramic group and started the Society for Post-Medieval Archaeology, one of today's most prestigious bodies of historical archaeologists. The general interest of the Society largely remains 1450 to 1750 history, but many post-medieval archaeologists also investigate the more recent era as well. Post-medieval archaeology in the United Kingdom is today a vibrant and active field.

The central idea that the "historical" period encompasses all those times for which written information is available is what ties the subfields together, and what makes them "historical." Pioneering historical archaeologist James Deetz, for example, argued that "the literacy of the people it studies is what sets historical archaeology apart from prehistory." In this definition, we may take the word "historical" to mean "literate," and the word "prehistoric" to mean "nonliterate." Clark's "secondary prehistory" is that time during which literate peoples came into contact with and wrote about nonliterate peoples. An archaeologist digging a sixteenth-century Portuguese settlement in Brazil would be engaged in the study of the "historical" period, but an archaeologist studying a site once inhabited by a group of nonliterate Tupinambá Indians—and described by the French friar André Thevet—would be researching the "protohistoric" period. An archaeologist investigating a Tupinambá site that shows no evidence of foreign contact and predates Portuguese involvement in Brazil would be studying "prehistoric" time.

Definitions of archaeology that divide time into two large periods make sense because "history" is, after all, widely understood as that part of the past for which documentation exists. In the Western tradition, we may imagine the historical period to begin with the Greeks and to continue, perhaps unevenly in places, until the present. In contrast, prehistory is literally that period *before* history. We may imagine that historical archaeology may be viewed as studying a period that extends from the focus of classical archaeology (from 1000 B.C.) to industrial archaeology (from A.D. 1750).

One can apply the same prehistoric/historical division to non-Western areas, like China. The Chinese past can be divided into "prehistory"—composed of Paleolithic (Old Stone Age: about 600,000–7000 B.C.) and Neolithic ("New Stone Age": about 7000–1600 B.C.) periods—and "history," beginning with the Shang civilization, around 1600 B.C. The earliest writings in China, the "oracle bones"— shoulder blades of oxen used to foretell the future and inscribed with royal divinations—serve to mark the beginning of Chinese "history." These inscriptions, corroborated by the later writings of the historian Ssu-ma Ch'ien in the first century B.C., document the uninterrupted development of Chinese writing since about 1000 B.C. Using the first definition, then, we may say that historical archaeology in China focuses on sites dating from any time since the Shang Dynasty.

### Historical Archaeology as a Method

A second, common definition of historical archaeology focuses on the methodological aspects of the field. Proponents of this approach view historical archaeology as unrestricted in time; they see the field as a research method that rests on the combined use of historical sources and archaeological data. In a study of the town of Silcott, a late nineteenth- and early twentieth-century village in Washington State, William Adams explained this approach as a diagram with two intersecting circles, "history" and "archaeology." Adams, however, also defined a second kind of archaeology, which he termed "ethnoarchaeology." In this kind of archaeology, the researcher uses written documents, archaeological findings, and even recollections of living informants to interpret the history and culture of a community. Adams illustrated this approach as three intersecting circles, labeled "history," "archaeology," and "ethnography" (Figure 1.4). Today, most archaeologists would consider his "ethnoarchaeology" simply to be historical archaeology, and they would use the term "ethnoarchaeology" in place of his "living archaeology" (which combines archaeology and ethnography).

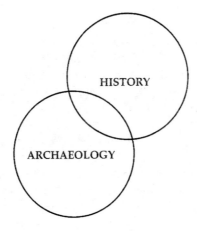

"HISTORICAL ARCHAEOLOGY"

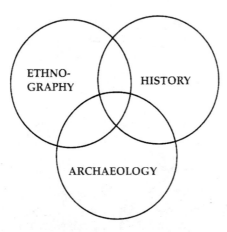

"ETHNOARCHAEOLOGY"

**Figure 1.4**   Adams's view of historical archaeology.

As an example of the rich information that living informants can offer, Adams learned that the fruit pickers in the Silcott's orchards referred to their boss, Hiram Werst, as "Hiram Fire Em." They said that he would sometimes sack a worker because he did not like the cut of his hair. Hiram could "curse for twenty minutes without repeating himself once," but he did not hold a grudge for long and would usually rehire the fired man. Adams's informants also told him that when two other Silcott residents, Weldon and Jennie Wilson, decided to build a new home using store-bought plans, they adamantly refused to place the bathroom next to the kitchen. They were dead set against an indoor toilet, and so they converted the room into a pantry.

In Adams's view, research in Mayan civilization, classical archaeology, and Egyptology all constitute historical archaeology (see Figure 1.4). The periods of history are different in each field of inquiry, but each allows archaeologists to combine so-called "nonarchaeological" materials with archaeological data, in essence working both as a historian and as an archaeologist.

Definitions that focus on the methodological aspects of historical archaeology give written records precedence over chronology. Under this rubric, we may consider Heinrich Schliemann's use of Homer's texts in his excavations at Troy in 1871 as an example of historical archaeology, as were Neville Chittick's excavations at the fourteenth-century Swahili town of Kilwa on the East Africa coast in the 1960s. We could conclude that Chittock was acting as a historical archaeologist, under Adams's definition, because he combined Islamic chronicles with archaeological materials. By the same token, Robin Birley has recovered letters written on thin slivers of wood from the Roman frontier fort at Vindolanda on Hadrian's Wall in northern Britain. These writings provide priceless information on Roman garrison life in the first century A.D.

The dates of a site's occupation are not important under the second definition of historical archaeology. What takes precedence is the presence of some form of written text—transcribed on paper, clay, stone, or whatever—that may be used by archaeologists in their efforts to interpret the past. In the late nineteenth century, British classical archaeologist David G. Hogarth distinguished between "literary documents" (that is, writings) and "material documents" (artifacts) in an effort to explain how archaeologists use "nonarchaeological" pieces of information in their research. The combined interpretation of these different kinds of "documents" defines how historical archaeology can be viewed as a methodology.

The methodological definition can be drawn even wider by including some alternate but valuable sources of historical information obtained from ethnohistory and oral history. *Ethnohistory is the study of the past using non-Western, indigenous historical records, including oral traditions.* Like historical archaeology, ethnohistory rests upon the combined use of different sources of information. It often focuses on peoples who are known to have existed in the past but who are recognized largely through the writings of outsiders. Ethnohistory became vitally important in the United States with the creation of the Indian Claims Commission in August 1946. Native groups and governmental agencies required the testimony of experts when the government began the process of terminating native tribal status. Anthropologists began to work as historians in archives and other documentary repositories, and historians started to work as anthropologists as they researched the histories of nonliterate peoples and used ethnological language. In the case *Sac and Fox Tribe of Indians, et al.* v. *The United States*, filed in 1955, for example, the Native American defendants hired ethnohistorians to prepare scholarly reports about their history and culture. Defendant's Exhibit 97 is entitled "An Anthropological Report on the Indian Occupancy [of land] Ceded to the United States by the United Tribes of Sac and Fox under the Treaty of November 3, 1804." These legal documents were terribly important to the case, and they provide significant cultural information. For instance, Defendant's Exhibit 57, "An Account of the Manners and Customs of the Sauk Nation of Indians," begins: "The original and present name of the Sauk Indians proceeds from the compound word Saw-kie alias A-saw-we-kee literally Yellow Earth. The Fox Indians call themselves Mess-qua-a-kie alias Mess-qua-we-kie literally Red Earth." Claims Commission reports are crammed with invaluable ethnohistorical information about Native American history and culture, ranging from games and dances to cosmology and language. When originally written, the documents demonstrated the power of ethnohistorical interpretation, and they pushed the study of oral sources to the cutting edge of anthropology and history.

When Hernán Cortés and his conquistadors entered the Aztec capital, Tenochtitlán, in 1519, they marveled at the sophisticated, cosmopolitan city. Its market was larger than Constantinople's (today's Istanbul). Cortés overthrew the Aztec rulers in 1521, bringing centuries of American Indian civilization to an end. Fortunately, however, Dominican friar Bernardino de Sahagun later developed a passion for Aztec culture and devoted his lifetime to recording their history. He assembled informants at strategic missions and recorded many details of a culture that were transmitted with picture signs and oral recitations. Sahagun's *History of the General Things of New Spain* was considered so heretical by his priestly superiors that it was not published until the nineteenth century. But his work is a mine of priceless ethnohistorical information for today's archaeologists and cultural historians. When Mexican archaeologist Eduardo Matos Moctezuma excavated the Templo Mayor (Great Temple) of the Aztec gods Huitzilopochtli and Tlaloc from beneath modern Mexico City, he found that many details of the structure and its history were corroborated by both Spanish accounts and Sahagun's informants.

Ethnohistory is a powerful tool for historical archaeologists, especially when combined with archaeological and conventional historical sources. It is a truly multidisciplinary form of research.

*Oral history* is *historical tradition, often genealogies, passed down from generation to generation by word of mouth.* It is transitory history in the sense that it lives in the memory, destined to vanish if not written down or passed on to the next generation. Much oral history is understandably related to family history, for tracing ties back to ancestral kin is a major concern of many societies. Maya lords were obsessed with establishing their royal legitimacy back to divine ancestors, and many Africans think of the past in terms of links to ancestors who are intermediaries with the spiritual world. Many men and women in Western societies are equally interested in understanding their genealogies and many of them spend their vacations toiling over faded manuscripts and census rolls in the world's archives.

Oral traditions treat far more than genealogies, however. They include vivid personal memories of major events like solar eclipses, wars, floods, and famines, of nineteenth-century family migrations from east to west or west to east, and so forth. Only in recent years have we fully appreciated the value of the historical memories of elderly people. In far too many cases, these valuable repositories of personal history pass away unnoticed, and their priceless legacy of historical information is lost forever.

The study of oral history has achieved great sophistication in numerous places around the world, including sub-Saharan Africa, which is rich in eighteenth- and nineteenth-century oral tradition. Many of the accounts were recorded early in the twentieth century, when memories were still vivid. Such traditions are a historical minefield, for they require careful critical analysis before they can be accepted as accurate reflections of the past. When archaeologist Peter Schmidt studied the ancient Buhaya kingdoms in East Africa, he combined oral traditions with data from archaeological and historical sources. Schmidt had to spend two to four hours with each of his informants as he learned the art of extracting relevant information from individuals who had acquired a lifetime's experience. He had to learn how to evaluate the Buhaya's rich mythology about the people's cultural origins and early migrations, and then he had to correlate them with the archaeological sites he had discovered in the field. Schmidt used the myths to tie the sites together, and in combining archaeology with oral history, he provided a truly insightful study of Iron Age metalworking.

Oral history is a vital tool in more recent American history, especially when studying the experiences of ethnic groups and working class families. Beginning as a kind of local history focused on what people could remember about themselves and their times, oral researchers, working in places like an urban neighborhood, realized that much about recent history was not written down. Instead, this history was almost entirely remembered. Tracking down the oral traditions required adopting the field methods of anthropologists and folklorists, scholars who had long experience with collecting and interpreting oral information. During his time in Tanzania, for example, Schmidt heard several stories about the founding of the Buhaya kingdoms and many accounts of their royal lineages. In one tale, he learned how the king Rugomora Mahe traveled through his domains, eventually arriving at a place where some people were smelting iron, a prehistoric technology documented by Schmidt's research. "They failed to welcome Rugomora, who, then, out of pique, changed their clan name to *Bahuge*, or 'the dull ones.'" Traveling further, Rugomora saw more people making iron tools, and he became inspired to "draw up a plan to build a tower to the heavens to see what they looked like." Schmidt's informant told him that he knew the precise spot where the iron for Rugomora's tower was smelted.

Thinking of historical archaeology as a methodology brings out a critical point. Like prehistoric archaeology, historical archaeology is a multidisciplinary enterprise. Prehistoric archaeologists draw on the researches of botanists, chemists, and zoologists, as well as many other scientists. Historical archaeologists do the same, but they use an even greater diversity of sources, including everything from documents to oral traditions, from photographs to the minute details of the technology of making nails. Historical archaeology is truly multidisciplinary detective work, the only limit being the archaeologist's creativity and ingenuity.

### Historical Archaeology as the Study of the Modern World

A third definition of historical archaeology focuses not only on chronology and on methodology, but also on a specific historical topic. In a now-classic definition, James Deetz defined historical archaeology as "the archaeology of the spread of European culture throughout the world since the fifteenth century and its impact on indigenous peoples." Although Deetz's definition contains an element of time—"since the fifteenth century"—his main idea is that historical archaeology is the archaeology of a specific subject, namely the spread of Europeans and European culture and institutions throughout the world by adventurers, explorers, merchants, and traders. As these Europeans traveled outward from their homelands and into Africa, the Far East, the New World, and the Pacific, they carried with them the ideas, perceptions, and material things with which they were familiar. Scholars sometimes refer to the interconnected network of European outposts, trading ports, and towns as a "modern world system." Historical archaeology is unique as the archaeology that studies this system and the spread of ideas and people that were part of it.

The third definition assumes that historical archaeology is a combined anthropological and historical study of the modern world. By "modern world," historical archaeologists mean the world that contained the earliest elements of our own world, such as large-scale urbanization, complex industrial production, mercantilism and capitalism, widespread literacy, long-distance travel, and contacts between large numbers of people from vastly different cultures. If there is one overriding assumption behind Deetz's definition, it is that of interconnectedness between different peoples.

The interconnectedness between far-flung human societies is nothing new, for it dates back at least to the beginnings of early civilizations in the Near East. By 2500 B.C., long-distance trade networks connected Mesopotamia with the Mediterranean and the Persian Gulf with northwest India (Figure 1.5). By 200 B.C., coastal routes around the Indian Ocean connected the Red Sea with India, Sri Lanka with China, and East Africa with Arabia. The voyages of discovery and trade created

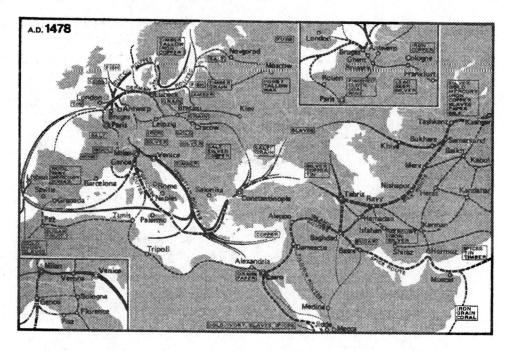

**Figure 1.5** Trade routes through the Near East.

in Asia in the fourteenth and fifteenth centuries, and the European Age of Discovery between the fifteenth and twentieth centuries expanded international trade routes to every corner of the world. In archaeological terms, these burgeoning connections are reflected in artifacts such as Ming porcelain bowls from China and majolica plates from Spain that were traded all over the world and found by archaeologists far from their places of manufacture. Ideas and spiritual beliefs, and new ways of doing things and different ways to see the world, accompanied the traders on their voyages. As a result, historical archaeologists can study Portuguese colonial settlements in central Africa, Brazil, and India, or English outposts in Virginia, South Africa, and Australia, with the understanding that each nation's settlements were part of the same global "system." In this way, many objects found by archaeologists at colonial sites in Massachusetts, and in equally dated towns in South Africa and southern England, can be expected to look similar or to be identical. The people who made, used, and discarded them were members of the same cultures who, for various reasons, lived in different parts of the globe. Deetz termed the archaeological interest in these large-scale, modern connections the "comparative international perspective" because this approach is a conscious attempt to examine the spread of Europeans across historically changing national boundaries.

Anyone who attempts to study any global issue soon discovers what geographer Peter Haggett learned: The "problem posed by any subject which aims to be global is simple and immediate: the earth's surface is so staggeringly large." To which should be added, "and its people so diverse." The use of an overt international perspective means that historical archaeologists face a formidable task, not only because of the complexity of their data, but also because they research complex interactions between rapidly changing societies.

When Portuguese explorer Bartolemeu Diaz rounded the Cape of Good Hope at the southern tip of Africa in 1488, he anchored in a bay with low hills where Khoi Khoi herders grazed their cattle (Figure 1.6). Dutch colonists settled at the Cape two centuries later, and usurped lands used by the Khoi Khoi for centuries. The Dutch forcibly evicted many Khoi Khoi from their lands and forced them to become indentured servants. This appropriation catastrophically disrupted the herders' ancient lifeways. The disruptions continued for more than a century. As a result, an archaeologist excavating a seventeenth-century colonial Dutch settlement in southern Africa must not only achieve an understanding of European history and material culture, but also must be sensitive to the complex social dynamics that governed the indigenous cattle herding in the area. The artifacts found in the region will provide unique information about social dynamics of the period.

As was the case with African American slaves in the New World, the anonymous servants came from a radically different physical and spiritual world than those people who sought to control them. Did the Khoi Khoi perpetuate their beliefs, or did they adopt the alien faith of their masters? Did they perceive advantages in adopting a European diet? Did they maintain contacts with their people still living outside the Dutch settlements? Excavators can seek answers to these important questions, but to begin their investigation they would need to know something about the complex history of at least two disparate peoples—the Dutch and the Khoi Khoi, the ever-changing nature of their cultural contacts, the material cultures used by both, and the ways in which each group exploited the natural environment (see Chapter 11).

As a result of the historical interactions of culturally distinct peoples from Europe and elsewhere, historical archaeologists see the study of the modern world as constituting the study of a process. The influence of the indigenous peoples on the foreigners who settled among them is what keeps the various colonial villages of each nation from being identical copies of cities at home. Non-Westerners reacted to, embraced, rejected, and fought against the Spanish, Dutch, English, Portuguese, French, and other colonizing cultures in diverse ways, depending on their individual circumstances, cultural traditions, and outlooks (Figure 1.7). Thus, even though Deetz tended to focus on European cultures in his definition, historical archaeologists today give equal weight to the actions and reactions of the many non-Westerners who accepted and rejected European social mores, economic ideas, political organizations, and religious beliefs and traditions. Under

**Figure 1.6**  Sixteenth-century drawing of the Khoi Khoi.

the third definition, a historical archaeologist may wish to study a particular settlement of native North Americans, not because these people lived in the "historical" or "modern" period, but because they constitute part of the history of the modern world. The actions, beliefs, and attitudes of these native peoples throughout the world are as important to the telling of world history as were the actions, beliefs, and attitudes of the powerful nation-states that are the usual stuff of basic history courses.

**Figure 1.7**   The massacre at Cholula by the Spanish, according to the Aztecs.

## DEFINING TODAY'S HISTORICAL ARCHAEOLOGY

Historical archaeologists have grappled with the complexities of these three definitions for more than a generation. At the beginning of the twenty first century we have a better understanding of the special strengths of historical archaeology, of the ways in which the field can enhance our understanding of the recent past. Current definitions of the field, which usually combine elements of the three formulations noted above, can be summarized as: *Historical archaeology is a multidisciplinary field that shares a special relationship with the formal disciplines of anthropology and history, focuses its attention on the post-prehistoric past, and seeks to understand the global nature of modern life.* Each clause in this definition is particularly important to developing a clear understanding of the nature and direction of contemporary historical archaeology. Let us dissect it a little further.

### *Historical Archaeology Is Multidisciplinary*

All modern archaeology can be said to be multidisciplinary because all archaeologists, regardless of specialization, routinely use information from a huge array of related fields, including anthropology, botany, geography, geology, sociology, and zoology. What makes historical archaeology unique is that it is *by nature* multidisciplinary. It is virtually impossible for a historical archaeologist to conduct any serious research without consulting information from other disciplines, most notably history and cultural anthropology. With their feet firmly planted in both history and anthropology, historical archaeologists regularly draw on the letters, maps, diaries, and governmental records that modern historians use, as well as the cultural anthropologist's culture histories, ethnographies, and insights. Historical archaeologists also must rely on the site maps, soil profile drawings, and artifacts that are common to all archaeological research.

Historical archaeology is text-aided archaeology because documents are a primary source of information. Documents and texts of all kinds support and supplement archaeological information to such an extent that historical archaeologists must be as adroit at archival research and documentary interpretation as they are at site research and artifact analysis. Like historians, they must be adept at locating and dissecting textual sources, but they must also be able to relate these sources to their archaeological evidence. They must decide whether a group of documents is an independent source of information on their site or region or whether it only supplements the archaeological evidence. If their assessment is that the sources are entirely independent, then the two sources—one archaeological, one documentary—will shed light on the same problems, with each possibly having equal weight. If the documentary sources are supplementary, however, then the archaeological and the historical information may cast light on the same issue in slightly different ways. In such cases, the archaeological evidence is often the most revealing of the two. Disagreement will sometimes occur between the archaeological data and the historical information, and only meticulous analysis can resolve the issue.

Suppose, for example, that we are involved in the excavation of a plantation slave cabin in the American South, dating to about the year 1800. We have excavated the cabin and found that it has a limestone foundation measuring 12 by 16 feet (3.7 by 4.8 m), and that it contains numerous artifacts—glass bottle fragments, sherds of ceramic dishes, brass buttons, clay pipes, and so forth. We also have access to a series of letters written by the plantation's owner. In one or two of these letters, the owner describes the slaves' cabins and mentions some of the articles the occupants used in their daily lives. Depending on the data at hand, we may consider the letters to supplement what we have learned from the archaeological remains, or we may think that our finds amplify what we have learned from the documents. In either case, the two sources of information work to complement one another. The letters help us understand the material remains of the excavated slave cabin, and the physical remains are a tangible amplification of the owner's comments about the slaves on his plantation.

Imagine for a moment that we decide the archaeological data and the letters are completely independent sources, with each providing a different view of the actual historical reality of the slave experience. We know that through their activities the slaves created the archaeological deposits found at the cabin site. This creative process was probably not exactly a conscious one. When a dish was broken, a button lost, or a hog bone discarded, the slaves were only living their daily lives, not seeking to leave a record of their lives for future generations. It was almost accidental that the artifacts became part of the archaeological record at all. But the plantation owner, a descendant of a different culture than his slaves, *was* consciously attempting to create a record of life at his plantation in his letters. The owner may have misrepresented the lives of his slaves, either purposefully or through his own misunderstanding of them. He may simply have written down his plans for how they might live according to his future designs for his estate. Here, we must conclude that the archaeological and the documentary sources of information are not supplementary but are actually quite distinct. Each source was created by a different sort of person for a unique reason, and each reflects the past in a disparate way.

The interpretive controversy noted above is important for historical archaeology because it forces us to continue exploring various ways of using "nonarchaeological" materials in our research. That most of the nonarchaeological sources used by historical archaeologists derive from the formal discipline of history means that text-aided archaeology has a special relationship with history, a relationship whose boundaries must be continually tested by new ideas and innovative approaches. This part of our definition draws on the idea that historical archaeology provides a useful method for examining the past, a method that combines "historical" and "archaeological" sources of information. The basic assumption is that historical archaeologists have many sources of information available to them and the failure to use them is simply bad historical archaeology.

### Historical Archaeology Focuses Its Attention on the Post-prehistoric Past

This element of our definition assumes that historical archaeology focuses on historical times rather than prehistory. Most historical archaeology described in this book concentrates on the "modern age"—the age many historians say began in A.D. 1415 with Portugal's successful capture of Ceuta in North Africa. This event was the catalyst for Prince Henry the Navigator's African explorations and the Age of Discovery that took Portuguese and other Western navigators throughout the globe. The date 1415 is, however, somewhat arbitrary, because many institutions of the "modern age" developed much earlier. For instance, some elements of modern mercantilism may be found in the ways in which Europe's Knights Templars—the powerful religious-military organization of the Middle Ages—trafficked in fabrics, wool, spices, dyes, porcelain, and glass. The link between these medieval entrepreneurs and modern industrial capitalists may be weak, but historical archaeologists understand that the practices of modern peoples can constitute tenacious traditions that extend backward in time beyond A.D. 1415. In this sense, then, we may expect some overlap between historical archaeology and European medieval archaeology based not solely on a similarity of method—although both make extensive use of written records—but on a similarity of subject matter. By the same token, the researches of historical archaeologists may overlap with investigations into the Chinese explorations of the early fifteenth century. Our basic point is that the term *post-prehistoric* signifies that historical archaeology finds much of its subject matter in those places that explorers and settlers visited in the "modern age," however we wish to define it. The term *post-prehistoric* is only meant to stand in contrast to *prehistoric*, and is meant to suggest that the world was a different place after the intercontinental spread of cultural institutions beginning sometime before A.D. 1500 and expanding dramatically after that date.

We accept the special place of literacy in helping to transform the modern world, but we do not give it a primary role in shaping recent history. Without question, the adoption in the West of a movable type printing press in 1451, after centuries of use in China, made knowledge available to more people than simply the elites of society. The effects of printed books and increasing literacy eventually did change the world, but many of the individual Europeans who traveled into the non-Western world were illiterate. The actions of these people and the ideals of the nations that drove them forward were more important than whether they could read and write.

### Historical Archaeology Seeks to Understand the Global Nature of Modern Life

Perhaps the most important facet of historical archaeology is its focus on modern life. No matter where we choose to set the beginning of "the modern world," the fundamental point is that the world of today was shaped in considerable part by compelling historical forces. The exploration of the New World, the African slave trade, the Industrial Revolution, the invention of the steamship and the railroad—these are but a few of the developments that have created our world. Many of these events and inventions affected hundreds of diverse human societies throughout the world. The invention of the steamship alone sparked human migration on a hitherto unheard-of scale in the nineteenth century. Mass cultural migration is one reason that historical archaeology is a global field that shuns often-arbitrary political boundaries in favor of large-scale events and broad processes that cemented together people and groups by their involvement in a common enterprise (such as colonial settlement, economic trade, or diaspora) or by common, historical circumstances (such as slavery or membership in a social class).

But for all this global perspective, historical archaeologists also work on a small scale, investigating in detail military forts, mining villages, colonial taverns, isolated shipwrecks, and slave cabins (Figure 1.8). They focus on the minute and the particular, on the humblest of artifacts, and on the usually anonymous people who made and used them. From these small-scale researches come new insights into the larger issues of world history.

The nations of the modern world were neither isolated nor necessarily inward-looking. Europe, for instance, was not a monolithic empire during its Age of Discovery. It was an ever-changing mosaic of competing nation-states, each with its own goals, histories, and traditions. Each had its own agenda, its own ambitions, and its special values, and each was affected by the actions and technological achievements of societies across the world. The technological innovations that helped to make it possible for Portugal to become a major world power in the sixteenth century included the astrolabe from the Near East and the magnetic compass from China. Thus, in using the term *international*, historical archaeologists generally refer both to a rising internationalism within the modern era, and to a globalization that took men and women into diverse and often remote parts of the world. This openly international focus means that historical archaeologists frequently study issues of vital concern today: multiculturalism, gender roles, the effects of exploration and settlement on native peoples and environments, racism, ethnicity, social inequality, consumerism, and the rise of the global mass market.

The prominence of these contemporary issues in our field means that historical archaeologists constantly negotiate between the past and the present. Many archaeologists now acknowledge that archaeology, although it studies the past, is part of the contemporary world. Our interpretations of the past are always bound within and constrained by our perceptions and attitudes of the present. The linkage between present and past is also the subject of much debate among prehistoric archaeologists, for some argue that archaeologists with a Western cultural perspective, however well trained, cannot legitimately interpret indigenous history. The situation is somewhat different in historical archaeology because it is obvious that our current perceptions of the recent past are shaped by our own

**Figure 1.8** Excavation of a slave cabin in Virginia.

histories and ideas. For example, the history of mass consumerism that many historical archaeologists are working diligently to document is still being played out, and we are all actors in this continuing drama. Because much of the past studied by historical archaeology is still unfolding, its practitioners find it difficult to argue that the past they study is too remote to be of relevance to the present.

The conscious internationalism of historical archaeology means that the field studies a vast array of people. Rather than focusing on an archaeological record that is essentially anonymous—as prehistorians must do because of prehistoric archaeology's general inability to identify specific individuals—historical archaeology often has the ability to concentrate on named people from the past. A great deal of archaeology has been conducted at Monticello, Jefferson's stately mansion, and on the properties of other people well known in history. More importantly, historical archaeology also has the ability to document the lives of people whose general histories may be known, but whose daily lives remain a mystery. We can explore the daily lives of slaves, factory workers, native peoples, public works laborers, farmers, colonists, and fur traders by excavating their humble abodes and workplaces. Archaeology writes the history not only of the rich and famous, but also of the common folk. Historical archaeology thus makes a priceless contribution to human history (Figure 1.9).

Douglas Armstrong's excavations at Drax Hall, Jamaica, provide a perfect case in point. Drax Hall was built on St. Ann's Bay, on the north coast of the island. This bay is where Columbus and his crew were marooned for a year and five days after his ship became infested with wood borers during his fourth voyage to the New World. During his survey of the plantation estate, Armstrong found some sixty possible house locations lying behind the mansion. These dwellings were the residences of slaves (1760–1810), transitional laborers (1810–1840), and fully freed slaves (1840–1925) (Figure 1.10). Rather than focus only on the mansion, as some earlier historical archaeologists might have done, Armstrong sought to give voice to the laborers, the people who actually provided the wealth for the William Drax family. Armstrong examined both sides of the social fence, the rich and the poor, the literate and the nonliterate.

The focus of historical archaeology means, too, that archaeologists can have a vital role to play in helping to foster national identity and ethnic pride. In the United States alone, archaeologists have uncovered African American cemeteries under the streets of New York and Philadelphia, they have documented the survival of traditional African beliefs at slave communities, and they have chronicled

**Figure 1.9**    African-American slaves at work on a plantation in the eighteenth century.

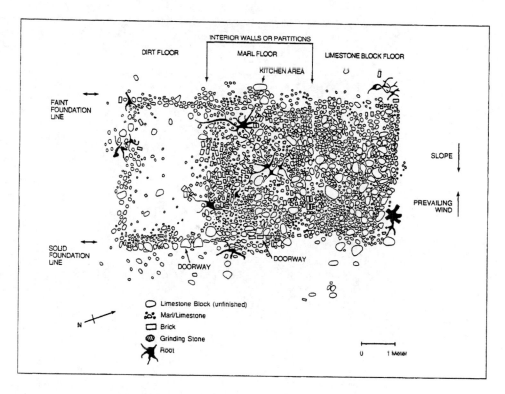

**Figure 1.10**   House remains at Drax Hall, Jamaica.

daily life at Catholic missions throughout the Southwest. Humble, day-to-day artifacts, food remains, house ruins, and myriad other seemingly insignificant finds combine into complicated jigsaw puzzles of history as compelling as any document or faded nineteenth-century photograph. It is from such finds that historical archaeologists infuse into history a human element that has too-often been ignored, pushed aside, or just plain forgotten.

Historical archaeology is far more than historic preservation and the reconstruction of stately colonial homes. It shines a searchlight into the recent past, clothing the deeds of common people with historical perspective, examining changing gender roles, and investigating ethnic communities and technological innovation. The archaeology of the recent past is more than a fascinating curiosity; it provides us with a truly multifaceted view of history during those centuries when everyone on earth became part of an ever-closer web of interconnectedness. Historical archaeology offers unrivaled opportunities for understanding the complex and often subtle forces that shaped our own evermore diverse world. Historical archaeology is changing the way we perceive our ancestors and ourselves.

## TIME TRAVEL

### *La Isabella, Hispaniola, 1493–1498*

In 1493, the Spanish built a medieval town in the New World. Columbus's second voyage across the Western Sea had been harrowing, and he, his crew, and his animals were feeling the effects of sickness and exhaustion. The weather had been harsh and unforgiving, and the crew of over one thousand were growing restless and rebellious. Columbus's goal was to build a Spanish city in the New World, a place that would serve as a central outpost of what would become the powerful Spanish empire. Knowing he had to decide a location for his town before his crew revolted, he chose a rocky promontory on the north shore of Hispaniola, in today's Haiti. He named his ill-fated town La Isabella, after the Spanish queen.

Hispaniola, like most places in what the Europeans called the New World, was neither new nor uninhabited. The islands of the Caribbean were home to the Taínos, a people who had lived in the region for generations. Inhabiting settlements that were both small hamlets and large towns (with as many as one thousand houses), the Taínos had a vibrant culture, a rich religious tradition, and leaders who could be either male or female.

Columbus and his European crew did not know what to think of the non-Christian Taínos, but they knew they would have to rely on them, at least during the first few months, for food, if for nothing else. The Taínos grew maize and manioc, and caught and ate fish, mammals, birds, rodents, and snakes. The Spanish, however, had not gone to the New World to meet strange peoples and to learn their ways. Their goals were mostly imperialistic and economic: They wanted gold and, to a lesser extent, souls for God. Given the

cultural gap between the Taínos and the Spanish invaders, it was not long before open hostilities erupted.

The design of La Isabella reflected the Spaniards' European mindset and their plans for Hispaniola. Even though he and his men were feeling the effects of sickness—either influenza or syphilis, historians disagree—Columbus immediately ordered the construction of a walled town. The wall, which they made of packed earth (called *tapia*), was clearly a defensive feature. Inside the wall they placed five structures: a customshouse and storehouse, a church, a powder house, Columbus's house, and a circular, stone watchtower. Built of stone rather than the wood and grass of the Taínos's houses, these buildings implied that the Spaniards' intentions meant that they would require defense against the Taínos. They also oriented the buildings to command the cliff and the beach. The church was the only building they had not defensively oriented; it conformed to the higher principles of Christianity and was sited east to west.

The Spanish had located Columbus's house to give it spectacular views of the area and to make it open to the fresh, ocean breezes that could temper the island's intense, tropical heat. The house served as the southwest corner of the town's defenses, and it incorporated a small watchtower on its northeast corner. The main room of the house measured over 18 by 39 feet (5.5 by 12 meters) and had a plaster floor. The house had four doors, all of which gave access to a patio or courtyard enclosed by a surrounding wall.

*(continued)*

*Source:* Kathleen Deagan and José María Cruxent, *Columbus's Outpost Among the Taínos: Spain and America at La Isabella, 1493–1498.* (New Haven: Yale University Press, 2002).

The Spanish residents of La Isabella, though far from home, lived in many ways like their countrymen and women in Spain. They surrounded themselves with plates and bowls in forms that were familiar to them, they wore finger rings and buckles, and they practiced Christianity in the settlement's church. They wore chain mail and spurs, and they armed themselves with crossbows, swords, and firearms. When their fellows died, they buried them in a manner that was completely consistent with Spanish practice. They lived a Spanish life in the Caribbean, making only a few concessions to local circumstances.

By 1497, the troubles in the colony—mostly over the scarcity of food and their deteriorating relations with the Taínos—came to a head, and a Spanish settler revolted. This man, named Roldán, questioned the authority of Columbus's administration and made alliances with groups of Taínos and disaffected Spaniards. By this time, however, the Spanish crown largely gave up on La Isabella, choosing to set their eyes on other parts of the New World. By 1498, Columbus's dreams for his colonial outpost were dashed and this town was quickly forgotten by the Spanish crown.

# Chapter 2

# A BRIEF HISTORY OF HISTORICAL ARCHAEOLOGY

*"A good half of all we see is seen through the eyes of others."*

Marc Bloch, 1953

In 1855 a Jesuit father named Félix Martin traveled westward from Montreal, Canada, to the eastern edge of Georgian Bay in what is today Ontario. Carrying with him an official commission from the Canadian government, Father Martin planned to explore and excavate the site known as Sainte Marie I, a location as important as any in early Canadian history (Figure 2.1). The Jesuit fathers had built this tiny mission, deep in the country of the Hurons, in 1639, with the hope of bringing these powerful people to the altar of Christianity. The Jesuits had established their mission with promise and hope, but only a decade later they abandoned it and burned it to the ground. Devastating smallpox epidemics and constant attacks by the more powerful Iroquois, who lived to the southeast, decimated the Huron as a people and forced the missionaries to evacuate Sainte Marie. Father Martin journeyed to Georgian Bay, as had his religious forebears 216 years earlier. Instead of going there to save souls, however, Father Martin went to record history. He drew a map of the famous mission's remains and documented the presence of the Jesuits at Georgian Bay.

The following year, similar activities were underway further south in the United States. James Hall decided to excavate the home of his famous ancestor, Miles Standish, the renowned leader of the Pilgrims of the *Mayflower*. Hall, a trained civil engineer, made careful excavations of Standish's home, faithfully recording the soil layers he found. He also mapped the stone foundation and even plotted the locations of several artifacts he uncovered during his dig.

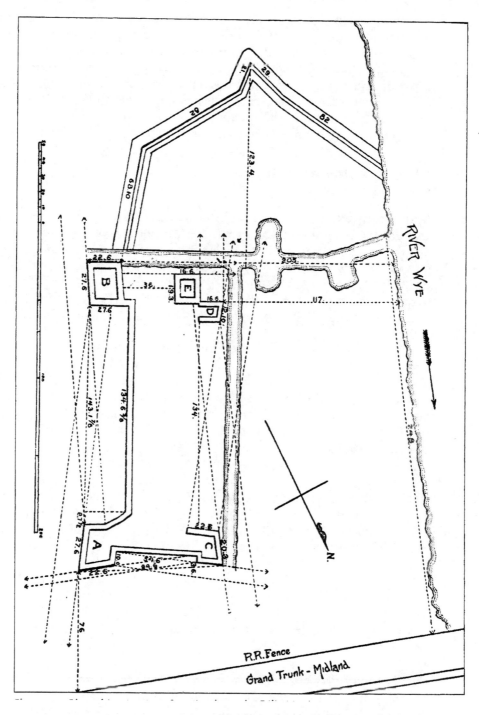

**Figure 2.1** Plan of Ste. Marie I, Ontario, drawn by Félix Martin.

These nineteenth-century investigations are the first known examples of historical archaeology in North America. This kind of exploratory archaeology has a short history compared with the more scientific, classical, and prehistoric excavations which had begun somewhat earlier. This chapter describes the early history of historical archaeology, and some of the general trends of the field as it developed in the United States and Canada. Our focus on North America is simply one of convenience. The broad trends outlined here have generally been played out in other countries where historical archaeology has developed.

## THE IMPORTANT AND THE FAMOUS (1855 TO THE 1960s)

Martin's excavations in Canada and Hall's in the United States more than a century ago would not meet the rigorous standards of today's scientific archaeology. Each man paid little attention to the minute details that fascinate archaeologists and that often disclose startlingly new information. These early excavations are nonetheless significant, not simply because they represent the first historical archaeology in North America, but also because they neatly define the scope of much of the historical archaeology that was conducted before the mid-twentieth century.

The earliest excavators tended to investigate sites associated with famous people or with events important in American or Canadian national history. In the United States, this kind of historical archaeology was sanctioned by the Historic Sites Act of 1935, which declared it a national policy "to preserve for public use historic sites, buildings, and objects of national significance for the preservation and benefit of the people of the United States." This act came five years after the Canadian National Parks Act, which stipulated the same protection for historical landmarks and objects having "national importance."

The writers of the 1935 act were undoubtedly aware that archaeology was already underway at sites having national significance. Jamestown, Virginia, was the first permanent English settlement in America (1607), the seat of the country's first legislative assembly (1619), and the locale of Bacon's Rebellion (1676–1677). President Herbert Hoover proclaimed Jamestown to be a Colonial National Monument in 1930. The first systematic excavations began there only four years later. Before the Second World War, the excavations were conducted with the support of two governmental public works agencies active during the Depression: the Emergency Conservation Work group and the Civilian Conservation Corps. In 1938, the government built an archaeological field laboratory and a storage building at Jamestown. Excavations resumed in 1954, as part of a larger plan to celebrate the town's 350th anniversary in 1957.

The archaeology at Jamestown was always dedicated to interpreting and presenting the site to tourists. Archaeologists used the excavated iron hinges and door locks, the white ceramics etched with delicate blue lines, and the foundations of the settlement's glasshouse to help interpret the history and the daily life of the town's residents. The reconstructed buildings, furnished with excavated remains or reproductions from the appropriate period, enabled visitors to experience something of what it meant to live in the seventeenth century. Jamestown's archaeologists focused on all the men and women who built and lived in the settlement, even though we most often read about the famous people we know from there—John Smith, Pocahontas, and John Rolfe. Jamestown is famous because these people lived there, but the archaeology was more about the *entire* Jamestown community.

During this period, a number of historical archaeologists specifically focused their attention on sites associated with famous people. When archaeologist Richard Hagen first thought of excavating Abraham Lincoln's two-story frame house in Springfield, Illinois, he went immediately to a reliable historical source: Lincoln's insurance policy, written by the Hartford Insurance Company on February 8, 1861. This policy protected "Abraham Lincoln of Springfield Illinois against loss or damage by fire to the amount of . . . Three Thousand and Two Hundred Dollars." Three thousand dollars protected the house, the remainder covered the carriage house and the privy. The policy carefully described Lincoln's home just in case the company had to replace it. Hagen began his excavation armed with this valuable document. He hoped to discover objects that he could directly associate with Mr. Lincoln, but he was disappointed. When he unearthed an 1857 penny and a large brass key, he could imagine that the penny had fallen from Lincoln's pocket and that some careless member of the family had lost the key. He could even "hypothesize the Lincolns' temporary distress at being locked out!" but his research could not provide the evidence for Lincoln's exact behavior. The best contribution he could make was to provide architectural details for interpreting the house and grounds. His excavations provided information about the size, shape, and location of Lincoln's carriage house and woodshed. He also provided information about the kinds of objects used by the Lincoln family, as represented by artifacts recovered from the two excavated privies.

During this period of historical archaeology's development, several archaeologists interested in Canadian history investigated a major early industry—the fur trade. Starting in 1938, archaeologist Emerson Greenman studied the trade that existed between French settlers and Native Americans who lived in Ontario's Georgian Bay region. The Ottawa River served as a convenient highway for canoes traveling west from Montreal to Lake Huron, and the route passed close to Old Birch Island, a tiny island in Georgian Bay. Greenman used written records to document the presence of both European fur traders and Native Americans in this area. The *Jesuit Relations*—letters and reports Jesuit fathers sent home to Rome to explain their missionary activities—related much of the history of the region between 1608 and 1760. Using these documents as a guide, Greenman conducted a field survey of the island. He found a Native American cemetery that included the remains of sixteen individuals in twelve graves. His discovery of brass pails, iron butcher knives, and brightly colored glass beads in the graves of these deceased men and women told him that this group of Native Americans had indeed conducted commerce with French traders from Montreal. The objects also told him that the native traders had adopted at least some European artifacts and technology into their traditional way of life.

Further west in North America, the Flood Control Act of 1944 mandated the construction of a series of dams along the Missouri River in North and South Dakota. These projects spurred the archaeological investigation of several locales important in the history of the American West. For instance, agents of the powerful Columbia Fur Trading Company built "Kipp's Post"—sometimes called "Fort Kipp"—on the Missouri River in the fall and winter of 1826–1827. The post, about fifty miles (eighty km) east of present-day Williston, North Dakota, was named for its builder, James Kipp, a Canadian fur trader of German descent who traded with the Assiniboines at this site. Traders occupied Kipp's Post until about 1828, when the larger, more important Fort Union was constructed nearby. Kipp's Post was then abandoned. Historians of the fur trade knew that Kipp's Post had been built, but they knew little else about it. European American traders only occupied the post for a short time, and they left painfully few records about their activities there. As a result, the archaeology conducted at the site provided a rare opportunity to learn about life at an important frontier outpost.

Archaeologists Alan Woolworth and Raymond Wood excavated Kipp's Post in July and August 1954 (Figure 2.2). Their careful research documented the post's long-forgotten architectural details. They learned, for instance, that the stockade around the post was 96 feet (29.3 m) on a side, with a rectangular bas-

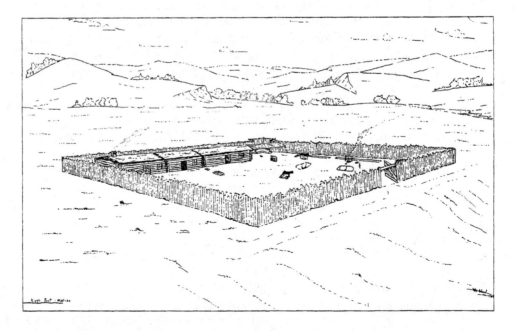

**Figure 2.2**   Artist's reconstruction of Kipp's Post, North Dakota.

tion extending 5 feet (1.5 m) beyond the northeastern corner of the enclosure. The wall posts were badly rotted, but the dark postholes that remained in the ground showed they were about 6 inches (15.2 cm) in diameter. The entrance to the post was on the south side and measured 9.5 feet (2.9 m) across. The fort's builders had placed four structures of various sizes along the back of the stockade, facing the gate. The traders must have had a cannon, but it was apparently of questionable use. Woolworth and Wood found several cannon fragments around the fort, suggesting that it had exploded during use!

The excavations at Kipp's Post also documented the commodities imported to the post. The traders ate from plain, white plates and drank from glass tumblers and white cups, but their stores contained a far wider range of artifacts that they bartered for furs—white clay smoking pipes, pieces of gold braid, small brass bells, and brass arrowheads. There were also tiny, glass beads of green, amber, blue, black, and white, spherical brass beads, and delicate, conical-shaped, silver ear bangles.

Woolworth and Wood used their extensive research to present a wonderfully detailed picture of this one small trading post on the Missouri River. Kipp's Post is but a footnote in the larger story of the North American fur trade. The two archaeologists' pioneering work, however, added remarkable detail to local history.

Even though much of the historical archaeology conducted during the field's formative years was directed toward sites of national importance, some archaeologists did turn to the study of sites that were associated with less prominent people. For example, in 1943, Adelaide and Ripley Bullen excavated the home of Lucy Foster, an African American slave who lived in Andover, Massachusetts. The Bullens published a short statement of their research in 1945, but in 1978 a larger report was presented under the authorship of archaeologist Vernon Baker.

As is true of most people who are neither prominent in the community nor wealthy, little documentary information exists about Lucy Foster. Baptismal records on file at the Andover South Parish Congregational Church include the following brief note: "July 14, 1771, Sarah, a child given to Job Foster and Lucy, a Negro. Child was baptized." These few words place Lucy Foster in Massachusetts in the 1770s. Lucy was apparently freed sometime in the early 1800s, and lived for thirty years in her cabin. She survived her later years in desperate poverty until her death of asthma in November 1845.

When the Bullens excavated Foster's home, they discovered that the house had burned and that someone had apparently rummaged through the rubble looking for something, perhaps useful building materials. The archaeology of the cellar foundation, made of dry-laid fieldstone, showed that the house was small, only 10.5–11.5 feet (3.2–3.5 m) on a side (Figure 2.3). This size of building may represent an African American tradition, because folklorists have demonstrated that the narrow, long houses built in West Africa, Haiti, and in the American South—called "shotgun" houses—generally have twelve-foot dimensions. The Bullens also excavated a shallow well, an oval pit about 3.6 feet (1.1 m) deep, and

**Figure 2.3**   Artist's reconstruction of Lucy Foster's Home in Massachusetts.

a trash dump, located just west of the cellar. When Baker compared the ceramic vessels from these archaeological features with those from a slave cabin at Cannon's Point Plantation, Georgia (see Chapter 10), he made a startling discovery. The percentages of vessel forms from the slave cabin matched those from Lucy Foster's house. At the plantation there were 44 percent serving bowls; at Foster's there were 41 percent. The slave cabin had 49 percent serving flatware (like plates), and Foster's home had 51 percent. Both sites also had a low percentage of other shapes.

Baker was unable to determine whether the similarity between the ceramic collections was an element of the African American heritage of the residents of both sites, or whether it resulted from a condition of extreme poverty (see Chapter 10). In any case, the Bullens' pioneering research, like that at Kipp's Post, showed the potential of archaeology for attacking basic historical problems.

## Theoretical Foundations

A number of archaeologists provided the theoretical foundation for much of the historical archaeology of the early period by arguing that historical archaeology was a historical pursuit. As early as 1910, archaeologist Carl Russell Fish, in a paper presented before the Wisconsin Archaeological Society, observed that "Nearly every historian should be something of an archaeologist, and every archaeologist should be something of an historian." Fish knew about the discoveries that archaeologists had made in Egypt and Assyria, and he was impressed by recent research on the Roman colonization of Britain. Viewing these excavations as historical archaeology—because the archaeologists had combined historical sources of information with excavated remains—he reasoned that the same attention could be given to American history: "we have monuments which are worthy of preservation, and which can add to our knowledge of our American ancestors."

Forty years later, J. C. Harrington, famous for his excavations at Jamestown, defined historical archaeology as an "auxiliary science to American history." He vigorously argued that the archaeology of the historical period was an "important historical tool" that should be developed and used by historians. In the early 1960s, Ivor Noël Hume, the famed excavator of Colonial Williamsburg, referred to historical archaeology as "the handmaiden of history." These authorities all viewed historical archaeology as a way to contribute unique and tangible information to the study of history.

The idea that archaeology could provide information for historians rather than for anthropologists made historical archaeology unique but not truly unusual. In fact, the view that historical archaeology is about "history" was generally consistent with the way in which prehistoric archaeologists conducted their research during this period. They thought of themselves as a "special kind of anthropologist," directing most of their efforts toward the construction of cultural chronologies. These chronologies were actually broad-brush histories of nonliterate peoples based on artifacts—stone axes, clay pots, and the like—and other archaeological evidence, rather than on written documents. Under this "culture historical approach," past cultures were defined on the basis of the artifacts collected from a certain number of key sites of the same approximate age. For instance, one archaeological culture might be defined on the basis of pottery incised with an "S" pattern, crescent-shaped copper ornaments, and the use of small, conical burial mounds. A separate archaeological culture might be identified by its undecorated pottery, round shell ornaments, and the use of large, flat-topped burial mounds. To this day, prehistorians still construct culture histories of prehistoric societies largely by using the artifacts these peoples left behind.

The creation of cultural chronologies forms the foundation of much archaeological research, whether historical or prehistoric, but the situation for historical archaeology is slightly different. The societies studied by historical archaeologists usually do not require construction by means of stratified artifacts because their histories are generally known from documentary sources. Father Martin knew that Jesuit fathers had traveled to the country of the Hurons, that they had built Ste. Marie Mission in 1639, and that in 1649 they burned it to the ground. Martin did not need to establish these historical facts because they were well documented in the available Jesuit records. His archaeological research was important, however, because he could use it to substantiate the facts and to flesh them out. How large was the mission? How did the Jesuits actually build it? Did they place the chapel in the center or near the gate? What kinds of religious objects did the Jesuits give to the Huron men, women, and children who visited the mission? These, and many other questions, are ignored in the historical records.

Two short case studies will show the way in which historical archaeology was conceived before the mid-1960s—J. C. Harrington's research at Fort Necessity, Pennsylvania, and Edward B. Jelks's excavations at Signal Hill, Newfoundland.

*Fort Necessity, Pennsylvania.* The history of Fort Necessity began in 1754 when George Washington, then a lieutenant colonel in the Virginia militia, took about 160 poorly trained men to what is today southwestern Pennsylvania. Washington was sent to this area because of French encroachments on land "notoriously known to be the property of the Crown of Great Britain." The French paid no heed to the warnings of the British because they, too, had established forts at strategic locations in North America. They were as eager as the British to control this territory. Washington's orders were to reinforce the English detachment at today's Pittsburgh and to improve the trail to the British stronghold. He did not originally plan to construct a fort, but after his troops attacked a small French force in the vicinity of Great Meadow, south of today's Pittsburgh, and killed their leader, he decided that a small fortification was needed. He and his men thus built the aptly named Fort Necessity, and so began the French and British contest for North America.

The location of the fort had never been forgotten, but its exact shape was a mystery. In 1816, a professional surveyor drew the fort as triangular, but a local historian in 1830 described it as shaped like a diamond or flattened square (Figure 2.4). The fort's precise design became important when the U.S. National Park Service decided to reconstruct it in 1932. Since documents could not settle the question of the fort's shape, the Park Service found "it necessary to supplement the scanty documentary information by archaeological exploration." When excavations finally got underway in 1952—after the Great Depression and the Second World War had considerably slowed the historic preservation movement—the objectives were "1. to settle, once and for all, the 'triangle versus

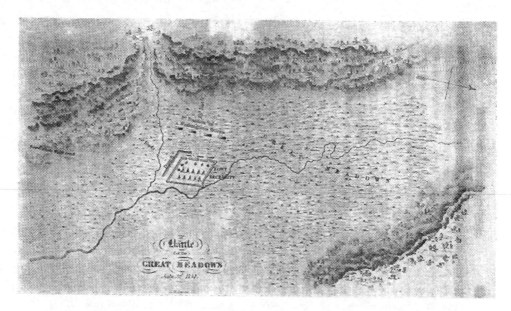

**Figure 2.4**   Map of Fort Necessity, Pennsylvania, published in 1837.

square' controversy, 2. to establish the 1754 location of the stream bed, and 3. to secure additional objects for museum display."

    J. C. Harrington's excavations proved that the fort actually consisted of two design elements: a diamond-shaped earthwork with a circular stockade inside it. The charred posts of the stockade were still visible in the soil of the old fortification trench and inside was a log storehouse. Harrington combined his archaeological findings with a deposition by John Shaw, a member of Washington's regiment, which explains the way the fort was built. Although this document had great relevance to the reconstruction of the fort, it was not taken seriously until the archaeological findings demonstrated its accuracy. In this way, then, Harrington used a combination of archaeological findings and historical documents to establish the size and shape of Washington's strategic frontier fort.

    *Signal Hill, Newfoundland.*   Like Fort Necessity, Signal Hill figured in the history of the French and British campaigns for control of North America. Situated on a strategic point overlooking the Atlantic Ocean and the harbor leading to St. John's and Fort William (established shortly before 1700), settlers used the promontory from 1750 to the mid-nineteenth century as a signal station to identify arriving ships. The British lost the area to the French in 1762 but then quickly regained it. Signal Hill, for all its strategic importance, did not have any fortifications built on it until 1795. The British had made numerous plans to construct fortifications on the hill, but many of these efforts were never carried out. During its greatest period of activity—from 1795 until the mid-nineteenth century—three batteries, or cannon stations, and several other buildings were built on the hill. Signal Hill also had other uses. On December 12, 1901, wireless pioneer Guglielmo Marconi used it as the base from which to make his first trans-Atlantic Morse code transmission. His message, simply the letter "s," sent all the way from Cornwall, England, showed that ships could communicate with one another and with the shore for at least 2,000 miles (3,200 km).

The number and locations of buildings on the hill became extremely important when the Canadian government decided to build an interpretive center for the new Signal Hill National Historic Park. When archaeologist Edward Jelks was commissioned to conduct the excavations in 1958, his objective was to dig in the area of the interpretive center to ensure that no archaeological remains would be destroyed by construction. He was also to determine the development potential of the park for future visitors, and to recover "artifacts and other data of general value to archaeological studies of British colonial sites."

Jelks's excavations were successful. He was able to document the complex construction history at Signal Hill and to locate buttons, bottles, coins, and other objects used by the soldiers there. The story of what happened at Signal Hill would be much less well known had these excavations not occurred.

## HISTORICAL ARCHAEOLOGY OF PEOPLE (1960s TO TODAY)

Archaeologists have long used their excavations to construct the broad culture histories of past peoples, but not every archaeologist accepted that this was all archaeology had to offer. American archaeologists, having been trained mostly in departments of anthropology, began to think in the early 1960s that archaeology could be something like cultural anthropology, in the sense that it could provide information about people's daily lives. As a result, archaeologists trained since the mid-1960s often envision themselves as anthropologists of the past, working to reconstruct past people's ways of life instead of simply adding to their cultural histories.

In 1962, archaeologist Lewis Binford presented one vision of anthropological archaeology in his essay "Archaeology as Anthropology." He proposed that archaeologists—instead of simply following paths that led only to large-scale cultural histories based on the identification of "archaeological cultures"—could be pathfinders who could lead the way to understanding past cultures. Rather than viewing culture as something statically represented in a collection of artifacts, Binford adopted the anthropologist's perspective that culture represents a changing adaptation to an environment. From this point of view, archaeologists could work like anthropologists and provide information about economics, kinship, religion, social interaction, and almost all other elements of past daily life. Archaeologists would simply study cultural processes in the past instead of in the present.

Binford used an archaeological expression called the ancient Old Copper Culture in Wisconsin (3000–500 B.C.) to illustrate his argument, but he also believed that an anthropological approach would serve historical archaeology well. Unlike many of his contemporaries, he had obtained personal experience in historical archaeology, serving in 1959 as a field assistant for excavations at Fort Michilimackinac, an eighteenth-century French and British military post in Michigan (Figure 2.5).

### Theoretical Foundations

The impact of Binford's article was immense. Prehistorian Paul Martin proclaimed that Binford had created a "revolution" in archaeology by proposing an entirely new theoretical paradigm for studying the past. Before long, archaeologists were referring to anthropological archaeology as the "new archaeology," because it represented an attempt to introduce greater scientific and theoretical rigor into field and laboratory research.

The furor over the study of cultural process instead of strict chronological history spilled over into historical archaeology. A year after the publication of Binford's essay, a number of archaeologists held a symposium entitled "The Meaning of Historic Sites Archaeology" at the annual meeting of the Society for American Archaeology in Boulder, Colorado. Binford was a panelist for this symposium, but the chair was Bernard Fontana. Fontana, an anthropologist who had conducted historical archaeology in Arizona, was inspired by the session and wrote an essay entitled "On the Meaning of Historic Sites Archaeology," which appeared in 1965.

As an anthropologist, Fontana understood the important role that non-Europeans played in creating the modern world. In line with this thinking, he designed a classification of historical sites that stressed the degree of Native American influence. His scale extended from a "protohistoric" site (one occupied after 1492 and that may contain some European artifacts, but that predates actual face-to-face contact between Native Americans and Europeans) to a "nonaboriginal" site (one that had little or no Native American influence).

Robert Schuyler reinforced Fontana's anthropological message in his paper "Historical and Historic Sites Archaeology as Anthropology: Basic Definitions and Relationships," published in 1970. Schuyler proposed that historical archaeology had much to offer to anthropology and that historical archaeology was not simply a way to reinforce or to substantiate historical facts.

By the early 1970s, then, many historical archaeologists had realized that their main theoretical foundation should be anthropological, but the question of whether anthropologists or historians should conduct historical archaeology became a topic of considerable debate. The controversy revolved around two central issues: first, whether the subject matter of historical archaeology was "history"—the realm of historians—or "culture"—the realm of anthropologists; and second, whether artifacts were historical documents—because they "told"

**Figure 2.5**    View of Fort Michilimackinac, Michigan.

about the past—or whether documents were really artifacts—because they were made and modified by conscious human effort. Traditional wisdom held that historians study written documents and that archaeologists study artifacts, but this neat distinction was not at all clear for historical archaeology.

Proponents of both sides of the argument tended to caricature the other. Some portrayed historians as narrow-minded scholars who wore tweed jackets while blissfully rummaging through stacks of dusty documents oblivious to the outside world. Others described archaeologists as brash adventurers who knew nothing about written records and who would go to any lengths to obtain rare artifacts. In 1962, Bernard Cohn published an article entitled "An Anthropologist Among the Historians: A Field Study." In this seemingly tongue-in-cheek study, Cohn said that "Historians are older than anthropologists." He also said that "A historian is usually regular in his work habits. The archives are open only certain hours," but that "An anthropologist often works in great bursts." Cohn also contrasted the relevance of each discipline's work: "A historian usually studies a topic which, even if somewhat obscure, is intrinsically important" but "An anthropologist may study intrinsically insignificant things"!

In hindsight, the history-or-anthropology debate raised a false issue by attempting to draw too fine a line between two closely related fields. Some of the debate's participants promoted stereotyped characterizations of historians and anthropologists and misunderstood the theoretical bases of both history and anthropology. The debate was important, however, because it forced historical archaeologists to consider seriously the theoretical foundations of their field and to help them define its boundaries.

At about the same time that historical archaeologists were debating history versus anthropology, many professional historians "discovered" anthropology (largely as ethnohistory) and began to employ concepts and ideas from ethnography in their historical interpretations. Rhys Isaac, for example, won a Pulitzer Prize in history for his highly anthropological *The Transformation of Virginia, 1740–1790*. Isaac's first word in this "historical" book is "Anthropologists." He was specifically interested in explaining how society in Tidewater Virginia had changed from 1740 to 1790, or before and after the American Revolution. Virginia's social hierarchy had become more rigid during this half century for reasons that were hard to discern. Hoping to understand this change, Isaac stayed away from politics and economics, choosing instead to examine such "anthropological" topics as architecture, interior design, furniture, silverware, dance, dress, manners, and the use of space (Figure 2.6). Isaac drew two important conclusions from these lines of evidence. First, he said that rich planters made common cause with poorer farmers to claim independence from England and to forge a new government. This conclusion was not entirely new, but his second, related conclusion was pathbreaking. He concluded that planters became increasingly threatened with the rise of American independence and liberty during the course of the eighteenth century. To maintain their elite positions in the social order, the planters tightened their control over society. One way they expressed this control

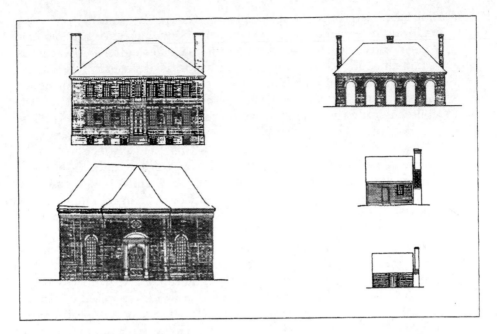

**Figure 2.6**  Hierarchy of buildings in eighteenth-century Virginia, ranging from mansion to slave cabin.

was the so-called "Georgian Order," a perspective that had significant relevance to material culture. House styles became more symmetrical and neat; dining and dance became more structured and orderly (see Chapter 9). Isaac had to look toward the material expressions of daily life to find evidence of these changes. He had to examine them as an anthropologist would investigate a foreign culture.

As some historians were turning toward anthropology, some archaeologists were leaning more toward history. In 1986, British prehistorian Ian Hodder wrote that "archaeology should recapture its traditional links with history." As a prehistorical archaeologist, Hodder had not thought too much about "history" until the writings of eccentric Australian-born archaeologist V. Gordon Childe again became popular in archaeological circles in the early 1980s. Childe considered archaeology to be a form of history, and in the 1930s and 1940s he wrote tremendously popular books about Europe's remote past, using archaeological objects to explain his main points. Hodder sought to reemphasize Childe's view that archaeologists were adding to historical knowledge.

Historical archaeologists have explored the connections between history and anthropology in numerous ways. Their inquiries have forced them to acknowledge and appreciate the multidisciplinary foundation of their field. In 1982, Kathleen Deagan, renowned for her research on colonial New Spain and Columbus's settlement on Hispaniola, noted that the "debate over the proper orientation of historical archaeology has not altogether been resolved." Deagan has repeatedly demonstrated, through her many important projects, the power of using historical records in archaeological research to study such topics as domestic architecture and changing gender roles. As was the case during her study of Fort Mose, Florida—the earliest free African American settlement in North America—she often closely collaborates with professional historians in a further attempt to link anthropology and history.

One of the most forceful statements for the adoption of an overt anthropological and scientific perspective in historical archaeology was Stanley South's *Method and Theory in Historical Archaeology,* published in 1977. South had been a graduate student with Lewis Binford at the University of North Carolina in the 1950s. He was a confirmed believer in the theory of cultural evolution as explained by anthropologist Leslie White. Following White, South believed that cultural progress could be measured by the amount of energy a culture could harness. The captured energy could be evaluated in terms of any human technological achievement, extending from the controlled use of fire to atomic power.

South agreed with Binford's ideas about archaeological reasoning, and argued that historical archaeologists could work more scientifically by making regular use of hypotheses, laws, and scientific testing procedures. South proposed that historical archaeology could be quantifiable, meaning that the artifacts found at different sites could be counted, grouped into categories, and then compared in a scientific manner with the artifact groups from other sites. The comparisons would reveal cultural information about the people who once lived at the different sites. Although archaeologists have been conducting comparative analysis for years, South's "pattern" concept was unique because of its strong anthropological and scientific basis (Chapter 5).

## People Without History

Historical archaeology truly came of age in the late 1960s and 1970s, when both archaeologists and historians realized the potential of the humblest of artifacts for studying people whose daily lives are not well documented in historical sources. These "undocumented" people came from diverse ethnic groups, including African American slaves, Chinese railroad laborers, Métis fur trappers, Welsh miners, and Irish farmers.

The realization that historical archaeology provides a unique way in which to study the men and women of history who seldom left detailed, written commentaries on their lives probably stemmed from two different yet related directions. First, by the late 1960s and early 1970s, it had become clear that most new historical archaeologists would be trained by anthropologists rather than strictly by historians. Most of these freshly minted archaeologists would have formal training in, or at least experience with, archival research methods, but they also would have extensive knowledge of the ethnography of nonliterate peoples. These archaeologists realized that they could successfully combine their anthropological perspectives with their knowledge of archival materials. Historical documents, for all of the information they contain about the construction of railroads through the American West, tell us virtually nothing about the daily lives of the Chinese people who actually did the construction. In the absence of archaeology, we would not know what kind of housing the railway companies supplied to the workers or what ceramic dishes and other objects the laborers used. Did the workers retain elements of Chinese culture in North America? If so, which elements did they keep and which did they surrender? Historical archaeology is the only discipline that can address such basic questions in minute and exacting detail.

The general revival of ethnic pride throughout the world in the 1960s and 1970s was a second factor that convinced many historical archaeologists that their discipline was relevant to society at large, and that their specialized knowledge was meaningful well beyond the sometimes narrow confines of professional archaeology. In other words, it became clear that historical archaeology, seeking to document the undocumented, could be invaluable for providing abundant detail about the daily lives of peoples whose contributions to history might otherwise be forgotten. Two examples will illustrate this important point.

*Yaughan and Curriboo Plantations, South Carolina.*   Yaughan and Curriboo were two eighteenth-century slave plantations in coastal South Carolina, a part of the southern United States that was home to thousands of African slaves. Historical records make it possible to reconstruct the basic histories of ownership and family association within Yaughan and Curriboo. But even for all their usefulness, these records only tell the "official" history of the plantations and provide no information about the enslaved men, women, and children who actually performed the manual labor that helped to amass the riches of the slave-owning families.

Thomas Wheaton and Patrick Garrow excavated twenty-nine dwellings on the plantation and added an entirely new dimension to the history of the region. They showed that between the 1740s and 1770s, the slaves lived in rectangular, mud-walled buildings that may have resembled their traditional houses in Africa or the Caribbean (Figure 2.7). From the 1780s to the 1820s they lived in smaller, square buildings placed on brick piers. Wheaton and Garrow believed the change reflected slave acculturation. In their view, as a result of constant interaction, enslaved Africans slowly learned the customs of those people who enslaved them. To put this another way, the enslaved men and women slowly replaced their African traditions with those of their owners. This interpretation is debated, because it can just as easily be argued that slaves who had once lived in African-style houses moved into European houses because they were forced to do so. They may have had no choice in the matter. Nonetheless, the view presented by Wheaton and Garrow causes archaeologists to think about the meaning of the housing change, rather than simply to accept it.

Yaughan and Curriboo yielded a wealth of information on slave nutrition. The slaves housed there lived on corn, rice, beef, and pork, supplemented with

**Figure 2.7**  Artist's reconstruction of slave cabins at Curriboo Plantation, South Carolina.

some wild plants and game. Musket parts found at several dwellings indicate that they used firearms to kill game. In addition to using a variety of European objects in their daily lives, the enslaved people also made their own pottery and probably also used some pots made by local Native Americans. Archaeologists currently think that the coarse, low-fired pottery found at many slave plantations, including Yaughan and Curriboo, were produced by mixing African, Native American, and European pottery traditions.

Historical archaeology adds an incredible richness to our knowledge of slave life and gives these largely undocumented people a chance to be heard. The lives of wealthy slave owners tend to be revealed by a combination of archaeological and written sources, but only archaeology can document the daily lives of slave men and women.

*Gold Bar Camp, Nevada.*  Gold Bar Camp in Nevada was a classic western mining settlement inhabited between 1905 and 1909. Only about one hundred gold and silver miners and their families lived there. The camp is largely invisible in official documents because it was settled after the 1900 federal census and abandoned before the 1910 count. Only a few newspaper articles refer to the place. These limited accounts mention the presence of boarding houses, bunkhouses, and a superintendent's bungalow (Figure 2.8). The homes of the miners' families must also have existed in the camp because the records state that eighteen school-aged children lived there in 1908. Photographs of the camp present general views of it while occupied, but like contemporary writings, they reveal little about daily life.

Historical archaeologist Donald Hardesty used excavation and survey to add an entirely new dimension to life at the Gold Bar Camp. He showed that the miners lived in houses measuring from 400 to over 1,000 square feet (37.1 to 92.9 sq m), that many of these residences seemed to have special functions, and

**Figure 2.8**   The Gold Bar Camp, Nevada, as it looked in 1908.

that the people at the camp used a huge variety of artifacts, including tin cans. These lowly cans, considered merely trash by nonarchaeologists, tell us that the residents of the mining community imported fruits and vegetables, meats, coffee, and milk for their meals. Glass bottles and lamp chimneys document the drinking of whiskey, wine, and beer, and the lighting of homes with kerosene lamps.

The people of Gold Bar maintained regular contact with the outside world—they wrote and received letters and were visited by traveling merchants and salespeople—and lived much like other people throughout the United States. Their difference, of course, was that they worked as hardrock miners, toughened laborers whose daily lives have been largely forgotten in written history. Without historical archaeology, their lives, though merely a footnote in the broad sweep of world history, would forever be shrouded in mystery, and our understanding of the past would be much less complete.

## TODAY'S HISTORICAL ARCHAEOLOGY

Historical archaeologists' interest in the rich and famous, as well as in the poor and undocumented, helps define the history of the discipline. Their interests reflects their growing awareness about the increase in cultural interactions after about A.D. 1500. The changing attitude is easy to identify in the literature. Whereas before the early 1960s the archaeologists' focus was almost exclusively on a slave owner's opulent mansion, by the late 1960s their emphasis had mostly shifted to the humble cabins of the enslaved. This change in orientation, though not absolute, is nonetheless striking.

As the number of historical archaeologists continues to grow, historical archaeology is quickly becoming an international discipline. Once confined largely to North America and Great Britian, historical archaeology today flourishes on all continents, from South America to the South Pacific, from Cape Town to the Arctic Circle.

## Theoretical Foundations

Historical archaeology continues to mature. A number of archaeologists are playing a major role in this intellectual growth by experimenting with diverse ideas and theoretical points of view at a large variety of sites. It is thus virtually impossible to provide a single theoretical theme to describe the field after the mid-1980s (see Chapter 10). Today's historical archaeologists use ideas and concepts from numerous disciplines, including anthropology, sociology, philosophy, material culture studies, social history, political economics, and geography. Most archaeologists are no longer content with simply describing collections of artifacts or preparing archaeological reports that document the undocumented. Many of them are beginning to examine the deeper meanings of artifacts and the complex relationships that exist between people and the things around them, including buildings and landscapes. These new concerns are taking the field in fascinating new directions. Four examples will help demonstrate the intellectual vitality of today's historical archaeology.

*The Paca Mansion, Annapolis, Maryland.* Annapolis, Maryland, has a rich history, and that city has been the subject of intense archaeological investigations for over two decades. Mark Leone has investigated the eighteenth-century residences of the city, including a large mansion built by William Paca, a wealthy lawyer and signer of the Declaration of Independence. In one element of his fascinating research at Paca's house, Leone provides an in-depth and innovative interpretation of Paca's magnificent garden.

Many wealthy elites in Europe and European America built luxurious pleasure gardens behind their spacious mansions. Like many of his contemporaries, Paca commissioned a large and rigidly structured, formal green space to stretch behind his mansion in four distinct terraces (Figure 2.9). The garden's designers symmetrically planted the first three platforms with trees and shrubs to give the garden a neat, manicured appearance. At the back of the property they designed a "wilderness," an area in which they let the plants grow wildly and without attention. In amongst the wilderness, the designers placed a fish-shaped pond.

Most researchers have viewed such formal gardens as an architectural feature designed simply to enhance the appearance of the house itself. Scholars tend to consider these gardens to have had a purely aesthetic function. In a departure from this widely held view, however, Leone argued that Paca actually used his garden to reinforce symbolically the existing social order of early America. The garden, though indeed aesthetically pleasing, had a much more serious meaning. Leone interpreted the difference between the garden and the wilderness as representing increased chaos as one moved further away from (and physically below) the order

**Figure 2.9**   William Paca's Garden, Annapolis, Maryland.

and symmetry of the mansion. In addition to the manicured trees and shrubs, the designers had also incorporated a number of optical illusions into the plan that altered the visitor's perspective of space and distance. Leone believed that the garden's designers wished to use these illusions to hide, in a symbolic sense, both the contradictions in Paca's own life—as a passionate defender of liberty and also an owner of slaves—and in American society at large, contradictions that could assign inalienable rights to some people and demand lifelong bondage from others.

Leone could easily have used his archaeological research simply to define the limits of the garden and to document the exact locations of trees and shrubs. Paca was an important historical figure, and architectural information about his mansion and its garden would interest many people, just as does Abraham Lincoln's house in Illinois. Leone chose, however, to offer an innovative interpretation by using the archaeological information in a new way. The importance of Leone's article, whether or not one accepts his interpretation—and it has been much discussed—is that it demonstrates that historical archaeologists are deeply engaged in important anthropological and historical debates about the past.

**Boott Mill, Lowell, Massachusetts.**   In 1835, when a group of Boston entrepreneurs decided to build a mill to produce cotton and woolen goods, they settled on a location in Lowell, Massachusetts, near the New Hampshire state line. They called their industrial complex the Boott Cotton Mills, after Kirk Boott, the first mill agent. The mill site, now a museum, operates as part of the Lowell National Historical Park. In the 1980s, the U.S. National Park Service sponsored an extensive archaeological study of the mill. Written records indicated that most of the "mill girls" were New England farm girls and immigrants' daughters, but little else was known about them. In an effort to learn something about these mill workers, the team of archaeologists turned their attention to their boardinghouses (Figure 2.10).

As a way to understand the meaning of the artifacts collected from the mill's boardinghouses, archaeologists Mary Beaudry, Lauren Cook, and Stephen Mrozowski decided to envision the artifacts in the same way that we understand a language—as a complex discourse incorporating a huge number of diverse and often-subtle meanings. Beaudry and her colleagues proposed that undocumented people such as mill workers, although they may be uncounted in many historical records, did communicate through the artifacts they used. Such individuals only remain undocumented if historical archaeologists fail to study the ways in which they documented themselves. In the researchers' view, the object of such analysis is not to study the undocumented from the "top down" (from the perspective of their social "betters") or from the "bottom up" (from the peoples' own viewpoint), but rather from the "inside out," meaning from the place in society in which they document themselves. For Beaudry and her colleagues, the most enlightening way to learn about the undocumented is to discover how they created their own worlds on their own terms.

The objects found during the excavation point to the ways in which ordinary men and women took the things around them and documented themselves. When Beaudry and her collaborators unearthed liquor, wine, and beer bottles—along with beer mugs and wine glasses—they knew that the boardinghouse residents flagrantly violated the corporation's strict sobriety rules. When they found flowerpot fragments it became clear that the workers attempted to brighten their often dreary lives, to reclaim a small bit of beauty in their otherwise monotonous and regulated work routines. The presence of marbles and doll parts suggested that children were also able to breathe life into the daily grind.

The men and women of Boott Mills, as consumers much like us today, were forced to purchase the objects they used. Like us, they had neither the technology nor the knowledge to make their own ceramic plates and glass bottles. The mill workers had to enter into relationships with others, notably merchants and grocers to obtain their possessions. Beaudry, Cook, and Mrozowski viewed these relationships, just like the relationships the workers maintained with the mill's agents and owners, as a discourse or dialogue between people occupying different social positions.

*The Chesapeake.* Some historical archaeologists are using information from individual sites to provide new insights about whole regions. The Chesa-

**Figure 2.10**   Lauren J. Cook excavating at Boott Mills boardinghouses, Lowell, Massachusetts, 1985.

peake region, which centers upon Chesapeake Bay and includes parts of Maryland and northern Virginia, is just such a place (Figure 2.11). This environmentally rich region was home to numerous prehistoric Native American villages,
and it was one of the lush environments first sought after by European settlers.
The region contains some of the most important historical archaeological sites in
North America, including Annapolis, Mt. Vernon, Williamsburg, and St. Mary's
City, to name but a few. Not surprisingly, then, the region has been the subject of
intense archaeological research.

In one study, archaeologist Anne Yentsch used ceramics and animal bones,
in conjunction with written records, from sixteen sites in the Chesapeake region
to identify small-scale social change in the period from about 1680–1740. Yentsch
used the information she assembled to examine the changing use of food by the
region's residents. By adopting a regional and long-term perspective, Yentsch
was able to observe a marked shift from wooden and pewter plates to ceramic
dishes, an increase in the number of plates used, a greater variation in plate sizes
in individual households, and a trend away from communal servings to individualized portions. The cultural issues involving changes in food preferences are
complicated, but Yentsch's focus on them allowed her to think like an anthropologist interested in cultural continuity and social change, instead of thinking like an
antiquarian concerned only with the appearance and beauty of the artifacts.
Yentsch provided an interesting way for historical archaeologists to examine the
transition from a pre-modern to a modern way of life through an analysis of
mundane artifacts.

In another important study of the Chesapeake region, archaeologist L. Daniel
Mouer investigated the creation of culture in the region during colonial times.
Mouer preferred not to adopt a view of culture that rested on the idea that separate cultures are completely autonomous in their actions, beliefs, and traditions.
He instead opted for an understanding based on the anthropological notion of
"creolization." A creolized culture is one in which several strands from two or
more cultures are consciously blended into a new expression, one that bears resemblance to the ancestral cultures, but is itself new. Mouer was specifically interested in showing how the men and women of the seventeenth-century
Chesapeake created a way of life that contained elements of English, Native
American, and African American cultures. To illustrate his idea, he examined dietary habits, methods of food preparation, the use of tobacco, the manufacture of
pottery, and the decoration of European-made smoking pipes. He learned that
the residents of villages throughout the Chesapeake selected from various cultural elements to invent new ways of doing things. They created a folk culture
unlike anything that had previously existed.

*The Blue Mountains, Jamaica.*   In addition to examining specific regions,
historical archaeologists also tackle special topics that have broad and often international significance. New World slavery and its aftermath clearly fit the bill as

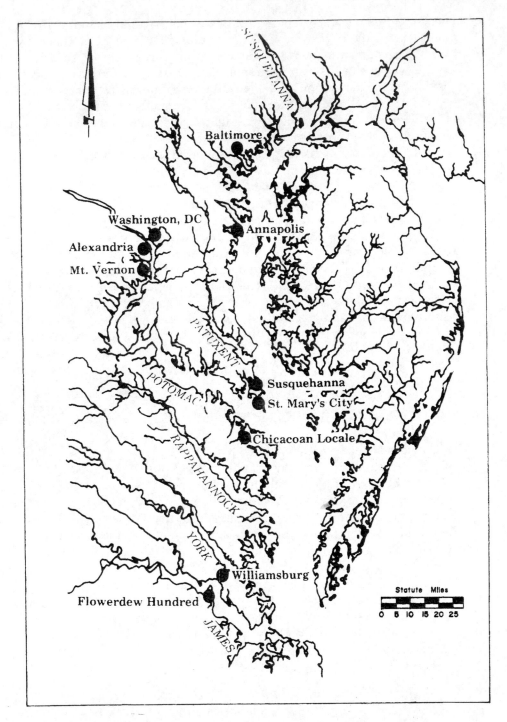

**Figure 2.11**   Chesapeake Region of the eastern United States, showing key sites.

subjects of analysis that have intercontinental meaning and which are guaranteed to provide archaeological remains that can be studied in detail.

In an important investigation of New World enslavement and freedom, historical archaeologist James Delle examined the changes that occurred in the coffee plantations of Jamaica between 1790 and 1865. These years bracketed a time of great social upheaval on the island. The emancipation of thousands of slaves and the resultant transition from slave to wage labor spelled the end of the old regime. The transition from enslavement to freedom is complicated because diverse social, economic, and political variables may have played different roles in the process. Archaeologists do not know beforehand how best to study these complex features of history. One of the ways that Delle sought to examine the monumental transition of Jamaican plantation society was through the use of space.

Archaeologists like Delle know that space is profoundly significant in all cultures because houses, roads, schools, and other features built on the landscape are not randomly placed. Any real estate agent will tell you that location is everything, and the situation was not much different in the past. Knowing this, Delle set out to learn how the buildings and other features of Jamaica's coffee estates were situated. One thing he learned, for example, was that the construction of the planters' houses were considerably more durable and larger than the slaves'—and later, the workers'—cabins. The owners had ordered that the houses of the plantation overseers (later foremen) were situated to increase surveillance over the workforce. Numerous maps commissioned by plantation owners provided mute testimony to the way plantation owners sought to manage and control the physical space of their plantations. The maps also substantiated how the owners struggled to use space as a measure of social position on their estates. Without question, the use of space on Jamaican coffee plantations was not accidental or mere happenstance.

In-depth studies of past settlements allow historical archaeologists to examine cultural complexity with everyday objects. Such investigation requires the careful construction of the people's context—the cultural, social, and natural environments within which they lived. As shown in the projects mentioned above, historical archaeologists now view artifacts—which also include buildings and roads—as active objects that helped create, structure, and maintain life rather than merely as passive, inanimate objects that yield information only about the date they were made (see Chapter 4). Before we can move to consider how historical archaeologists study artifacts, we must first explore culture and society. These notions form the core of most modern-day archaeological research.

## TIME TRAVEL

### Smith's Fort, Bermuda, 1613

The islands of Bermuda, of which there are over 300, lie about 670 miles (1,080 km) southeast of New York City in the Atlantic Ocean. The islands are named for a Spaniard named Juan de Bermúdez, a seafarer who may have sailed with Columbus on his first voyage of exploration. The European superpowers would dispute ownership of the Caribbean and its islands for many years, and by the middle of the sixteenth century, the British had staked their empire-building claim on the Bermuda islands. They sought to control them, believing that the islands could serve as a sanctuary, a convenient and much-needed respite for ocean-weary colonists on their way to Virginia. Because other European powers could view the islands in the same way, between 1612 and 1957 (when the British garrison finally withdrew), ninety forts had been raised on the islands. One of the earliest was called Smith's Fort.

British colonists at Bermuda feared attacks from their Spanish enemies, whose ships regularly patrolled the Caribbean seeking new conquests. The British, seeking to stress their seriousness in holding Bermuda, built a fortification on a tiny island on the eastern end of the archipelago. The spot, called Governor's Island, provided excellent defensive terrain, because it guarded the harbor of the English town of St. George. The idea for the fort had began with Governor Richard Moore, and he worked feverishly to defend the islands and transform them into a viable British colony. Soon, however, the fortification became known as Smith's Fort, a name it retains today. Captain John Smith, indefatigable self-promoter and friend to Pocahontas, published a map of Bermuda that depicted its forts in 1624, including one he modestly named for himself.

Smith pictured the tiny fort as triangular in shape with two circular towers facing seaward. A small house, possibly a power magazine, sits inside the walls, and five soldiers, with swords and early seventeenth-century firearms, patrol around it. A neat row of defensive loopholes appear along the wall facing the viewer and in the nearest tower. He depicted the fort's back wall as straight with a large doorway at its mid-point. In overall appearance, then, the fort as drawn by Smith approximated a truncated triangle; one point was sliced off, and the other two had circular towers on them. Outside the fort's front wall, and between it and the shore, are arranged a row of five cannon pointing outward in a semi-circle. A three-masted ship (friend or foe?) approaches from the lower right.

Military engineers always understood the defensive importance of Governor's Island. In the eighteenth century, long after Smith's Fort was abandoned, Captain Andrew Durnford, of the Royal Engineers, arrived to construct a new installation on the island. The new fort, called Durnford's Redoubt, was in place before 1811. Henry Lauzan, one of Durnford's surveyors, drew a plan of Smith's Fort as it looked to him in 1790. His plan, since confirmed by archaeology, depicts a fort that was more square than triangular, with a back wall that was bowed out into a semi-circle rather than flat as Smith had shown it. Lauzan had also drawn a D-shaped "sea battery" that extended outward from the front wall of the fort, with the curved part of the D pointing toward the sea. Once we

*(continued)*

*Source:* Edward Cecil Harris, *Bermuda Forts, 1612–1957* (Bermuda: Bermuda Maritime Museum Press, 1997); Norman F. Barka and Edward C. Harris, *Archaeology of Smith's Fort and Durnford's Redoubt, Governor's Island, Bermuda: Final Season, 2001* (Williamsburg, Virginia: Department of Anthropology, College of William and Mary, 2002).

know about this battery, we can see something that may be it in Smith's drawing.

The maximum dimension of Smith's Fort was only about 56 by 82 feet (17 by 25 m). The two circular towers were located where both Smith and Lauzan had drawn them. They were made of cut limestone, and each had an interior diameter of only about 6.5 feet (2 m). The distance from the mid-point of each tower was only 24 feet (7.5 m). The builders of the fort had chiseled a flat surface into the bedrock between the towers, along the fort's outer wall, and had hewn steps into the east side of the western tower to allow access from the sea battery.

Smith's Fort is one of the few examples of early English forts built in the New World of which traces can still be seen above ground. Most forts, being made of timber, have long since disappeared from the earth's surface. As a historical monu-ment, part of the significance of Smith's Fort derives from its being one of the last truly defensive "castles" to be constructed anywhere in the world. Its designers worked during an important time of transition in the technology of warfare from medieval to modern. Castles were mostly abandoned with the development of firepower because they could not withstand attack from cannons. Castles came from an age of crossbows and rudimentary firearms. The towers of Smith's Fort were too small for cannon; they had been designed for archers and men with muskets. The small cannons depicted by Smith on the shore could possibly have defended against lightly armed ships, but its defensive might could have easily been tested. The coastal defensive fortification, first designed by Romans in Britain, received one of its final expressions at Smith's Fort.

# Chapter 3

# HISTORICAL
# CULTURE, SOCIETY,
# AND HISTORICAL SITES

*"Not a having and a resting, but a growing and a becoming is the character of perfection
as culture conceives it."*

Matthew Arnold, 1869

Most people have an interest in what archaeologists do. When they meet them in the field, perhaps at a place they have driven by day after day without noticing or at a nearby historic site, they usually have a number of questions to ask: How do you know where to dig? What is so special about this place? How do you know what to look for? How deep do you dig, and how do you know when to stop? Archaeology seems so scientific and meticulous that it holds a mystery all its own. Even the most casual onlooker is fascinated by how archaeologists carefully strip away the layers of dirt and sand to reveal the objects made and used in a distant time and by people long dead.

One question frequently asked of modern-world archaeologists is seldom posed to archaeologists who study the ancient past: Why excavate history? Why should historical archaeologists spend scarce grant funds, endure long, tiring days in the hot sun—often in unsafe or even dangerous environments—and teach students to excavate a period of history that is documented in written records? Wouldn't it be less expensive and safer to go to an archive to learn about this more recent past? People can readily understand why archaeologists may be drawn to the study of the ancient Egyptians or the pyramid-building Mayas of Central America, but they may find it more difficult to understand why archaeologists would wish to excavate the home of an early twentieth-century coal miner. Surely, historical records provide us with enough information about coal mining to make archaeology unnecessary?

We could provide many philosophical reasons why all archaeology is important in helping us to construct knowledge about the past, and we have presented some ideas about this subject in Chapter 1. The value of excavating history was neatly summarized, however, by prominent historian and the Librarian of the U.S. Congress, Daniel Boorstin: "We know more about some aspects of daily life in the ancient Babylon of 3000 B.C. than we do about daily life in parts of Europe or America a hundred years ago." Boorstin's comment is perceptive. In Chapter 2, we touched upon some of the values of excavating the recent past. In this chapter, we explain more fully that it is an interest in "culture" and "society" that makes the excavation of history important. The information about historical culture and society collected by archaeologists helps us explain why today's world is the way it is.

## ANTHROPOLOGY

*Anthropology*—defined broadly as the study of humanity—is generally said to begin with the Greek historian and traveler Herodotus, who was born in 484 B.C. (Figure 3.1). Herodotus wrote at length about many aspects of the ancient Greek world, including trading and market customs, the differences in peoples' dress, and the division of labor between men and women in different cultures. He also made note of several more unusual practices, such as how ancient Egyptians mourned the death of a house pet: "If a cat dies in a private house by a natural death, all the inmates of the house shave their eyebrows; on the death of a dog they shave the head and the whole of the body." Scholars disagree about the veracity of many of Herodotus's observations, but everyone who reads him cannot help but be impressed with the diversity of the world's cultural traditions.

Many talented thinkers, like Thomas Jefferson, have pondered the human condition since the days of Herodotus, but as an actual field of inquiry anthropology only acquired its scientific credentials in the late nineteenth century. During the earliest decades of the twentieth century, numerous luminaries such as Franz Boas, Margaret Mead, Bronislaw Malinowski, and Ruth Benedict made anthropology a household word. These pioneering anthropologists were engaging writers who put their discipline on the map. Their writings about exotic peoples have convinced many readers that an anthropologist is a person who goes to remote corners of South America, Africa, or New Guinea to live with "primitive" peoples to learn about how they live.

Today's cultural anthropologists do indeed spend long periods living among non-Western cultures. They conduct *participant observation*, a method whereby they attempt to strike a balance between watching the peoples' activities and taking part in them. But anthropological fieldwork among non-Western peoples does not tell the entire story of anthropology.

Anthropology is generally taught in the United States as a four-field discipline. The four fields are cultural or social anthropology (sometimes called "sociocultural" anthropology), physical anthropology, anthropological linguistics,

**Figure 3.1**   Herodotus, the great traveler.

and archaeology. If we define anthropology as the study of humankind, past and present, then we can well imagine the breadth of the modern anthropological project. American anthropologists view each subdiscipline as an integral part of the larger study of humanity.

Cultural or social anthropologists study the ways in which current people live: how and what they eat, what stories they tell one another, how they practice religion, how they decide to whom they are related, and every other aspect of daily life that we can imagine. Cultural anthropology is quite simply the study of custom. A cultural anthropologist may study the customs of the Karaja in central Brazil as they were practiced while he or she lived with them. The anthropologist also may write about how the Karaja are adapting to or resisting the cultural changes caused by the construction of the Belém-to-Brasília Highway.

Physical anthropologists study humans both as biologic and social animals. Physical anthropologists study everything from the very earliest appearance of humans—by examining the fossils of our earliest ancestors, such as the famed "Lucy" found in Ethiopia by Donald Johanson—to the genetic compositions of living peoples. The study of physical characteristics, primate behavior, the development of bipedal locomotion, and the creation of human social organization all fall within the realm of physical anthropology.

Anthropological linguists study human speech, how language is used by people, the history of language, and nonverbal communication. Anthropological linguists may study what it means to cross one's arms while talking or what English speakers mean when they say "blue" and "green." They may study the adoption of English words by modern-day speakers of Japanese and Spanish, or the ways in which different peoples give meaning to specific sounds.

Archaeologists contribute to this larger study of humanity by conducting research that differs from that of their anthropological colleagues only in their interest in the past and the remains of past peoples. The contribution of historical archaeology derives from its explicit interest in recent history.

The idea of "culture" is the common thread that binds together the four subfields of anthropology. The concept of culture is no less important for historical archaeologists than it is for cultural anthropologists.

## CULTURE AND SOCIETY

We all use the word *culture*, but we employ it in many ways. For example, we may describe someone who goes to the opera as "cultured," and someone who makes rude noises while eating soup in a restaurant as "uncultured." When used in this popular way, the word *culture* often says more about the individual using the term than about the person or group to which that person is referring. In a popular sense, the term *culture* only means what one person (or perhaps one group of people) views as appropriate behavior in a certain setting. Some behaviors reflect "culture"; others reflect a lack of it. This popular use of the term may be widespread, but it is not anthropological.

Another popular sense of the word *culture* is closer to the anthropological meaning. We all know that other cultures exist. We can see what to us is their strange dress and odd customs in TV documentaries, and we can go to museums and examine the unusual objects they made and used. We can even directly experience something of another culture by eating their native dishes in restaurants and by meeting people from other cultures in the world's largest cities. We know that these people, often called "foreigners" to indicate that they come from someplace else, may speak odd-sounding languages, they may prefer unusual foods, and they may even worship a deity other than our own. These differences allow us to sense that "foreign" people are indeed different from us—but how do we really know their true differences? What are we really sensing when we meet "foreign" peoples? Surely we are not observing any real biologic difference in the people themselves because physical anthropology teaches us that humaninty constitutes only one species. What we are encountering is simply a difference in culture.

The concept of culture is at the core of anthropology and all anthropologists seek to contribute something to its understanding. The diversity of the world's cultures and the multitude of ways that culture can be studied has meant, however, that anthropologists have formulated numerous definitions for this one important concept. One might reasonably expect all anthropologists to agree on the definition of a concept that is so central to their field, but this is not the case. In 1952, Alfred Kroeber and Clyde Kluckhohn, two renowned American anthropologists, collected all the definitions of culture that had been used by their colleagues. We might expect that they only found a handful of different definitions, but they collected more than 160 of them!

In the face of such overwhelming disagreement, the best definition is perhaps the first one ever proposed. In his book *Primitive Culture*, published in 1871, Edward Tylor defined culture as "the complex whole which includes knowledge, belief, art, morals, law, custom, and any other capabilities and habits acquired by man [humans] as a member of society." Tylor's definition captures three important elements of culture: first, that culture is composed of many diverse elements—from the shape of clay pots to beliefs about the afterlife—that are brought together in unity; second, that culture is not instinctual, but must be learned; and third, that people learn culture in societies, groups of people who are bound together by a shared way of life and who engage in social interaction. From the members of our culture, we learn how to sit at a table to eat, how to arrange the place setting in the "correct" way, what is acceptable to serve at a meal, how to interpret what is served, and how to eat. Much of our culture is internalized during our enculturation process, an often unconscious way of learning what is "right" and what is "wrong." Sometimes, though, we also learn the rules of our culture purposefully. Formal schooling provides a good example. During our first years of attendance, we learn many of the rules of our culture in a fairly structured way. We learn how to sit, how to address figures of authority, and when to speak. On the playground during recess we also learn the rules of our culture, but in a nonstructured, informal way. Both ways of cultural instruction are equally important for teaching individuals what is expected of them and how to behave toward others.

Humans use their cultures to help them adapt to their environments. In this sense, human culture is unique. People use their intelligence, traditions, and experience to feed themselves, to shelter themselves from the heat and cold, and to protect themselves from predatory animals. All of these ways of surviving in the environment are determined by culture.

Anthropologists have learned that they cannot really understand culture without also comprehending society. Men and women do not simply practice their cultures unaware of the other individuals around them. In fact, the enactment of culture always involves many people. All human culture must have men, women, and children to engage with one another. Anthropologists and sociologists refer to the linkages between individuals as *social relations*. Emile Durkheim, the great French sociologist whom students of anthropology and sociology continue to study today, wrote in 1915 that "There is no people and no state which is not part of another society, more or less unlimited, which embraces all the peoples and all the states with which it first comes in contact, either directly or indirectly." Durkheim is telling us that we must understand that cultures involve real people and that these real people must regularly interact with one another to live in society.

The social relations of any society create a *social network*. We may think of a social network as a web of connections between the individuals in a specific culture (Figure 3.2). Individuals who live in today's large, highly complex, industrialized states are enmeshed in many complicated social networks. In addition, individuals who have formed themselves into groups—age grades, secret societies, clubs, classes, and so forth—also maintain social relations with other groups. These groups complicate matters considerably for archaeologists, but we are fortunate because social groups are usually associated with material objects that can be excavated and analyzed (see Chapter 10).

We must not confuse culture with behavior because not everyone in a culture acts exactly alike. Individuals will act differently based on many factors,

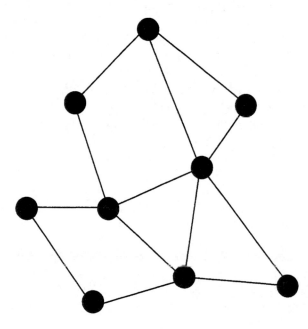

**Figure 3.2** Graphic representation of a simple social network.

including their social relations with others and their position in various social networks. Ants and wolves have societies—because they engage in social interaction and have a shared way of life—but they do not have culture. Culture structures the rules and standards that are deemed acceptable, but it provides for variability within the limits of acceptability. If culture were not variable, then everyone would act exactly the same.

## HUMAN BEHAVIOR IN THE PAST: ANALOGIES AND DIRECT HISTORICAL APPROACHES

The concepts of culture and society help archaeologists explain what they find at archaeological sites. The material objects and the other remains archaeologists find, however, do not represent culture as such, but rather the results of behaviors of people acting within culture and society. Archaeologists cannot directly observe past behavior, so they must infer actions and even ideas from what they find during excavation. All archaeologists can infer the past by using ethnographic analogy and the direct historical approach.

*Ethnographic analogy* refers to the archaeological use of a past observer's comments about a living people as added support for an inference about past behavior. The cultural anthropologist's ethnography and the accounts filed by nonprofessional direct observers (such as missionaries and travelers) can provide the source of the analogy. In a famous example, when archaeologist Lewis Binford found shallow, basin-shaped pits filled with charred corncobs at the prehistoric Toothsome Site in southern Illinois, he used ethnographies of Native Americans to infer that these pits were used during the process of tanning hides. The tanners placed the hides over the pits, and the smoke from the smoldering corncobs made the hides pliable and more easily worked. Binford was willing to make the connection between what he read in the ethnographies about the use of shallow pits and the archaeological pits he discovered in Illinois. He was unable to interpret the function of the pits without relying on the ethnographic material. Archaeologist Patrick Munson later questioned Binford's conclusion, stating that the shallow pits may have been used simply to put a blackened surface on clay pottery. Munson also used ethnographic analogy to make his claim, but he used a different set of Native American cultures for the analogy.

The *direct historical approach* is similar to ethnographic analogy except that here a direct link exists between the "ethnographic" and the archaeological cultures. In this approach, the archaeologist uses a culture that still inhabits the region in which the archaeological site is found to show the connections between the two cultures. The direct historical approach is as old as the European invasion of the New World. Spanish explorers in Middle America and Peru used it to connect the stone monuments they saw with the native cultures around them. A classic example in modern archaeology is A. V. Kidder's use of the approach in the 1910s and 1920s. Excavating at Pecos Pueblo in northern New Mexico, Kidder correlated the stratified layers of prehistoric occupation (with their painted potsherds) with artifacts used by modern Pueblo Indians in the region (Figure 3.3). Kidder's methodology was a blueprint for all subsequent research in the Southwest and much farther afield as well.

Direct historical research is based on the establishment of a cultural link between past and present. Once this link is made, archaeologists can use information from the present-day or historically described culture to infer the past with greater confidence than is possible with ethnographic analogy. If a Southwestern archaeologist finds smooth, flat stones at an archaeological site and native people 60 miles (96 km) away grind corn using flat stones, then, using the direct historical approach, one may reasonably conclude that the ancient flat stones were also used for grinding corn. From this material evidence, the archaeologist can infer the behaviors of growing, grinding, and eating corn in the past.

Historical archaeologists regularly use both ethnographic analogy and the direct historical approach. The analogies used in historical archaeology often derive from historical documents or from other materials that date to the exact time a site was inhabited. Historical archaeologists know from their own archival research and from the studies of historians that slave owners expected certain behaviors from the enslaved—deference, ignorance, a willingness to work—and

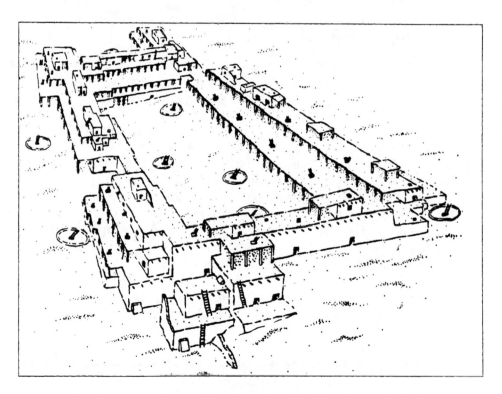

**Figure 3.3**  Artist's view of how Pecos Pueblo, New Mexico, looked when the Spanish colony was established in 1598.

that slaves, for their part, cherished other images—bravery in the face of bondage and cruelty, the ability to trick the master, the skill to leave the plantation surreptitiously at nightfall, and even the power to harm the planter's family with charms, spells, and more serious measures. In the 1760s, the *Charleston* (South Carolina) *Gazette* complained that "The negroes have again begun the hellish practice of poisoning."

Where documents or historical studies exist, historical archaeologists need not rely on ethnographic analogies or the direct historical approach to help them devise their interpretations. Rather than referring to these kinds of analogies as ethnographic, we may think of them as direct analogies, because exact agreement exists between the archaeological site and the text-based material. When used in combination, these two sources can permit a great deal of interpretation. Historical archaeologists can make direct analogies because the people being written about and the people who lived at the archaeological site being excavated are often one and the same. Archaeologists who do not have recourse to texts cannot make direct analogies because the people they study did not write about themselves or the times in which they lived and neither were they written about by anyone else.

## CULTURAL SYSTEMS

Tylor's idea that culture is a "complex whole" makes the point that culture is composed of many elements. These elements are both tangible (erasers, chairs, and notebooks) and intangible (religious beliefs, economic attitudes, and folklore). They work together as a system, or interconnected network, in which the various spheres of life are related. The cultural system allows individuals to adapt to another system, the natural environment (the ecosystem).

An important feature of any system is the idea that when one of its elements changes, other elements change as well. This sort of change is easy to understand in an ecosystem. Deforestation allows rain to strike the ground directly, causing erosion and increased sedimentation in nearby rivers and streams. The change in one part of the ecosystem—in this case, the trees—has brought about changes in another—the soil and the nearby watercourses. These changes can in turn affect human life, particularly if the rainfall destroys houses and agricultural fields.

The idea that change in one part of a system causes changes in others is easy to envision in small, relatively simple cultures where little social stratification exists. We may easily imagine how a change in the leadership rules of a small culture may affect a people's way of life. If the leader, who was once selected only by heredity, is now chosen on the basis of his or her material wealth, we may well imagine that some changes may also occur in the people's trading habits.

Systemic change is more difficult to envision in highly complex, hierarchical cultures, such as those studied by historical archaeologists. Neat one-to-one correlations between changes in one sphere and changes in another are often extremely difficult to make in complex cultures because too many interacting factors exist.

Consider the case of Henry the Navigator, Prince of Portugal (Figure 3.4). Born in 1394, Henry was a studious young man who had a strong interest in mathematics and astronomy. He and his two older brothers, to prove themselves worthy of knighthood, raised an army in 1415 and captured Ceuta, an Islamic commercial town across the Straits of Gibraltar in Morocco. Ceuta was a major center of the Saharan gold trade. Once he had a foothold in North Africa, Henry aimed to control the gold trade and to obtain more African wealth. He thus sponsored several naval expeditions southward along the African coast, with the long-term objective of outflanking the Saharan trade routes controlled by his Islamic enemies. In 1441, one of his captains, Antão Gonçalves, returned to Portugal with two black African captives, one male, the other female. These individuals were the first African slaves taken to Europe. As Portuguese ships navigated southward, they found Madeira and the Cape Verde Islands. On these tiny islands, they developed labor-intensive sugar plantations worked by slaves. These plantation outposts were also relatively close to a seemingly unlimited supply of African captives. The Portuguese soon became obsessed with the economic

**Figure 3.4**   Prince Henry of Portugal, The Navigator.

potential of the African slave trade, not only for human cargoes to work the fields at home, but, eventually, for export to sugar plantations in Brazil and elsewhere.

The African men and women taken to Portugal caused Portuguese citizens to think differently about their world. Instead of seeing the world composed simply of "Christians" and "non-Christians," as before, Portuguese men and women began to see the world as being divided between "slaves" and "nonslaves," "black" and "white," "our culture" and "their culture."

The presence of Africans on the cobbled streets of Lisbon forced the Portuguese to think about new categories of people, to contemplate the men and women among them who were from completely different, non-Portuguese cultural systems. Did the influx of Africans affect *every* part of Portuguese life? Did the presence of Africans in Portugal change the Portuguese system of government? Portuguese strategies and plans for their empire changed over time, but to say that these changes were the direct and sole result of African slavery denies the complexity of Portuguese culture. The Portuguese were undoubtedly changed forever because of their involvement with African slavery, but the true extent of this change to their cultural system and their many social networks must be studied for years to be understood.

All cultural systems are complex, no matter how large the population. At first glance, the Tiwi hunter-gatherers of northern Australia appear to be a "simple" culture. Living on two islands off the northern coast of Australia, they maintained minimal contact with the outside world before 1890. Early European visitors to the islands found them living in small bands, armed only with boomerangs and stone-tipped spears. The Tiwi are by our standards a "simple" people. Their "simplicity," however, is highly misleading.

The complexity of Tiwi culture is amply demonstrated by something we take for granted: our names. Personal names among the Tiwi are bestowed on a child by its father or the man currently married to the child's mother. Whenever a husband dies and the widow remarries, the child receives a new name. In fact, all names given by the dead man are taboo and are never spoken again. Women can marry several times in their lives, so their children may have several different names during their lives. A person would not typically receive a permanent name until his or her mother was dead and could no longer remarry. The Tiwi solved this problem by only exercising the name taboo for a short time. After what was judged to be a decent period, most people slipped back into calling the person by their most familiar name. For men, this generally meant the one they received in their twenties and thirties, and for women the most familiar name was derived from early adolescence. Studies of material culture prove that cultural complexity cannot be measured by artifacts and food remains alone, because many societies, like the Tiwi, enjoyed elaborate and highly sophisticated belief systems and ceremonial lives that may seem more "advanced" than their material possessions.

The archaeologist's job of interpreting past cultural systems is made especially difficult because most of the archaeologist's information about cultural complexity comes from material remains—artifacts, food remains, building ruins, and so forth. Even in the case of exceptional preservation, the intangible aspects of human culture, such as language and religious beliefs, have vanished with their users. Historical archaeologists often have an advantage in being able to interpret past cultural systems because of the presence of written texts and other "nonarchaeological" materials, such as photographs and maps.

## CULTURAL CHANGE

All cultures and societies constantly change, regardless of their size and complexity. Transformations occur in all spheres of culture because people are active beings who invent new ways of doing things, who find new ideas more acceptable than old ones, and who come into contact with other peoples from whom they can learn. Change can be endogenous, originating within the culture, or exogenous, originating outside the culture.

Archaeologists view change primarily through the material remains people left behind. One advantage of archaeology is that it allows anthropologists to study change over long periods. Archaeologists excavating sites inhabited for three centuries may observe a change in pottery decoration from red-painted to black-and-white-painted. The archaeologist task is to seek a plausible interpretation of this process of change. Was the change caused by a switch from male to female potters? Was a religious ban on red-painted pottery enforced by powerful priests? Did red pigment sources become depleted? Did foreigners who made black-and-white pottery acquire more influence in the society? Or did a combination of several factors account for the change in pottery decoration? The search for solutions to such questions makes archaeology an exciting but challenging discipline.

Historical archaeologists face similar problems in understanding cultural change, even though they seldom study sites that were inhabited for several centuries. Cultural change in the modern era was often truly exogenous and far beyond the control of most peoples who experienced it. For example, as we discuss in more detail in Chapter 4, changes in ceramic usage may be mandated by the factory's owner. In the early 1760s, famous English potter Josiah Wedgwood introduced a ceramic he called "cream-colored ware." This ware, with its soft, creamy appearance, enjoyed quick and widespread popularity. Even today, collectors scour dusty showrooms and out-of-the-way antique shops hoping to find the odd example. Not every late-eighteenth-century English consumer could have liked the cream-colored ware, but many of them may have felt forced to buy it at a time when choices were far more limited than they are today. Even then, however, smart factory owners listened to the marketplace, in a lesson that industrialists have repeatedly experienced many times ever since.

The origin of some cultural changes can originate thousands of miles from an archaeological site. For instance, the changing fashions in beaver felt hats in seventeenth- and eighteenth-century Europe had a profound impact on the Native American cultures who lived in Canada's rich, fur-bearing landscape.

Archaeologists can see the pressure exerted by the fur trade at countless native village sites throughout northern North America. The tiny glass beads, the once-shiny copper kettles, and the dull brass buttons provide mute clues to the impact of the European fur-based economy on the native communities.

A family's preference for blue-banded or red-banded plates would, of course, have little effect on culture change outside the narrow confines of a single household. But many changes have lasting significance. A shift from communal planting of crops using horse-drawn plows to the use of diesel-powered planting machines by individuals would ripple through even a complex culture and affect everything from threshing technology to crop yields. The change would affect the operation of social networks through the discontinuance of relations between once-cooperating individuals and groups.

One strength of historical archaeology lies in its ability to assess the impact of what may appear at first to be a minor cultural change. It may be that Wedgwood's cream-colored plates were rejected by some people who chose instead to build their own kilns so that they might continue to produce the earlier styles. Such action is difficult to document. The continuation of traditional pottery styles, however, has been demonstrated by historical archaeologists. In New Hampshire, for instance, archaeologists David Starbuck and Mary Dupré used archaeological specimens to show that the potters of Millville, an area on the western edge of Concord, produced traditional redware ceramics (somewhat resembling terra-cotta flowerpots in material) from 1790 until about 1900. This pottery tradition was virtually unchanged during this 110-year period.

The change in plate color may be so subtle, or unrecognized for its importance, that authors of historical records may have completely ignored it. Starbuck and Dupré pointed out that even though 250 potters operated in New England before 1800, and more than 500 after 1850, they were seldom mentioned in written documents. The conscious, combined use of archaeological and nonarchaeological sources of information makes it possible for historical archaeologists to study both large and small cultural changes.

## GOALS OF HISTORICAL ARCHAEOLOGY

In Chapter 2, we indicated that historical archaeology unfolded in three broad stages. The historical development of the field has resulted in its increasing sophistication, a maturation that is also reflected in three of its major goals:

- to provide information useful for historic preservation and site interpretation;
- to document the lifeways of past peoples; and
- to study the complex process of modernization and all the cultural and social changes, adaptations, and non-adaptations that accompanied it.

Historical archaeologists can meet these goals at a single site or at many different sites throughout a vast area, depending upon the archaeologist's plan of research.

### Preservation and Site Interpretation

Historical archaeology has a large role to play in documenting how buildings looked in the past. Excavation can provide unique information about building size, when room additions were constructed or removed, and where fence lines and outbuildings were located in yards. Homeowners of the past often made reference in their letters and diaries to room additions or to the construction of new buildings on their property and, in many cases, they may have even kept sketches or plans of them. Many people may have made the effort to document the buildings in which they lived, but most homeowners did not. Some people wrote about how they *hoped* to improve their property, but this does not mean that they necessarily could realize their plans. Few people recorded where they located their privy or how often they moved it, thinking perhaps that the subject was too delicate or perhaps too unimportant to be mentioned in writing. As Benjamin Franklin wrote his wife, Deborah, from London in 1765: "I cannot but complain in my mind of Mr. Smith that the house is so long unfit for you to get into, the fences not put up, nor the other necessary articles got ready." We cannot know precisely what these "necessary articles" were, but it is possible that Franklin was referring to the privy behind the house. Archaeologist Paul Schumacher found one of these "necessaries" near the back of this very house in 1953.

Living history museums—old houses and settlements where history is actively interpreted for the public, often with guides wearing period costumes— and historical organizations that try to preserve or restore old buildings are usually interested in knowing "where things were" and "what they looked like." This detailed information enriches the stories interpreters can tell about the past. Historical archaeology, even where abundant historical records do exist, is often the only way to document the full history of a building, from the day it was built to the day it was abandoned, to when it was torn down. Archaeological excavation can provide exacting details that permit the better interpretation and understanding of a site by tourists, thereby promoting the study of history by putting a human face on it.

In addition to providing basic details about when structures were built, how they were built, their size and design, and the location of their associated outbuildings, historical archaeologists also have been able to provide unique information about the furnishings inside homes and other buildings. When archaeologists compare these kinds of archaeological findings with *probate inventories*—lists of a person's possessions at the time of death—a more complete picture of a property can emerge (Chapter 4).

### Undocumented Lifeways

We indicated in Chapter 2 that in the 1960s historical archaeologists developed a strong interest in providing information about people not well represented in historical records. Many historical archaeologists have since provided important information about past lifeways, how people in the past actually lived. Research into the lifeways of people from the recent past is generally thought to be most effective in shedding light on the disfranchised or forgotten men and women of history—slaves, factory workers, miners, farmers, and so forth.

The search for information about past lifeways can be expanded to include people well known in history. Historians have told us a great deal about the large industrialists, financiers, and international merchants who used their wealth to help build today's economic superpowers. Almost every public library has more than one biography of men like Henry Ford and J. P. Morgan. Although we may know where such people went to school, where they lived, or on what boards of directors they served, what do we really know about their day-to-day lives?

Henry Ford's assembly line production methods and his vision to provide affordable automobiles to the public forever changed our lives and our landscapes. Concerned in the 1920s about preserving the nineteenth-century world his automobiles were helping to alter, Ford built a living monument to mythic America called Greenfield Village, in Dearborn, Michigan. His plan was to identify and purchase buildings he deemed either important to American history or associated with famous American citizens. Once acquired, Ford had the buildings disassembled and moved to Michigan, where his workers carefully and accurately reconstructed them. When the invented village was completed, Ford proudly declared: "We have no Egyptian mummies here, nor any relics of the Battle of Waterloo nor do we have any curios from Pompeii, for everything we have is strictly American."

The research conducted by Ford's team was not systematic or consistent with today's professional standards. Ford's workmen did use archaeological methods to compile architectural histories of the individual buildings, but his interest was purely architectural. He was concerned only with the bricks, the clapboard siding, and the floorboards of places like the Armington and Sims Machine Shop, the Logan County Courthouse where Abraham Lincoln practiced law, Edison's Menlo Park laboratory (Figure 3.5), and the other two dozen buildings he ordered reconstructed. Ford was definitely not interested in documenting anyone's lifeways. An archaeologist *could* have excavated around Ford's birthplace (the first home Ford restored, but the last he had moved to Greenfield Village). They could have collected valuable information about the daily life of the Ford family during Henry's formative years, but this was not done. If historical archaeology had been conducted at Ford's birthplace, it would have underscored the discipline's ability to answer questions about all past peoples, regardless of social position, sex, or ethnic affiliation.

### The Process of Globalization

The greatest challenge faced by historical archaeologists is in the area of studying globalization, the worldwide spread of material objects, people, cultures, and ideas. Globalization includes such complex topics as the spread of urbanization, industrialization, capitalist economics, and the expansion of nations and their in-

**Figure 3.5**   The reconstruction of Thomas Edison's laboratory complex at Greenfield Village, Michigan, in January 1929.

stitutions to all parts of the world. Archaeologists can study these processes using a diverse storehouse of information, including artifacts, architecture, food remains, personal letters, governmental records, and travelers' account to mention but a few.

The European Age of Discovery brought peoples of diverse cultures in contact for the first time. The interactions that developed were complex and bi-directional in their impact, meaning that culture change occurred between both parties. As both sides borrowed from one another, they created the modern world. One only has to mention the American potato, which became a staple of European peasants, or tobacco, to get the point. At the same time, the European nations built forts, missions, and small colonies in distant lands, settlements that were transplanted but altered versions of communities at home. Portugal became a global superpower in the sixteenth and seventeenth centuries by virtue of its international trade in gold, spices, sugar, and human beings. Its agents planted colonies along the coasts of Africa, in India, throughout Asia, and across the Atlantic in Brazil. In each place, the colonists erected buildings that were copies of prototypes back home. For example, their late fifteenth-century fort at Elmina, on the Ghanian coast in West Africa, was built according to the latest European ideas on fortification, with no concession to local conditions. Even entire town plans were imported to foreign lands. The eighteenth-century town of Ouro Prêto in Brazil looks as if it were mail-ordered from Portugal. The streets are narrow and cobblestoned, the houses are small and have red-tiled roofs, and the language heard in the shops is Portuguese. Minute details of architecture and material culture often disclose telling differences between colonial towns and their homeland's prototypes, details that are never mentioned in documents of the day.

## HISTORIC-PERIOD SITES

Historical archaeology, like all archaeology, is based on the recovery of information from sites. A *site* is any place that contains traces of past human activity. The site constitutes the archaeologists' basic source of information, the place were they can get a glimpse of past culture and society. Many different kinds of sites exist, ranging from those occupied for a few hours to those inhabited for hundreds of years. Archaeologists often classify sites in terms of their past function.

### Domestic Sites

Domestic sites are places where people lived. These sites can include an array of habitation types ranging from the smallest, simplest structures to the grandest mansions. Archaeologists are interested in domestic structures because they provide the clearest information about how past peoples lived. Domestic sites tell archaeologists about the kinds of objects people used, the varieties of foods they ate, whether they traded with other peoples, the nature of their religious beliefs and ceremonies, and how they chose to discard their broken and unwanted articles.

Archaeologists can study domestic sites either alone or in groups. Numerous individual sites can be clustered in cities and towns, and in such cases the archaeologist may consider the entire city to be a single site. When archaeologists from a private consulting firm excavated a small Chinese immigrant village at Rincon Point, California, they learned a great deal about mid-nineteenth century Chinese life in one part of the American West. The village was inhabited from about 1850 until only about 1865, but today it lies beneath the western approach to the San Francisco Bay Bridge. The archaeology at the village site filled many blank spots in our knowledge about Chinese domestic life in America. The research team at the site found bones and shells to prove that these immigrants had become California's first commercial fishermen. These immigrants were the first to recognize the commercial potential of abalone, and so they used the sea as a way of adapting to American life. They ate the meat from the abalone and sold the colorful shells to craftsmen, who were soon making popular jewelry for northern California's shoppers. The archaeologists also discovered that the Chinese who lived at the Rincon Point village used equal proportions of American and Chinese objects, ranging from brown stoneware jars used to store traditional Chinese foods to American beer bottles and tooth powder. Rising real estate prices and increased taxes (imposed only on the Chinese) soon drove the Chinese away from their town, and by 1870, the area had become part of the booming San Francisco waterfront. Only careful archaeology could provide the details of life at Rincon Point.

Long before the creation of public landfills, many historic peoples threw their trash into their yards, tossed things under their houses, or swept their refuse against the back fence. Many people also used their privies as places to discard objects they did not want others to know about, such as alcohol bottles.

A privy excavated by Kenneth Lewis, now of Michigan State University, provided a unique perspective on the consumption habits of the planters who lived on a late seventeenth- and early eighteenth-century sugar plantation near Charleston, South Carolina. Henry Middleton founded Middleton Place Plantation in 1675 upstream from the city. He owned no less than eight hundred slaves and twenty individual plantations. Middleton Place prospered for nearly two centuries. It had two beautifully landscaped formal gardens, a spring house, and a long drive leading to the mansion. General Sherman's troops destroyed all the main buildings at the plantation when they cut their scorched path through the South in 1865 (Figure 3.6). The privy was the only building they left unharmed. Over one hundred years later, the archaeologists carefully removed the accumulated rubbish in the privy and recovered priceless information about its users. They learned, for example, that the plantation residents used blue and white porcelain imported from China; other dishes with a pattern of delicate flowers, called French Bourbon Sprig, popular before the French Revolution; and finely cut glass decanters and stemware. The jumble of broken medicine bottles in the privy revealed that the plantation's residents suffered a variety of ailments, ranging from upset stomachs to night sweats associated with consumption.

The Middleton Place privy, like all such facilities, provides an imperfect picture of past life because it encapsulates only the things that people meant to throw down the open hole. Nonetheless, long-sealed privies can be a revealing source of information about every level of society.

Historical archaeologists often use their techniques to reconstruct the architectural history of standing buildings, in a more scientific way than did Henry Ford's workmen. When archaeologist Theodore Reinhart took a crew of students from the College of William and Mary to Shirley Plantation, Virginia, in 1980, one of his objectives was to reconstruct the mansion's history. Many historians thought that this stately brick mansion, overlooking the James River about 35 miles (56 km) west of Williamsburg, was built in the seventeenth century, probably after 1660. Because no one knew for certain, Reinhart decided to dig next to the mansion's wall to look for a builder's trench.

Construction workers who built brick walls needed to excavate linear trenches along the path of the walls to allow them space to construct the wall's lowest courses. Laborers often lost coins or dropped broken bottles and other objects inside the trench as they worked. The trenches, which would be forever covered over with earth, where also convenient places to throw the trash from their

**Figure 3.6** Ruins of the main house at Middleton Place Plantation, South Carolina.

lunches. Archaeologists can use the objects buried in the builder's trenches to help determine the date of a building's construction (Figure 3.7).

The known manufacturing dates of the English ceramics found by Reinhart's team inside the Shirley mansion's builder's trench convinced him that it was not erected in the seventeenth century, but that the mansion "was built by John Carter, sometime before his death in 1742 and possibly in the years 1738 and 1739." In the case of the Shirley mansion, then, archaeology was the only way to answer a seemingly straightforward historical question.

### Industrial Sites

Places once used for manufacturing or production are known as industrial sites. The study of industrial sites is a subfield of historical archaeology, known as industrial archaeology. Industrial archaeologists study a variety of manufacturing sites that include mills, factories, kilns, and mines. Such sites can range in date from the earliest days of manufacturing to the present. Industrial sites are often

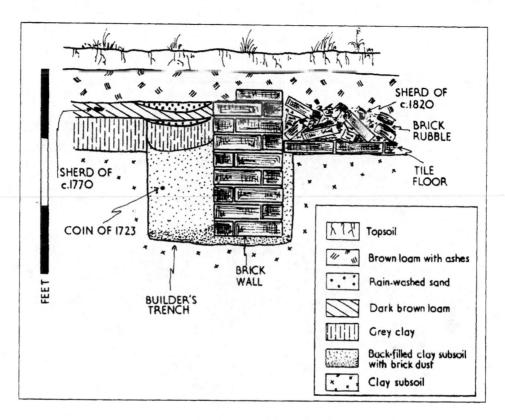

SHERD OF
c.1820

BRICK
RUBBLE

TILE
FLOOR

SHERD OF
c.1770

COIN OF 1723

BRICK
WALL

BUILDER'S
TRENCH

FEET

| | Topsoil |
| --- | --- |
| | Brown loam with ashes |
| | Rain-washed sand |
| | Dark brown loam |
| | Grey clay |
| | Back-filled clay subsoil with brick dust |
| | Clay subsoil |

**Figure 3.7**  Builder's trench.

complex and require full documentation using photographs and accurately scaled architectural renderings.

Industrial archaeology need not always involve excavation. Many individuals who are not archaeologists—but were trained as industrial architects, engineers, or in another field—often refer to themselves as industrial archaeologists. In a great many cases, these researchers are storehouses of information. For example, as documented by archaeologist Donald Linebaugh, the amateur archaeologist Roland W. Robbins was the leading authority on seventeenth- and eighteenth-century industrial sites in New England. Robbins investigated numerous iron works in the northeastern United States from 1948 to 1984. Professional archaeologists did not always approve of his methods of excavation, but his knowledge of industrialization in the region was unparalleled.

Researchers sometimes only wish to document the remains at the site without disturbing the soil. At large, standing industrial sites—such as the Silver King Ore-Loading Station in Park City, Utah (Figure 3.8)—archaeologists may be called in to assess what might remain buried at such sites. They may be asked to excavate one or two small areas to search for specific details about construction techniques and

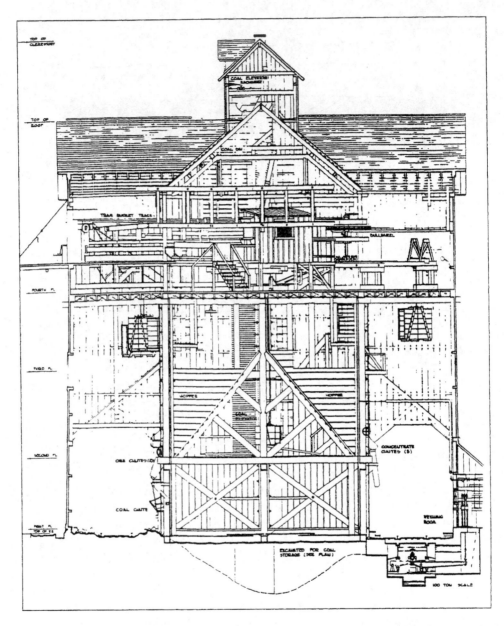

**Figure 3.8**   Measured drawing of the Silver King Ore-Loading Station, Park City, Utah, built in 1901.

dates. Such research typically involves not only industrial architects, but also the collaboration of historians of technology, experts on such arcane subjects as iron bridges or nineteenth-century railroad stations.

Archaeological research sometimes provides an important way to learn about small-scale technologies. A prime example is the arrastra found in the western United States. Arrastras were circular, stone-lined depressions ranging in size from 8–20 feet (2.4–6.1 m) in diameter. Prospectors used arrastras to crush stones during their often-frenzied search for gold and silver. They performed the actual crushing with heavy grinding stones that would turn about ten revolutions per minute. Contemporary photographs show that miners used horses, steam engines, and water wheels to turn the massive grinding stones. Archaeologists Roger Kelly and Marsha Kelly studied an arrastra site in northwest Arizona. Built sometime in the early twentieth century, this site consisted of the arrastra itself, a long, narrow trough made of flat stones extending outward from the arrastra, a stone wall, an ore pile, and a possible camp area. Laborers at the site had scratched dates of between 1910 and 1916 on stones, and someone had etched "Hello Bill" on one of them. The study of this one arrastra will not change the way we think about the large sweep of world history. But, as the Kellys correctly point out, arrastras challenge archaeologists to think about industrial sites, regardless of size, as storehouses of information about technological development and the people who made industry possible.

Archaeologists sometimes research industrial sites to learn about the production of artifacts. As one important example, Edward Heite studied the Collins, Geddes Cannery Site, in Lebanon, Delaware. The site of the cannery is largely forgotten by today's local residents, but more than one hundred years earlier it was an important industry. A local reporter wrote in 1873 that "The large fruit canning establishment of Collins & Co. at Lebanon, near Camden, is now running day and night in manufacturing sixty thousand gallons of catsup for parties in Philadelphia and New York, at one dollar per gallon." Cans, such as those that contained catsup, are common finds at late-nineteenth-century archaeological sites (Figure 3.9). As an archaeologist, Heite was concerned, not with the production of catsup, but with the manufacture of the tin cans themselves.

Heite was called in to study the cannery because the site was slated to be destroyed by construction. The site was overgrown with trees and brush and stood in the path of a much-needed new bridge over the Tidbury Branch of the St. Jones River in central Delaware. Heite examined the site using a combination of surface survey and small test pits (see Chapters 6 and 8). He also used a backhoe to help him expose the cannery's brick foundations. During the course of the fieldwork he found many of the wall foundations (discovering in places that someone had robbed much of the brick for use elsewhere), the brick foundations for two boilers, the building's cellar, and a dump.

Many of the most interesting artifacts from the site were small scraps of tin. Most people might consider these fragments to be junk, but they told the story of tin can production at the Lebanon cannery. Heite learned by examining the scraps

**Figure 3.9**   Three tin cans produced at Collins, Geddes cannery of
Lebanon, Delaware.

that two methods existed for making the ends of the cans. In one process, the
metalworker cut the circular top from a sheet of tin with a stamping die. The die
also cut the "fill hole," the spot through which the can's contents were later
added. In the second method, a die first cut the top and then the fill hole was
punched in a separate process. Heite discovered the second method by observing
that the fill holes were off-centered and not systematically placed on the lids. He
also learned that the tin can producers had cut their cans from sheets of tin that
averaged about 16 inches (40.6 cm) square, though they sometimes used sheets
half this size. The size of the sheets seems irrelevant, but it is not. Tin can producers made cans based on the size of the sheets. The ideal was to cut four can bodies
from one sheet. Tin can producers still make cans in the same sizes as those found
in Delaware, but the tin now comes in rolls instead of sheets.

Heite's research on tin cans may strike many as trivial. After all, he only
studied a few cans produced at a single cannery in one U.S. state. But it is
through such detailed research that historical archaeologists expand our knowledge about all aspects of history. Even the lowly tin can is part of history. Heite
was correct when he wrote that his research provided "a laboratory in which to
study the changes in canneries over the past century." Industrial sites of all kinds
provide important laboratories for such research efforts.

We may often think that industrial sites occur as individual factories or even
a complex of closely spaced buildings, all of which are dedicated to the production of a specific product, like tin cans. But in addition to studying individual
sites, industrial archaeologists can also examine large regions where the inhabitants were engaged in a multitude of industrial activities. In his study of the Bas-

sar, an iron-working society living in the tiny nation of Togo, West Africa, archaeologist Philip Lynton De Barros investigated a region that contained villages inhabited by numerous industrial specialists. Archaeological research indicates that West Africans started working iron during the 900–800 B.C. period. The people of the Bassar region had adopted iron production sometime after A.D. 500, and they continued it until the early years of the twentieth century. During the seventeenth century, the region developed specialized villages dedicated to iron smelting, iron smithing, charcoal making, and pottery manufacture. De Barros's research showed that the slave raids into the area during the late eighteenth and nineteenth centuries had a significant impact on the region's people, because they had to invent new political institutions to adapt to the changing circumstances of the times. The new organizations in turn caused a change in the location of population centers in the region as people sought safety in numbers.

De Barros's research indicates that industrialization is not simply technological. Adopting new ways of producing things—from smelted iron to tin cans—has social and cultural implications that industrial archaeologists can also investigate.

### Military Sites

Military sites are places associated with armed conflict or with military occupation. Forts, blockhouses, earthworks, and locations where battles were fought are all classified as military sites.

Traditional historians have always used military actions as a way to explain international politics and world events, and so it is perhaps not surprising that military sites were some of the first places to attract both amateur and professional historical archaeologists. From 1918 until 1940, the New-York Historical Society sponsored a Field Exploration Committee whose goal was to investigate military sites used from colonial times until the War of 1812. The committee was the brainchild of military historian William Calver. Working in collaboration with civil engineer and amateur historian Reginald Bolton, Calver wrote a series of articles on his findings for the *New-York Historical Society Quarterly Bulletin*. These articles were later collected together and republished in 1950 as the book *History Written with Pick and Shovel*. The publication of Calver and Bolton's study was an inspiring event for many amateur historical archaeologists. Just to name one example, in the early 1950s Stanley Gifford began excavating at Fort William Henry, the military installation made famous outside archaeology by the 1992 epic film *The Last of the Mohicans*.

In 1959, the State of Michigan began archaeological excavations at Fort Michilimackinac. These excavations have been conducted every year since (see Figure 2.5). Archaeologists have examined much of the fort's interior, unearthing over one million artifacts, including glass bottles, religious medals, brass kettle fragments, glass trade beads, dish fragments, keys, and military buttons. Professional excavations, like those at Fort Michilimackinac, help provide significant information about how fortifications were built, what modifications in ideal forti-fication design were required in certain environments, and how forts were en-larged and rebuilt to adapt to changing circumstances. Site managers and restorationists use the archaeological evidence to help interpret the site to tourists.

In addition to providing important details for site reconstruction and restoration, historical archaeologists can also show how individual companies of soldiers lived. The soldiers' unit may be well known, but their actual everyday lives may remain a mystery. In North America, the Royal Canadian Mounted Po-lice—the redoubtable Mounties—is among the world's most famous law enforce-ment service. The Canadian government created the North-West Mounted Police in 1874 to protect Canada's sovereignty over its most-western territories, and to keep the peace between the region's European and Native American inhabi-tants. The Mounties built several outposts along the frontier, including Fort Walsh, which they erected in 1875 in today's southwestern Saskatchewan. They dismantled the post in 1883, selling its logs to ranchers who were just moving into the region.

Canadian archaeologists started excavating the hospital at Fort Walsh in 1973. Their diggings showed that the Mounties built the hospital 16.4 by 44.5 feet (5 by 13.6 m) in size, and included a wing measuring 12.5 by 13.5 feet (3.8 by 4.1 m). They divided the hospital into three equal-sized rooms. The rooms on both ends were used as sick wards, and the post's doctors used the central room as an office and examination room. The excavations yielded 150,000 artifacts, in-cluding numerous medicine bottles.

Historical records indicate that the Mounties were often beset with sickness, including a malady they called "mountain fever." Today we know this illness as Rocky Mountain spotted fever. Many of the townspeople who lived near the fort died of the fever, but during its eight years of operation, only one Mountie died at Fort Walsh. The excavated medicine bottles hold the key to the different rates of death. The presence of 2.5-gallon (9.5-1) bottle fragments in the hospital's remains prove that the fort's doctors had bulk medicines shipped to the post. Specimens of smaller medicine bottles suggest that they dispersed their own prepared reme-dies to the Mounties. The excavators did not unearth a single patent medicine bottle from inside the hospital. The absence of these commercial remedies is note-worthy because patent medicines were considered the wonder drugs of the nine-teenth century. Government agencies did not regulate the patent medicine industry, so its practitioners were free to infuse their "medicines" with high quan-tities of cocaine, alcohol, codeine, and even arsenic. The archaeologists did dis-cover numerous patent medicine bottles outside the hospital. These bottles imply that the fort's residents actually did consume great quantities of self-prescribed miracle drugs, but only out of sight of the post's doctors. The doctors, for their part, may have refused to use patent medicines, recognizing them for what they were: long on advertising fluff and short on restorative power.

Archaeological research can even document how battles were fought. By recording and examining patterns of bullets and matériel found in the ground, archaeologists can provide important information about military tactics and can even document what weapons were used in a battle.

A dramatic example comes from just south of Fort Walsh, in the fields of Montana where George Custer fought his famous battle with the Sioux and Cheyennes in 1876. By examining the distribution of cavalry equipment and Native American artifacts on the battlefield, archaeologist Douglas Scott was able to reconstruct the sequence of the battle (Figure 3.10). The distribution of spent cartridge cases showed that Custer, or someone in command, deployed a line of men facing south from Custer Ridge to meet the onrush of Cheyennes from the west and of the Dakotas (Sioux) from the south. At the same time, another group of Sioux attacked from the east against the end of the soldier's line. Scott's team of archaeologists found at least fifteen Springfield carbines and two Colt pistols in this part of the field. In the course of the battle, the solders formed themselves into a broad V, with Last Stand Hill to the north. When the soldiers' position on the east gave way, the Sioux on the east began a two-pronged attack toward the main body of soldiers, who, as the cartridges prove, were already under intense attack from the west and south. The physical evidence also proved that several

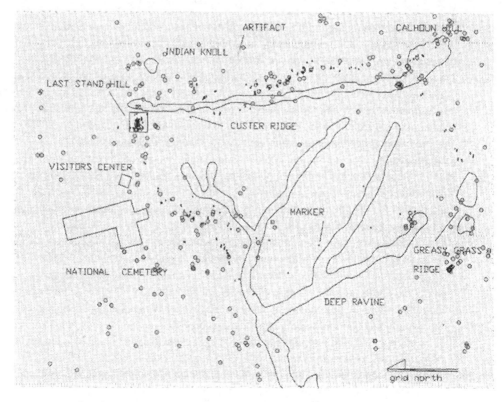

**Figure 3.10** The distribution of army-related artifacts on the Custer Battlefield.

Native Americans used captured arms to shoot back at the soldiers. At the end, the remaining soldiers were on the west end of the ridge and were completely surrounded by the hostile force.

In a related study, archaeologist Richard Fox used artifact finds and Native American testimony to shatter the Custer myth. Fox showed that the Seventh Cavalry entered the battle in a disciplined manner, in full accordance with their training. When they met the stiff resistance of the overwhelming enemy, the soldiers' order suddenly broke down. The famed "Last Stand," far from being a heroic battle-to-the-death, was characterized by chaos and panic. The soldiers, in complete disarray, engaged in little determined fighting.

The research by Fox and Scott at the famous Little Big Horn battlefield, and by numerous archaeologists working at other less well-known battle sites, does more than simply fill in the gaps in knowledge about specific military engagements. These archaeologists challenge us to think about how archaeology can be used to study warfare, tactics, and strategy.

## Burial Sites

Places where the dead are buried are understandably some of the most controversial sites archaeologists can study. Excavating a skeleton necessarily means disturbing the grave site, and many would consider excavation a form of desecration. The study of modern-era burial sites have the ability to generate widespread controversy because many descendants of the deceased may still be living. It is reasonable to conclude that they may not be entirely enthusiastic about archaeologists excavating their ancestors' remains and subjecting their bones to study in a university laboratory. Archaeologists have thus learned to be sensitive to the desires of descendants when they seek to unearth the remains of the dead.

The investigation of historic burials is often expressly forbidden or highly regulated by law. These regulations have not been universally applied, however, and only in recent years have laws been enacted to control the investigation of ancient burials in many countries.

Archaeologists are interested in grave sites because they can provide a mine of unique information about past societies. Archaeologists who study grave sites and cemeteries usually work closely with physical anthropologists, specialists who can provide information about diets, growth rates of children and adults, the prevalence of dental cavities, disease rates, and the effects of devastating afflictions such as lead poisoning from water pipes.

In the mid-1980s, anthropologist Jerome Handler used a collection of excavated African skeletons from a slave plantation in Barbados (dating from about 1660–1820) to study the effects of lead poisoning. Handler discovered that the ailment, dry bellyache—of which the slaves constantly complained—was actually the effects of lead poisoning. When teetotalers said that "there was a demon in the rum," they did not know how right they were. As it turns out, the apparatus used in making rum was constructed with lead seams. Lead would leach into the rum during the fermentation process and those imbibing would unknowingly ingest it. The rate of lead poisoning was accordingly high among Caribbean populations that relied heavily on rum for entertainment and refreshment.

Non-African skeletons are not available from Barbados to compare with those of slaves. Another dramatic example, however, demonstrates that no one in the historic period was immune to lead poisoning. When Sir John Franklin left England in 1845 with 129 crewmen and officers to find the elusive Northwest Passage through the Canadian Arctic, people widely considered his expedition one of the most exciting of the day. England was thus stunned when Franklin and "his gallant crew" (as they were immortalized in song) vanished without a trace. What had happened to them? The answer to the Franklin mystery was not known until the 1980s, when the bodies of several crewmen were discovered, in an almost perfect state of preservation, in far northern Canada. Upon examining the bodies, Owen Beattie discovered that the expedition's massive supply of canned foods had in fact killed them. High-tech atomic absorption analysis of soft tissue from the buried crewmen showed that they had suffered from acute lead intoxication. The heavy solder seams on their food cans had leached into the food, causing lead poisoning. The chance that the Franklin crew would be poisoned was high because each man had 248 pounds (111.6 kg) of canned meats, stews, soups, and vegetables allocated to him. Arctic explorers and historians who had studied the Franklin expedition since the mid-nineteenth century had always been puzzled by the crew's apparent aimless wanderings as evidenced by the rock cairns they built and by their irregular scatters of abandoned supplies. Neither hostile natives, the Arctic deep freeze, nor bad leadership was the cause of the crew's demise; tin cans killed Franklin and his men.

As noted above, the excavation of burial sites is not always without quarrel. A recent controversy surrounded the study of an eighteenth-century cemetery in lower Manhattan, near Wall Street, provides a stark example. A cemetery, historically known as the "African Burial Ground," came to light during the construction of a 34-story federal office building. Archaeologists discovered the remains of over 400 individuals located from 16–28 feet (4.9–8.5 m) below the current street level. The human remains were those of New York's enslaved men, women, and children of African descent. The discovery of this rare archaeological find caused a broad outcry from members of the African American community. Whereas some people favored the academic study of the remains, others thought that any examination was unnecessary. Activists proposed that more African American participation was needed in the excavation, and in September 1993, an African religious ceremony was held to commemorate the transfer of the remains from Lehman College in New York City to Howard University in Washington, D.C. In October, a second ceremony marked the final "homecoming" of the remains, as the last skeletons were transferred to Howard University. At Howard, the remains are the subject of an intensive, multiyear, scientific study by a team of physical anthropologists. The team's research is providing important new information about the daily lives of hundreds of eighteenth-century men, women, and children of African descent who resided in New York City.

### Special-Purpose Sites

Places where people once performed tasks that were not related to industrial production, military activities, or domestic life are termed special-purpose sites. Churches, stores, mental hospitals, and other special-purpose sites give archaeologists the chance to interpret chapters of the past that are often overlooked.

Historical archaeologists have excavated several special-purpose sites. An intriguing example is William C. Hoff's store in San Francisco, California. William Hoff, from New York, was one of thousands of "forty-niners" who traveled west during the great California Gold Rush. Hoff's dreams of wealth lay not in prospecting but in merchandizing, and less than a year after his arrival in the West he had established a general store and ship supply house on the bustling San Francisco waterfront. Unfortunately for Hoff, however, about a year later, on May 3–4, 1851, the "Fifth Great Fire" completely engulfed his store, destroying it along with hundreds of homes, hotels, and other businesses.

In early 1986, archaeologist Allen Pastron led a group of investigators to the site of Hoff's Store. After almost a full year of excavation, the research team had pulled thousands of artifacts from the old store remains, encapsulated 15 feet (4.6 m) beneath the streets of San Francisco. These artifacts offer a rare glimpse of the actual merchandise purchased by the optimistic forty-niners: leather shoes, brass military buttons, books of matches, ceramic crocks, patent medicine bottles, silver forks, brass spoons, and ceramic crucibles used for melting gold. The archaeologists even found a charred wooden bowling pin. They also discovered numerous foodstuffs in the store deposits, including cut pork bones, perfectly preserved olives still in their tightly closed jars, coffee beans, walnuts, peach pits, and even cakes, breads, and crackers.

Another interesting example comes from the King's Arms tavern site in England (Figure 3.11). The inn was located in Uxbridge, Middlesex, and during the height of the inn's operation in the 1780s and 1790s, the town was the first major coach stop between London and Oxford. As reported by Jacqueline Pearce, the archaeological research at the King's Arms was important for two major reasons. In the first place, few tavern sites have been excavated, either in Great Britain or elsewhere. As a result, even the briefest analysis significantly increases our knowledge of one kind of site important in the lives of past people. Second, because the excavated remains had been deposited as a single "clearing operation," they offer a rare, snapshot view of the objects that patrons used while at the inn. Finds of encapsulated archaeological deposits are unique and archaeologists are always pleased to find them.

Pearce concentrated her analysis on the ceramics, glassware, and clay smoking pipes from the inn. The ceramics alone showed the variety of objects purchased by the innkeepers. The collection includes at least thirty dinner plates (with five different raised patterns along the rims), two oval serving plates, four

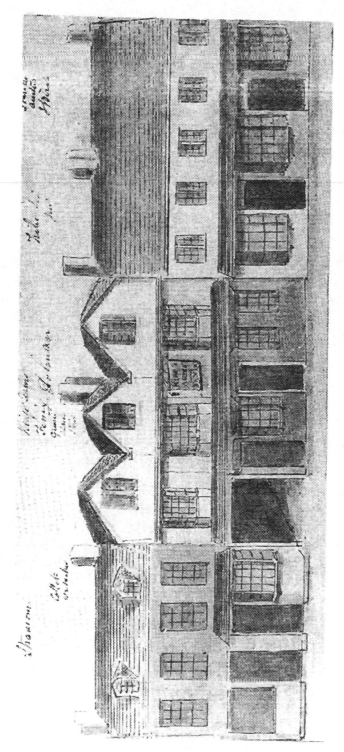

**Figure 3.11** The King's Arms Inn, around 1790.

sauce boats, and at least seven mugs, all of English manufacture. Also included are bowls and plates made of English and Chinese porcelain, heavy stoneware mugs, teapot lids, and punch bowls. As we might expect at an inn, the collection also contains fragments of numerous glass bottles, goblets, tumblers, and other bottles, as well as at least seventy-five clay smoking pipes. At that time in history, individuals could purchase a pipe of tobacco along with their spirits.

## Multipurpose Sites

Multipurpose sites are complex places where the occupants carried out several often equally important tasks. Multipurpose sites cannot be classified simply as domestic, industrial, or special purpose because their former inhabitants performed all of those tasks there. Historical archaeologists often encounter several kinds of multipurpose sites. Richard Beavers of the University of New Orleans found that Destrehan Plantation, Louisiana, was the perfect example of a multipurpose site. The estate's owners built Destrehan in 1787 as an indigo plantation, but three-quarters of a century later they converted it into a more profitable sugar-producing property. An inventory made in 1792 lists the following buildings on the plantation's grounds: a mansion, a detached kitchen, a storehouse, two hospitals for sick slaves, a pigeon house, a coach house, three cabins, a "Negro camp" of nineteen cabins, a blacksmith shop, a drying house for indigo, a hay shed, a pump house, a series of sheds needed for churning indigo during fermentation, and an engine house for the indigo grinder. With the conversion to sugar cultivation, the plantation's owners built a sugar boiling house and a mill. Beavers and his research team investigated several different domestic buildings, numerous special-use structures, and many buildings associated with production. Plantations, because they housed so many different kinds of people, doing so many different tasks, are perfect examples of multipurpose sites, but archaeologists can classify many different kinds of sites as multipurpose.

## Maritime Sites

Maritime archaeology, once referred to as underwater archaeology, is a highly specialized kind of archaeology that is not restricted to historic sites. Maritime archaeologists have been extremely successful in documenting past ship designs, routes of trade, and many aspects of technology among Phoenicians, Romans, and other ancient, seagoing cultures. The change in designation from "underwater" to "maritime" has developed because many archaeologists interested in seaborne history are as interested in coastal sites, like docks and shipping villages, as they are in the ships that brought goods to land. Like their colleagues who explore sites from ancient history, historical archaeologists also regularly conduct excavations underwater and along coastal areas with maritime connections.

A superb example of the connection between land and sea comes from Labrador. In the mid-sixteenth century, Basque whalers from northern Spain pursued their giant prey in the Strait of Belle Isle off southern Labrador. They hunted and processed whales with great efficiency from a shore base in a sheltered anchorage at Red Bay. A true understanding of the work of the Basque whalers could only come from linking their activities on land with those at sea. James Tuck of Memorial University in Newfoundland examined their near-industrial whaling operation on land, while Robert Grenier of Environment Canada searched the bay floor for the wreck for the whaling ship *San Juan*. Basque archives indicate that this vessel sunk off the whaling station in late 1565, just as she was about to leave for home with a full cargo.

After eight years' work, Grenier's team located the wrecks of three whaling ships, one of them almost certainly the *San Juan*, a mid-sized sailing vessel, and several small boats. All were well preserved by the area's cold water and fine silt. After months of diving on the *San Juan*, the archaeologists recovered more than two-hundred whale oil barrels, parts of the ship's rigging, some navigational instruments, and details of the 250-ton (227 mt) ship. The team drew and photographed every timber, joint, tool mark, and hole before the wood was returned to the favorable preservation conditions on the sea floor. The result of their labors was a detailed reconstruction of a sixteenth-century whaling vessel.

Meanwhile on land, the terrestrial archaeologists exposed the remains of twenty "tryworks," or refineries where the whalers processed the blubber into marketable oil. They also found the cooperages, the places where the barrel workers had made the casts used to transport the oil to market. In among the remains were also many personal possessions the whalers used in their daily lives in the Far North.

Whether on land or underwater, historical archaeologists study past human culture and society in all its many forms throughout the world. To do so they must rely heavily on artifacts, the topic of Chapter 4.

## TIME TRAVEL

### Palmares, Brazil, c. 1650

Resistance will exist wherever men and women are kept in forced bondage. The plantations of the New World were certainly no exception. Thousands of enslaved men and women ran away from their captors, and in their flight, sought lives elsewhere on their own terms. The communities of fugitive slaves appear throughout the slave-holding world, including Jamaica and the southern United States. One of the earliest and largest runaway slave communities in the New World was Palmares, in northeastern Brazil. Like all maroon communities (or, in Portuguese, *quilombos*), Palmares was created as a direct response to the horrors of human bondage and the harsh treatment received by enslaved men and

*(continued)*

Source: Charles E. Orser, Jr. and Pedro P. A. Funari, 2001. Archaeology and Slave Resistance and Rebellion. *World Archaeology* 33:61–72.

women who cultivated cash crops for someone else's benefit.

Portuguese colonists had established a number of sugar plantations along Brazil's lush Atlantic coast by 1570, or about seventy years after they had first encountered the continent. They built their plantations between the white, sandy beaches of the coast and the dense forests that appeared further inland. A row of mountains created a natural barrier to the spread of colonial plantations. At the time of the Portuguese arrival, Native South Americans either lived throughout the forests or along the coast. Those on the coast were pushed inland by the clearance of land and the harsh practices of the European settlers.

When slaves ran away from the coastal estates, they inevitably headed inland toward the mountains. By 1605, several fugitives had established Palmares, about 50 miles (80 km) from the coast. The Portuguese called it Palmares because of the palm groves that grew in the area, but the inhabitants may have called it "Angola Janga" (or Little Angola), after the African homeland of most of its people. The area encompassed by Palmares may have been as large as 10,400 square miles (27,000 square kilometers).

Slave owners regarded the unwelcome departure of slaves from their plantations as a serious affront to their power and finances. As a result, they did everything they could to destroy maroon communities when they sprang up. Their goal was to recapture their former slaves as fast as possible and return them to their plantation labors. Dutch explorers trying to acquire Brazil and Portuguese planters trying to keep it, both perceived Palmares as a substantial threat to their authority and safety. They thus began almost annual attacks on the community's villages in 1612. These assaults had little affect, and Palmares had continued to grow and prosper. At the height of its development (1650–1670), the community was reported to be composed of ten separate villages and a population as high as twenty thousand.

The people of Palmares succeeded in creating a new culture in Brazil. It was a complex mixture of diverse strands from Africa, Europe, and South America. Their religion was a combination of African and Roman Catholic beliefs and rituals, but they had a political organization that had a king at its head. He lived in a capital city, and was supported by a number of lords, or sub-rulers, who lived in the smaller hamlets. The material culture of Palmares also blended together various traditions. Their pottery, for instance, portrayed a mixture of Ovimbundu (African) and Tupinamba (Native South American) traits.

The people of Palmares made their houses using the materials they found around them, so they resembled the local Indians' homes. They erected wooden stockades around their towns, because they were under frequent attack. The only contemporary drawing of Palmares, made in 1647, indicates that the people also built high watchtowers, from which they could signal the approach of a hostile, enemy force.

Even with all their attention to defense, the men and women of Palmares had to maintain a number of alliances to survive. They traded with the local Native South Americans for food, clay pottery, and other materials, and also with the Portuguese settlers who lived on the frontier. From these Portuguese colonists they received wheel-thrown, glazed ceramics, possibly locally made and from Europe.

The Portuguese finally succeeded in destroying Palmares in 1694. They captured the community's king, a popular leader named Zumbi, took him to the Portuguese-controlled coast, and beheaded him. His memory is still very much alive in Brazil, and he is widely revered for his bravery, leadership skills, and defiance.

# Chapter 4

# HISTORICAL ARTIFACTS

*"For life and joy, and for objects and knowledge curious."*

Walt Whitman, 1855

In the "Adventure of the Blue Carbuncle," Dr. Watson arrives at 221B Baker Street, London, to find Sherlock Holmes contemplating "a very seedy and disreputable hard-felt hat, much worse for wear, and cracked in several places." From this hat, judged by Watson to be rather ordinary, Holmes brilliantly deduces a wealth of information, as only he can do. The great detective concludes that the owner of the hat was an intellectual man, that he was once prosperous, that he is middle-aged, and that he recently has had his hair cut. Holmes also figures that the owner's wife has ceased to love him and that the man has no gaslight in his house.

Almost everyone in the Western world is familiar with the exploits of the illustrious, though fictional, Sherlock Holmes. His deductive methods will live forever. Some readers may be surprised to find his name in a book about historical archaeology, but though Holmes was only the literary creation of an English physician, the insightful sleuth has much in common with modern archaeologists. When Holmes says in "The Boscombe Valley Mystery" that his method is "founded upon the observation of trifles" he could have been speaking as an archaeologist. Archaeologists, no matter what time of history they study, focus on what archaeologist James Deetz memorably termed the "small things forgotten." These "small things" are the many mundane objects ordinary people used in their daily lives, things sometimes so trivial that their users may never have consciously thought about them. They may simply have taken the objects for granted, much as we do with many of the things around us. For historical archaeologists, the trifles bear a striking resemblance to things the average Westerner uses every day today: glass bottles, ceramic dishes, mirrors, buttons, thimbles, and a hundred and one other things. The similarity between the things used today and those used in the recent past are part of the mystique and appeal they hold for historical archaeologists.

## ARTIFACTS AND MATERIAL CULTURE

Archaeologists are known for using the terms *artifact* and *material culture* and sometimes they use them interchangeably. They often talk about the "material culture" of a particular site when they refer to collections of artifacts, and sometimes they say "artifact" when they mean "material culture."

In its simplest sense, an *artifact* is anything that is made or modified by conscious human action. A stone arrow point, a soft drink bottle, a carved wooden mask, and a table are all artifacts. Humans are constantly surrounded by artifacts: we cook with them, eat from them, drive in them, sleep on them, and get buried in them. The artifacts we use help to define who we are. The term *material culture* includes artifacts, but is generally conceived of more broadly. Material culture includes all elements of human expression that are consciously created, including landscapes, words, a marching band's design on an athletic field, the distance we stand from someone when speaking to them, and so forth.

The stone circle known as the Big Horn Medicine Wheel lies in the mountains of northern Wyoming (Figure 4.1). Most Americans know of the Big Horn Mountains because of their association with "Custer's Last Stand" (see Chapter 3), but they were more importantly home to Native Americans for thousands of years before Custer was born. These Native Americans built the Big Horn Medicine Wheel some time in the prehistoric past. The wheel looks like a wagon wheel with a central "hub" of stones out of which radiate a series of "spokes." A stone "rim" connects the ends of the spokes. Archaeologists today hotly debate the exact reason Native Americans built the wheel, and they have put forward a number of interpretations. Ancient Native Americans may have used the wheel as an observatory, or it may have served as a monument to deceased, revered leaders. It may have been the focal point for the vision quests of adolescents who fasted and prayed in the hope that the Great Spirit would lead them to adulthood, or its designers may have built it as a symbolic representation of the universe. Many Crow people on the northern Plains today regard the wheel as a sacred site, and argue that no one needs to "explain" it to them; they know its meaning the way any believer understands what is sacred within their belief system.

The Big Horn Medicine Wheel is a fascinating object, but is it an artifact? The stones of the wheel cannot be considered artifacts in the strictest sense of the term because they were not actually modified by human action. Only their place on the earth's surface was changed. The only difference between the stones of the wheel and others nearby is that the former are arranged in such as way as to resemble a wheel. If any one of these stones were found someplace else, an archaeologist would not consider it to be an artifact. Arranged as a medicine wheel, though, these stones can be considered to be an example of Native American

**Figure 4.1**  Big Horn Medicine Wheel, Wyoming.

material culture. The medicine wheel makes a cultural statement about past ideas even though archaeologists do not agree on its precise meaning. Material culture thus includes objects that may have been shaped by humanity but not necessarily physically altered. A gravel road is an example of material culture, but the thousands of pebbles in the road are not artifacts by themselves.

A house presents more of a challenge for an historical archaeologist to classify as either an artifact or as an example of material culture. A house is clearly something that was made by conscious human activity, but is it an artifact? Houses are composed of hundreds of things that clearly *are* artifacts: nails, roofing tiles, floor boards, and plaster walls—but should we consider a house an artifact in the same way as a bottle?

In the final analysis, the difference between an artifact and material culture is perhaps not all that significant. To simplify matters here, we consider an artifact to be any readily *portable* object, and material culture to be all the physical expressions created by human action.

What is important about artifacts and material culture is that both require interpretation. Artifacts need interpretation because they are not simply passive creations.

People do not simply make tools, use them, and then forget about them. In fact, artifacts impose structure on people's lives in the same way that people impose structure on an artifact in the process of fashioning it. The relationship between humans and things may best be considered by thinking about a small farmhouse.

Farmhouses, like all buildings, are built in ways that make cultural sense to their builders. When War of 1812 veteran Charles Ames moved from New England to Indiana in the early nineteenth century, he built a house that was true to his memories of New England. Let us suppose that Ames was used to looking at his fields out of his back door in New England, but that in Indiana the topography made it impossible for him to see his pastures from home. We can readily see how the house in Indiana would "structure" Ames' life. He could adopt a number of strategies to survey his fields in the manner in which he was accustomed: He could design his house differently, he could alter the landscape, or he could change the way he checked his fields. Regardless of his decision, we can easily see that part of Ames's material culture—his new house in Indiana—has affected his behavior.

Material culture can structure human actions in powerful ways. In an innovative study, archaeologist Gregory Monks argued that the architecture used by the Hudson's Bay Company at Upper Fort Garry in today's Manitoba, Canada, served as a form of nonverbal communication. The mighty Hudson's Bay Company built the fur trading and commercial post in 1836 and used it as an administrative center for their activities in the Red River/Assiniboine River region. Monks did not accept the conventional idea that the fort was built simply to be used by traders and governmental officials in their daily affairs. In other words, he rejected the interpretation that the structure was merely functional. He proposed instead that Upper Fort Garry was an active participant in promoting the quasi-military and economic goals of the Hudson's Bay Company. The placement of the flagpole—with its British Red Ensign proudly emblazoned with "HBC"— standing directly opposite the entrance; the construction of an interior wall to separate living quarters from storehouses; and the expansion of economic areas at the expense of living and administrative zones were not simply done for convenience. Monks believed that these changes were meant to symbolize something much more profound: that the Hudson's Bay Company gave its economic motives greatest importance. The movement of the outer wall to make the once-interior sales area accessible from outside the fort was perhaps the clearest nonverbal message the Company could send. They were saying in effect that they wanted local trade, but only on their terms. The quality of material culture to embody several meanings, such as at Upper Fort Garry, make them a centrally important, though frustratingly complex, subject for historical archaeologists.

## INTERPRETING ARTIFACTS

In his intriguing book *Reading Matter: Multidisciplinary Perspectives on Material Culture*, Arthur Asa Berger presented a hypothetical situation in which the offices of six scholars look down upon and surround a small courtyard. On a picnic table in the center of the courtyard the scholars can see a McDonald's hamburger, some French fries, and a milkshake. The scholars are a semiotician (someone who studies signs or symbols), a psychoanalytic psychologist, an anthropologist, a historian, a sociologist, and a Marxist political scientist. On looking at the objects, each scholar perceives something quite different. The semiotician views McDonald's as a symbol of America, its standardization, and its efficiency, and the psychologist sees the success of McDonald's as an example of the need for individual gratification and of creeping depersonalization. The anthropologist perceives the hamburger and fries ritualistically and contemplates how the McDonald's experience has entered American folklore. The historian considers the food an example of the history of a successful corporation and as a visible reminder of the growing importance of corporations in American history, but the sociologist sees in the same meal a representation of the youth culture and the way in which immigrants work their way into the America social order through low-paying jobs. Finally, the Marxist political scientist sees the objects as examples of how different classes of people are exploited by multinational corporations and how McDonald's hides the class differences inherent in capitalism by equally providing inexpensive products to all members of society.

Berger's hypothetical situation vividly shows how scholars from diverse disciplinary backgrounds and with disparate perspectives can variously interpret the same objects. The intricate process of interpretation can be made even more complex by adding, for example, a number of historians, each of whom have a slightly different slant on history, or a group of anthropologists who see culture in different ways. No matter how many scholars are added, what is missing from Berger's mix is a historical archaeologist. How would an historical archaeologist see Berger's fast food meal?

The easy answer is that historical archaeologists can see the objects in all the ways as Berger's scholars. We showed in Chapter 1 that because historical archaeology is a field that reaches across disciplines, its practitioners are perfectly free to borrow ideas from numerous perspectives. American studies expert Thomas Schlereth outlined nine of the diverse perspectives—what he terms "conceptual positions"—that students of material culture can adopt: art historic, symbolist, cultural historic, environmentalist, functionalist, structuralist, behavioralist, nationalist, and social historic. He placed historical archaeology in the cultural historic category, but it is obvious today that the field has much more to offer than simple historical reconstruction. In fact, historical archaeologists have conducted research in all of Schlereth's categories, choosing to examine artifacts from various perspectives.

For the sake of brevity, we present the interpretation of artifacts from just three broad perspectives: as historical documents (Schlereth's art historic, cultural historic, nationalist, and social historic), as commodities (Schlereth's functionalist and behavioralist), and as ideas (Schlereth's symbolist and structuralist). These three categories of interpretation are not mutually exclusive, because each builds upon the other, starting with the use of physical things as historical documents.

## ARTIFACTS AS HISTORICAL DOCUMENTS

All archaeology is based on the fundamental assumption that artifacts provide information about the past. For more than a century, most archaeologists have considered artifacts as the equivalent of historical documents. John L. Stephens, the nineteenth-century American explorer of Copán, the majestic city of the Maya, understood this usage. On beholding a finely carved stela, or upright stone slab, Stephens remarked that it proved "as a newly discovered historical text might have done, that the peoples who once occupied the American continent were no savages." He likened the stelae of the Maya to historical documents in that they provided important information about life in ancient Mexico. Historical archaeologist Ivor Noël Hume once gave Stephens's comment a more modern twist by proclaiming artifacts to be the "signposts of the past."

The idea that artifacts can be read as historical texts has much to do with the technology of artifact production. People who made artifacts in prehistoric times probably relied almost exclusively on cultural conventions when it came to design. They developed the technology, the decorations, and the styles of their objects over many years. Prehistorians can chart changes in artifact design or decoration, but only broadly. For instance, when Donald Lehmer compiled the cultural chronology of a region in the United States archaeologists call the "Middle Missouri"—the Missouri River valley in North and South Dakota—he knew that pottery with surfaces roughened with cord-wrapped sticks characterized the Initial Coalescent Variant of the Central Plains Tradition. He also knew that the people who lived during the more recent Extended Coalescent Variant did not cord-roughen their pottery. "Cord roughening is so rare," said Lehmer of the Extended Coalescent Variant, "that it cannot be considered an integral part of the ceramic tradition." Archaeologists of the American Plains generally agree that the Initial Coalescent Variant dates from about A.D. 1400–1550 (150 years) and that the Extended Coalescent Variant dates from about A.D. 1550–1675 (125 years). In South Dakota, therefore, an archaeologist could date a cord-roughened sherd she found along the Missouri River to sometime within a 150-year period. The precise placement of this sherd within this time span, however, will probably remain a mystery.

Historical archaeologists often have a distinct advantage over their prehistorian colleagues when it comes to using artifacts as historical documents. Historical archaeologists can often recognize changes in artifacts in individual years, or sometimes even days, rather than in generations or centuries. The fine-grained understanding of artifacts as historical documents often exists, particularly in the most recent years, because most historical artifacts were manufactured by factories or corporations. These corporations, because they were economic concerns, usually kept careful, detailed records as part of their responsibilities to their shareholders. Corporate archives can thus provide abundant information about the changes in design, style, and decoration of specific artifacts.

A famous designer of eighteenth-century ceramic artifacts was Josiah Wedgwood, a man widely celebrated for his beautifully crafted wares and for his business acumen. Wedgwood, who justifiably viewed his ceramic paste formulas and his decorative innovations as trade secrets, is known to have kept detailed records of his patterns, shapes, and decorations. His decorative designs on plates, called "Old Feather Edge," "New Feather Edge," "Queen Pattern," and "Royal Pattern," are well known today because of his factory records (Figure 4.2). Archaeologists conducting excavations throughout the British colonial world have repeatedly found ceramic sherds bearing these patterns.

Historical archaeologists use artifacts as historical documents in many ways. They most frequently use them to date specific occupation layers in the soil. The common Coca-Cola bottle provides an excellent case in point.

### The Coca-Cola Bottle

Coca-Cola was invented in Atlanta, Georgia, by pharmacist John S. Pemberton in 1886. Pemberton's creation became such a popular beverage that in 1892 he called his business "The Coca-Cola Company." With the prospect of Coca-Cola

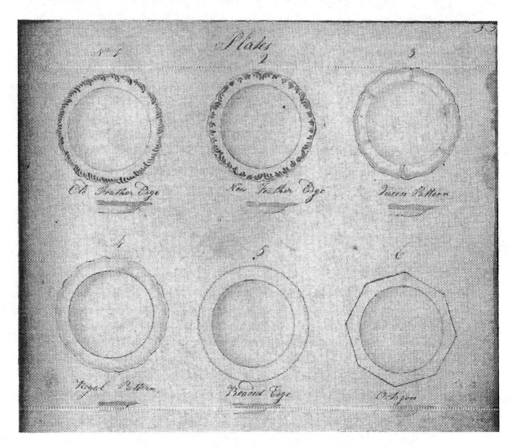

**Figure 4.2** Plate drawings from Wedgwood's 1802 drawing book.

becoming a major sensation, the company registered the now-classic "Coca-Cola" logo with the United States Patent Office in 1893. In the earliest years of production and distribution, bottlers paid little attention to the packaging in which Coca-Cola was sold, and they indiscriminately used straight-sided bottles of whatever color they could get. In 1916, however, the company decided to adopt a standardized, patented bottle design to protect its popular product from the countless imitators who sought to cash in on Pemberton's soft drink gold mine.

Many early twentieth-century manufacturers of liquid foodstuffs chose to patent their bottle designs rather than the bottle's actual contents. To patent a bottle's contents required announcing the product's formula, something that few manufacturers of highly sought-after products wished to do. All Coca-Cola sold between 1916 and 1923 thus came in bottles that read on the base "Bottle Pat'd Nov. 1915." This bottle had a classic shape that we now associate with the drink (Figure 4.3). The company patented a new design on Christmas Day, 1923, so all Coca-Cola sold between 1924 and 1937 came in bottles reading "Bottle Pat'd Dec. 25, 1923." Other design innovations followed in 1937, so that all Coke bottles sold between 1937 and 1951 read "Bottle Pat. D-105529." The company had the word "Coke" first used on their bottles in 1941, and between 1963 and 1965 they also included "6½ oz." on one side panel.

The changes in the common Coca-Cola bottle form the official patent history of one of the world's most widely known products. With their relatively tight dates, Coca-Cola bottles, when found at archaeological sites, can function as documents in a way not often duplicated by prehistoric artifacts. When David Gradwohl and Nancy Osborn found a bottle with the easily identifiable "Coca-Cola" script painted on it at Buxton, Iowa—a coal mining town with a large African American population—they immediately knew that the bottle dated to after 1893.

In addition to tell-tale designs and identifiable product names, many mass-produced objects contain manufacturers' marks that can serve as valuable chronological markers. The manufacturers' symbols were company icons and identifiers, but archaeologists can use them as time markers. Ceramics and glass bottles are two noteworthy examples.

### Ceramic Makers' Marks

The practice of placing makers' marks on the bottom of ceramic dishes goes back centuries. A Roman potter named M. Perennius lived sometime between 100 B.C. and A.D. 100. He was renowned for his skill at copying Greek designs and was widely considered a ceramic genius. He stamped his pottery "M. PERINNI," "M. PEREN," or "M. PERE." Classical archaeologists have found his marks to be a wonderful time marker, for his wares have come from digs in Rome, northern France, and Spain. Perennius is said to have employed seventeen slaves in his pottery works, the most famous being a man named Tigranes, who was so proud of his work that he stamped it "TIGRAN," "TIGRA," or just plain "TIGR." Following a tradition that dates from classical times, potters

**Figure 4.3** 1915-prototype of the classic Coca-Cola bottle.

have etched their wares with a variety of initials, shapes, and symbols that forever serve as their personal, unique marks. Archaeologists also call maker's
marks *bottom marks* because potters usually placed them on the outside bottom of
their vessels.

Large pottery houses in operation during the Industrial Revolution of the
late eighteenth century adopted the same procedure to mark their products. The
most well-developed set of makers' marks appear on post–Industrial Revolution
British ceramics, but American potters quickly followed suit by marking their
wares as well. Potters on both sides of the Atlantic soon compiled a massive array
of unique and distinguishing marks. As may be expected, the numbers of symbols expanded with the rapid growth of the ceramics industry and the increase in
competition between potteries. Before 1770, English potters seldom marked their
wares; after this date, they almost always did. Ceramic scholars have spent years
compiling catalogs of pottery marks, and many published catalogues are currently available for use by historical archaeologists. Geoffrey Godden's
*Encyclopaedia of British Pottery and Porcelain Marks,* published in 1964, is a standard
reference work.

Historical archaeologists use these catalogues to identify and to date the
marked ceramics sherds they find. For example, a sherd that is marked with a
globe with the word *MINTON* written across it was a product of the Minton pottery of Staffordshire, England. Established in 1793, the Minton pottery used the
globe from about 1863 to 1872. In 1873, the Mintons added a crown to the top of
the globe and an *S* to the word *MINTON* (Figure 4.4). In addition to such individualized marks, many English potters incorporated the British Royal Arms into
their marks. These logos are characterized by a lion (on the left) and a unicorn (on
the right) flanking an oblong shield with a crown on top of it. The marks included
a quartered shield with a smaller shield in the middle before 1837, but the small
shield was removed after this date.

Ceramics from Victorian England, made from 1842–1883, carry one of the
most diagnostic bottom marks a historical archaeologist can find. These are
diamond-shaped symbols with a small circle on top; numbers and letters appear
on the inside corners of the diamond. These distinctive marks indicate that the
pottery factory registered the design or shape of the vessel with the British
Patent Office. Because the purpose of the symbol was to protect the pottery from
piracy for at least three years, the bottom mark contains an exact date of registry.
The Patent Office assigned codes to ceramic manufacturers and required that
they place them in the corners of the diamond. An archaeologist can date a piece
of English pottery made during the 1842–1867 period and marked with "C" in
the left corner of the diamond, "I" in the right corner, and "X" in the top corner
as having been registered at the British Patent Office on January (C), 1 (I), 1842
(X) (Figure 4.5). This date has little to do with when the ceramic vessel may have
been used, except that it serves as a *terminus post quem*, or "date after which" it
was made. We know, because of the 1842 date on the vessel itself, that this piece

**Figure 4.4** Marks from the bottom of Minton ceramics. Without crown: about 1863–1872; with crown: about 1873. The word England was added below the crown in 1891. The symbol on the right was used from about 1912–1950.

could not have been used *before* 1842. Only more detailed knowledge of the site itself will provide a *terminus ante quem*, or "date before which." If we knew for certain from other sources that the site was completely abandoned in 1862, then we can date the ceramic sherd with the diamond-shaped mark from 1842 to 1862.

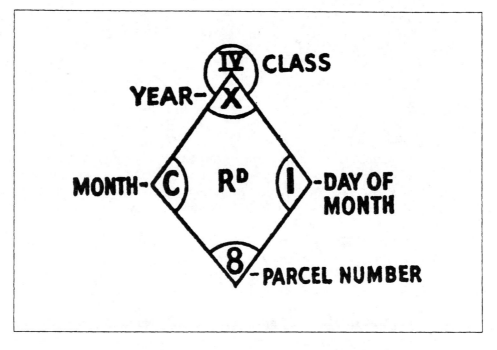

**Figure 4.5** British registry mark, used from 1842–1867.

A recognizable portion of the mark must remain visible on the sherd to be useful for archaeological dating. Archaeologists are often frustrated by only finding a tiny (and thus unidentifiable) corner of a mark.

## Bottle Makers' Marks

Glass bottles can also carry makers' marks. The first known marked glass reads in Greek "Ennion made it." Happily for historical archaeologists, most glass manufacturers have followed Ennion's lead. To identify makers' marks on glass, historical archaeologists can use catalogues of marks complied by glass specialists in the same way that they employ books of ceramic marks.

Glass manufacturers, like potters, often used distinctive marks to identify their wares. Glass specialists have told archaeologists, for example, that a "C" with a square around it on the bottom of a bottle indicates that the Crystal Glass Company of Los Angeles, California, made the bottle between 1921 and 1928. The words *KEARNS & CO.* identify a bottle made by the Kearns, Gorsuch Bottle Company of Zanesville, Ohio, between 1864 and 1876; and the letters *ABGM Co.* indicate that a bottle was manufactured by the Adolphus Busch Glass Manufacturing Company of Belleville, Illinois, sometime between 1886 and 1928.

As is the case with marked ceramics, archaeologists can use the glass marks to identify the object's producer and the date ranges of its manufacture. Historical archaeologists can also use the marks in conjunction with ceramic marks to understand the distance that artifacts had to travel to reach the archaeological site. This information sheds important light on marketing and artifact distribution, information that may exist in no other source.

## Technological Attributes

The prevalence of artifacts like bottles and plates that have clearly identifiable marks increases with time, so that late-nineteenth- and early-twentieth-century sites are more likely to contain marked and readily datable objects. As a result, historical archaeologists who study sites that date before the late nineteenth century often do not have the advantage of discovering easily identifiable, marked ceramics and glass. With the lack of supporting documentation, historical archaeologists have had to learn from prehistorians how to date artifacts by their *attributes*, or physical characteristics.

The physical attributes found on prehistoric objects are largely the result of culturally recognized and understood conventions. The beautifully decorated Mimbres black-on-white pottery from southwestern New Mexico (A.D. 1000–1130) is emblazoned with bold geometric designs and delicately drawn animal figures that would be widely and immediately recognized by every member of that culture. The physical attributes of these ceremonial bowls are culturally expressive; they depict legends of the creation and other aspects of long-forgotten Mimbres belief.

In contrast, the physical attributes of historical objects seem to relate more to a manufacturer's efforts to produce objects that consumers find pleasing and appealing, or to simplify and streamline a costly manufacturing process. As a result, physical attributes of historical objects have much to do with technological change and innovation.

Glass bottles provide an excellent example of how technological change can be documented through time with artifacts. Since antiquity, makers of glass objects have produced bottles by using a blowing process. The glassblower places a ball of molten glass on the end of a hollow rod, then blows a bottle from the ball of glass. Glassblowers could "free-blow" the bottle, using just their skill and experience to shape it. Tell-tale, stretched air bubbles remain within the glass for all time. Also visible is the distinctive rough mark on the bottle's base, called the *pontil scar*, where the glassblower broke the glass rod free from the bottle. Glass blowing was a slow and laborious process, and the uniformity of the individual bottles rested with the skill of the glassblower.

As producers of recognizable liquid foodstuffs began to link their products with their containers, like Coca-Cola, they began to require standardized bottles. To meet this demand, glass producers began to make their bottles in molds. Around 1750, glassblowers started to blow their bottles in a hinged, two-piece mold. The protrusions on the bottle mouths (called the "finish") were made by hand using a shaping tool run around the outside of the glass before it cooled. When the vessel had sufficiently cooled and hardened, the completed bottle was removed from the mold and the blower repeated the process with a new lump of molten glass. Such molded bottles contain evidence of the mold as a seam line running from near the top to bottom of the bottle, and diagonally across the base. The seam does not appear where the bottle maker ran the shaping tool around the bottle mouth.

Glass factories used the two-piece mold until about 1880. English bottle-maker Henry Ricketts patented a three-piece (or "Ricketts mold") in 1821. Manufacturers used this mold, characterized by a seam running around the bottle's shoulder, until about the 1920s. Michael Owens, then general manager of the Toledo Glass Company, invented the first fully automatic bottle-making machine in 1903, and today, after a series of improvements, we have the modern bottle. Today's bottles show evidence of their manufacturing technique by the presence of a seam that extends from the tip of the mouth down to the base. Even the finish is machine-made. Given the bottle's technological history, their visible attributes—seam lines, pontil marks, and bubbles—all serve as valuable chronological indicators.

Even inconspicuous attributes, such as bottle closure type, are chronologically significant. Bottle makers used threads on bottle necks only after about the mid-1850s. Before then, they capped their bottles with wax, corks, or some other clever method designed to keep the liquid inside. The greatest innovation in bottle closure came in 1892 when William Painter patented the "crown cap," readily recognized today because of the familiar bottle cap. Painter called his invention the "crown cork" because it "gives a crowning and beautiful effect to the bottle." Painter's official patent for his "Bottle-Sealing Device" gave a less poetic description of his achievement, calling it "a metallic flanged sealing-cap adapted to receive the head of a bottle and containing a concavo-convex sealing disk"! (Figure 4.6).

Even the common, everyday nail has a well-documented manufacturing history. The round-headed, fully machine-made wire nail we know today only dates to the 1850s. Before then, nail producers used a variety of other methods to make their products. One can recognize completely handmade nails by their hammered heads, flattened points (when viewed from one side), and irregular shapes. Blacksmiths who made nails completely by hand found it a tiresome and monotonous process. With the rise of greater industrialization, nail manufacturers, like their glass- and ceramic-making colleagues, sought more efficient and quicker ways to mass produce uniform nails. Nails made between the 1790s and the 1820s were thus cut with a die from a flat, solid sheet of "nail plate." We can recognize these nails by their rectangular, rather than round, cross sections and by their hand-hammered heads. By the 1880s, our modern wire nails (with round heads and

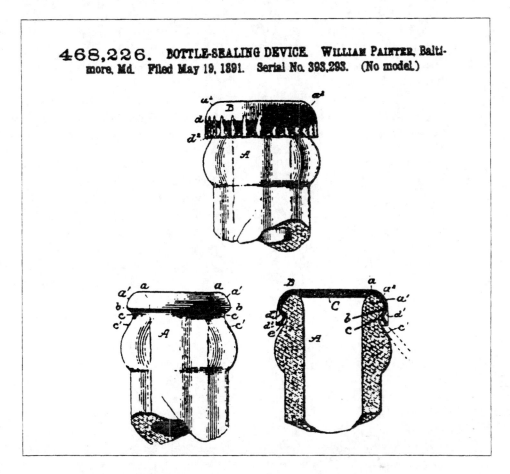

**Figure 4.6**   Patent information for common bottle cap, 1891.

shanks) were much less expensive to manufacture than their machine-cut cousins, and so they were cheaper to sell. Most builders shifted to using the less expensive, round nails at about that time, though many building restorationists still prefer to use old nail styles for the sake of authenticity. Historical archaeologists must therefore be careful when attempting to use nails for dating purposes.

The list of potentially datable artifacts is enormous. Lighting devices, locks, horseshoes, smoking pipes, glass beads, tin cans, hair combs, and many other objects were all produced with different technologies through time. Historical archaeologists can use these artifacts to help date soil layers, wells and privies, and even entire sites. Even the most prosaic of artifacts can become important historical documents for the archaeologist.

## ARTIFACTS AS COMMODITIES

Artifacts produced during the most recent decades were mass-produced and were intended for sale on a large scale. Most historical artifacts were thus *commodities*, objects created specifically for exchange.

The manufacture and sale of commodities extends back thousands of years. British prehistorian V. Gordon Childe remarked how the presence of cylinder seals throughout ancient Mesopotamia and the Indus Valley provided the "earliest recorded instance of the transmission of manufactures over such vast distances." Many archaeologists think the Kulli merchants, early traveling salesmen, of the third millennium connected the Mesopotamian world with the Harappans in the Indus Valley. The Kulli lived in Baluchistan, a region that now straddles western Pakistan and southeastern Iran.

Most communities, no matter how small and self-sufficient, generally maintained a series of connections with the outside world. These linkages might include connections with nearby neighbors, with communities across a region, and with a world market. They might entail the trade of both necessities and luxuries. Archaeologists are interested in studying short- and long-distance connections because of their commercial, political, and social significance. Historical sites offer a rich potential for such research, because historical archaeologists can use historical and archaeological sources to learn about commodities.

### *Using Historical Records in Commodity Research*

Some historical records can provide abundant information about the kinds of commodities that were available and the ways in which people selected them. Probate records, store advertisements, business catalogues, and even storekeepers' inventory books can be a mine of information about consumer preference and market availability.

Historical archaeologists have found probate records to be an important source of information. Shortly after a person's death, assessors would walk through the deceased's home and record the objects they saw. The inventory provided a list of objects that could be assessed for taxes, valued for inheritance purposes, or evaluated in preparation of an estate sale. Probate inventories can be extremely informative for archaeologists for three reasons: They can help to identify objects found in archaeological deposits, and they can describe perishable household effects (such as books), that leave no durable archaeological evidence. They can even provide information about objects that were never actually at the site at all, like cattle herds, farm implements, or carriages. Probate inventories tell us what objects surrounded a person immediately before his or her death. The probate list of James Edward Calhoun, of rural Abbeville County, South Carolina, makes the point.

James Edward Calhoun was the cousin of the ardent defender of the American South's slaveocracy John C. Calhoun. James Edward—world traveler, speaker of seventeen languages, and scholar—served as the astronomer with the Stephen A. Long expedition of 1823 as it traveled along the old fur trading routes of the Upper Midwest. Settling down on two cotton plantations in northwestern South Carolina—named Midway and Millwood—Calhoun promised to become a full-fledged member of the South's antebellum slave-owning elite. When his young wife died in 1844 during a horrific epidemic, Calhoun gave up the life of the high-born southern gentleman and soon became known as the "Hermit of Millwood." Upon his death in 1889, assessors carefully inventoried Calhoun's personal property. Millwood Plantation was located in South Carolina's backwoods, but Calhoun's probate list includes numerous objects that belie his seclusion: a pair of dueling pistols, three gold watches, a telescope, two surveying compasses, a Chinese clothes basket, a silver dog whistle, a silver tea service, $100 worth of Confederate war bonds, and the usual assortment of buttons, dishes, tools, rifles, and agricultural implements that one might expect to find in a southern planter's home.

As an added bonus for historical archaeologists, auctioneers held an estate sale after the inventory, and this additional list can be used to assess the relative value of the items Calhoun owned. The Chinese clothes basket sold for $1.55, the dog whistle for $5.00, and the gold watches for $22, $40, and $41. All told, Calhoun's estate sold for $1,644.27, not a paltry sum in rural South Carolina in 1889.

Calhoun obviously cared for the valuable items he owned, otherwise they could not have been available for sale after his death. Archaeologists who excavated his homesite found little of extraordinary value there. The archaeology did tell them, however, that he ate from dishes decorated with a blue pattern called "Italian Flower Garden," that he used a variety of patent medicines, and that he smoked a small pipe that had a face etched into it. These less-valuable objects did not appear in the probate inventory because Calhoun had discarded them. The archaeology—in conjunction with the probate inventory—was needed to provide a full picture of the range of objects Calhoun used during his lifetime.

Our fast-moving, rapidly changing modern world seems to operate because of advertising and aggressive marketing. Inventive merchants devised the now-classic methods of modern advertising in the late nineteenth century. A classic example is the Sears Roebuck Catalogue. Back in the 1890s, Sears executives reasoned that if most American consumers could not visit their store in Chicago, then they would take their store to their customers "through the agency of Uncle Sam's Mail." Their method was the now-ubiquitous mail-order catalogue. Sears used over seven hundred tightly packed pages to list everything from underwear to cast iron pots, from shovels to French bust developers. Calling themselves the "Cheapest Supply House," the Sears executives bragged that "Nearly all our customers send cash in full. It's the best way. If you send too much money we will always refund the balance with the bill." And so they did, ushering in a revolution in retailing.

Archaeologists can use contemporary advertisements, such as those in the Sears catalogue, to develop ideas of what goods were available in different regions at various times. These sources also provide interesting information about consumer attitudes because marketers wished to capitalize on the public's widely held perceptions. The selling of St. Jakob's Oel, a popular late-nineteenth-century patent medicine, provides an excellent example of nineteenth-century advertising techniques (Figure 4.7).

Charles A. Voegeler of Baltimore, Maryland, first marketed St. Jakob's Oel in the 1880s under the name of "Keller's Roman Liniment." Voegeler used a picture of Caesar on the label to imply that his product went back in time to the ancient Romans. He rested his hope on the idea that people would assume that what was good for the world-conquering Romans would be good for them as well. But when the Roman motif did not sell as Voegeler had hoped, he changed the name of the product first to "St. Jacob's Oil" and then to "St. Jakob's Oel." The spelling change allowed him to market the oil as if it were made by German monks living in the fabled Black Forest.

Advertisements in the *Chicago Tribune* show the way in which Voegeler adjusted his claims for the sake of sales. An advertisement dated January 1, 1880, stated that St. Jakob's Oel cured "rheumatism, neuralgia, pains, soreness, stiffness, cuts, [and] sores." Three days later, advertisements claimed that the medicine cured "backache, toothache, headache, swellings, sprains, bruises, burns, [and] scalds." Two days later, Voegeler added "chilblains [the inflamation of the hands and feet because of exposure to the cold], wounds, [and] corns" to the maladies cured by his remarkable elixir. Did the readers of these ads realize that St. Jakob's Oel was getting better day by day? In any case, Voegeler was definitely not shy about promoting his product. On one of his promotional cards, he depicted a red-robed and hooded, white-bearded monk standing in New York Harbor in place of the Statue of Liberty. Instead of a torch, the monk holds up a shining bottle of St. Jacob's Oel!

Historical archaeology shows that Voegeler's cure-all sold well. Excavations at the Drake farmstead in northern Illinois (inhabited from 1838 to 1896) proved that the Drake family bought at least fifty-one bottles of this "German" remedy in the decade it was available to them. At the documented price of 50 cents a bottle, the Drake family spent over $25 on this one patent medicine, a not inconsiderable sum at the time!

**Figure 4.7**   A St. Jakob's Oel
patent medicine bottle.

### *Using Artifacts in Commodity Research*

Apart from historical records, the artifacts themselves tell us much about their
roles as commodities, not only from their labels or attributes, but also from their
distribution within sites and across entire regions. Historical archaeologists often
have a unique opportunity to obtain a good understanding of the kinds of material objects that consumers purchased over wide areas. Perhaps even more revealing, they can often discover things that were intended to be hidden from public
view. For example, while excavating at colonial Jamestown, Virginia, John Cotter
was surprised to find the left half of a male pelvis and the bones of the left leg

and foot in a seventeenth-century well! Are the bones evidence of an unsolved, or even undetected, murder of a person dismembered after death? Cotter was at a loss to explain why part of a human body lay in the well, for there were no obvious signs of violence. These bones cannot be considered commodities, but they demonstrate how wells and other archaeological features can be used to hide elements of daily life, and how they can provide archaeologists with important, often unique, information.

It may be possible to hide some things from your neighbors, but the prying eyes of the archaeologist can see into every corner of a site. When David Hurst Thomas excavated Spanish colonial and Native American sites on St. Catherine's Island, on the Georgia coast, he discovered that the Franciscan missionaries there required their Indian charges to accept all the outward trappings of devout Christianity. The archaeology shows that the priests encouraged the Native Americans to adopt the Christian manner of burial: unmarked graves beneath the church floor, hands crossed over the chest with feet pointed toward the altar. But the priests also compromised because they allowed the Native Americans to deposit objects in the graves. The placement of artifacts within the graves of the dead was a common custom among many Native American cultures. Many of the artifacts excavated on St. Catherine's Island were clearly aboriginal in nature—a shell gorget, several stone projectile points, and a "chunky" stone, possibly used in a game. Other grave objects were European commodities—whole ceramic vessels, mirrors, and bronze religious medallions (Figure 4.8).

Church leaders frowned on the deposition of objects with the dead, but the missionaries at St. Catherine's Island apparently decided to overlook this traditional practice in their efforts to convert the natives to Christianity. Not every colonial Spanish site, however, indicates a willingness to accede to native practice. Graves found at mission sites in Florida are often devoid of artifacts. The precise reason for this difference remains a mystery, but it does illustrate an important reality of Spanish colonialism—that the missionaries' approach to conversion was flexible. Local priests apparently had some latitude when enforcing Church regulation, or else they simply turned a blind eye to some traditional, Native American practices.

Archaeologists have studied the flow of commodities through large trade networks by calculating the distance artifacts had to be transported to reach the site of their use and final deposition. Studying the distribution of imported obsidian among the prehistoric Mayas, for example, archaeologist Raymond Sidrys found that people living during the Classic Period (A.D. 250–900) transported obsidian in greater amounts to ceremonial centers than to smaller settlements, regardless of the distance to the natural sources. In the Postclassic Period (A.D. 1000–1450), the Mayas distributed obsidian more widely as they developed sea canoe routes of trade and built ports of call.

Historical archaeologists, by using company records, patent information, and other sources of information—in addition to direct information from artifacts themselves—are often able to establish exact manufacturing locales of artifacts

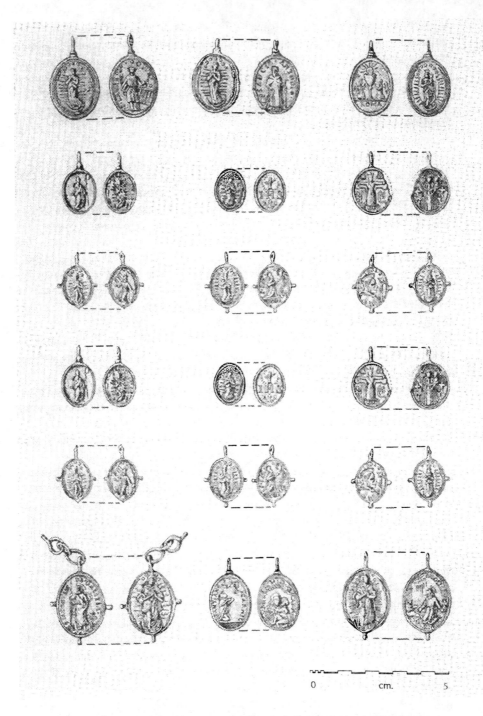

**Figure 4.8**   Religious medallions from St. Catherine's Island.

found at archaeological sites. The historical information can reveal clues about the long-distance connections maintained by people who lived in past settlements.

Excavating at the Moser farm in extreme northwestern Arkansas, occupied from about 1875–1919, archaeologist Leslie Stewart-Abernathy discovered that people in the remote Ozark Mountains maintained diverse connections with the outside world. The site itself was rather small, but the cultural boundaries of this homestead extended "well beyond the fences of the farm." In fact, the Moser site yielded artifacts from all over the world. The farmers who once lived there ate from dishes made in Ohio and England, administered to their ailments with "Dr. King's New Discovery for Consumption" from Chicago and "Dr. Jayne's Expectorant" from Philadelphia, and canned the vegetables from their gardens in fruit jars that had zinc lids with white glass lid liners made in West Virginia and New York. Stewart-Abernathy's excavations show that the Ozarks, a region often assumed to be well out of the commercial mainstream, was as much a participant in the world's marketplace as anywhere else.

The presence of exotic commodities at archaeological sites of recent date is easy to understand because the roots of our own economic lives were forged during the fifteenth and sixteenth centuries. In her long-term study of historic St. Augustine, Florida, for example, Kathleen Deagan has documented the wide range of goods available to colonial settlers. Spanish settlers founded St. Augustine in 1565, and the town served as the headquarters for Spain's economic, military, and religious activities in eastern North America, called "La Florida," until 1821. The main cultural ties of the citizens of St. Augustine were with Spain itself, but Deagan's excavations proved that the residents also received goods from many other places. She found several kinds of Native American pottery from throughout Florida, red-painted wares from Mexico, redware ceramics from Italy, and porcelain from Asia. Such research demonstrates that the residents of even remote colonial settlements on the fringes of an empire could use artifacts imported from far afield.

A residence excavated in Plymouth, England (called the Kitto Institute site) demonstrates that the distribution of commodities was widespread. An examination of the 201 ceramic vessels found at the site, which dates to the 1625–1630 period, indicates that the residents used commodities from all over Europe. Included in the collection are six blue and white porcelain vessels from China, vessels of five different decorative types from Spain and Portugal, and eight different types from France. Also included are ceramics made in Germany, the Netherlands, and throughout England.

Our understanding of the number and kinds of commodities used at specific sites, like the Kitto Institute site and St. Augustine, allow archaeologists to investigate lines of inquiry that may never had occurred to them without understanding the important role of commodities in the modern world. But even commodities were never simply economic objects, meant only to be purchased, used, and then discarded. Throughout the time of their use, all objects—including commodities—were imbued by their owners with various meanings. The search to discover these meanings is one of the most challenging and yet exciting elements of today's historical archaeology.

## ARTIFACTS AS IDEAS

One of the most interesting, yet difficult, aspects of understanding artifacts of any date is to determine what they actually meant to the people who made and used them. It may be relatively easy for us today to envision how artifacts serve as historical documents—objects that tell us about the past—or as commodities—things bought and sold in the marketplaces of the past. But it may be more difficult to understand that the meaning of artifacts may not be so obvious or straightforward. Many archaeologists now think of artifacts as "signs." A sign, as defined by the Italian semiotician Umberto Eco, is anything that "can be taken as significantly substituting for something else." Eco has become famous outside the narrow field of semiotics for his novels, especially *The Name of the Rose and Foucault's Pendulum.* Although Eco's books can be read simply as good stories, semioticians pore over them in search of much deeper meanings reflected in the deeds and dialog of the main characters.

Signs are strongly associated with physical things, especially when objects are defined as bits of information that are intended to invoke an image. The Coca-Cola Company's famous red and white sign is an excellent example. On one level it simply advertises the soft drink product, but on another level it has become synonymous with the United States. When Americans see this symbol in distant lands, they may be reminded of home; when non-Americans see the red and white logo, they may think of the creeping presence of American consumer products. In both cases, the Coca-Cola sign stands for something that is not embodied by the drink itself.

Ideas underlay all physical things and give them meaning. Even our early human ancestors who lived at Olduvai Gorge, East Africa, put ideas into their simple stone choppers and flakes. They made such artifacts to be multipurpose tools, designed to accomplish tasks related to survival, such as breaking bones during food preparation. Archaeologists can understand the functional value of such artifacts through experiments. They can replicate the tools with authentic methods of stone chipping, and they can use the tools to smash bones and scrape meat from them. These experimental archaeologists can examine the tools through microscopes, looking for the telltale signs of edge wear they may also have seen on the actual, prehistoric stone tools. If the edge wear patterns match, then there is a good chance that both tools were used in the same manner.

But what about other, apparently non-functional attributes of artifacts, elements like decorations on pottery that have no obvious connection with physical survival? What do these things mean? Without supporting documentation, archaeologists are on their own when it comes to providing an interpretation. In these cases, they might decide to use an ethnographic analogy (see Chapter 3), but in other cases they may be completely mystified. The first farmers along the

Danube River in ancient Europe etched spirals and meandering designs into their pottery, and today, no one knows precisely what these designs were meant to represent.

The meaning of artifacts from the historic past can be somewhat easier to interpret because of the role of most historical objects as commodities. We can thus assume that artifact designers produced artifacts that would become "objects of desire," things people wanted but did not always actually need. The question that archaeologists, as well as modern advertisers and product manufacturers ask, is: What makes an artifact desirable? Does an object's appearance alone, often meant to represent something else, make people willing to pay for it? Do ideas exist behind artifacts that allow them to become expressions of something else?

## Different Interpretations of the Ideas Behind Artifacts

Many archaeologists who study artifacts as ideas have used a theory called "structuralism." Structuralism is a complex and hotly debated theory that has as one of its main goals the understanding of the basic, universal patterns that structure human ideas and, thereby, actions. The most fundamental universal pattern is binary opposition, an idea structuralists propose as basic to the production of meaning. Some of the opposites that material culture specialists have used in studying objects are: bright/dull, light/dark, modern/classic, expensive/cheap, hand-crafted/mass-produced, and fashionable/everyday. When exploring the role of binary opposites in structuring Anglo-American material culture during the colonial period, James Deetz used the categories private/public, artificial/natural, and complex/simple (see Chapter 9). Deetz proposed that the distinction between individual and shared table settings represented the private/public dyad; the difference between blue and white ceramics and brown, green, and yellow ceramics represented the artificial/natural opposite; and multicolored versus blue and white dishes represented the complex/simple binary opposite.

Deetz used these binary opposites to illustrate the "oppositional structures" that underlay the Anglo-American world view. Deetz's plan was not to perceive artifacts as historical documents—merely found in the ground instead of in an archive—or as commodities, but rather as an avenue for understanding the mentality of English men and women during colonial times. His foundation for such an approach stemmed from his belief that "Material culture is certainly more democratic than documents, and it is less sensitive to the subjectivity that every person brought, however unconsciously, to his or her accounting of peoples and events." What Deetz meant is that people in the past did not create deposits of artifacts with the same intentions that they had when the wrote documents. In fact, they could never have imagined that anyone would care about their discarded trash! They undoubtedly could imagine, however, that they were leaving written documents for posterity.

Ann Smart Martin, a material culture specialist who has used archaeological materials in her research, has adopted a different way of exploring artifacts as ideas. Like Deetz, Martin investigated eighteenth-century sites in the eastern

United States, but her focus was on objects made of pewter rather than ceramic. Pewter, an alloy made with a combination of lead and tin, was a common material for the manufacture of drinking and eating utensils during colonial times (Figure 4.9). When thinking about pewter and its widespread use in the past, Martin was struck by the archaeological collections she studied: while they were typically rich in ceramics sherds, they were usually devoid of pewter objects. Colonial chroniclers, on the other hand, often mentioned artifacts made of pewter in probate inventories and other writings. So why do historical archaeologists find so few pewter objects in their excavations?

The scarcity of pewter in relation to ceramics may relate to simple physics: Ceramics break and are discarded, pewter dents but does not break. A person can drink from a dented pewter mug, but he or she cannot eat from half a ceramic plate (at least not very easily). This simple reality is no doubt true, but Martin also sought a deeper meaning for the relationship between pewter and ceramics. Her research convinced her that the meaning of the different proportions of ceramics and pewter may relate to simple consumer preference for ceramics over pewter, or else to a deeper meaning in which pewter represented "conservative stability and wealth" in a rapidly changing society. Martin concluded that the difference between the presence of pewter (as traditional objects) and ceramics (as modern objects) was not based on physical differences alone, but on a subtle idea of social standing. Pewter and ceramics were chosen by people because of the ideas behind each.

In another significant study, archaeologist Paul Shackel described how many of the mundane objects of daily life can provide unique insights both about artifact meaning and how artifacts present and encapsulate ideas. Shackel used a combination of historical and archaeological sources to show how one object, the common toothbrush, can be immensely important in helping archaeologists to understand past ideas.

Archaeologists usually give toothbrushes little thought. When they find them during excavation they quickly give them a functional meaning: People used toothbrushes for dental hygiene. But by using historical records, Shackel was able to show a deeper importance for the way in which toothbrush manufacturers made their products. He specifically investigated the placement of the bristles into the head of the toothbrush and its relation to the larger concerns of social order and discipline (Figure 4.10). Most people would find such a topic to be unusual and perhaps not worthy of intensive study. But that was precisely Shackel's point: that there is meaning in the most commonplace objects.

Chinese inventors created the toothbrush, but Western travelers did not bring them home until 1498. Today we use synthetic-fiber toothbrushes, but European toothbrush makers in the past used boar hair bristles that came from Poland, Russia, China, Japan, and Tibet. Rather than simply viewing the change from hog bristles to nylon as merely technological, Shackel proposed that the change in bristle placement on the toothbrush—from widely haphazard to neatly in rows—reflects a deeper understanding of social and workplace order. He believed that an *idea* of orderliness began to permeate society to such an extent that

**Figure 4.9**  Pewter objects made in colonial America.

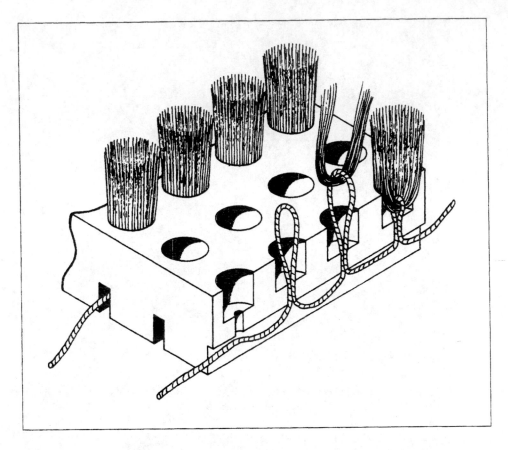

**Figure 4.10**  Putting the bristles in a toothbrush.

people *expected* orderliness in all elements of society, including in their tooth-brushes. Shackel envisioned the neat rows of bristle holes in the common toothbrush as a sign of the increased importance of personal discipline in Western society. The toothbrush symbolized discipline and order.

Not all archaeologists agree that accurate meanings of past ideas can be discerned from artifacts. One school of thought holds that all perceptions and perspectives about the past are filtered through our own life experiences and education. They argue that because no one can ever really "know" the past, most of what we say about it actually derives from our own times. In other words, we construct a past that has meaning to us.

"Critical archaeologists" of this school argue that no matter how much we may wish to understand the past, we can never truly know it. This point was made as long ago as 1926 by historian Carl Becker in a paper before the American Historical Association. In a memorable phrase, Becker said that "the historical fact is in someone's mind or it is nowhere." Critical archaeologists have used this idea to provide meaning to artifacts from prehistoric times. How can anyone alive today know the ideas of a prehistoric potter who lived along the banks of the Danube River and put designs on her pots? But ideas about the meaning of the designs on the pots come from someplace and, for many archaeologists, the only place can possibly be the "here and now."

In contrast, historical archaeologists can rely on numerous pieces of well-documented information to study the meaning of artifacts in the past. Contemporary writings do much to help us "get inside people's heads" and to see something of the world as the writers saw it during their time. The presence of documents, however, does not mean that the search for meaning in past artifacts is either straightforward or readily agreed upon. On the contrary, this kind of research will always provide controversial interpretations. But rather than being put off by the points of contention, historical archaeologists embrace them because they provide intriguing insights into past life. The study of meaning—from the lowly toothbrush to the grand formal garden—will continue to attract the historical archaeologists' attention for many years.

Having introduced some of the ways in which historical archaeologists can think about their data, we must now turn to the critical issue of archaeological context. Context anchors all artifacts and other archaeological finds in dimensions of time and space, the key aspects of research about the past.

## TIME TRAVEL

### Mobile, Alabama, 1702–1711

The French, not to be outdone by the other European superpowers who were harvesting the riches of the New World, strove to establish their own empire in North America. In addition to their successful efforts in Canada, they also cast their eyes on the Gulf of Mexico, and settled in a region that would come to be called French colonial Louisiana. The French sought to establish themselves between the Spanish at La Florida (on the east) and Nueva España (Mexico) on the west. So, in 1702 Pierre Le Moyne d'Iberville began a settlement that was designed as the military, economic, and political linchpin of the French empire in Louisiana. This settlement is known today as Old Mobile. This French center lasted only nine years, when the decision was made to move the town to the location of today's Mobile, on the mouth of Mobile Bay.

As was true of all colonial adventures, the new settlers had to decide how they would interact with the native peoples who had lived in the region for generations. The French at Mobile encountered several cultures, including the Mobiles, Tomés, Creeks, Choctaws, and Chickasaws. These long-time occupants of the region had developed histories interwoven with intermittent trade contacts and warfare.

*(continued)*

Source: Gregory A. Waselkov, ed. 2002. "French Colonial Archaeology at Old Mobile: Selected Studies." *Historical Archaeology* 36(1):1–148.

In one of those strange twists of historical fate, the French and the Spanish (whose nearest settlement was the presidio at Pensacola, just west of Mobile) were uneasy allies throughout the life of Old Mobile. Their connection was uniquely European, because they were drawn together by the War of Spanish Succession (1701–1713). Their uncertain relations along the Gulf coast in far-away North America derived from two circumstances: They were both seeking to control land in North American (often the same land), and they had different ideas about how to interact with the local Native Americans. But, even so, the French at Mobile and the Spanish at Pensacola learned that they had to depend on one another because of the chronic shortage of supplies caused by the unreliability of supply ships coming from Europe. They undoubtedly also shared some sense of being culturally European in an environment in which they were surrounded by indigenous peoples who were certainly not European in behavior or tradition.

French Mobile was in many ways a typical European colonial town. The colonists designed a settlement that made cultural sense to them. They built over one hundred houses on a regular grid of streets, and gave the streets names that would not have been out of place in Paris. They constructed their houses using a method called *poteaux sur sole* (post-on-sill). In this kind of construction, a wooden sill was laid on the ground and hewn wooden posts (like today's wall studs) were set on top of them. They filled the interstices with a mixture of clay and other materials that would provide both strength and insulation. The houses also had several rooms and fireplaces. Smaller houses, possibly used for soldiers, had only one room and were made with the less-substantial *pieux en terre* method, in which upright posts were set into narrow trenches. These buildings were less-substantial and more temporary than the residential dwellings. At one edge of town, the colonists constructed Fort Louis, a simple wooden stockade overlooking the river.

The residents of Old Mobile were mostly men, but with time the colony's promoters were able to convince a few French women to emigrate to the settlement. The residents also purchased slaves—mostly Native American women and children—to serve as domestic servants. Enslaved Indians thus comprised a large percentage of the population, perhaps as much as a quarter. Priests in the colony disapproved of the cohabitation of French settlers and Native American women, and so they promoted the emigration of more French women and even the introduction of African slaves.

Given the high percentage of native peoples at Old Mobile, it is not surprising that the objects used every day were a combination of Native American and French in manufacture and design. In addition, the town's linkage with La Florida meant that much of the material culture was Spanish. The members of a household at Old Mobile may have used an equal amount of French tin-glazed faience, Spanish tin-glazed majolica, and unglazed pottery made by the Apalachees in Florida. The residents also used a substantial amount of fine Chinese porcelain, the quality and styles of which were comparable to examples found throughout Europe.

The food consumed by the residents of Old Mobile was also a cultural blend of New and Old World species. They ate native maize and European fava beans, and they learned to harvest the wild foods around them. The ate white-tailed deer, as well as muskrat, beaver, opossum, and squirrel, and lesser amounts of fish.

# Chapter 5

# TIME AND SPACE

*"Time is central to archaeology."*

Michael Shanks and Christopher Tilley, 1987

*"It has slowly emerged that there is archaeological information in the spatial relationships between things as well as in things themselves."*

David L. Clarke, 1977

In Chapter 4, we explored some of the ways historical archaeologists examine and use artifacts. The subject of artifacts automatically brings up the issue of time and space. Time and space are essential aspects of archaeological research and we must now examine them closely.

## TIME

We humans are obsessed with time—with its passage, with using it wisely, and with the evils of "wasting" it. We "spend" time like money and find, like money, that there's never enough of it. Men and women have measured time for thousands of years, first using the rising and setting of the sun and the passage of the seasons to regulate their lives. The invention of the clock standardized time and made people think in terms of hours, minutes, and seconds. Peter Henlein's creation of the first spring-wound, portable clock around 1500 ultimately made it possible for us to carry time around with us on our wrists and in our pockets. We now take time zones for granted, but they were not invented until 1883 to satisfy railroad companies in the United States, who were concerned about standardizing their schedules. Today's train, bus, and airplane schedules all owe their invention to our modern desire to depart and to arrive "on time."

Unlike many societies, Westerners have always thought of time in linear terms, extending far back into the distant past, to more than 2.5 million years of human existence. Many Native American and African cultures, however, conceive of time in cyclical terms, as an endlessly repeating passage of seasons, years, and longer periods of time. The Aztecs of central Mexico measured time in fifty-two year cycles, and the pueblo dwellers of the American Southwest used the movements of heavenly bodies to mark planting and harvesting seasons.

Linear time forms the foundation of all archaeological research, with history representing the passage of time through centuries and millennia. The celebrated Roman orator Marcus Cicero put it well when he wrote that "History is the witness that testifies to the passing of time; it illuminates reality, vitalizes memory, provides guidance in daily life, and brings us tidings of antiquity." Cultural achievements and events act as signposts to the passage of time. Excavations in East Africa indicate that early humans roamed the tropical savannas more than two million years ago. A combination of archaeological and historical sources sets the unification of Egypt and the beginnings of ancient Egyptian civilization at about 2900 B.C. More recent events are accurate to the day. Columbus landed on the island of San Salvador on October 12, 1492. On April 9, 1865, Confederate General Robert E. Lee strode up the steps of Appomattox Courthouse and surrendered to the Union army.

The more recent the event, the more accurate is its recorded date. For instance, the exact time of every space shuttle launch in Florida is chronicled to the second by advanced computers and atomic clocks. Columbus's movements in the Indies are known to within the day and sometimes to the time of day. Roman history is accurate for the most part to within a year or a decade, and the reigns of the ancient Egyptian pharaohs are accurate to within a quarter century or so. Rudimentary documents extend back some five thousand years in the Near East. Prehistoric archaeologists are forced to measure cultural developments in centuries and often in millennia. Their colleagues examining text-aided history can use shorter scales of time, and the history they study is often further advanced with the collection of artifacts of known age (see Chapter 4). Historical archaeologists satisfy their obsession with time by using four dating techniques—relative dating, dating with objects of known age, formula dating, and dendrochronology.

### Relative Dating

All objects in the world have a different temporal relationship with every other object. Even today's mass-produced objects—bottles being filled with catsup on a mechanized assembly line, for instance—individually can be said to have a different "date." These dates may differ only by seconds, but they are different nonetheless. We may not be aware of the difference in date between the individual bottles, but we would certainly notice it once the bottles were filled, capped, and boxed for shipment. Factory workers would stack the boxes of bottles in the warehouse, as they waited to ship them. Simple common sense dictates that the boxes on the bottom of the stack are older than the ones on top. The lower the boxes in the pile, the earlier their date of manufacture.

Suppose you are walking down a street that is in such bad condition that a number of potholes expose three layers underneath. The top layer is a relatively new, brilliantly black, smooth surface. Beneath this layer is the gray, weathered surface of the old, worn blacktop, and below this a layer of red paving bricks. At the very bottom is a layer of grayish-white gravel. Based on common sense, you would immediately know that the uppermost, black surface is more recent in date than the paving bricks, but you would not know *precisely how much later*. You can only say that the uppermost surface is *relatively more recent* than the bricks.

Archaeologists refer to these kinds of time differences as "relative chronology." They only know, as with our imaginary street, that relationships of time exist between stratified soil layers, but they do not exactly know how much time is represented. Was the placement of the bricks and the black pavement separated by months, years, or even decades? How much time elapsed between the laying of the gravel and the bricks?

Relative chronology is based on a classic principle from geology, called the *Law of Superposition*. This law holds that under normal circumstances deep layers of soil, sediment, or rock are older than those above them. Relative chronology is thus devised from *stratification*, the sequences of layered deposits. The deposits found at an archaeological site resemble the exposed face of a cliff that contains numerous rock strata; the difference is that at an archeological site, the deposits will usually be layers of soil rather than layers of rock. Another important difference is that many of the archaeological layers encountered at an archaeological site will have been created through the conscious and unconscious activity of the site's past inhabitants. Other soil layers will indicate the natural action of wind and rain, as well as the activity of various animals.

Archaeologist Michael Schiffer has referred to the creation of archaeological strata—through the action of both human and natural forces—as "formation processes." These processes work together to "make" an archaeological site. Once the residents of a site leave that particular place and move someplace else, nature's effects on that site do not cease. Suppose that a small society lived at a village site from 1550–1650. We may easily understand that the effects of nature on that site did not cease when the villagers left. Its remains were constantly acted upon by the chemicals in the soil, the effects of drought and flood, the burrowing of mice, and the steady work of earthworms. The archaeologist first arriving at this site 350 years later will discover the activities at the site since its abandonment, even if no one else ever lived there!

Nature exercises a powerful affect on every archaeological site. When you walk through a suburban neighborhood, take a close look at a neglected yard and you will see how nature is slowly reclaiming it. After a few months, unkempt grass slowly creeps over the edges of the sidewalk and the front path. The grass, and even a thin layer of soil, will eventually cover the concrete, causing them to disappear from view. This same process is repeated at thousands of archaeological sites throughout the world. Strong winds blow fine sand over collapsed adobe dwellings, and unstoppable floods deposit a thick layer of soft mud over houses.

Complete devastation is even possible. On August 25, A.D. 79, an erupting Mount Vesuvius in Italy buried the nearby Roman towns of Herculaneum and Pompeii in a mountain of fine ash. Dramatic excavations have chronicled the last moments of Herculaneum. The sudden eruption trapped hundreds of people as they fled the throat-clogging ash. Families jostled their neighbors to reach the harbor and the safety of the boats moored there. Dozens of sprawling skeletons—people who did not reach the boats—wear their finest jewelry: rings with precious stones and bracelets of gold with beautiful glass beads. Nature's fury has the power to obliterate archaeological sites. It can work either quickly and dramatically or slowly and barely noticeably.

Humans can be powerful and destructive agents. Major cities like London and Boston have undergone massive development in recent decades. Such large-scale construction projects slice deeply into underlying strata and disturb the archaeological deposits that lie underneath. Newly excavated foundation trenches often reveal layer upon layer of earlier occupation, buried in the haste of urban renewal.

The remains of London's venerable Rose Theatre unexpectedly came to light in 1989 in the foundations of a new high-rise office building on the south bank of the Thames River. It was in this modest, circular theater that Elizabethan actors first presented William Shakespeare's *Henry VI* in the 1590s (Figure 5.1).

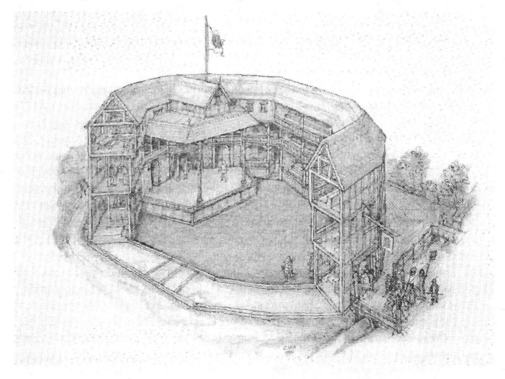

**Figure 5.1**  Reconstruction of the Rose Theatre, London.

Four hundred years later, worldwide public outcry greeted the news that what was left of the remaining wooden foundations were to be bulldozed away. Teams of archaeologists worked day and night to record details of the theater before the remains were covered over and lost forever. The discovery of the remains of the Rose Theatre, lying beneath so much of modern-day London, provides a dramatic example of stratification and relative chronology.

Relative chronologies in archaeology derive from the close study of human occupation layers. The Koster site in south-central Illinois reflects more than nine thousand years of prehistoric human activity. It contained no less than twelve separate layers of occupation, dating from modern times to about 7000 B.C. and extending to a depth of 34 feet (10.4 m). The Koster Site provided a perfect example of how superposition works in archaeology. Archaeologists at the site immediately knew that the sixth layer of human occupation, located about 7 feet (2.1 m) below ground, was more recent than the eleventh living surface, located almost 30 feet (9.1 m) down. Simple common sense and a knowledge of superposition told them this even before they found the first artifact.

The Koster Site is dwarfed by some Near Eastern cities, like Jericho or Ur, but its stratified layers cover a much longer period and extend to a greater depth than the vast number of historic-period sites. Historical archaeologists often work at sites that may have been inhabited for a couple of brief decades rather than for hundreds of years. When historical archaeologist Ivor Noël Hume excavated Martin's Hundred, a seventeenth-century settlement in colonial Virginia associated with Jamestown, he found the remains of the town almost directly beneath the present ground surface. The three and a half centuries that had passed since Martin's Hundred was abandoned was only time for a thin layer of soil to accumulate over the remains of the settlement. Koster's stratigraphy was well defined, with the occupation zones separated by natural layers accumulated during periods of abandonment that often lasted many centuries. In contrast, Martin's Hundred had thin strata. The presence of these delicate layers required meticulous recording and observation. Archaeologists often use the term *microstrata* to refer to the thin soil layers they encounter.

Noël Hume and his archaeologists at Martin's Hundred found microstrata inside the remains of a subterranean "cellar" dwelling. Excavation revealed that this house had a steeply pitched, A-frame style roof supported by large, upright, interior posts (Figure 5.2). During the life of the dwelling, its inhabitants deposited a thin layer of gray clay on the floor. Subsequent to its abandonment, additional clay and earth washed into the building, creating about 4 feet (1.2 m) of gently sloping soil. The archaeologists worked for several months to understand the chronology of this dwelling as presented by its soil layers.

The stratification of soil at archaeological sites, both human-made and natural, can be complex and confusing. Field archaeologists may be quickly able to understand the most basic relative chronology through a quick appraisal of the soil layers, but they may need assistance in unraveling all the relationships that may exist between the various soils. Archaeologists generally hold it as a rule of

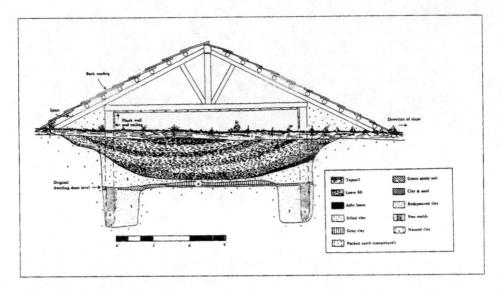

**Figure 5.2**  Seventeenth-century A-frame house at Martin's Hundred, Virginia.

thumb that the more soil strata at a site, the more confusing and difficult it is to interpret.

To help archaeologists better envision the relationships between the various soil strata they might encounter, archaeologist Edward Harris invented the ingenious *Harris Matrix*. Working at a complicated site in England, Harris was given the post-excavation task of interpreting the relative chronology of the site's many excavated soil layers. This monumental task led him to create a visual way of understanding the relationships between the strata and the human-built features at a site. Harris's method has many important elements, but its foundation rests on the idea that units of archaeological stratification may have three relationships. They may be unrelated, meaning that they do not touch one another; they many exhibit superposition, or be layered on top of one another; or they may be correlated, but no longer associated (such as when a ditch cuts through a soil strata and creates two sections of the once-whole layer).

Harris's breakthrough was that he envisioned a way that archaeologists could visually display these relationships through the use of a diagram (Figure 5.3). In this diagram, boxes represent the various archaeological units (soil strata, brick walls, and so forth) and vertical and horizontal lines represent their relationships. Archaeologists around the world immediately recognized the Harris Matrix as a significant tool, and his method is now part of every archaeologist's toolkit.

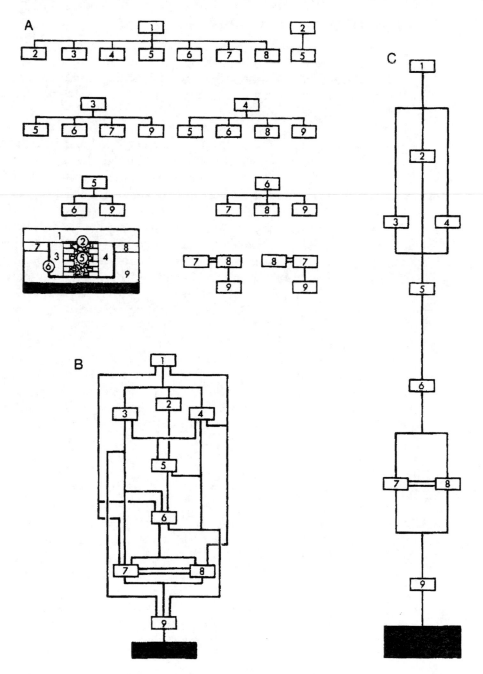

**Figure 5.3** Construction of a Harris Matrix.

### Dating with Objects of Known Age

Historical archaeologists are fortunate because they usually excavate sites where objects of known age can provide accurate calendar dates for buildings, graves, stratified layers, and other features. Such items include common, everyday artifacts like dated coins, domestic table wares, objects bearing telltale manufacturers' marks, and bottles.

Ivor Noël Hume's Martin's Hundred excavation provides a superb example of such dating, using depictions of the objects, rather than the objects themselves, as chronological markers. After carefully digging through the silted clay that had washed into the foundation of the abandoned A-frame house (see Figure 5.2), the excavators reached the building's original floor, which appeared as a thin, fairly even layer of gray clay. The artifacts within the clay included tiny pieces of blue and white fireplace or wall tile, probably imported from the Netherlands, known to date after the 1630s. Noël Hume's research revealed that Pieter de Hooch depicted similar tiles in his painting of 1660. In another painting, Dutch artist Jan Olis (1644) illustrated a pair of fireplace tongs exactly like those found on the floor of the A-frame house. Other objects—such as a green-and-yellow-glazed pot intended for kitchen use—can be seen in paintings from the mid-1660s. Noël Hume used these pictures to help him establish the occupation period of the house as the mid-seventeenth century.

Another dating problem resolved with objects of known age arose at Millwood Plantation, a nineteenth- and early-twentieth-century cotton plantation in the South Carolina upcountry. Archaeologists working under the author's direction documented twenty-one stone building foundations among the dense underbrush that had grown up at the site since its abandonment in the 1920s. Census rolls, court records, and personal papers written by the historic plantation's owner, James Edward Calhoun (see Chapter 4), established the occupation dates of these buildings from 1832 until about 1925. The author's team excavated the foundations in an attempt to date them more closely with artifacts.

One foundation was a roughly rectangular pile of red bricks and granite stones set in the middle of a large depression. The depression appeared to represent the wall line of a former building, with the rubble pile being what was left of the central chimney support. When the archaeologists excavated the rubble, they discovered that it was indeed a stone chimney support that had been faced with brick. Because the floor of the cabin was undoubtedly raised off the ground, the brick facing must have been visible under the house. The archaeologists decided to excavate inside the brick-lined support in an attempt to establish its construction date, because it could have dated to the plantation's slave period (1832–1865) or to its postwar era (1865–1925). The excavators found three layers of stones inside the chimney support used to reinforce and strengthen its foundation (Figure 5.4). A layer of loose, small cobbles appeared first, followed by a slightly thinner layer of small pebbles mixed with red clay. On the bottom was a layer of large, tightly packed stones. The excavator discovered a Seated Liberty quarter dollar, dated 1876, pressed within a tiny space in the deepest stone layer. This coin could not

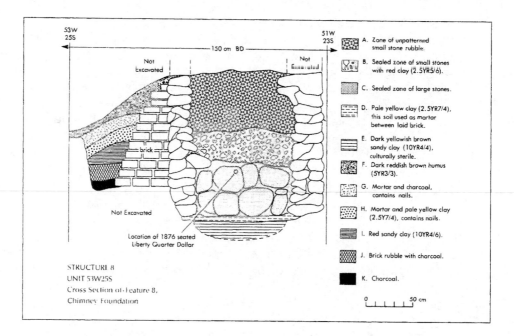

Figure 5.4 Position of 1876 quarter at building support, Millwood Plantation, South Carolina.

have fallen into the chimney support after the feature was constructed because the two stone layers above it were so tightly sealed. The coin was either lost or purposely placed among the stones sometime after 1876, or in other words, during the construction of the chimney support. The archaeologists could not tell exactly when the support—and the building itself—were built, but they did know that it dated between 1876 (the date of the coin) and 1925 (the date of the site's abandonment).

The use of artifacts to date sites, human-built features, and soil layers at Martin's Hundred and Millwood Plantation involved only one or two key artifacts. The archaeological use of artifacts to refine relative chronologies more often includes the interpretation of several soil layers and possibly thousands of artifacts. The additional data increases the complexity of dating.

When they excavated part of a city block in Sacramento, California, archaeologists Mary and Adrian Praetzellis used the artifacts they found to construct a chronology for the block. As is typical of most urban settings, a mix of people had lived and worked on the lots during the block's existence. A careful search of historical records told the Praetzellises that members of four individual households lived on the block: the Reeber family of German bakers; an unknown Gold Rush–era trader; James Meeker, a carriage lumber merchant; and the Goepel family from Germany. The Praetzellises assumed that each family contributed to the artifacts they discovered in the block. In an excavation 18 feet long and 3 feet wide (5.5 by 0.9 m) called Trench 3 West, the Praetzellises found at least eleven different soil layers that could be dated with their associated artifacts (Figure 5.5). They dated the deepest layer at about 1852, based on the eighteen coins they found there. Some of the coins were earlier in date—a tenpence, Irish coin, dated 1806; a five lire, Italian coin dated 1811; and an Indian rupee, dated 1840—but, for obvious reasons, they dated the layer on the basis of the *latest* coin—an 1852 ten-dollar gold piece issued in San Francisco. They dated the next highest soil layer to the late 1850s, based on a bottle of "Mrs. Winslow's Soothing Syrup," a well-known elixir bottled in New York City beginning in 1849. The Praetzellises dated a small soil lens above this layer to about 1862, based on the "Davenport" registry mark (see Chapter 4) of November 14, 1856, they found on the bottom of a white saucer. They assumed that it would have taken a few years for the syrup and the English plate to have reached Sacramento. They assumed that the Davenport plate, registered in late November, probably did not reach the city before December. The next highest soil layer they assigned a date of 1861–1863. They based this interpretation on the dates of the glass and ceramics within it. One difficulty with this interpretation, however, was their discovery of a bottle marked *ELLENVILLE GLASS WORKS* in the same deposit. This company used this mark only between 1866 and the 1880s. Rather than causing them to rethink their date, they concluded that the bottle was an *intrusion*, something that was not part of the original deposit but was deposited later. This find indicated that people continued to toss broken and unwanted objects in the area until at least the late 1860s. They dated a thin transition zone and the soil layer above it to 1863–1868

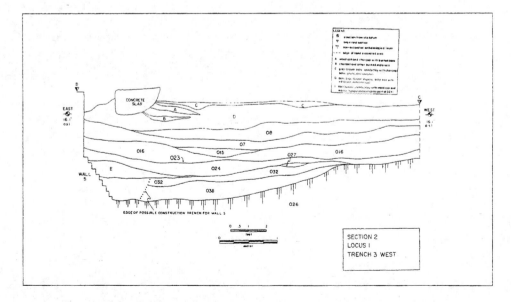

**Figure 5.5**   Soil layers in Trench 3, Sacramento, California.

using the embossed "Corn and Oats" pattern they found on pieces of white ceramics. The famous Wedgwood factory in England produced this pattern during the mid-1860s. These pieces also carried a registry mark of October 31, 1863. The Praetzellises dated the soil lens directly above the last layer to 1868 using the same "Corn and Oats" ceramics. The next highest soil layer they dated to about 1875, based on a small piece of a brown bottle marked "Dickey Chemist." This bottle originated in San Francisco and dates to the 1873–1920 period. The soil layers above the 1875 layer consisted of urban debris and artifacts dating from the mid-1870s to the present.

This example from Sacramento, California, demonstrates the value of having artifacts available with known dates of manufacture, sale, and use. Even in this instance, though, the plausibility of the interpretation rests on the archaeologists' research skills, abilities to identify various artifacts, and wide knowledge of artifact dates. In some cases, the archaeologists may find thousands of artifacts that by themselves can be assigned no particular date. In such instances, they can turn to two methods of formula dating, analytical methods that are wholly unique to historical archaeology.

### Formula Dating

Many historical archaeologist have turned to formula dating to help them date large white clay smoking pipe and glazed ceramic collections. Formula dating works on the idea that historic artifacts change over time and that these changes, no matter how imperceptible they may be, are sometimes amenable to measurement in years. The steady changes in the attributes of long-stemmed smoking pipes and mass-produced ceramics can be represented in mathematical formulae.

The white clay smoking pipe was in the past what the disposable razor is today—used for a few days or weeks, then thrown away. They date roughly from the mid-sixteenth century to the early twentieth century. Historical archaeologists excavating colonial sites usually unearth hundreds, even thousands, of fragments of white clay smoking pipe bowls and stems. For example, excavations at the eighteenth-century Fort Michilimackinac in Michigan yielded no fewer than 5,328 pipe fragments from between 1959 and 1966 alone. Excavators at the seventeenth- and eighteenth-century Ferryland site in Newfoundland found tens of thousands of pipe fragments in only seven years! As is the case at Ferryland, many of the pipes contain identifiable maker's marks (see Chapter 4), but in the vast majority of cases, the pipes exhibit no obvious markings.

A clay smoking pipe consists of two parts: a bowl and a stem (Figure 5.6). Fortunately for historical archaeologists, the bowls of these white, long-stemmed pipes were altered over the decades, beginning with the late 1500s. Pipe experts have charted these changes, showing the years in which each style was popular. Sixteenth-century pipe makers typically produced undecorated and simple bowls that had a sharp angle to the pipe stem. They straightened the sides of the bowls over time and made the angle with the stem smoother. By the early eighteenth

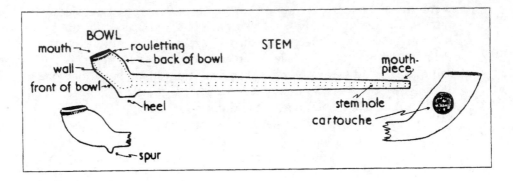

**Figure 5.6**   Parts of a clay smoking pipe.

century, their pipes had straight, smooth bowls. Also in the early eighteenth century, pipe makers began to put intricate symbols and decorations on their bowls. By the late eighteenth century, even short-stemmed pipes were becoming popular. These pipes were smoked by inserting a reed or stem into the short, stubby bowl (Figure 5.7).

The fine, white clay pipes were fragile and easily broke into small pieces when dropped or tapped to remove the old tobacco plug. Whereas the bowls might break into only two or three pieces, the stems generally fractured into several sections each measuring about 1 inch (2.5 cm) long. A broken pipe usually produced more pieces of stem than of bowl. Of the pipes found at Fort Michilimackinac between 1959 and 1966, fully 4,347, or almost 82 percent, were pipe stems.

On the face of it, pipe stems are hardly promising dating material. In the 1950s, however, pioneer historical archaeologist J. C. Harrington, in a monumental display of patience and dedication, examined more than 50,000 pipe stems he had excavated from the colonial site of Jamestown, Virginia. After examining hundreds of stems, he noticed that the size of the hole, or bore, appeared to get smaller through time. Harrington concluded that "if this represented a definite and consistent trend, then it might possibly be useful as a dating criterion." So inspired, he measured 330 stems from colonial sites in Virginia, and discovered that between 1620 and 1650, most of the bores measured $8/64$ ths of an inch (31.7 mm), whereas between 1750 and 1800, they were only $4/64$ ths of an inch (15.9 mm) (Figure 5.8). Harrington used 64ths of an inch as his scale because he had measured the pipe stem bores with the only tools he could think of that were available in different, highly accurate sizes: a set of drill bits.

Seven years after Harrington's breakthrough, Lewis Binford made the first strides in what is now called formula dating. He believed that Harrington's observations could be converted into what mathematicians call a regression formula. A regression formula is a mathematical way of representing the relationship between two variables, in this case, bore diameter and date. With

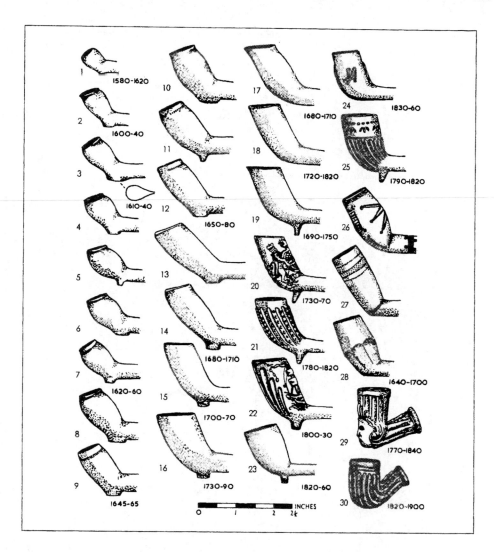

**Figure 5.7** The evolution of the pipe bowl 1580–1900.

bore diameter plotted on the X axis of a graph and date on the Y axis, the regression formula will show the precise relationship between the two variables. According to Binford, the formula Y = 1931.85 − 38.26X could be used to date collections of broken pipe stems, with Y being the mean date to be calculated, 1931.85 being the statistical date that pipe stem bores would theoretically disappear, and 38.26 being the number of years that it took for a pipe stem bore to be reduced by $\frac{1}{64}$ of an inch (1.6 mm).

Historical archaeologists immediately recognized that they could use Binford's creative formula to determine the date of any collections of pipe stems. The

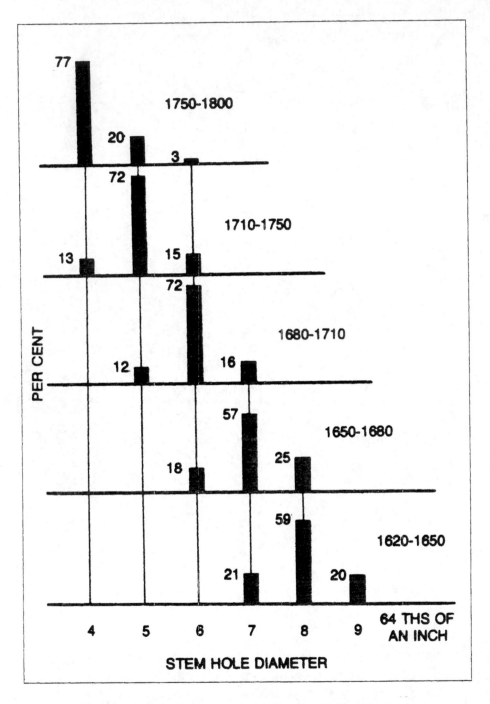

**Figure 5.8**   Harrington's pipe stem measurements.

X is calculated by multiplying the number of pipe stems by the number of 64ths of an inch in their measurement (7 stems measuring $^6/_{64}$ = 42; 35 stems measuring $^7/_{64}$ = 245), and then adding the products together and dividing by the total number of pipe stems.

Many enthusiastic archaeologists began to experiment with Binford's formula. Robert Heighton and Kathleen Deagan discovered that the regression line was not straight as Binford thought, but curved. They reasoned that pipe stem bores reached a minimum diameter and then stayed constant after about A.D. 1800. Ivor Noël Hume also discovered that the formula works best with samples of more than 900 stems deposited between 1680 and 1760. These refinements have strengthened Binford's original pipe stem formula.

Perhaps encouraged by the promise that formula dating held for historical archaeology, Stanley South devised a mean ceramic dating formula (or MCD) for use with eighteenth-century British ceramics. He reasoned that if English ceramic types have recognizable dates of manufacture, then it should be relatively easy to add all the ceramic date ranges at a site and calculate a single midpoint for all the individual ranges. South's formula is easy to compute (Table 5.1), and it has the advantage of yielding an actual calendar year. The year calculated represents the mean date of the combined ceramics in the sample.

To present a simple example, suppose we had a ceramic collection from a site that only contained ten sherds. Our knowledge of British ceramics tells us that seven of them were manufactured from 1800–1850, giving a mean date of

**Table 5.1**  *Calculating a Mean Ceramic Date using South's Method*

| Ceramic Type | Type Median ($X_i$) | Sherd Count ($f_i$) | Product |
|---|---|---|---|
| 22 | 1791 | 483 | 865,053 |
| 33 | 1767 | 25 | 44,175 |
| 34 | 1760 | 32 | 56,320 |
| 36 | 1755 | 55 | 96,525 |
| 37 | 1733 | 40 | 69,320 |
| 43 | 1758 | 327 | 574,866 |
| 49 | (1750) | 583 | 1,020,250 |
| 44 | 1738 | 40 | 69,520 |
| 47 | 1748 | 28 | 48,944 |
| 53, 54 | 1733 | 52 | 90,116 |
| 56 | 1733 | 286 | 495,638 |
| 29 | 1760 | 9 | 15,840 |
|  |  | 1960 | 3,446,567 |

The mean ceramic date formula

$$Y = \frac{\sum_{i=1}^{n} x_i \cdot f_i}{\sum_{i=1}^{n} f_i} \qquad Y = \frac{3,446.567}{1960} = 1758.4$$

*Source:* Stanley South, *Method and Theory in Historical Archaeology* (New York: Academic Press, 1977), p. 22.

1825. Suppose that the other three sherds were produced from 1830–1860, for a mean date of 1845. This means that the entire manufacturing range of the ten sherds is from 1800–1860. The computation of the mean ceramic date yields 1831, just about what we would expect. The formula works by weighting the collection by the number of sherds of different manufacturing dates. Our sample of ten sherds would produce an MCD of 1839 if we had three sherds with a mean manufacturing date of 1825 and seven with a mean manufacturing date of 1845. The date is weighted in the direction of 1845 because there are more sherds of that date. To get a better idea of how this formula works, simply use the ten sherds and South's formula from Table 5.1.

The ceramic mean dating method works best with large collections, just as does pipestem formula dating. Even so, South's dating formula has found a wider audience than the pipe stem dating, but only because potsherds of all kinds are more common finds. Where its results have been tested against historically documented occupations, the mean ceramic dates have been generally consistent. It works just as well at sites of unknown historical date.

All formula dates should be checked against other dates—preferably documentary ones. If we are excavating a site with a historically documented date range of 1690–1740, and the ceramic formula yields a date of 1770, something is amiss. Either we have misidentified the ceramics or the historical sources are wrong or incomplete. Sometimes the mean ceramic date can provide unexpected information.

Archaeologists from the University of Delaware excavated at the Williams Site in Glasgow, Delaware, a residence once occupied by an African American farm laborer named Sidney Stump. Legal records set the mean historic date of the site at 1887, but the mean ceramic date yielded 1844. How can such a discrepancy be explained? One possible answer is that Stump may have used second-hand or hand-me-down ceramics. This interpretation is plausible because he was a farm laborer for the entire time he lived at the Williams Site. We will never really know for certain why such a date discrepancy exists between the ceramic collection and the known dates of site occupation, but the calculation of the mean ceramic date allowed the archaeologists to suggest an interpretation they may never have otherwise imagined.

### Dendrochronology

An astronomer named A. E. Douglass invented dendrochronology, or tree-ring dating, in 1904 when he was studying ancient sun spot activity in the American Southwest. Douglass soon extended his method to the ancient beams he saw preserved in prehistoric pueblos, and in so doing, provided archaeologists with an elegant and extremely accurate dating method.

Trees grow seasonally, and the affects of rainfall and the number of frost-free days means that the trees' seasonal growth varies from year to year. The different rates of growth, especially in environments with well-defined wet and dry seasons, leaves a series of concentric growth rings of various thickness in the trunk. Dendrochronologists take sequences of growth rings from ancient logs and match them by computer with a master tree-ring sequence previously documented within a region. The master sequences are based on ring counts from living trees, and they provide an extremely accurate chronology that in some places extends back thousands of years. Even a small log from a site can be matched with the master sequence. Archaeologists in Europe have linked living trees to church beams and farmhouse timbers, as well as to ancient logs found in bogs, and have provided an archaeological tree-ring chronology that goes back to before 5200 B.C. in Ireland, and almost as far in Germany.

Historical archaeologists find dendrochronology to be a powerful dating tool when they can use it. Archaeologists used the method to date the historic Pueblo of Acoma, the famous "Sky City" in New Mexico, the oldest continuously inhabited city in the United States (Figure 5.9). Spanish explorers first visited the pueblo in 1540 during Coronado's efforts to locate the legendary, golden Seven Lost Cities of Cibola. In 1599, the Spaniards destroyed Acoma as part of their plan to control the pueblo peoples in the region, but the residents soon rebuilt it. Modern Acoma is a tapestry of building and rebuilding going back many centuries. In 1987, the people of Acoma invited the Laboratory of Tree-Ring Dating at the University of Arizona to date the oldest part of the village. They planned to restore the rooms of the old pueblo, and they wished to be certain of their construction dates. The Laboratory's core samples from well-preserved beams enabled them to date fifty rooms. They found that the pueblo was begun in 1646, and that it had achieved its current form by 1652. In 1934, the Historic American Buildings Survey (see Chapter 7) had completed accurate architectural drawings of the pueblo.

**Figure 5.9**   Acoma Pueblo, New Mexico.

When the archaeologists compared the buildings on this detailed map with their tree-ring dates, they were surprised to discover that the pueblo had changed little between 1652 and 1934, a span of 282 years.

## SPACE

Space in archaeological terms refers to the precise location of any find, site, or structure. One way to understand the archaeological use of space is to think of the word "position." Position is a key element in understanding how things were related in the past. Sherlock Holmes solved many of his most challenging mysteries because of his careful understanding of where things were located in relation to one another. In "The Adventure of the Priory School," he ponders the disappearance of Lord Saltire, the ten-year-old son and heir of the Duke of Holdernesse. The young lord had disappeared one night, along with Heidegger the German master. Holmes was called in because, in characteristic fashion, the police had already thrown up their hands in despair. But understanding the significance of space, Holmes drew a sketch of the landscape to help him solve the baffling mystery. With this map in hand he was able to reconstruct the route taken by the abductors, was led to the body of Heidegger, and deduced—from the bicycle tracks, also on the map—that young Saltire was being held at the Fighting Cock Inn, on the top of the map near Holdernesse Hall.

Archaeologists are not scientific versions of the fictional Sherlock Holmes, but his methods are instructive. Holmes is like an archaeologist because of his intense interest in where things are located, and he could even have been speaking as an archaeologist when he told Watson, "I want you to realize those geographical features which may have a good deal to do with our investigation." Archaeologists refer to the analysis of location—from the placement of artifacts at a site to the placement of the features on a landscape—as *spatial analysis*. Archaeologists have adopted many of their methods and perspectives on spatial analysis from geographers, and this borrowing and adaptation represents another important instance where archaeologists, including historical archaeologists, have relied on scholars from other disciplines.

Spatial analysis proceeds on many levels, or scales. Archaeologists can examine the location of artifacts and features within an individual house. Intra-site analysis can focus on the spatial associations of artifacts, houses, and other features present at a site. Archaeologists can concentrate inter-site analysis on the presence of artifacts within many sites, and so may learn important insights about past trading patterns. They can also conduct larger-scale, macro analyses of entire regions. All of the spatial relationships have the potential to yield valuable cultural and historical information. The placement of sites in relation to natural resources—fertile soils, stands of good timber, streams and rivers that run cold and clear the year around, and sun-drenched hillsides—also provide abundant information about what natural features past peoples sought out. Equally important are the placement of sites in relation to objects of human construction—mills, bridges, roads, and major settlements.

Historians have documented that railroads were an important, and indeed central, determinant of settlement in the flat, fertile prairies and plains of North America. On the plains of Saskatchewan, the Canadian Pacific Railroad gobbled up the best land and then convinced immigrants to settle on it. Author James Minifie recalls the irresistible pull this land had on his father in 1909: "The last, best West was filling up fast; my father determined to get in while he could. He closed down his business and decided to go as far west as his money would take him." Old maps of Saskatchewan show the network of railroads in the southern half of this province with settlements appearing as beads on a necklace, strung out along the rail lines. It was not unknown in the nineteenth century for a town's residents to pick up their buildings and move them next to a railroad. They knew that isolated towns could die.

The scale, or level, of a spatial analysis is determined by the research questions being posed. The transportation of commodities from one place to another is essentially a problem in spatial analysis, with a scale that can extend to whole continents. When British archaeologist Peter Danks studied the distribution of late-eighteenth-century ceramics made by the Lowestoft factory on the east coast of England, his region of interest was the entire British Isles. No written records or pattern books survived for his perusal, so he was forced to rely strictly on artifacts to establish the spatial distribution of the Lowestoft wares. The only way he could perform this kind of study was by examining the ceramic collections from several sites. Once he had identified Lowestoft pieces in various collections he could be reasonably certain that some sort of linkage had operated between the factory and the sites.

Most spatial analysis occurs on a far smaller scale than the continent level. When Stanley South became interested in the spatial placement of pins and beads at the eighteenth-century Public House and Tailor Shop in Brunswick Town, North Carolina, he focused only on this one 3,600 square foot (324 sq m) building. A careful analysis of the location of the artifacts indicated that all the beads and pins occurred in five of the six rooms (Figure 5.10). These tiny objects had apparently fallen through the cracks in the floorboards during the building's use. The unequal distribution of beads and pins led South to conclude that "Room 6 must have been used for merchandising the objects sewn together in the five other rooms" because he found almost no pins and beads there.

### Space at Archaeological Sites

The study of space is based on another fundamental principle of archaeology, the *Law of Association*. This principle holds that an artifact or other find is contemporary with the other objects found along with it in the same soil layer or human-built feature.

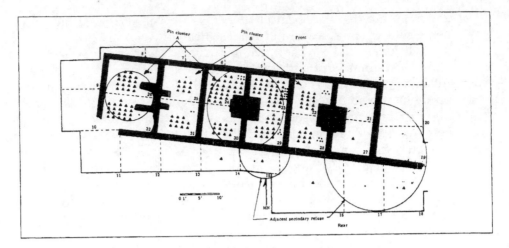

**Figure 5.10**   Plan of the Public House and Tailor Shop show the location of pins and beads.

We mentioned above how Mary and Adrian Praetzellis dated the different soil layers in one city block in Sacramento, California, using one or two datable artifacts. Using the Law of Association, we would say that all of the finds within the layers were contemporaneous with the datable artifacts. This conclusion is particularly reasonable when the deposits are sealed, or closed to intrusions, like the chimney support at Millwood Plantation.

Burials accompanied with grave goods provide an excellent example of the Law of Association. Interment is a single event that takes place at a particular moment in time. Given the nature of burial, we can be certain—in the absence of intrusions—that the artifacts deposited with the deceased were used in the society at the time of the person's death. Once the grave is filled over, it becomes impossible to place anything further with the deceased. Cultural anthropologist Jerome Handler and archaeologist Frederick Lange excavated the skeletal remains of several seventeenth-century slaves from Newton Plantation, Barbados. Their careful excavation of the remains conclusively demonstrated that the artifacts placed alongside the dead—glass bottles, white clay smoking pipes, brass buttons, glass beads, and glazed ceramics—were all used together when these individuals were alive. Such tightly enclosed collections of artifacts help archaeologists to construct the contexts of past daily life. By knowing the range of materials placed in graves, archaeologists can develop at least a partial understanding of the kinds of goods the people had available in their society.

Beyond such simple contexts as burials and individual soil layers, the Law of Association permits archaeologists to perceive the sites they routinely study as being arranged within a spatial hierarchy. The hierarchy extends from small spaces to extremely large ones. The idea behind these levels of analysis is that people use space in regular ways because spatial use is culturally determined. We can discern something of a culture's patterns of spatial use by studying the spatial distribution of artifacts, features, and whole sites on a landscape. The hierarchy of spatial analysis in archaeology extends from activity areas to entire communities.

*Activity Areas.*   The activity area is the smallest spatial unit studied by archaeologists. These zones are places within a site where people conducted specific activities. Archaeologists can usually identify them by the clusters of artifacts they contain. These artifacts typically indicate the range of past activities carried out at that spot. At a prehistoric site, the presence of a pile of stone debris may indicate a place where the people manufactured their stone tools.

As part of her investigation into the archaeology of activity areas, Susan Kent examined a number of site locations in the American Southwest. She identified five archaeological sites associated with the Navajo. One site had an occupation date from about 1890 to around 1930. She found littered across the site coffee can lids, porcelain doll parts, glass bottle fragments, sheep and cow bones, and a 1927 New Mexico automobile license plate. She could identify several activity areas through dense concentrations of wood chips and ash (Figure 5.11). These spots were obvious places where people had performed activities: probably

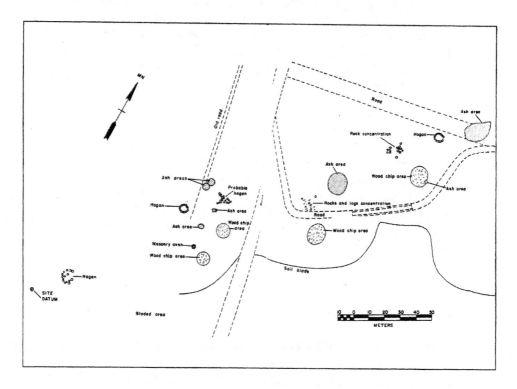

**Figure 5.11**   Activity areas at a Navajo site, 1890–1930.

chipping wood and building fires. The presence of at least three traditional Navajo dwellings, or hogans, suggested to Kent that three related families, perhaps members of the same extended family, had created the activity areas.

The presence of historical records and the construction of analogies based on activities performed today often allow historical archaeologists to use site labels that are more descriptive than the generic "activity area." For example, while excavating at Jamestown, Virginia, in the 1950s, John Cotter found a cluster of three kilns used by the settlers to make pottery, perhaps once housed inside a building. Cotter's crew unearthed two other archaeological features nearby: the foundation of a seventeenth-century workshop or brewhouse and a shallow pit, probably dug for clay during the construction of the kilns and later filled with refuse. The workshop/brewhouse was located only 20 feet (6.1 m) to the east of the kilns; the pit was only 10 feet (3.1 m) to the south. The excavators located three additional features within 160 feet (48.8 m) of the three kilns—a large dwelling, a small outbuilding, and a smaller house. At this one spot in colonial Jamestown, Cotter found what may be described as eight separate activity areas: a large house, a small building associated with it, a small house, a workshop or brewhouse, three kilns, and one pit. Each area represents the remains of activities that produced archaeological evidence. Cotter was able to use his knowledge of colonial history to assign functional terms to the activity areas.

Kent's identification of the three Navajo hogans in the American Southwest and Cotter's discovery of the two house sites at Jamestown illustrate an important point: In historical archaeology, the word "site" often equates with "household." Much historical archaeology is focused on such residential units.

*Households.*   The U.S. Bureau of the Census defines a household as "all the persons who occupy a housing unit." Houses, apartments, groups of rooms, and even a single room all qualify as housing units. Many of us may think of a household as being composed of men, women, and children who are related by kinship. We often thus equate "household" with "family." Within the past several years, Westerners have witnessed dramatic changes in the composition of the traditional male-centered family. The once so-called "nontraditional" families are becoming ever more commonplace. But as early as 1900, the U.S. Census Bureau defined the "family" in broad terms, as "a group of individuals who occupy jointly a dwelling place or part of a dwelling place." They said further that "All the occupants and employees of a hotel, if they regularly sleep there, make up a single family." Given this historic definition, coupled with the changes that family structure has recently undergone, perhaps the best way to think about households is to view them simply as a group of people who live together.

Households are particularly interesting to historical archaeologists because their members were the consumers who bought, used, and discarded the artifacts and food remains that chronicle history. The spatial distributions of these finds have the potential to tell us a great deal about the activities of the household.

In their archaeological history of Philadelphia, John Cotter, Daniel Roberts, and Michael Parrington describe excavations at 8 South Front Street. Located about one and one-half blocks from the Delaware River and not far from Independence Hall, this address was home to three different households from 1683–1833. Historic plats show that Letitia Penn, of the prominent Penn family, lived there from 1683–1713 (Figure 5.12). From 1713–1736, a bricklayer named Joseph Yard lived on the property with his family, but in 1736, Joseph's son, John, sold the property to Andrew Bradford. Bradford's son, Thomas, would later become a lieutenant colonel in the American militia fighting for independence. Thomas lived much of his later life in the house. The Bradfords sold the property in 1833 to John Moss, a prominent shipping merchant, who never actually lived there.

The preliminary analysis of the archaeological remains discovered at 8 South Front Street indicates that the occupants of the house dug three deep pits on the property. Near the end of their residence, the Yards dug an eight-foot-deep (2.4 m) privy pit near the back of the house. Later, they filled this relatively shallow pit with trash. The pit contained only one datable artifact, a gray stoneware chamber pot bearing the mark "A.D." These letters indicate that the pot had been made at the pottery shop of Anthony Duché, between about 1720–1730.

When the Bradfords purchased the residence from the Yards, they did not bother to have the privy cleaned. They simply dug a second one, 15 feet (4.6 m) deep, directly adjacent to the old one. Excavation of the second privy yielded a

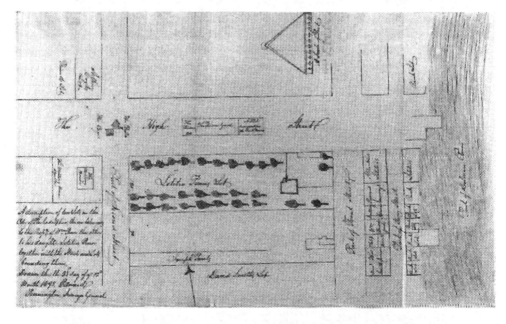

**Figure 5.12** Section of a 1698 survey map of Philadelphia showing the location of Letitia Penn's lot and those of her neighbors.

1734 British coin. Sometime between 1736 and 1756, the Bradfords added a
kitchen to the house. Space considerations forced them to build this addition over
the privy. As a replacement, they used an old brick-lined, 26-foot-deep (7.9 m)
well, also in the backyard. As Cotter, Roberts, and Parrington note, "With its
greater depth, it would have served the needs of the site's occupants better than
either of the previous privy pits. The health of anyone using water from wells in
the vicinity of this deep privy would, however, have been ill-served." We unfortunately know nothing about the health of the members of these households or
that of their nearby neighbors. But the archaeological research at 8 South Front
Street has cast light on some of the household activities of the three families who
inhabited this one house site.

Households formed the basic economic unit for Letitia Penn, the Yards, and
the Bradfords at 8 South Front Street, just as they have for millions of people
around the world for centuries. But households, no matter how tightly knit, did
not exist in a vacuum. Individual households were part of a larger unit, called a
neighborhood.

*Neighborhoods.* Neighborhoods are simply collections of households.
Going back to a definition posed by the U.S. Bureau of the Census, neighborhoods are composed of several "housing units": single-household dwellings,
apartment buildings, and hotels. Neighborhoods in cities can be tightly com-
pacted spaces, with people virtually living on top of one another in apartments
and tenements. Neighborhoods in more rural settings may cover much larger
areas, with individual dwellings being widely separated.

The families who once called 8 South Front Street home were members of a
larger neighborhood. When Thomas Holme, William Penn's general surveyor,
drew the lots on Front Street, he listed not only Letitia Penn, but also Daniel
Smith, Charles Pickering, Thomas Harriet, and other landowners who were her
neighbors. All of these people were both members of households and members of
the neighborhood. They probably nodded to one another on the street, perhaps
they took tea in one another's houses, and perhaps they even knew some of their
neighbors' personal business.

Historical archaeologists can often use historical documents and maps to
help them understand neighborhoods. They can link this textual information with
their archaeological findings to provide a rich picture of neighborhood life. In
large American cities, invaluable neighborhood maps were once published by the
D. A. Sanborn National Insurance Diagram Bureau, later called the Sanborn Map
and Publishing Company. The Aetna Insurance Company hired Sanborn in 1867
to make maps of several cities in Tennessee, to show their appearance after the
devastation of the American Civil War. Sanborn saw the potential for a profitable
business and soon created a company to specialize in producing these so-called
"fire insurance maps." By the time the company stopped produced them one hundred years later, they had published 700,000 maps of 12,000 cities and towns in the
United States. In Great Britain, similar maps were produced by Charles E. Goad,

Ltd., and in Australia, newspapers sometimes published panoramic views of cities, often showing details of various houses around their borders.

Memories of the highly devastating fires, like those in London in 1666, Lisbon, Portugal in 1755, and Chicago in 1871, convinced city- and town-dwellers of the wisdom of knowing where buildings were located, their materials of construction, and their owners' fire precautions. Maps like those produced by the Sanborn company showed the spaces between buildings and noted whether the buildings were constructed of brick, stone, or wood. They distinguish between residences, stores, stables, and special-use buildings, such as glasshouses. In an era of coal and wood fires, the maps inventoried chimney designs for firefighters combating the many chimney fires of the day. The maps also show porches, outbuildings, and lot lines. In short, where they are available, urban insurance maps are priceless archives of the spatial relationships of late-nineteenth- and early-twentieth-century neighborhoods.

Historical archaeologists also find the aptly named "bird's-eye views" of cities and towns to be as valuable as maps. Such views are really "artistic maps" because they provide a three-dimensional perspective on an urban area. Buildings appear as actual structures with windows, doors, and roofs. They also depict trees and landscaping, boats sailing on rivers, and horse-drawn buggies on busy thoroughfares. These images may at first appear more realistic than simple maps, but they also display far more artistic license than the sober diagrams of the insurance plats. Many artists of the bird's-eye views made their drawings look better than the towns they portrayed.

When used together, maps and bird's-eye views provide historical archaeologists with a compelling picture of old neighborhoods. Historical archaeologists can use these sources to construct an image of a neighborhood long before their excavations begin.

When Mary and Adrian Praetzellis investigated the Sacramento city block mentioned earlier, they excavated the household of a woman named Mary Collins, who once lived at 808 I Street. The first family to live at this address was the Leonard Kellogg family, who were there by 1858. Mary Collins, a widowed Irish woman, soon followed them. Her family lived there until sometime before 1910. The 1900 census indicates that Mary had three children who lived with her. The Praetzellises used both the 1869 bird's-eye view (Figure 5.13) and the 1895 Sanborn map of the block (Figure 5.14) to reconstruct the history of the neighborhood in which the Collins family lived. They learned that a small dwelling was adjacent to the Collins's yard on the right (at 810 I Street), and that a narrow alleyway was placed on the left. Next to the alley were two small buildings, behind which was a large house situated on the corner (at 901 8th Street). A large "Wood & Coal Yard" was directly behind the Collins home. Next to the coal yard was the "A. Meister & Sons Carriage Mfg." company. Further behind the house, fronting J Street, were one or two other dwellings. All of these properties—the dwellings, the coal yard, the manufacturing company—were part of the Collins's neighborhood in 1895.

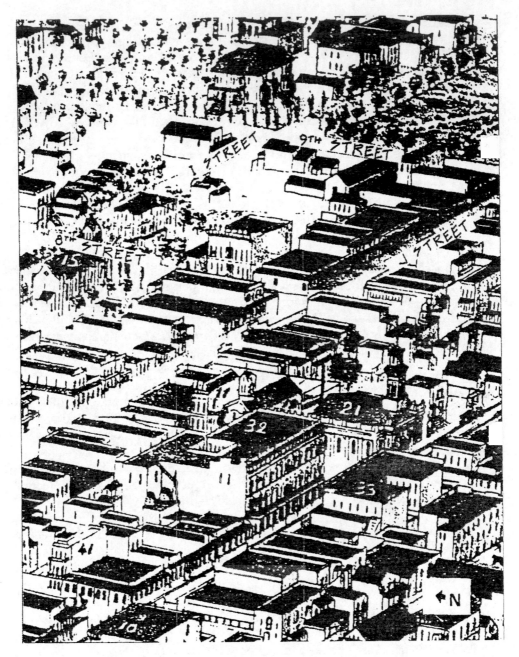

**Figure 5.13**  Bird's-eye view of Sacramento, California, in 1869.

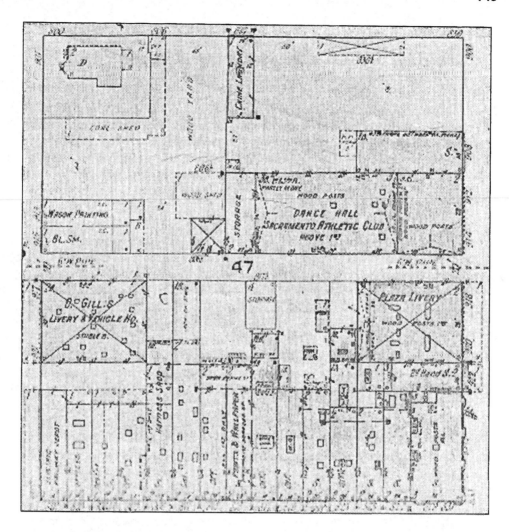

**Figure 5.14**   1895 Sanborn map showing the location of Mary Collins's home at 808 I Street, Sacramento, California.

This one block in Sacramento, California, shows the many different kinds of buildings that can exist in a neighborhood. Historical archaeologists can study each of them: domestic, commercial, and manufacturing sites. The 1869 bird's-eye view also proves that the Collins neighborhood did not exist in a vacuum. It was one element of a much larger, vibrant community.

***Communities.***   In Chapter 1, we mentioned the research of William Adams at Silcott, Washington, a late-nineteenth- and early-twentieth-century town in eastern Washington. Adams's study focused on Silcott strictly as a community: a collection of households and neighborhoods. In his words, "We sought information from which inferences could be made on the basis of the community as a whole, rather than on individual sites within it." His plan called for the excavation of several sites to get some sense of the community.

His research team began with Bill Wilson's Store because they viewed the old general store as a microcosm of community life. All of the manufactured things the people of Silcott bought in town would have come through Wilson's Store. Adams's team also excavated three households. Many of the artifacts they found during their excavations—cups and saucers, pitchers, crocks, marbles, tin cans, medicine bottles—appeared at all four sites. Using these artifacts in conjunction with oral histories and old pictures, Adams constructed historical vignettes of the community as it may have appeared in 1917. For example, one of the excavated dwellings, the Ireland Place, was commented on as follows: "Strange the way names stick to a place. The first house you come to from the ferry is known as the Ireland Place, even though Richard Ireland only lived here about a year or so and that was over fifteen years ago, in 1902. But somehow his name stuck to it. Right now Jim Stanfill and family live here."

Historical archaeologists have also learned that communities are more than merely a collection of people and buildings. Residents of communities can develop feelings of belonging and group identity through the creation and encouragement of common traditions. Archaeologist Heather Burke illustrated this process in her detailed examination of Armidale, Australia. By examining the 1840–1930 period, Burke learned that the working-class men and women who moved into the more upscale part of town created a sense of shared community among themselves as a strategy for cohesion. Their sense of togetherness fostered group identity (see Chapter 10) and made the residents feel that, even though they were not at the top of the social order, they nonetheless shared a social rank with their neighbours. The creation of the ideological community also helped to level, or at least to downplay, the internal differences that existed *within* the physical community, between households with more income and perhaps wider social connections.

The households of the Yards of Philadelphia, Collinses of Sacramento, and the Stanfills in Silcott were members of neighborhoods and communities. Communities are larger than neighborhoods, but they are not the largest spatial unit that historical archaeologists can study. Above the community is the settlement pattern.

### Settlement Patterns

The study of *settlement patterns* involves analyzing ways in which archaeological sites are distributed across a landscape. This specialty is also called *settlement archaeology*.

The archaeology of settlement patterns is based on the assumption that people with free choice make informed decisions about where they choose to live, and that they live in specific locales because they seek to satisfy some want or need. Ancient Egyptian farmers founded their villages on high ground on or just outside the Nile floodplain, so that only the surrounding farm lands, not their homes, were inundated by unusually high floods. Some people lived on the edge of the desert because fertile land was so important that they wasted none of it on their village sites.

More recent historic peoples tended to locate their sites with careful regard for such factors as the availability of water, the slope of hillsides, protection against hostile attack, and so on. In Silcott, Washington, in the late 1890s, Richard Ireland situated his homestead on the banks of the Snake River to take advantage of the ferry. During the days of widespread fur trapping in Canada, archaeologist Scott Hamilton has demonstrated how fur traders were forced to change the locations of their posts and other settlements once they had depleted the fur-bearing mammals within the nearby environmental zone. The miners who built the Dolly's Creek settlement in south Australia not surprisingly situated their town where they hoped to find gold.

Settlement decisions can be complex issues that may involve many buildings and other properties. When the American Civil War ended in 1865, most of the enslaved families on James Edward Calhoun's plantation decided to remain on the 15,000-acre (6,073 ha) estate as semi-autonomous tenant farmers. This place had been their home for decades, and most of them wanted to stay there. Archaeologists working under the author's direction realized that the site presented a rare opportunity to study the settlement pattern of the emancipated men and women because as freedmen and women they could no longer be told where to live. As tenant farmers they did not wish to live in their old slave cabins, and they were free to establish their homes anywhere they wished on the estate. The important archaeological question thus became: What criteria did the tenant farmers use when deciding where on the plantation they should live? The archaeological team used old maps to identify sixty-six tenant homes within the plantation's boundary (Figure 5.15). They next assessed these sites in terms of a number of factors, including agricultural potential, distance above mean sea level, degree and direction of land slope, and the distances to nearest stream, road, railroad, neighbor, and town, Calhoun Falls.

The Millwood researchers soon discovered that most of the tenant farmers located their homes 475 feet (148 m) above sea level, and oriented them to the southwest, west, or southeast, $^3$10 of a mile (0.5 km) from the nearest stream, and 1 $^1$2 miles (2.4 km) from the Savannah River, which bordered the plantation. The typical farmer was located less than $^1$2 mile (0.8 km) from his closest neighbor, less than 1 $^1$2 miles (2.4 km) from both the nearest road and the nearest railroad, and more than 1 $^1$2 miles (2.4 km) from the town. The Millwood tenant farmers thus established their homes on high ground close to a neighbor and a road, but not too near town. Through the placement of their farms, the tenants appear to have been saying that their community was designed to look inward, toward one another, rather than outward, to the wider world around them. Oral recollections collected from former tenants confirmed this interpretation, for the people preserved a strong sense of community on the plantation.

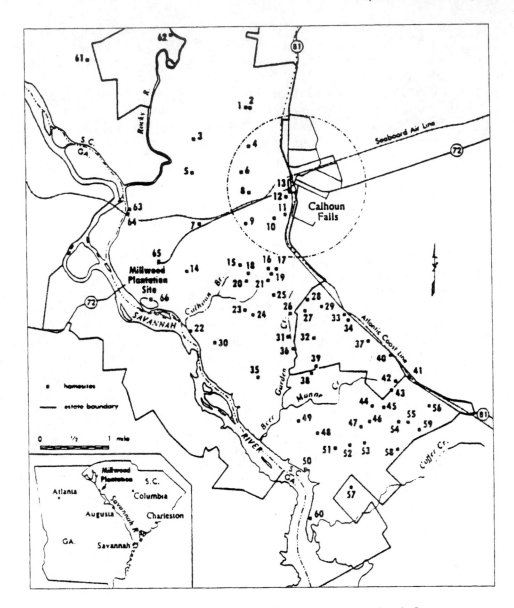

**Figure 5.15**  Settlement pattern at Millwood Plantation, South Carolina, after 1865.

Historical archaeology is of immense value in understanding past settlement patterns. Telltale house foundations, scatters of distinctive artifacts and food remains provide unique information about settlement patterns and the cultural values that shaped them. Again and again, the archaeological record amplifies impressionistic, often superficial accounts of life in the past.

People actively create space, and once created they give it meaning. People invent networks of physical things—rooms, sites, houses, towns—with a logic that is consistent with their cultural beliefs and attitudes. Their way of situating things makes sense to them.

Time and space are the two most important dimensions archaeologists study. Having explained them, we must now proceed to the heart and soul of archaeology: finding and excavating historic sites.

## TIME TRAVEL

### Limehouse Porcelain Manufactory, London, 1745–1748

On the north bank of the fabled Thames River, just east of London's city center, is an area of wharfs not unlike those found at the water's edge throughout the world. The area was a growing industrial section, with the picturesque, though descriptive names of nearby features: Rope Makers Field Road, Lime-Kiln Dock, Limehouse Bridge. The waterfront was alive with ships of all sorts, from ocean-going, three-masted sloops to small rowboats.

The bank of the Thames was an obvious place to develop new industries, and as early as 1363, a man named John Dik had operated a lime kiln on the spot that would later house the porcelain factory. Lime from Dik's kilns was undoubtedly used throughout the area for plaster and mortar for the buildings that were going up in the area. Lime continued to be important in this part of town, and in fact the last lime kiln at this location did not close until 1935. From 1745–1748, the site of Dik's kilns housed Joseph Wilson's porcelain factory.

The manufacture of porcelain was something of a mystery to Europeans during the early eighteenth century. Chinese potters had perfected their beautiful blue-and-white, hard-paste porcelains during the fifth and sixth centuries, and once Asia

and Europe developed lasting trade relations, the fine porcelains became all the rage for those consumers who could afford to purchase them. Eager Europeans coveted the exquisite porcelains, and so desperate were they, that they even regarded the poorest-quality Chinese porcelains with reverence.

It was increasingly clear, however, that the importation of porcelains from Asia would not satisfy the European market. Being delicate, porcelain was often difficult and expensive to ship. In addition, as greater numbers of Europeans began to enjoy the second great Asian import—tea—it was clear that more porcelain would have to be made available. The thick-bodied, tin-glazed European earthenwares could not withstand the high boiling temperatures needed for good tea. The obvious solution was for Europeans to invent their own porcelains. The Italians, in the 1570s, began the task of trying to manufacture thin-bodied, hard-paste porcelains, but the secret was elusive. Several others worked feverishly to find the secret combination of clay, glaze, and firing temperature, but it was not until the first decade of the eighteenth century that a brilliant German chemist named Johann

*(continued)*

Source: Kieron Tyler, Roy Stephenson, J. Victor Owen, and Christopher Phillpotts, *The Limehouse Porcelain Manufactory: Excavations at 108–110 Narrow Street, London, 1990.* (London: Museum of London Archaeology Service, 2000.)

Friedrich Böttger cracked the porcelain code. His discovery meant that German porcelains quickly became world famous for their quality and beautiful decoration, a reputation they still rightly enjoy. England lagged woefully behind in their commitment to porcelain manufacture, and in the 1740s, only two porcelain manufactories existed in there: one in Chelsea, the other Joseph Wilson's Limehouse kiln. Chelsea thrived where the Limehouse factory failed, and by the 1770s, at least thirteen other factories rivaled the Chelsea works.

The centerpiece of any pottery manufactory was the kiln. The Limehouse kiln was circular in shape with an interior diameter of 11.8 feet (3.6 meters). Its walls were made of brick, and its floor was composed of limestone flags. Its chimney was probably bottle-shaped like most kilns of the day. Charred areas on the flagstone floor indicated that it probably had six fireboxes. These were the places the potters would add fuel to maintain the kiln's internal temperature. Control of the heat was a key element of making a successful batch of ceramics, and porcelain was no exception.

Like all potters, the Limehouse artisans used a number of saggers, special kiln furniture intended to keep the individual vessels from fusing together during the firing process. Their saggers were made of fine, hard white clay tempered with coal and fine particles of grit. The smooth, fine-grained surfaces of the saggers were designed to keep them from fusing to the vessels, but many of them became glazed during firing. The lack of other pieces of kiln furniture at the Limehouse kiln—pieces potters know as stands, pipes, bobs, and stilts—indicates that the potters there were not engaged in the production of small, decorative items (like flowers and leaves) that could be applied to the most expensive wares.

The potters at the Limehouse kiln produced a number of different kinds of vessels during the short time of their factory's operation. They made polychrome sauceboats with enameled floral designs and pastoral scenes, white octagonal platters with blue decorations, and white cat figurines with blue eyes, whiskers, and claws. The potters were also fond of making blue-and-white pickle dishes molded in the shape of scallop shells. They also made boxes, butter boats, jars, teapots and lids, mugs, various-sized plates, and many other vessels. Some of the craftsmen in the factory would sign their initial to the bottom of their vessels.

Wilson undoubtedly understood the consumerist desires of his English customers, because many of his products were decorated with Asian motifs. Some of his favorite Asian designs showed Chinese fishermen with fishing rods in hand, men sitting on square divans being attended to by servants, and men hunting with their dogs. All of these designs had Asian-looking trees and other foliage in their backgrounds to add to their non-European character. Leaf-shaped pickle dishes, complete with molded veins, could be decorated with blue butterflies or with vases holding exotic-looking plants. All of the designs were hand-painted by skilled artisans.

# Chapter 6

# HISTORICAL SITE
# SURVEY AND LOCATION

*"Simply walking around the countryside in the hopes of stumbling on an archaeological site is good exercise, but the rewards are likely to be small unless the searcher knows what to look for and approximately where to find it."*

Ivor Noël Hume, 1969

Some historic sites are easily recognizable by ruins and even standing buildings that may still be visible. But this is not always the case. Many archaeological sites, even those inhabited during the recent past, can be hidden from view, silently lying beneath the earth's surface. How do archaeologists know where to look for hidden historic sites? Does training in archaeology give field workers special knowledge about sites and their locations? Special knowledge, often based on experience, does play a part in archaeological site location, but archaeologists most often rely on sophisticated techniques they have either developed on their own or else borrowed from scientists in related fields. This chapter presents some of the ways in which archaeologists find archaeological sites of all kinds.

The Pyramids of Giza in Egypt, the city of Teotihuacán in Mexico, the Mission St. Xavier del Bac near Tucson, Arizona—all of these are conspicuous archaeological sites because they still contain monumental standing structures that have survived into modern times. Most historical sites are much more inconspicuous, and even often invisible. Egyptologist Howard Carter spent seven years searching the Valley of Kings before he found Tutankhamun's tomb in 1922. It took years for archaeologists to locate L'Anse-aux-Meadows, a Norse settlement of about A.D. 1000 in northern Newfoundland. In both cases, even a trained eye faced formidable difficulties in locating such important places. Many archaeological sites, such as the Elizabethan Rose Theatre mentioned in Chapter 5, come to light by accident during the course of construction (Figure 6.1). Archaeologists

**Figure 6.1**   Rose Theatre, London, on the last day of excavation,
May 14, 1989. The large objects in the open area are modern building
foundations.

often locate sites using a combination of common sense, a well-designed research
plan, and sophisticated techniques and equipment.

## KNOWN SITES

Historical sites are often conspicuous features on the landscape. Many places—
missions, mansions, and mills—have been continuously inhabited or otherwise
maintained since their construction. Historical archaeologists have studied these
kinds of known sites since the earliest days of their profession (see Chapter 2). Archaeology at well-known historical sites is often directed at providing architectural details that preservationists can use to restore or reconstruct famous
properties. Colonial Williamsburg, Virginia, provides a perfect example.

Henry Wetherburn built his tavern in 1743 on Duke of Gloucester Street just
about midway between the Capitol of Virginia on the east and the colonial courthouse on the west. Wetherburn enlarged his tavern in the early 1750s as his busi-

ness thrived and expanded. Over the next two centuries, the owners of this eighteenth-century building used the old tavern as a store, a dwelling, a boarding house, and as a girls' school. But in its prime, Wetherburn's tavern was most-famously the site of numerous public meetings and scientific lectures. When the Colonial Williamsburg Foundation decided to renovate this notable landmark in the 1960s, they called on a team of architects, historians—and historical archaeologists—to help them. Their chief archaeologist, Ivor Noël Hume, dug along one wall of the tavern to answer specific questions about the design of the entrance porches. He also excavated in the tavern's backyard in the attempt to find outbuildings (Figure 6.2). His efforts revealed the presence of the foundations of two kitchens, a dairy, and two buildings of unknown use, as well as evidence of several old porches. Noël Hume's field crew collected over 200,000 artifacts, including tiny pieces of brass from the bases of small chafing dishes and pieces of the

**Figure 6.2** Archaeology in progress behind Wetherburn's Tavern, Williamsburg, Virginia, in the mid-1960s. A dairy foundation appears on the left; that of a kitchen on the right.

"white flowered China" listed in Henry Wetherburn's inventory of 1760. They also discovered stems from delicate wine glasses and white plates reading around their edges "SUCCESS TO THE KING OF PRUSSIA AND HIS FORCES" in raised letters. These plates, popular from 1757–1763, commemorated King Frederick the Great's victory in 1757 against the combined armies of Austria, France, and Russia at Rossbach.

Known sites can yield detailed information indeed. The Battle of the Little Bighorn matched George Custer's Seventh Regiment of U.S. cavalry against the combined forces of the Dakota (Sioux) and the Northern Cheyenne in 1876. The engagement lasted only an hour or so, but it is today notorious in the history of the American West. An enormous historical literature surrounds the battle. Drawn from contemporary records, eyewitness accounts, and minute-by-minute reconstructions of the battle, these textual sources help us understand the incident in detail. "Custer's Last Stand" has been immortalized in many highly imaginative paintings, and has been the subject of many fanciful motion pictures. In recent years, it seems that the true story of the encounter has been overtaken by myth. Until recently, it never occurred to anyone to use archaeological methods in addition to the eyewitness and textual accounts.

Many questions remain about the famous battle. Some historians have long argued, for example, that cartridge extraction failure on the part of the cavalry's carbines may have been one cause of Custer's defeat. This meant that his soldiers were unable to defend themselves properly because their rifles constantly jammed. To address this and other historical questions, a National Park Service research team led by archaeologist Douglas Scott made a detailed study of the battlefield site (also see Chapter 3).

Scott's team first conducted excavations around several of the marble markers that commemorate fallen soldiers, as well as on Calhoun Hill, south of the place where the famous "last stand" occurred. They also surveyed the entire battlefield with metal detectors to locate spent bullets and other significant artifacts. They plotted the position of every artifact, even individual spent cartridges, with meticulous care. Back in the laboratory, Scott and his team members examined the excavated cartridges for telltale signs of jamming. They found that *both* sides had problems with jamming carbines, to the point that malfunctioning weapons were not a significant factor in the battle's outcome.

Movies and pictures have given many history buffs a mental picture of Custer's final moments. One famous image finds him defiantly standing amid his fallen comrades, pistols in both hands, golden hair flowing behind him. We imagine from such paintings that Custer was the last to fall and that he withstood the onslaught for a relatively long time. The archaeological research shows, quite the contrary, that the battle was a brief firefight and that most of the cavalry dead were wounded—either by bullets or metal-tipped arrows—and then were killed at close range by a deadly blow to the head. Even at a famed place like the Little Big Horn Battlefield, archaeological research has yielded vital, unique information about an historical event. Without the archaeological efforts of Scott and his team, we would know much less about what actually happened in that field that bloody day.

## ACCIDENTAL DISCOVERIES

Historical archaeology at such well-known places as Colonial Williamsburg and the Little Big Horn Battlefield National Monument demonstrates the field's interpretive power. But not all sites are so famous and well-located, and accidental discoveries represent a significant proportion of major archaeological finds, especially in urban settings, where construction, demolition, and rebuilding is almost constant.

One of the most spectacular, accidental discoveries made in recent years occurred in New York City in 1991. The General Services Administration planned to build a thirty-four story office building to house a number of federal offices in lower Manhattan. When the archaeologists hired to examine the building site examined old city maps, they found that a "Negro Burial Ground" had existed at this location in the mid-eighteenth century. As many as twenty thousand individuals could have been buried in this five to six-acre (2 to 2.4 ha) lot. Archaeologists had assumed before the discovery that the digging of several deep basements in the nineteenth century had destroyed any burials that may have remained in the cemetery. Their report could not have been more explicit: "The construction of deep sub-basements would have obliterated any remains within the lots that fall within the historic bounds of the cemetery." Six weeks before construction was scheduled to begin, the cautious General Services Administration hired archaeologists to check the lot just in case one or two odd burials still remained. Officials at the General Services Administration were stunned when the archaeologists found dozens of undisturbed graves over the next two months. The government had spent $104 million on the property, and the offices they planned to build were slated to cost another $276 million. By law, the GSA had to remove the burials (or leave them undisturbed), arrange for their scientific study, and make arrangements either for their reburial or permanent safe storage. In the end, archaeologists removed 420 skeletons from the cemetery, the largest sample of historic African American remains ever discovered. Physical anthropologists are now engaged in a long-term, intensive study of the skeletal remains.

Even well-known historic sites can yield unexpected discoveries. The Spanish Presidio in Santa Barbara, California, was founded in 1782 and remained in use for seventeen years. Over the next two centuries, the fort and its buildings fell into disrepair, and much of it vanished beneath the nineteenth-century Chinatown. In 1967, archaeologists and local volunteers under the direction of Richard Humphrey excavated the foundations of the Presidio Chapel to provide architectural and historical information for future reconstruction. During their otherwise routine excavation to trace the building's foundations, the excavators found three burials under the church floor. When archaeologist Julia Costello and physical anthropologist Phillip Walker studied the bones, they discovered that Humphrey had actually found the remains of four people. They compared the physical remains with Presidio records and tried to associate the graves with actual individuals. They did not know the exact identity of each skeleton, but they could suggest one or two candidates. This close a match is remarkable, and it demonstrates the power of historical archaeology to combine archaeological and textual sources of information. Burial 1 was a middle-aged adult of unknown sex whose teeth suggested either Native American or Asian ancestry. The chapel's registry showed that Domingo Carrillo died in 1845 at the age of forty-five, and that José Antonio Ortega also died that year, but at an unknown age. Records show that Ortega was called "El Chino," or "The Chinaman," and so he is the best candidate for Burial 1 because of his teeth. A newborn baby and a young child were interred in Burial 2. The records indicated that four infants, between the ages of three and twenty-five days, were buried in the chapel after 1797, so the exact identity of the remains remain a mystery. The older child, however, was probably María Dominga Carrillo, who died in 1840 at age two years six months. Burial 3 was that of a woman between the ages of sixteen and twenty. The Presidio records suggested to Costello and Walker that the remains could be those of one of two unmarried young women: Soledad Carrillo (who died in 1837 at age seventeen) or María Antonia Carrillo (who died in 1844 at age sixteen years nine months). The woman in Burial 3—Soledad Carrillo or María Carrillo—had been placed in a redwood coffin wearing a long cape ornamented with sequins, glass beads, and flower bundles. Parts of her cape were preserved.

## FINDING HISTORICAL SITES

Historical archaeologists use three techniques for locating sites—historical maps and other textual sources, formal archaeological survey methods, and, mainly on-site, sophisticated subsurface surveying techniques. The archaeologist will decide which method is most appropriate based on numerous criteria including limitations of time and funding.

### Using Maps and Other Sources to Find Historical Sites

In Chapter 5, we made reference to the use of Sanborn and other maps for developing ideas about past urban neighborhoods. These sources are but the tip of a rewarding historical iceberg, for maps can be a mine of information on potential archaeological sites of all kinds. Some written records can also be used to help locate historic-period sites.

   Where do historical archaeologists find useful maps and other sources? Many of them come from well-known reference works and repositories (Chapter 7), but others appear in the most obscure and unsuspected places. The records kept by city governments, military bodies, land management agencies, and other groups can be remarkable sources of information. Detailed plat books and property titles can also contain invaluable information about site locations. But anyone serious about using historical maps and records to locate archaeological sites has a great deal of patient detective work in front of them.

The U.S. National Park Service created the Minute Man National Historical Park in Massachusetts in 1959 to commemorate "the significant events, structures, and sites of the opening day of the War of the American Revolution" in 1775. This park protects the famous sites of Lexington and Concord, where "the shot heard round the world" rang out, but it also includes a number of other, less well-known sites, such as the Brooks "tanyard." The Brooks family operated their tannery on the Concord road west of Lexington from about 1700–1829. The business, though locally important, had little regional significance. After its demise, the buildings fell into disrepair, and the old tannery was quickly forgotten. In 1984, the National Park Service decided to conduct a full archaeological survey of the sites within the boundaries of the Minute Man park, under the direction of archaeologist Alan Synenki.

When historian Martha Holland combed through old newspaper accounts, notes and maps of boundary surveys, tax rolls, and census lists, she found three maps of the area that included the Brooks property. One, drawn in 1749, provides a sketch of the Brooks property and shows the "Tan House" located next to the "High way." The map depicts the tanyard as a simple, small square with a cross in the middle, like a window with four panes. An earlier document, dated 1745, notes that the tannery included "a Tann House and Tann pits." These buildings may be what the cartographer meant to show in the 1749 map. A second map, made nearly a century later, in 1830, shows no sign of the tannery whatsoever. Twelve years later, and two years before he published *Walden*, nearby resident Henry David Thoreau drew a third map. He showed only an empty "Meadow" where the tannery once stood (Figure 6.3). As often happens, the archaeologists were unable to match precisely the old maps with the current landscape, and their limited excavations did not yield clear evidence of the tannery. They found instead the remains of a house, probably demolished in the nineteenth century, before 1875. The archaeologists' failure to locate the tannery does not negate the importance of the historical maps. Quite the contrary, these maps are useful because they help document the history of the area and show how the Brooks property was used throughout the late-eighteenth and early-nineteenth centuries.

Not all maps are useful for site location. Many early colonial maps, for example, often show forts, missions, trading posts, and the villages of native inhabitants as simple, large dots or squares. Archaeologists may thus know that certain sites once existed in the area, but the maps lack precise information about their exact locations. By tracking a series of maps through time, a historical archaeologist may use them to establish the dates of a building's construction, abandonment, or destruction. In most cases, however, only excavation will answer other questions.

Fort de Chartres was an important colonial French outpost near the tiny town of Prairie du Rocher in southern Illinois. During the eighteenth century, the

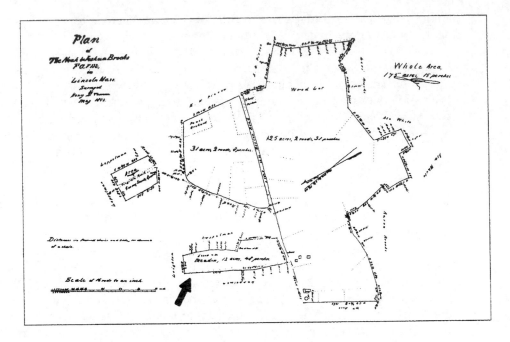

**Figure 6.3**   Thoreau map, 1852, of the Brooks Tannery area.

French established a number of towns along the Mississippi River in today's Illinois and Missouri as a means of connecting their Canadian settlements with those around New Orleans. They named one of their strongholds Fort de Chartres. They build their first fort as a simple wooden stockade, but later replaced it with a more elaborate structure. In the mid-1750s, the French replaced the wooden fort with an impressive stone-walled fortress. The first map to show Fort de Chartres was drawn by Francois-Benjamin Dumont de Montigny in the 1720s. He depicts the fort with four bastions in a form that was typical of the period. He shows only one small section of the Mississippi River Valley, and his map is not accurate enough to permit archaeologists to locate the first fort. A later map, drawn in 1755 by Jacques Nicolas Bellin, is even worse. He depicts the stone-built "Nouveau Fort de Chartres" as sandwiched between the town of Prairie du Rocher and a Native American village (Figure 6.4). Luckily for archaeologists, some of the massive stone fort stood the test of time and the site was easy to find. Without this physical evidence, archaeologists would have faced a difficult task of finding even the once-massive stone fort.

Archaeologists can also use images taken above the ground in their search for long-lost human settlements. They can consult the source materials of "aerial archaeology" to examine entire landscapes for major cultural features such as roads and trackways, agricultural field systems, and other features that may cover huge areas.

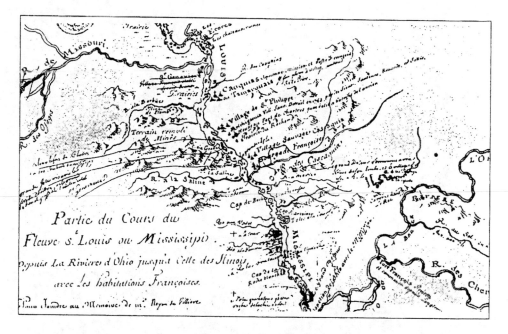

**Figure 6.4** Section of a map drawn in 1755 by Jacques Nicolas Bellin. It shows the area around Fort de Chartres.

Archaeologists have used aerial photography since the First World War, when excavators-turned-military observers realized that the bird's-eye view was an unrivaled way of identifying inconspicuous earthworks, forts, and other such locations. One great strength of aerial photography is that pictures taken from the sky can reveal hidden sites from all periods of history, many of which may not be recognizable from the ground. For example, aerial photography was essential in locating the site of the eighteenth-century Fort de Chartres. In 1981, U.S. Army Corps of Engineers' archaeologist Terry Norris found an aerial photograph of the fort's general area taken in 1928 (Figure 6.5). This picture just happened to show a rectangular stain which, upon excavation, turned out to be the foundations of the first fort, a small, wooden stockade that would have been difficult to locate in the absence of the old photograph.

Today's archaeologists can also use satellite images produced with the latest, cutting-edge technology. Aerial photography is limited to a number of atmospheric conditions, including cloud cover, but more sophisticated equipment can be used when aerial photography fails to obtain the necessary results. They can use color infrared film to detect minor variations in vegetation that may hide an archaeological site, though this film also requires good weather to be effective. Other high-tech tools include thermal scanners and various kinds of radar. Unlike the more straightforward aerial photographs, the more complex remote sensing techniques require an expert to analyze the data to look for archaeological "signatures."

**Figure 6.5**　Aerial photograph, taken in 1928, showing the rectangular stain of the first Fort de Chartres, Illinois.

These telltale clues may either be an archaeological site or may lead to one. Nicholas Clapp collaborated with NASA's Jet Propulsion Laboratory to locate the ancient city of Ubar on the Arabian Peninsula. He used Landsat imagery to find the otherwise invisible old roads that led to the ancient city.

## Archaeological Survey

Documents and maps, no matter how informative, provide only one method for finding archaeological sites. Historical archaeologists also rely on formal archaeological survey techniques—exactly those used by all other archaeologists. There is nothing glamorous about such methods, for they involve the systematic search for historic sites within a circumscribed area—whether a small urban lot, a neighborhood, a plantation, or even an entire geographic region.

Archaeologists usually begin their survey work in the library and laboratory, where they research archival sources, old maps, local histories, and even geological information—in other words, anything that provides a background for the fieldwork that follows. A survey of an empty lot destined for a warehouse might initially involve a title search to establish the ownership and use of the land before it was purchased by its current owner. Such preliminary investigations are vital because they provide clues to the possible character of the archaeological record. Did previous owners erect houses on the property or did they dig wells and privies? Did they corral cattle there or did they dig a cellar? The historical archaeologists' rule of thumb about background information is this: The more they gather before entering the field, the less likely they are to be surprised by what they find.

*Pedestrian Survey.* One of the most effective archaeological surveys are those carried out on foot. These surveys, usually referred to as "visual inspection" or "pedestrian survey," involve walking slowly over the ground while looking for telltale signs of human occupation. Such traces of human activity come in many forms—surface scatters of ceramics and glass, telltale black privy soil spilling from a gopher hole, piles of bricks or stones, old walls and fences, grassed-over cellar depressions, and capped wells. In the once-active logging areas of America's Upper Midwest, archaeologists can identify the remains of logging camps by the presence of one or two small mounds of earth, the occasional small depression, and a loose scatter of broken whiskey bottles and bent, corroded enameled tin plates and cups (Figure 6.6). The same evidence may reveal an abandoned mining community, such as those found in Australia, throughout the American West, and wherever people extracted precious metals.

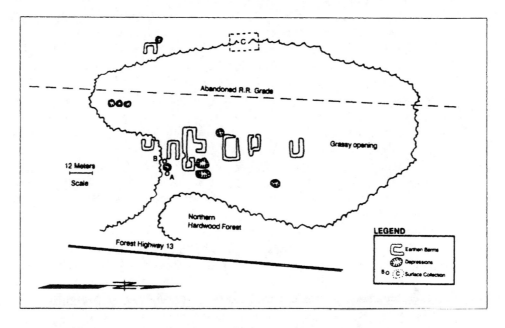

**Figure 6.6** Archaeologist's map of hardwood-era logging camp in Michigan.

Historical archaeologists can also use botanical clues to help them identify archaeological sites. The presence of large shade trees and domestic flowers, still blooming after years of neglect, may reveal the past location of a house. It is not unusual for archaeologists conducting field surveys to locate past house sites by the presence of lines of trees once planted as protection from the wind or by stands of stately elms and oaks. Even the presence of blooming perennials can indicate a past house site.

Historical archaeologists, like all archaeologists, must learn to "read the landscape" as part of their field education. Much information can be gathered by field surveyors who know how to recognize the faint wagon wheel ruts of a disused trail, a row of trees that may represent an old fence line (growth from seeds deposited by birds that once sat on the fenceposts), and the isolated pilings of a long-forgotten dock.

Historical archaeologists can also use oral interviews to tease out information about site location (Chapter 7). Most people, particularly in rural areas, will be familiar with the local topography. Farmers and local amateur archaeologists often know the precise location of numerous sites. In her research in the lowland region of Soconusco in Chiapas, Mexico, Janine Gasco learned that the information provided by local residents may sometimes help locate colonial-period sites. She also discovered, however, that local residents often did not know where sites could be found. As a result, she had to employ conventional survey methods that involved sampling the region.

*Sampling.*   Surveying a city lot may simply consist of intently combing over a small area of level terrain. Such surveys are easy to perform and they may take only a day or less to complete. Archaeologists understandably find it much more difficult to locate all the sites in a region. One hundred percent survey coverage is rare in anything but the smallest of areas, and sometimes even such complete a survey does not reveal everything. Archaeological history is full of cases where surveyors have returned to a well-trodden area only to find more sites! Heavy rain, wind erosion, and other natural factors can reveal the presence of sites that were once completely buried.

A field survey of anything but the smallest plot involves the use of formal sampling methods. The realities of fieldwork, often involving financial constraints and a lack of time, make complete survey coverage rare for most archaeological projects.

An enormous literature surrounds sampling methods in archaeology, because they remain both controversial and difficult to apply. Effective sampling depends upon the formal strategy adopted. The proper survey is intended to provide statistically valid, and hopefully representative, samples of sites within the survey units selected for detailed examination. Common strategies involve the use of transects (straight corridors), geometrical units (squares, hexagons), and nongeometrical units (polygons). Depending upon the project goals, an archaeologist might introduce variation into these strategies as well. Transects, for instance, can consist of parallel lines (where surveyors walk abreast of one another a predefined distance), intersecting (where the surveyors may make two passes of a survey unit, one at 45 degrees of the other), and undulating or wavy (where the surveyors do not walk in straight lines) (Figure 6.7). Regardless of their exact design, archaeologists employ all sampling strategies with an eye toward examining as much territory as possible with maximum efficiency.

In the late 1980s, a team of archaeologists under the direction of archaeologist David Benn conducted a systematic survey in the Big Sioux River valley in northwestern Iowa. They devised a careful sampling strategy to investigate the 8,000 acres (3,239 ha) in their project area. They divided the area into eight different sections and used systematic criteria based on the topographic features in the region (floodplain, river terrace, and upland). By the end of the survey, the crew had walked over 10,732 acres (4,345 ha), and had discovered 109 prehistoric Native American sites and 20 historic sites. The prehistoric sites ranged from small, temporary camp sites to larger settlements with mounds, and dated from about 500 B.C. to A.D. 1500. The historic sites included individual log cabins as well as the town of Beloit, whose first European-American settlers arrived in 1868.

This survey of northwestern Iowa illustrates an important point: Sampling designs are especially useful in situations where large numbers of inconspicuous sites may exist. Such sites can be stone-walled cattle enclosures on the grasslands of southeast Africa, medieval field systems in England, colonial-era settlements in the Mexican lowlands, or early nineteenth-century farmsteads in New York State. For the most part, however, a historical landscape consists of large, human-built features that can dictate the distribution of all kinds of sites large and small. Builders of roads, bridges, and mills knew exactly why they built such structures where they did. For example, when J. A. Carpenter built the Beloit Mill in 1871—within one of Benn's survey units—he knew exactly what he was doing. He erected it on the banks of the Big Sioux River because he needed to harness the energy of the water to grind flour. He followed conventional wisdom and built a dam to control the river's flow past his mill. Carpenter was obviously successful because the 1880 industrial census reveals that his mill had three water wheels with a daily grinding capacity of 250 bushels of grain. He would have been

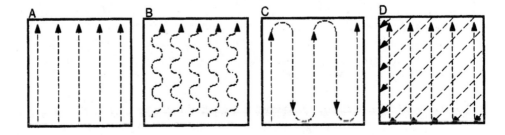

**Figure 6.7**   Different survey transects.

indeed shortsighted to have built his mill in the Iowa uplands, 20 miles from the Big Sioux River!

Pedestrian survey is often not the best approach for locating sites, and archaeologists must adopt more sophisticated survey methods. These methods can involve high-tech equipment that requires extensive knowledge and experience to operate. Historical archaeologists who are not specialists in these methods, but know their potential, must collaborate with specialists in "subsurface surveying" who can both operate the equipment and interpret the results.

### Subsurface Surveying

Subsurface detection methods are of critical importance to archaeologists because they allow them to acquire information about what lies underground before they begin to excavate. The noninvasive (or nondestructive) character of these methods of site assessment means that archaeologists need not disturb sites to gain some idea of their nature. They are able to use these techniques to protect precious archaeological remains from unnecessary disturbance.

The historical archaeologists' subsurface surveying methods include both geophysical and geochemical techniques. These methods extend in complexity from relatively simple to extremely sophisticated.

*Metal Detectors.*   Metal detectors are electromagnetic instruments that can be used to locate metal objects beneath the earth's surface. These tools were originally developed as landmine detectors, thus they can be expensive and sophisticated. The most expensive models can be set to distinguish between different kinds of metal and can penetrate further into the ground than their less expensive counterparts.

Metal detectors can also be used to find buried kilns, brick walls, and any human-built features that have been magnetized through use, such as burning. These machines typically issue a "beep" or electronic hum when they pass over a disturbance in the earth's magnetic field. Many detectors come equipped with a sensitive meter and headphones. Metal detecting is today a popular hobby, and many metal-detecting enthusiasts are skilled operators. Most hobbyists use their detectors to locate missing coins and rings. Beer can collectors sometimes use them to find early specimens to add to their collections. Historical archaeologists occasionally will call on a skilled operator to provide assistance because they offer an inexpensive and quick way to learn about a site's subsurface features.

Archaeologists can use metal detectors in conjunction with site surveying, employing the detector during their visual inspection of the ground surface. As noted above, the archaeologists who investigated the Little Bighorn battlefield successfully used metal detectors in their field survey.

Archaeologists working in the relatively new field called "forensic" or "crime-scene archaeology" can also use metal detectors to gather important legal information. Archaeologist Robert Sonderman collaborated with the U.S. Federal

Bureau of Investigation to survey Fort Marcy Park, Virginia, over the 1993 death of Deputy White House Council Vincent W. Foster, Jr. Sonderman ran a series of parallel straight lines across the area with string, and the operator of the metal detector then walked along these lines, swinging the instrument as he went. This string-line surveying technique provided for 100 percent coverage of the park and helped the authorities decide that Foster's death was a suicide.

*Proton Magnetometers.*   Like its cousin the metal detector, the more sophisticated proton magnetometer locates "anomalies," or disturbances, in the earth's natural magnetic field. They give readings as quickly as a metal detector but usually with more accuracy.

Historical archaeologists might use a metal detector to gain a fast understanding of the subsurface remains at a site, but they will usually employ a more systematic method when using a proton magnetometer. A proton magnetometer survey begins by laying out a grid of equal-sized squares over the site area. Next, the magnetometer operator measures the normal magnetization of the site's ground surface. Once the magnetic background readings are known, the surveyors take one reading from each spot the grid lines intersect. They then use the collected data to create a "map" of the magnetic readings. The various anomalies appear as "hot spots," or high magnetic readings, on the map.

Magnetometer surveys have proven effective at archaeological sites that contain large amounts of ferrous artifacts. At the eighteenth-century French Fort Ouiatenon in the American Midwest, the map of magnetic anomalies helped guide archaeologists to a number of subsurface features, including a cache of iron trade objects deposited outside one of the fort's buildings. The magnetic survey also helped to locate four eighteenth-century burials at the fort, proving that, like metal detectors, magnetometers can be used by forensic archaeologists.

Proton magnetometer surveys also can be conducted underwater to locate anchors, chains, spikes, cannons, and other ferrous objects associated with shipwrecks. Marine archaeologist J. Barto Arnold successfully used a proton magnetometer in a survey off the coast of Galveston, Texas. Historic records and maps revealed 327 known shipwrecks in Galveston Bay, many dating to the American Civil War (1861–1865). One of the most interesting wrecks was that of the ill-fated USS *Selma*, built of reinforced concrete by the U.S. Navy during the First World War. She sank on her maiden voyage after ramming jetties off the coast of Mexico, and the navy abandoned her a couple of years later in Galveston Bay. The wreck's general location had been known for years, but Arnold's magnetometer survey confirmed its precise placement on the Gulf floor.

*Soil Resistivity Surveying.*   All rocks and soils, being porous, absorb different amounts of moisture. All porous objects and features under the ground will thus conduct varying degrees of electricity. Archaeologists can use a soil resistivity meter to measure the amount of resistance encountered by an electrical current passing through these objects. A trash pit with many open spaces will hold more moisture than the dense clay surrounding it, just as a brick wall will retain more water than the surrounding sandy soil. An electrical current introduced into the ground will encounter greater resistance when trying to pass through the wall than through the soil.

Resistivity surveys involve inserting a grid of metal probes, or electrodes, into the ground. An electrical current is passed into the ground by the electrodes and the resistivity meter measures the resistance it encounters. The analyst plots the different resistance measures across the site. As with the proton magnetometer, the finished map has the appearance of a topographic map. Instead of showing differences in the elevation of the ground surface, the soil resistivity map illustrates the differences in the amount of soil moisture beneath the ground. Anomalies that appear may represent buried archaeological features.

Soil resistivity is useful under circumstances where excavation is impracticable. Archaeologists from the University of Texas used a soil resistivity survey to locate a series of lost graves in an early nineteenth-century Anglo-Texan cemetery in south Dallas. They established a grid over the site and, after conducting a resistivity survey, they were able to distinguish eight anomalies that were probably graves. They knew that early Anglo-Texans buried their dead with an east-west orientation, so any anomaly pointing north-south was probably not a burial. In this particular case, the archaeologists were allowed to test their findings by excavating the anomalies, because any located skeletons were to be re-interred in a more secure location. Excavations revealed the bones of four children in three anomalies (one contained two skeletons). The burials were about 6 feet (2 m) beneath the current ground surface, with the last 1.5 feet (0.5 m) chipped into the natural limestone underlying the cemetery. This research shows that soil resistivity surveying, like all nonintrusive survey methods, is particularly useful at cemeteries, locales that people usually do not want disturbed by full-scale excavation. Archaeologists can also employ such methods at historic home sites where excavation would be intrusive and unwanted.

***Ground-Penetrating Radar.***  Ground-penetrating radar works by transmitting a low-frequency electromagnetic signal into the ground by way of a radar system pulled along the ground. The path of the radar may be a series of transecting grid lines or parallel straight lines depending on the archaeologists' needs. When the radar signal encounters an anomaly beneath the ground it sends a second signal back to the receiver. This reflected signal indicates that it has struck something that is unlike the surrounding soil. Specialists can interpret the signal "profiles" to determine the locations of buried features.

Ground-penetrating radar was used effectively by a survey team led by geoarchaeologist Bruce Bevan in Virginia. Working in association with the U.S. National Park Service, Bevan and his researchers were attempting to find "Spring Garden," the home of a Mr. William Taylor in Petersburg. Taylor was a person of no particular historical note; he was simply a victim of circumstance, because his house was destroyed by the Union Army in their unsuccessful attempt to capture Petersburg in 1864. In 1978, the National Park Service wanted to establish the precise location of the home so that they could include it in their interpretive program, but test excavations came up empty. The archaeologists found one or two outbuildings, but failed to find the Taylor home. At that point, Bevan's team was called in.

Bevan ran the radar along the ground in a series of parallel rows across the suspected location of the home, in a spot where the outbuildings had been discovered. The radar beam used could detect anomalies 3 feet (1 m) to the right and to the left of the path at a depth of 3 feet (1 m). He surveyed an area of about 2.2 acres (slightly less than 1 ha) in four days. Using the radar, he was able to delineate a buried feature that measured about 20 to 25 feet by 50 to 55 feet (6 to 8 by 15 to 17 m). The anomaly was rectangular and was exactly parallel to a standing outbuilding. Two years later, when the National Park Service sponsored test excavations over Bevan's anomaly, archaeologists found the northeast and southwest corners of a brick-lined cellar. Remarkably, the cellar measured 19 by 55 feet (6 by 17 m), exactly the dimensions the radar showed. The archaeologists could date the ceramics they found in the cellar to the last years of the eighteenth century and to the first half of the nineteenth. The cellar was undeniably the foundation of Taylor's house.

*Sonar.*   Marine archaeologists use a technique related to ground-penetrating radar, called sonar, to locate lost shipwrecks. Sonar, whose name derives from SOund Navigation And Ranging, is a complex detection device that emits a sharp pulse of sound that produces an echo when the sound waves strike an object. A submerged submarine or a lost ship would produce a pulse indicating their presence.

Sonar was invaluable for studying the wreck of the USS *Monitor*. The *Monitor*, once referred to as a "tin can on a shingle," is famous for her battle with her Confederate counterpart, the *Merrimack*, on March 9, 1862, off the coast of Maryland. The *Merrimack* was actually a rebuilt Union frigate. Union forces had scuttled her at the Navy yard at Portsmouth, Virginia, when they evacuated the town in 1861. The Confederacy raised the vessel, encased her in iron plates, and renamed her *Virginia*. Most people today, however, continue to use her original name. The inconclusive engagement between the two ships became the stuff of legend, even though the battle did no serious harm to either vessel. But nature succeeded where the *Merrimack* had failed. The *Monitor's* ignominious end came as the ship filled with water during a violent storm, as she was being towed to safety by a more buoyant vessel. The *Monitor* lay on the floor of the Atlantic Ocean until 1973, when divers found the wreck site off the coast of Cape Hatteras, North Carolina. It was promptly declared a National Marine Sanctuary and a National Historic Landmark under the administration of the National Oceanic and Atmospheric Administration. The NOAA conducted extensive remote sensing at the wreck site in 1985 and 1987. The 1987 project used state-of-the-art surveying equipment, including high-resolution sector-scanning sonar imaging that produced a computer-generated, three-dimensional view of the entire wreck.

Historical archaeologists use ground-penetrating radar, soil resistivity, and magnetometer surveys whenever and wherever possible. These methods can be expensive and usually require the collaboration of a highly skilled operator who fully understands how to interpret the readings.

*Soil Phosphate Analysis.*   Soil phosphate analysis is a geochemical subsurface surveying technique used to locate old habitation sites. Chemical changes occur in the soil of past settlements simply through human occupation. Chemicals such as calcium, nitrogen, carbon, and phosphorus are added to soils through human activity, but only phosphorus is stable over time. Phosphorus plays a role in the composition of fluids in the digestive tract, is fixed with calcium in bones and teeth, and occurs in significant amounts in animal and human excreta. The presence of humans and even domesticated animals at a locale can increase the amount of phosphorus in the soil. Because phosphorus moves so little once deposited, archaeologists can even use phosphate testing to identify stratified habitation levels.

A soil phosphate analysis begins with laying out a site grid. A soil coring tool or auger is then used to collect samples below the topsoil at the many grid points. A rigorous quantitative laboratory analysis can reveal precisely how much phosphorus is contained in each soil sample, but a less accurate spot test is generally adequate for most archaeological research. In the spot test method, a small amount of soil from each stratum is tested for the presence of phosphorus, using first, a solution of distilled water, ammonium molybdate, and dilute hydrochloric acid, and second, a solution of distilled water and ascorbic acid (vitamin C). After applying the two solutions to a soil sample, the analyst checks for a blue color produced by the reaction of the phosphorous and the chemicals. Depending upon the intensity of the color and the length of the blue rays emanating outward from it, the analyst assigns a number from 1 to 6 to the test. When all of the soil samples are similarly tested, the values are placed on a map at the proper coordinates, making a contour map of phosphorus concentration. The locations of high phosphorus concentrations, or "hot spots," are likely to contain the remains of houses, yards, animal pens, fence lines, and privies.

Soil phosphate expert William Woods used a quantitative test to help locate the first Fort de Chartres in southern Illinois. While the reconstructed stone fort is a familiar landmark, the two earlier forts were buried under the featureless topography of agricultural fields. Their locations were unknown until the 1928 aerial photograph mentioned above revealed a large soil discoloration near the stone fort. The precise location of the first fort, however, was not known for certain until Wood's phosphate testing program located areas of high phosphorus concentration (Figure 6.8). Excavations confirmed the reliability of the tests by discovering the ditches that once contained the fort's palisaded walls.

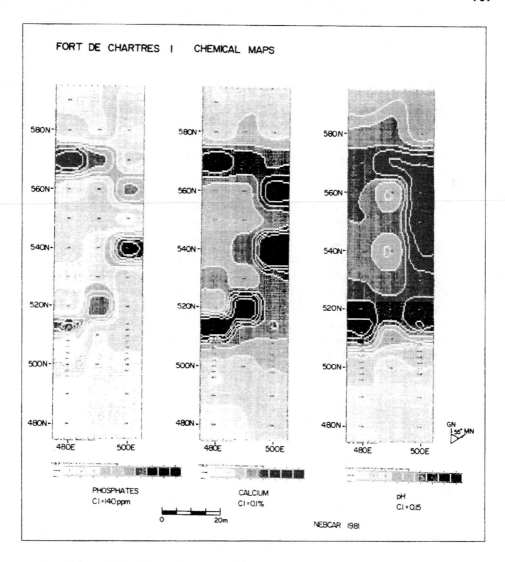

**Figure 6.8** Chemical map made at the first Fort de Chartres, Illinois.

*The Paranormal?* Before concluding this chapter, we should mention dowsing, a distinctly low-tech detection method that most people have heard about. Some people claim they can find underground water using a forked stick or even two bent, metal coat hangers called "angle rods." Renowned historical archaeologist Ivor Noël Hume introduced dowsing to the field in the 1950s and mentioned it in his book *Historical Archaeology*. He noted having success with the method at Colonial Williamsburg and, though he did not elaborate, he said he felt "a little idiotic walking across a field intently watching two pieces of coat hanger." His most curious discovery was that 80 percent of men can make dowsing rods work, but only 30 percent of women. Perhaps these figures say more about which sex is willing to walk around archaeological sites looking idiotic than about anything else!

Dowsing is more widely used in Britain, and Noël Hume, a British national, mentions the existence of a British Society of Dowsers. The book *Dowsing and Church Archaeology* describes the apparent successes dowsers have had on medieval sites in England. St. Mary's Church at Woodhorn in northern England dates to at least the Norman period (post-A.D. 1066), and exhibits thirteenth- and early-nineteenth-century design elements. In 1973, when the building was no longer needed as a house of worship, it was converted into a museum and cultural center. In 1982, two dowsers, Eric Cambridge and Richard Bailey, were given the opportunity to conduct a survey of the church. They found what they took to be possible foundation walls beneath the existing chancel. The location of these walls suggested that the chancel had once been smaller, probably having been enlarged in the nineteenth century. Given the opportunity to test their findings, Cambridge and Bailey set about excavating where their angle rods indicated the presence of a foundation wall. They quickly discovered a mortared, stone wall precisely where they said it would be! The wall was 8 inches (20 cm) below the paved surface of the chancel, and was approximately 39 inches (100 cm) wide. They were not able to provide an exact date for the wall, having found both medieval floor tiles and a white clay pipe bowl dating to 1650–1680.

Dowsers complain that professional archaeologists have "bitterly attacked" them as occultists because their technique has "no underpinning theoretical explanation." These British dowsers swear that their method of subsurface surveying works, and they provide what counts as a serious argument for it.

It is admittedly easy to be tricked by dowsing because it actually does appear to work in some cases. But can it really provide archaeological clues to buried sites? James Randi, famed professional magician and debunker of the paranormal, reported that all dowsing fails when it is tested using scientific methods. In fact, no dowser has ever passed the test. So why do they continue to believe in their method? The reason is that a powerful psychological phenomenon, called "the ideomotor effect," is an involuntary bodily movement that can be evoked by an idea or a thought process. In other words, the angle rods will move when we think they should. Most dowsers are not even aware that they are causing the angle rods to move. In the case of British churches, dowsers are familiar with church architecture and they undoubtedly evoke the rods to move where they expect to find a buried wall. Dowsers of water know how to read a landscape.

All paranormal methods claimed to be useful in archaeological site location are best left in the hands of mediums and other characters. Serious historical archaeologists seeking to locate buried sites would do infinitely better to employ one of the methods outlined in this chapter and leave dowsers to their own devices.

## TIME TRAVEL

### Pribilof Islands, Alaska, 1780s

The Aleut people had lived on the Aleutian Islands, stretching into the Bering Sea west of the Alaska Peninsula, for at least four thousand years before Europeans encountered them in 1741. They had lived as peoples in the far north had always lived, hunting wild animals from the sea and land and, when available, collecting wild berries and other edible plants. The Europeans who made contact with the Aleuts were Russians who had come to the region also for its animals. Their interest, however, was in precious furs and skins rather than subsistence. In the decades that followed, the Russians made several dozen expeditions to the land of the Aleuts and developed a substantial fur-trading empire.

The Pribilof Islands are composed of five tiny islands located north of the main Aleutian archipelago. The two largest islands are named St. Paul and St. George. The land is rocky, windswept, and only a light covering of hearty plants can survive there. But marine mammals were well adapted to the islands, with whales and fur seals predominating. In fact, at the time of Russian contact, as many as 3–4 million fur seals may have been in the Pribilof Islands. Russian fur traders promptly viewed the islands as a gold mine, and they quickly began to harvest the valuable seals with zeal.

The impact of the foreigners on the Aleuts was devastating. Diseases ravished them, and as many as 80 percent of them may have died as direct result of contact. As may be expected, profound social changes accompanied the steep demographic drop, and by the early 1700s, the Aleuts were no longer in control of their lives. Their population was devastated,

their traditional social networks were irretrievably disrupted, and their food supply was in danger of being destroyed by overhunting. Thus enmeshed in a transnational economic system that was not of their making, they were forced into work camps as laborers for the Russian fur trade.

Living conditions on the Pribilof Islands were understandably harsh. The changes in Aleut housing reflected the broader cultural transformations they experienced. Their earliest dwellings were usually fairly large, partly dug into the ground, and were either rounded rectangles or ovals in shape. Their residents would enter and leave them through holes in the roofs, which were made of either sod, wood, or bone. After the arrival of the Russian fur traders, the houses of the Aleuts were no longer truly semi-subterranean, and they had interior walls made from blocks of sod. They also had doors and windows placed on the outside walls, and their roofs were made of dried grass held down against the wind with nets. These buildings were undoubtedly crowded, damp, and bleak.

The task of living in such conditions was challenging. Harvesting fur seals was exhausting work, because the Russians designed it to have an almost factory-like efficiency. Their government granted the Russian-American Company, formed in 1799, exclusive rights to all hunting activities in the region, and the entrepreneurial fur traders planned to make the most of the opportunity. Their goal was to obtain as many pelts as fast as possible, and put them on the eager market while the prices

*(continued)*

Source: Douglas W. Veltre and Allen P. McCartney. 2002. "Russian Exploitation of Aleuts and Fur Seals: The Archaeology of Eighteenth- and Early Nineteenth-Century Settlements in the Pribilof Islands, Alaska." *Historical Archaeology* 36(3):8–17.

were high. The chronic shortage of Russians willing to do the work (and willing live on the cold, tiny islands) meant that the labor force would have to be composed of Aleuts. Not only were they present in the region, they also knew how to survive in the harsh climate and, more importantly, how to catch the precious animals. They would thus perform the work of the Company.

The Aleuts traditionally hunted marine mammals in a time-tested and ecologically sound way. Hunting individually or in a small group, they used their tracking skills, patience, and aiming proficiency to bring down one or two animals that they would then take back to their settlement. They used the pelts for clothing and other necessities, and consumed the meat. This time-honored practice dramatically changed with the development of economically based seal hunting. Under the direction of their Russian foremen, Aleut hunters were encouraged to conduct fur seal drives. Instead of killing individual animals on the spot, this new hunting method involved driving large numbers of seals overland to a specified killing ground. The killing ground was located close to the main settlement, so that the Aleuts would not have to haul the pelts far. This means of hunting was efficient and devastating to the ecosystem.

# Chapter 7

# Pre-Excavation Fieldwork: Documents, Interviews, Buildings

*"The past is everywhere. All around us lie features which, like ourselves and our thoughts, have more or less recognizable antecedents."*

David Lowenthal, 1985

Archaeology is a multidisciplinary enterprise. Whether studying the earliest humans in Africa or Inca road systems high in the Andes, archaeologists of ancient history rely both on artifacts, structural remains, and food residues, and on information from many sciences. Prehistorians often collaborate with biologists, climatologists, geologists, and chemists. Historical archaeologists also rely on the sciences, but their field is unique because of its strong reliance on sources of information not usually associated with excavation: historical documents, interviews with informants, and standing buildings. In this chapter, we explain how archaeologists use these so-called "nonarchaeological" sources in the study of the recent past.

## HISTORICAL FIELDWORK AND DOCUMENTS

Historians James Davidson and Mark Lytle state that "The writing of history is one of the most familiar ways of organizing human knowledge. And yet, if familiarity has not always bred contempt, it has at least encouraged a good bit of misunderstanding." This misunderstanding stems from the common assumption that "history" consists of a series of dry "facts." Many people believe the job of the historian is simply to discover the "facts"—like an archaeologist unearthing potsherds or a detective investigating a crime—and to compile them into a "history." Many people think that historians are just like archaeologists who reconstruct pots from their many broken fragments. It is a sad reality that many of us first encounter history as a dull, seemingly relentless recitation of sterile dates and facts. Many people confess to dislike history simply because of the way it was originally presented to them.

Modern historians have diligently worked to dispel the stereotype that history is dull and boring. In their fascinating book, *After the Fact: The Art of Historical Detection*, Davidson and Lytle demonstrate how historians actually work. Rather than merely searching for new facts about an old topic or simply rehashing a collection of old facts, historians engage in a great deal of evaluation and interpretation of their sources. Davidson and Lytle present several case studies, that range from colonial times to Watergate, to show that "what happened in the past" is not necessarily the same as "history." In their essay on early photography, for instance, they show how photographers of the past can affect our vision of past reality. We often imagine the camera to be an impartial observer, or what Davidson and Lytle call a "mirror with a memory." We point it at something, and it simply records the image on film. In actuality, though, the photographer behind the camera has the ability to insert his or her own biases into any picture. Images of lodgers in overcrowded, late nineteenth-century tenements or children playing in squalid alleyways may not truly represent "how things used to be." Some photographers may have staged their photographs or they may have removed important elements from the negative. Because these photographs are available today, we tend to accept them as truthful, and they become our visual reality of the past.

The great French historian, Marc Bloch—a member of the French Resistance during the Second World War who was captured and executed by the Nazis on June 16, 1944, only ten days after D-Day—wrote that the "faculty of understanding the living is . . . the master quality of the historian." The writing of history, technically termed "historiography," thus involves the interplay between the past (what actually happened) and the present (what the historian can document and is interested in studying). The past is not a huge file of dead facts, but a living body of knowledge from which we draw our interpretations using various changing perspectives and attitudes.

Nowhere does the interpretive task of the historian come across better than in T.H. Breen's brilliant study of East Hampton, a village located on the eastern end of Long Island, New York. Breen presented a history of this seventeenth-century town that appears as an "interpretive journey." As he made the journey, he held firm to the idea "that people like ourselves have ultimately decided what will or will not be treated as a historical 'fact.'" Breen realized that the existing histories of East Hampton are "products of an interpretive process that at the very best can generate only partial truths." When John Lyon Gardiner wrote the first history of the town in 1798, he portrayed East Hampton as a pastoral, idyllic place that stood tall and proud for American Independence and staunch in its support of democracy. Gardiner felt that the Native American Montauks were the blight on the town's history, because he saw them as living in a degenerate condition. He regarded their extreme poverty as the result of their own "idle disposition and savage manners." For Gardner, East Hampton would have been a perfect place without them.

Today, Gardiner's eighteenth-century history seems ill-informed at best and racist at worst. But in his view, he undoubtedly believed that he was simply writing down the town's historical "facts" for posterity. Other educated, literate members of his society (his audience) also probably assumed that the Montauks—and all other Native Americans for that matter—were degenerates that only had themselves to blame for their debased condition. We know now that what Gardiner recounted to his readers were not the "facts," but only his interpretation of certain elements of the past.

Historian Carl Becker told the assembled members of the prestigious American Historical Association in 1926 that "the simple historical fact turns out to be not a hard, cold something with clear outline, and measurable pressure, like a brick." He said that historical facts have a much more nebulous character; they change and mutate with our attitudes. A history written in 1926 would not be the same history written in 1996, even though both historians might cover the exact same period of history.

Breen understood this curious situation, and he became adept at writing several East Hampton histories at once. He saw the past from many different angles. He traveled easily between the past and the present, and he learned that history is written by looking back at the past with different lenses. He discovered a man named Samuel Mulford, East Hampton's most prominent citizen in the 1680s. Mulford owned a whaling company employing twenty-four men. He was also a Puritan and widely recognized for his dogmatic and rigid views on Calvinism. People who knew Mulford characterized him as "a long-winded, self-righteous bore." Using such comments, Breen developed an impression of Mulford's personality. As Breen said, the written accounts "allow us to imagine a person who was extraordinarily ambitious. They suggest other adjectives as well: tough, clever, articulate, blunt, and obstinate." Breen also discovered that Mulford had the curious nickname of "Fishhook."

The story told in East Hampton is that early in the eighteenth century, Mulford traveled to London in the hope of obtaining a personal audience with the king. While waiting outside the palace, a clever pickpocket lifted most of Mulford's money. So distressed was the penny-wise Mulford that he promptly sewed a series of fishhooks inside his coat to secure his remaining cash. The storytellers say that all of London, and even the king himself, was impressed by Mulford's ingenuity.

Breen doubted that the fishhook incident ever actually happened. He argued that its truth was less important than the story itself. In fact, he believed that the story was really about the entire East Hampton community. A small town in the process of being overwhelmed by the world around it, East Hampton used ingenious methods—like Samuel Mulford and the fishhooks—to protect and preserve itself. That the story uses Mulford as its focus merely shows how important he was (and still is) to the town's history.

Breen found it difficult to shake the image of Samuel Mulford, so he visited with a direct descendant, the Presbyterian Reverend David Mulford, to learn more about the eighteenth-century eccentric. David Mulford lived in the house the Mulfords owned for more than three centuries. The family genealogist, Breen hoped that Mulford could "add something to what I had found in the colonial town records." Breen also hoped that his visit might remind Mulford "of half-forgotten letters or documents from the seventeenth century now stored in some corner of the attic." During their discussion, Breen told Mulford what he knew about Samuel Mulford and the seventeenth century; Mulford in turn told him about East Hampton's three-hundredth-year celebration in 1948, and of his father's "outspoken belief that the automobile had ruined the village." It was in these conversations that Breen traveled, sometimes even unwittingly, between the past and the present. In the end, Breen had to admit that "months after this conversation took place, I still wonder how much of Samuel I saw in David." He also had to admit that he "had somehow constructed a mental image of Samuel Mulford." Clearly, the writing of history is not divorced from the experiences and attitudes of the present.

### The Historian's Craft

Breen's detailed and interesting account of how he unraveled the many histories of East Hampton, New York, illustrates that the act of writing history, really the art of interpreting the past, is an expert field of research in its own right. Few archaeologists have extensive formal training in its intricacies, or in the subtle nuances of historical research. Still, all historical archaeologists must understand the basics of historiography because at some point in their careers they will be called upon to conduct some original research of this kind, perhaps simply because no one else is available to do it for them. In many respects, an historical archaeologist's abilities will show from the quality of his or her documentary research. Breen's East Hampton study clearly illustrates that the best historians are not necessarily detached scholars who know everything, but merely curious people who simply know where to find the pertinent information they seek. Their real skills as historians are revealed in their interpretations of what they find. Being a historian is in this sense just like being an archaeologist. Glass bottles, ceramic teacups and bowls—like legal papers, personal diaries, and correspondences—do not speak; they must be interpreted.

Historians study both primary and secondary sources. *Primary sources* are contemporary records, generally written by eyewitnesses or people who may have a direct understanding or a personal insight into the events or attitudes of the day. Breen used many primary documents in his East Hampton research. One of these sources is especially intriguing. In the late 1600s, the economy of East Hampton depended on whaling. Many of the town's most prominent citizens— Samuel Mulford included—were involved in the "whale design," the economy of whaling. The local residents knew that to hunt for whales they would require the assistance of several common laborers, but the majority of able-bodied workers in late-seventeenth-century New England were Native Americans. In a bind for ready laborers, the whalers of East Hampton entered into binding contracts with the Indians for the whaling season. But, there were not always enough Native Americans to meet the demand, so the competition for their labor services was fierce. In April, 1678, the Reverend Thomas James—an ambitious whaler—wrote the following document, apparently because he did not trust his parishioners:

> I, Thomas James of East Hampton, having together with my copartners for the whale design made several contracts and agreements with the Indians. . . . I do by these presents both in my own name and name of my copartners enter a solemn protest against any person or persons who have or shall contrary to all law of God or man, justice or equity, go about to violate or infringe the above mentioned contracts or agreements without our consent.

This first-person document offers a clear picture of what Thomas James thought about people who would try to co-opt his Native American laborers out from under him.

*Secondary sources* are interpretations of primary sources, written long after the events they describe. Breen's history is now a secondary source. Breen also read a number of other secondary sources, including Gardiner's history, to learn about earlier interpretations of the town's history.

The historian's craft involves knowing precisely where to look for primary sources, a task that often requires tact and ingenuity. Primary sources come from government archives, from courthouse basements, from dusty trunks in Victorian attics, even from auction room lots. The search for sources never ends, even after the historian has compiled hundreds of them. Even letters of Abraham Lincoln— one of the most well-researched historical figures in world history—occasionally turn up in unexpected places. Not too long ago, the Circuit Clerk of Tazewell County Courthouse in Pekin, Illinois, discovered thirty-four previously unknown Lincoln papers by simply pulling out a file marked "Re: Lincoln." These documents were written by Lincoln when he was a circuit-riding lawyer in central Illinois, and they include instructions to juries, bills of indictment, affidavits, and pleas. Lincoln rode a fifteen-country circuit twice a year and worked day and night when he visited local courthouses. William Beard, the assistant editor of the Lincoln Legal Papers project, said that the new documents represent a "King Solomon's mine in Pekin." The discovery of these new papers, along with seventy-five others unexpectedly found at Illinois State University and at other Illinois courthouses, have sparked great excitement among Lincoln scholars around the world. Finding the Lincoln papers prove that documents from even the great figures of history, like important archaeological sites, still await discovery.

Archaeologists may not be as unrelenting in their search for primary sources as historians because their concerns are usually less specialized. Primary source materials, however, are of major significance in historical archaeology, and some of the common places where they may be located are:

- Federal repositories (official, governmental correspondence; government maps and charts; photographic collections; statistical reports; acts and statutes; business charters; newspapers; military records; census rolls; immigration lists);
- State and provincial archives (official correspondence; local statutes; personal letters and diaries; militia records; photographic collections; newspapers);
- Private and university archives (special collections of correspondence and records of prominent individuals and important places; rare manuscripts and books; maps and charts);
- Local repositories (personal correspondence; land ownership records and plat maps; local tax rolls; birth and death records).

This is an incomplete list. Fortunately for researchers, most large archives and special collections facilities publish up-to-date catalogues of their holdings. Most of these facilities now have websites and many have searchable databases. These computer sources are superb research tools, because they allow historical archaeologists to perform some of their research right from their laboratories and offices.

A project at the Adobe Walls trading post site in the Texas panhandle demonstrates the value of primary sources in historical archaeology. This remote trading post came into being in 1874, when enterprising merchants followed the buffalo hunters flooding onto the American Plains. The merchants only occupied their sod-and-picket post for six months, choosing to retreat to Kansas when local Native Americans began to harass them. When archaeologist Billy Harrison began to study the post in 1975, he collaborated with historian T. Lindsay Baker. Baker sifted through nineteenth-century newspapers, including those with the romantic names of the *Dodge City Times* and *Leavenworth Times*, personal papers, letters, reports, and books and articles housed in no less than fifty-five separate repositories. These archives ranged from the National Archives in Washington, D.C., to a personal library in South Croydon, England. The historical documentation for this one small site, inhabited for only one-half year, kept Baker busy for months as he located, read, evaluated, and interpreted the abundant material.

Harrison's excavations at Adobe Walls benefitted tremendously from Baker's historical research. While combing through the files of the National Archives in Washington, D.C., Baker discovered two sworn depositions relating to the trading post. In the first, made on October 11, 1892, Charles Rath, partner of the Rath and Company store, described his building at the post. As he remembered it, the store was built of sod, was 25 by 50 feet (7.6 by 15.3 m) in size, and had two "block houses" on opposite corners. He said these block houses measured 12 or 15 feet (3.7 or 4.6 m) square. The second deposition was made by Andrew Johnson, known as "Andy the Swede." In his statement, recorded the same day as Rath's, he recalled the Rath and Company store as being 24 or 25 feet (7.3 or 7.6 m) wide and about 50 or 60 feet (15.3 or 18.3 m) long. He said it was made of sod with a log roof. He also mentioned the two "block houses" as being about 12 by 12 feet (3.7 by 3.7 m) square. The presence of these eyewitness accounts meant that Harrison had some idea of what he would find when he began excavating at the store. He knew he was looking for a sod building that measured somewhere around 25 by 50 feet (7.6 by 15.3 m) in size. That the excavators found the actual building to measure 16.5 feet (5.0 m) by almost 53 feet (16.2 m) is not surprising (Figure 7.1). We should expect some error in the informants' memories. After all, how many people actually know the measurements of the rooms in their house? Also, because the Adobe Walls trading post was occupied for such a short time, we cannot expect its occupants to recall every minute detail about it. What is more surprising, however, is that Harrison found archaeological evidence for only one "block house," on the southeast corner. The building never had two block houses! The discrepancy between the residents' memories and the physical evidence cannot be explained. Perhaps another store built someplace else had two block houses, and the men were simply confusing the two. We may never know why the men mentioned two block houses.

The Adobe Walls research highlights some of the difficulties inherent in using primary documents in archaeological research. The problems become even more acute when international relations or trade are involved. Quite apart from an expertise in, say, sixteenth-century Spanish language and script, access to even official archives may be difficult to arrange, even with the cooperation of local scholars. The study of colonial sites in North America and elsewhere, for example,

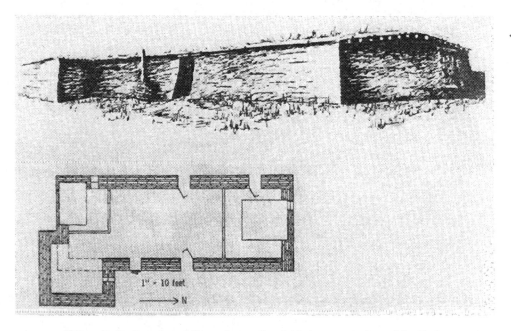

**Figure 7.1** Excavated floor plan and artist's reconstruction of the Rath and Company Store, Adobe Walls trading post, Texas.

usually means acquiring a familiarity with the colonial archives of Spain, Portugal, Great Britain, France, or the Netherlands, depending on the history of the site involved. Such was the case when historical archaeologist Kathleen Deagan teamed up with historian Jane Landers in the study of Fort Mose, outside the historic city of St. Augustine, Florida. St. Augustine was the first permanent European city in the United States, and Fort Mose, more properly called "Gracia Real de Santa Teresa de Mose," was the creation of African American escapees from British plantations to the north (Figure 7.2). The Spanish welcomed these people who had fled from their European enemies. They founded Fort Mose in 1738, and it became the first legally approved free black community in what would later become the United States. The residents of Fort Mose helped the Spanish defeat their former masters when the British attacked St. Augustine in the early 1740s. To learn something of the history of this important site, Deagan and Landers spent the first six months of their archaeological project becoming familiar with Spanish parish records held in Florida, and official governmental dispatches from Spanish archives. These Spanish records tell the "official" story of Fort Mose, or what the British derisively called simply a "Negroe Fort."

Deagan's archaeological research exposed some of the history of Fort Mose. The site of the fort was first identified in 1971 by a crew working under the direc-

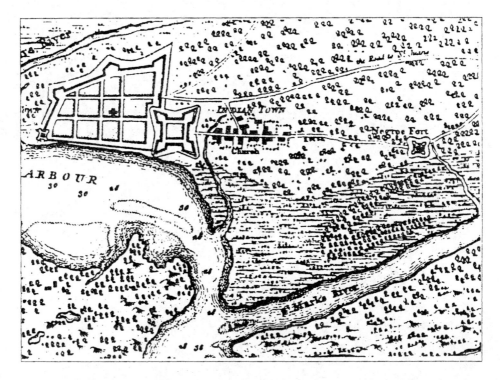

**Figure 7.2**   Detail of 1792 map of St. Augustine, Florida, showing "Negroe Fort."

tion of Charles Fairbanks, a pioneer historical archaeologist from the University of Florida. Deagan was a student on this crew, and she returned to the site in 1976 as a professor to conduct a more detailed examination of the fort. She confirmed the fort's location, but she was not able to obtain enough funding for a large-scale excavation until 1985.

The Fort Mose archaeology revealed several unique things about the fort, including details of its construction. The fort's walls were about 5 feet (1.5 m) tall, faced on the outside with marsh clay and planted along the top with prickly pear cactus. The fort's defensive moat was almost 7 feet (2 m) wide and about 2.5 feet (0.8 m) deep. It also had a watchtower or large building, and a smaller, circular wood and thatch building that may have been a dwelling. The artifacts from the site included lead shot, carefully chipped gunflints, white clay smoking pipes, brass buckles, bone buttons, and glass bottles. Native American pottery comprised a full 62 percent of the finds. Deagan identified these wares as coming from the local Timucuas. Most of the European ceramics in the collection are English, rather than Spanish, in origin. The English dominated the world ceramic market at this time, and smugglers were adept at bringing British goods into Spanish America. Deagan's archaeological program at Fort Mose, supported by Landers' extensive research in the relevant Spanish-language documents, provides exciting new information about early African American history.

## ORAL INTERVIEWING

Oral sources can be as valuable as written documentation. Anthropologists discovered early on that they would have to talk to people to learn about certain cultural practices. Anthropologists in the field thus asked numerous questions about kinship, genealogical terms, religious beliefs, attitudes about infanticide, and birth control methods, to name only a few topics. The anthropologists could not directly observe such aspects of daily life, and the people themselves seldom talked about them. Such practices were also not usually recorded by missionaries and early explorers. The only way to learn about oral cultures—those without writing—is to ask and to watch. This asking and watching is what anthropologists call "participant observation," and it is one of their fundamental research tools.

Polish-born Bronislaw Malinowski was one of the first professional anthropologists to spend a long period living among and studying the people of another culture. His work among the Trobriand Islanders, near New Guinea, produced many important works that are now classics in the history of anthropology. His *The Sexual Life of Savages in North-Western Melanesia* created a public sensation when it appeared in 1929 because of its frank discussion of Trobriand sexuality. Malinowski is perhaps best known among anthropologists for developing techniques of participant observation. His fieldwork involved extensive oral interviewing and face-to-face interaction. His diary entry for January 18, 1915, shows that he was well aware of the difficulty of obtaining oral information: "Yesterday before noon, Pikana came. With great effort—for he was sleepy, kept yawning, and I had a headache and felt poorly—I wormed out of him material relating to kinship." This information, "wormed" from Pikana with the greatest of difficulty, forms the core of what many anthropology students learn about kinship today.

Historical archaeologists often sympathize with Malinowski. They search for what historian Carl Becker called the kind of history people "carry around in their heads." Everyone, no matter what his or her station in life, knows some history that is unique, and sometimes private to that person. The layout and use of the rooms in our house, when we graduated from high school or started college, and what our first job was like are all part of our "history." We remember what we thought about important national or international events, and how these things affected us and the people around us. These things we know; they are part of who we are. Such personal history can be central to learning about the recent past.

Orally presented personal histories have been a part of anthropological research for many years. Several committed anthropologists, like Frances Densmore, sought to save them from being lost forever (Figure 7.3). Collecting oral history is today a central task for many professional historians, who use them to

**Figure 7.3**   Anthropologist Frances Densmore getting an interpretation of a Blackfoot song.

write about modern times. Oral anthologies have been compiled for events as distinctive as the Woodstock Festival and the attack on Pearl Harbor. Studs Terkel's bestselling *Hard Times: An Oral History of the Great Depression* is just one demonstration of how compelling oral histories can be. Even though Terkel modestly describes his book as "simply an attempt to get the story of the holocaust known as The Great Depression from an improvised battalion of survivors," his informants tell stories that have no equal. Before their collection, these deeply personal stories could not be culled from published articles, books, or newspapers. They existed only in peoples' memories. The oral historian, like the field anthropologist, commits these personal tales to the written page and gives them permanence.

Oral accounts are a nonrenewable resource. The people who remember Pearl Harbor, Woodstock, the Great Depression, or for that matter, the Boston Tea Party, have died, or will eventually die. The death of a generation is like the burning of an archive full of unique and nonretrievable information. Oral interviewing is thus similar to archaeology. The only difference is that when interviewing you can learn about the past directly from the people who lived it. You can ask them questions, elicit further information, clarify obscurities or ambiguous statement as you go along.

The lines between oral history, anthropology, and historical research are often fuzzy. When Baker and Harrison studied Adobe Walls, they used a number of interviews with still-living veterans of the post set down in the 1920s and 1930s. The transcripts were invaluable sources of personal information that could come from no one but a direct participant. Many of the informants—for example, J. Wright Mooar, a Chicago streetcar conductor turned professional buffalo hunter—remembered Adobe Walls and spoke about it in an insightful and personal way. "We had eleven outlaws hired," he recalled. "I remember some of them. They were good fellows. They stayed with us. We never had any preachers with us."

In 1922, during a visit to the old site, Andrew "Andy the Swede" Johnson and Orlando A. "Brick" Bond (Figure 7.4), two former residents of the post, drew a sketch map of the way they remembered the store. Billy Dixon was another man who remembered his experiences at Adobe Walls (Figure 7.5). Widely regarded as a hunter of rare ability, Dixon was awarded the Congressional Medal of Honor for his bravery at the Battle of Buffalo Wallow, a battle in which six soldiers and scouts held off an overwhelming number of attacking Native Americans. He recalled the area of Adobe Walls as "a vast wilderness, inhabited by game—truly a hunter's paradise." Describing a fellow hunter, Dixon said that he was a man "who had lots of nerve and knew all the ins and outs of frontier life." These priceless accounts seem to come from the pens of writers of western fiction, but they are real and invaluable.

We mentioned above how some of the eyewitnesses' comments about the construction of the Rath and Company store were confirmed by the archaeological excavations. In many cases, the combination of oral information and archaeological findings serves to flesh out the small details of daily life. Many of the

**Figure 7.4**   Orlando Bond and Andrew Johnson at the Adobe Walls Site in 1922.

post's men, interviewed in the 1920s, remembered the popularity of wild plums and coffee at the trading post. Accordingly, the archaeologists found sixteen plum pits and twenty-five coffee beans from excavations in the area of the mess hall.

Oral remembrances can provide a range of information. Archaeologist Peter Schmidt used oral history in a somewhat broader way than the Abode Walls team when he investigated farming villages among the Buhaya, who live on the shores of Lake Victoria in Tanzania, East Africa (also see Chapter 1). Schmidt called his research "historical archaeology," even though some of his sites date to the time of Christ or even earlier, far earlier than colonial sites in Florida, Australia, or South Africa. He used the term *historical* to mean the use of written and oral sources in conjunction with archaeological information in a way that is common to much historical archaeology.

Relying on local informants, Schmidt learned a great deal about the political history of the Buhaya, their religious traditions, and their present-day land tenure system. He conducted two- to four-hour interviews in Swahili and then used what he learned to guide his excavations. Collecting such histories required persistence and patience. He had to visit some informants several times before he could make them comfortable enough to talk freely. Even then, most informants would agree to but one interview, because "They reasoned that we had covered the subject already and that another discussion was an obvious waste of time."

Much of what Schmidt learned was not the kind of eyewitness information used by Baker and Harrison at Adobe Walls. Instead, his Buhaya informants

**Figure 7.5**   Billy Dixon in 1876.

spoke of the past by using mnemonic devices, mental images meant as memory aids. They used these mental tricks because they could not possibly have witnessed key events that unfolded centuries ago. They recited what they learned from their parents, and what their parents had learned from their parents, and so on, back several generations. After some experience with the informants and their way of thinking about the past, Schmidt came to understand how the people of this one part of Tanzania perceived their physical environment. He came to see the landscape as "a collage of mythology, folklore, and local legends of untold permutations."

The significance of Schmidt's study to historical archaeology lies in his understanding that people have many different ways of remembering the past. Some are direct memories—resting on actual events seen and recalled or on reminiscences of individuals known and respected. At times the informants talk of events shrouded in folklore and tradition, accounts of a mythic, long-vanished past that were passed from father to son, mother to daughter over the generations. Schmidt's research in Tanzania shows that long-told stories can be as useful as more recent information.

Oral information can sometimes contain a subtle mix of eyewitness account and oral tradition. Such is the case with Black Elk, holy man of the Oglala Sioux (Dakota), who at age thirteen witnessed the Battle of the Little Big Horn. His autobiography stands today as one of the most beautifully told oral accounts in the world. In beginning his life story, Black Elk said that it was a tale "of us two-leggeds sharing in it with the four-leggeds and the wings of the air and all green things; for these are children of one mother and their father is one Spirit." Black Elk recounted the events of his life with a mixture of eyewitness detail and Oglala tradition. Speaking of the famous skirmish with Custer, he recalled that "it seemed that my people were all thunder-beings and that the soldiers would be rubbed out." His account is both spiritual and factual, personal and cultural at the same time.

Oral accounts can provide great depth to our knowledge of the past. When used in conjunction with textual sources and archaeological data, they can be extremely powerful ways to interject a profoundly personal perspective on the past.

## ARCHITECTURAL FIELDWORK

Not all sites studied by historical archaeologists are empty fields or deserted city lots. The places that often provide the most exciting information contain standing buildings, pieces of complex machinery, bridges, and abandoned mills. Historical archaeologists, though perhaps often viewed only as excavators of the soil, do not ignore these "large artifacts." In fact, they are frequently called upon to conduct surveys of standing buildings and other extant structures. Historical archaeologists are as interested in what rests above the ground as they are about what lies underneath it.

Large-scale architectural surveys are often required when areas to be affected by whole-scale land modification projects are to change the landscape and everything on its surface, including existing buildings. Buildings, like oral interviews, represent a non-renewable resource. If preservation or moving the structure is an impossibility, then archaeologists or architects may be called upon to document them before destruction. When the U.S. Army Corps of Engineers constructed a huge dam on the Savannah River, between Georgia and South Carolina, they created a gigantic artificial lake that was about 25 miles (40 km) long. The reservoir behind the dam rose about 60 feet (18.2 m) above the former river banks, and inundated a large number of archaeological sites.

The Corps of Engineers hired teams of archaeologists to excavate both historic and prehistoric sites within the dam area before the reservoir was flooded. They also hired a group of historical architects to document the standing buildings that would be destroyed by the dam and lake. The area to be flooded had once been home to slaves and freedmen, to expansive plantations and small tenant farms.

Houses are pieces of material culture, and they have much to tell us about past daily life. Most houses are examples of *vernacular architecture*, buildings constructed in agreement with cultural norms and without the aid of trained architects and builders. Mansions and public buildings are typically built as examples of *formal architecture*, where highly trained architects will draw up detailed plans for skilled builders to follow.

Architect Linda Worthy, editor of the report detailing the buildings in the Savannah River area, stated that "The dwelling house is the most important component of the cultural landscape." It is thus impossible to overlook their significance. Historical architects and folklorists have repeatedly shown us that dwellings can be "read" like an old book or a landscape to reveal histories that would otherwise remain silent. You only need to know the language. Boarded-up windows, room additions and altered roof lines all tell part of a story that can be interpreted if one knows what to look for.

In compiling what they called the "more human history" of the Savannah River dam, architectural surveyors found and photographed ninety-three abandoned houses, including wood-framed farmhouses once inhabited by once-enslaved tenant farmers, two-story plantation mansions of slave owners, and hewn-log cabins of the region's earliest settlers (Figures 7.6, 7.7). Traveling an intertwined network of dusty backroads, they also discovered log barns and sheds, a blacksmith shop, and rusted iron bridges. These buildings collectively tell a story that covers the years from before 1860 to the mid-1950s: the region's initial European American settlement, its creation as a rich plantation region based on the

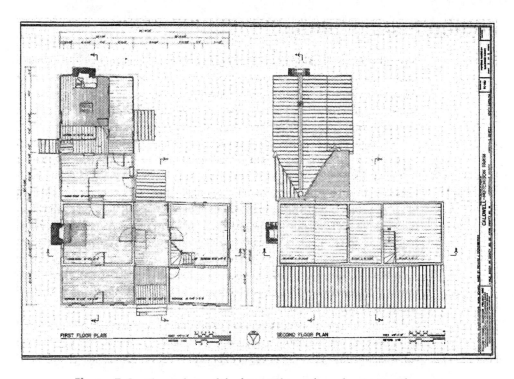

**Figure 7.6** Floor plans of the late-eighteenth–early-nineteenth-century Caldwell-Hutchinson Farm, South Carolina.

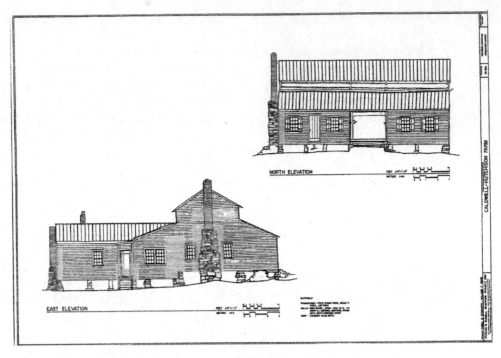

**Figure 7.7**   Elevation of the late-eighteenth–early-nineteenth-century Caldwell-Hutchinson Farm, South Carolina.

labor of enslaved African Americans, and its transition into a region of small tenant farmers clinging precariously to the near-exhausted red soil of the Upland South.

## Detailed Architectural Surveys

The conduct of architectural surveys is highly specialized work. It requires detailed and exacting mapping, and precise interpretation of the buildings' physical characteristics. Many nations have established precise standards for architectural surveys. In the United States, the standards are set by the Historic American Buildings Survey (HABS), founded in 1933, and the Historic American Engineering Record (HAER), founded in 1969. Congress formally combined HABS and HAER in 1983 as HABS/HAER. The staff of HABS/HAER execute their measured drawings to precise specifications, and they are intended to be a permanent, archival record of structures of historic significance. Precise measured drawings have been completed for the Statue of Liberty in New York, for the original Smithsonian Institution building in Washington, D.C., the steam-powered hoist at the Quincy copper mine in northern Michigan, and many other important buildings, bridges, mechanical systems, historic ships, and land-scapes.

HABS/HAER staff members were involved in documenting the architectural history of the White House in Washington, D.C. The removal of several layers of old paint laid bare walls that had not been exposed since 1798, and revealed scorch marks that provide silent testimony to the British attempt to burn the mansion in 1814. With the paint removed, architects from HABS/HAER made exacting measured drawings of the windows, doors, and building facades. Their drawing of the main entrance reveals an ornate design of oak leaves and roses that harkens back to an age when formally trained architects ornamented their masterpieces with such ostentatious adornments.

HABS/HAER recorders also create a photographic record to amplify their drawings. Photographs are often preferred to measured drawings because they are quicker, easier, and less expensive to produce, particularly in digital format. These photographs are not simple snapshots, but highly professional images intended to convey a building's three-dimensional qualities, its spatial relationships with other buildings, its condition or state of preservation at the time of the photograph, and the texture of the building's many surfaces. Many of these photographs are artistic and beautiful, but they actually serve as documents that constitute the formal record of the building.

In England, architectural surveying is handled by the staff of English Heritage's Architectural Investigation team. This highly skilled team includes architectural historians, building analysts, graphics specialists, and photographers, all of whom have the goal of documenting the nation's incredible storehouse of historic buildings. They regularly collaborate with local bodies interested in historic preservation, and they make their materials available through the National Monuments Record. They also serve as consultants to bodies seeking advice on how best to protect a significant example of architecture.

## Other Architectural Surveys

Not many historical archaeologists can prepare measured drawings that would meet the high standards of HABS/HAER or English Heritage's Architectural Investigation team without considerable, specialized training. Nonetheless, historical archaeologists are often called upon to prepare measured drawings and take architectural photographs of standing structures. The level of detail of their survey will depend upon the amount of available time and the requirements of the specific project. Some building surveys must be quickly completed. For others, the investigators may have the luxury of time and can provide thorough documentation of every aspect of a structure's architectural fabric.

In the 1980s, a new kind of historical archaeology, called buildings archaeology, began to emerge in England. Proponents of this non-excavation–based archaeology argued that archaeologists should be directly involved in the documentation, dating, and interpretation of the built environment. In *The Archaeology of Buildings*, Robert Morriss outlines the need for an archaeology of buildings and provides a useful guide for field archaeologists. Morriss explains how archaeologists should survey buildings, and he describes methods of conducting archival research that may help to date them. He explains how archaeologists should learn to evaluate the evidence provided by a bulding's walls, roof, flooring, and windows. The research, though focused on above-ground standing structures, is remarkably archaeological. Working much as field excavators, building investigators must learn to recognize significant features and to document the relationships of the features. They must also have considerable knowledge about the material culture used in buildings during various periods of history (bricks, tiles, flooring materials, framing, stonework, and so forth).

Archaeologists from Southern Methodist University in Dallas, Texas, performed an architectural survey in north central Texas as part of a larger study of the Richland/Chambers Reservoir project. Their work resulted in the documentation of twenty-six dwellings, four bridges, and twelve "special purpose structures"—storage sheds, various kinds of outbuildings, and even a store. Settlers in this part of Texas built these still-extant buildings between 1848 and 1945. The documentation provided by the survey team provided important information about the kinds of houses and other structures built in this region during an eventful, one-hundred-year period of history.

Building archaeologists can also document structures that no longer exist. Morriss details the research conducted at Caradoc Court, Herefordshire, England. The mansion was built in the 1600s as a timber-framed structure, and it was partially rebuilt in the 1860s. A devastating fire gutted the mansion before archaeologists could make an investigation of its history. Using an ingenious method of reconstruction, however, archaeologists salvaged what they could from the interior debris, and reconstructed the old house in the garden. They were able to move the various structural elements around in the garden to recreate much of the building's framing on paper. They were aided by the unique character of hand-cut mortise and tenon joints. They were also able to document remaining standing walls of the building once the debris was cleaned from the scorched interior. From all this evidence, the archaeologists learned that the builders had originally designed the mansion in a half-H plan, rather than the L-shaped plan that was once assumed.

Historical archaeologists can use historical records, oral interviews, and architectural information to create powerful, rich pictures of the past. These images, constructed with materials gleaned from numerous, diverse, so-called "non-archaeological" sources, add a more human, personal touch to our understanding of history. They help us appreciate a bit of the experience of living in the past. In the next chapter, we turn to the actual excavation of historic sites and the processing of the artifacts in the laboratory.

# TIME TRAVEL

## *La Surveillante, Bantry Bay, Ireland, 1797*

After a long and complex series of false starts, rumors, and international negotiations, the French military, under ultimate command of Napoleon Bonaparte, decided to assist the Irish in their quest for independence from Britain. Many radical Irish men and women had long wished to free themselves from their powerful neighbor to the east, and with the rise of the revolutionary United Irishmen in the 1790s, the dream seemed possible. The basic idea behind the plan, seen strictly from a miliary standpoint, was to have Irish citizens rise up against their English overlords and defeat them at home with the support of French allies. When the plan succeeded, the British island would precariously stand between two hostile powers: France on the east and the Hibernian-Franco alliance on the west. To bring the plan to fruition, the French planned to send a huge flotilla to rendezvous with the United Irishmen in Ireland.

The fleet left Brest under command of Vice-Admiral Morard de Galles in mid-December 1796. Their impressive armada was composed of seventeen lines of battle ships, thirteen frigates, six corvettes, and eight transports. One frigate specifically carried supplies of powder for the fleet. A force of thirteen thousand soldiers and cavalry were also on board under the command of General Lazare Hoche. They would comprise the landing party.

The passage to Ireland was doomed from the start. The formidable English navy had blockaded Brest for months, and so running the blockage was no easy matter at a time when ships' captains had to rely on the wind. Not knowing the precise location of the British vessels, and attempting to take advantage of favorable winds at night, the French armada was quickly thrown into confusion. One ship, armed with seventy-four cannons, was run aground, and over six hundred men were lost. The other ships became scattered in the dense fog, and the fleet became hopelessly separated. In the face of such chaos, the French captains agreed to meet off the coast of Mizen Head, on the extreme southwest corner of Ireland. They hoped to collect their accumulated strength and then to continue with the planned invasion. The French sought to land at Bantry Bay, in the southwest, because of its ready access to the city of Cork. If they could control this important town, the British forces in the Province of Munster would be in serious trouble, because the French could open an undefended gateway for the importation of more troops.

On December 21, the reduced fleet made for Bantry Bay, but overshot it, because of the ocean's haze. On finally making the bay, however, the fleet was once again plagued by foul weather. The snowy gales that blew against the fleet threatened to spoil the invasion for good. At least two of the ships were blown 300 miles into the Atlantic! Before long, a couple of British warships that had entered the bay merely added to the French's confusion and peril. *La Surveillante* was taking on water to such an extent that her crew decided to abandon and scuttle her. They did so on January 2, 1797, in 111 feet (34 meters) of water.

*La Surveillante* was a small frigate. She was built in 1765 and measured about 143 feet (43.5 m) long. She was triple-masted and had two decks; the lower deck was the gun deck. *La Surveillante* was one of only twelve French ships to have her hull

*(continued)*

Source: Colin Breen. *Integrated Marine Investigations on the Historic Shipwreck* La Surveillante: *A French Frigate Lost in Bantry Bay, Ireland, January, 1797.* (Coleraine: University of Ulster, 2001).

fitted with thin copper sheeting, installed to protect her from marine borers, barnacles, and other potentially damaging ocean-borne organisms. French naval engineers used bronze nails and bolts to fix the sheathing to the ship's wooden hull. They expected the protective cooper coating to last about five years.

The French ranked their warships based on the number of cannon they carried. First-rate ships had one hundred guns on three decks, and a second-rate ship had ninety guns on three decks. Third-rate ships had sixty-four to seventy-four guns on two decks, and fourth-rate ships had fifty on two decks. Smaller frigates carried between twenty-four and forty cannons, and so they were faster and lighter than the heavier, more well-armed vessels. *La Surveillante* had thirty-two guns, twenty-six 12-pounders and six 6-pounders.

It is possible that the crew scuttled the ship by raising the anchor up the main mast and then letting it crash into the deck and hull. The ship's appearance on the ocean floor indicates that the crew did not attempt to remove her heavy cannons. They also did not remove many of their supplies of muskets or many of the other artifacts they carried on board. The ship probably landed on her stern first and then listed slightly to starboard. With time, the wreck has worked its way into the seabed and now sits in Bantry Bay.

# Chapter 8

# Archaeological Fieldwork: Field and Laboratory

*"The excavator without an intelligent policy may be described as an archaeological
food-gatherer, master of a skill, perhaps, but not creative in the wider terms
of constructive science."*

Mortimer Wheeler, 1954

Archaeological excavation: The very words evoke images of heroes like Indiana
Jones hacking their way through dense forests in search of stone pyramids,
golden idols, and lost civilizations. Such stereotypes of the archaeologist are
today only the stuff of Hollywood fantasy; they reflect not what archaeologists really do, but only what someone thinks they do. Magazines like *National Geographic*, along with well-produced television programs, paint a far more realistic
portrait of archaeology today. Here, scientific excavation is the rule—instead of
directing armies of workmen, archaeologists use toothbrushes, dental picks, and
high-tech devices in pursuit of the past. The adventurer of yesterday is the time
detective of today, logging as many hours in the laboratory as in the field, tracking down ancient mysteries with all the scientific fervor of a latter-day Sherlock
Holmes. Scientific excavations may appear less spectacular than the more well-
funded, over-publicized treasure hunts of pseudo-archaeologists, but they are
much more significant. Our fascination with them comes not from the discovery
of buried gold, but from uncovering lost knowledge for future generations.

Archaeological stereotypes stress discovery and digging for the simple reason that exploration always engages the enthusiasm of a wide audience. However dazzling the finds, however significant the site, the archaeologist's most
important and time-consuming task is not the actual excavation. Excavation,
though infinitely exciting, is really a detailed record-keeping process. The
notepad and the computer database are as symbolic of today's excavation as the

spade and the trowel. This chapter presents some of the basic field and laboratory procedures used by historical archaeologists.

## ARCHAEOLOGICAL PROCEDURES

"All excavation is destruction." With these words, Sir Leonard Woolley, the British excavator of Ur—the great Sumerian city in today's Iraq—succinctly described archaeological excavation. Simply put, when archaeologists excavate a site, they destroy it. They generally destroy it carefully, taking it apart piece by piece, but nonetheless, they do demolish it. As archaeologist Kent Flannery once said, "Archaeology is the only branch of anthropology where we kill off our subjects!" This conscious destruction may be somewhat difficult to imagine. We generally do not think of archaeologists as people who destroy the very thing they love. Instead, we often envision archaeologists standing boldly in the face of a raging bulldozer, willing to risk life and limb as the last line of defense against the wanton destruction of an important archaeological site. We see archaeologists as front-line warriors in the battle for historic preservation. But it is still true: Archaeologists, usually strong advocates of historic preservation, nonetheless destroy the archaeological sites they excavate. Archaeologists use subsurface surveying methods (Chapter 6) to minimize the amount of a site's destruction. Site destruction is sad but inescapable.

To understand archaeological excavation, imagine an old library card catalog file, the kind used before the introduction of today's familiar computerized data bases. Imagine that the catalog has forty drawers arranged in four rows and ten columns. Each row represents one layer of earth. Each card within the drawers represents one piece of information. This information can be an artifact, a post hole, a stone foundation wall, a trench, a soil color or texture, or any other element of the archaeological record. If the archaeologist has planned to obtain a 10-percent sample of the site, then he or she will be able to look into only four of the drawers. Within these four drawers, our archaeologist will remove and keep the ones marked "artifact," but will only be able to record the information from the other cards before destroying them. For example, he or she will only be able to make notes about the information contained on a card marked "soil color." The archaeologist can only record the measurements written on a card marked "privy." Because all of the nonartifact cards must be destroyed, future investigators will only have thirty-six drawers left to examine. They also will have the "artifact" cards and the notes the original archaeologist took from the other cards: soil colors, thicknesses of soil layers, width and height of stone walls, the distance between a privy and a fence line, and so forth. Our researcher knows that once his or her study is finished, the destroyed cards will be lost forever. Only the archaeologist's record of the destroyed cards will remain.

This example is, of course, fictional; archaeological sites are not wooden file boxes filled with cards. Nonetheless, field archaeologists repeat much of the process just described. Some of the archaeological record vanishes forever (soil layers, delicate pit outlines), while some of it (artifacts, selected soil samples) ends up in a museum or storage facility. Archaeologists destroy many archaeological features by the realities of excavation. When Kenneth Kidd excavated Sainte Marie I in 1941, the seventeenth-century Jesuit mission in Ontario mentioned in Chapter 2, he was only able to measure, record, and photograph the small post holes that the mission's builders had placed beneath the still-visible wooden sill of the chapel's original wall. Kidd could not actually save the post holes themselves because they were simply dark stains in the soil. All we know about these post holes today derives from Kidd's records and archaeological report; the holes themselves no longer exist. When Kidd stated that the posts had an average diameter of "4 inches" (10 cm) and an average depth of "about 20 inches" (51 cm) we must believe him because we can never see the post holes ourselves.

Historical archaeologists generally follow the same excavation procedures as all other archaeologists. They would excavate a colonial tavern in Cape Town, South Africa, with the same basic methods they would use to excavate an eleventh-century Anasazi pueblo in Arizona. Excavation is an unfolding process of carefully applied scientific procedures, techniques that have been developed and refined by decades of archaeological research.

## The Process of Archaeological Excavation

Excavation, like other research procedures, is slow and meticulous. Each excavation is unique in some ways, but six stages are common to all of them, extending from the earliest ideas about how to conduct the excavation to the final process of publication.

*Research Design.* All archaeological fieldwork begins with a carefully developed *research design*. A research design is a carefully organized plan for carrying out the project, an explicit statement of the way in which the researcher seeks to answer questions posed before the excavation begins. The number of sites to be investigated, the size of the sample needed (Chapter 6), and the kinds of specialists to be involved are all specified in the research design.

In an ideal world, we may suppose that an archaeologist constructs a research design based solely on the needs and requirements of the research. It would be comforting to think that archaeologists can always conduct the sort of research that interests them in the best and most scientific ways. The reality is often quite different, however. Today's excavators must balance what they want to do with what they can realistically accomplish given the many constraints placed upon them. Funding limitations, the availability of students and other field workers, the difficulty of obtaining permits and licenses, the development of volatile, dangerous political situations, and environmental catastrophes—floods, volcanic eruptions, or droughts—can all affect archaeological research. Almost anything can happen to change the course of an archaeological field project. Even the most carefully and well-planned research design must be flexible enough to adapt to the changing conditions of fieldwork.

Archaeologists who work in the realm of cultural resource (or heritage) management are called upon every day to create research designs that are cost-effective and tightly scheduled (see Chapter 12). Cultural resource management (CRM) studies are completed to ensure that important archaeological sites and historical properties are not destroyed by construction projects before they can be adequately studied. Archaeologists in this environment regularly collaborate with private companies and governmental bodies, including those in charge of highways, forests, lakes and rivers, and environmental protection. CRM studies, being conducted for a specific purpose, are usually restricted to a particular, well-defined place, like the route of a new road.

In the 1990s, a team of archaeologists from Sonoma State University directed by Adrian and Mary Praetzellis, performed a study for the California Department of Transportation. The goal of the highway department was to upgrade and widen the San Francisco Central Freeway in San Francisco. Federal law required that the highway department engage archaeologists to examine the area to be affected by the construction so than any important features could be studied before their destruction. But, because the highway had a specific, predetermined route, the archaeologists were restricted to examining only those city blocks directly affected by it (Figure 8.1). They were able to dig only within the designated city blocks. This restriction meant that the archaeologists had to create a research design that took into account both the larger history of the city and the region, as well as more detailed information about those specific blocks that could be investigated. The archaeologists were able to overlay the route of the highway on historic maps of the city, and, along with their archaeological findings, they were able to reconstruct the entire history of their project area.

The research design created by the Sonoma State University archaeologists was highly successful because they planned it extremely well. They were able to use the limitations imposed on them to present a thorough study of the area. The abundant information they provided did not lead to the reconstruction of the buildings or the creation of a permanent museum exhibit. The highway department's requirements made this impossible. But the research design enabled the archaeologists to document the settlement and growth of a part of one of the world's most important urban centers.

*Implementation.*   Proposal and grant writing, fund raising, the hiring of a qualified crew, and the acquisition of all required permits—every archaeologist spends months on these mundane, often-frustrating tasks. But excavation can seldom be done without them.

The process of implementation involves proposal writing and perhaps even the refinement of the research plan to accommodate the realities of time and funding. Construction, such as for the San Francisco highway project, is expensive, and construction engineers do not have the luxury of waiting while archae-

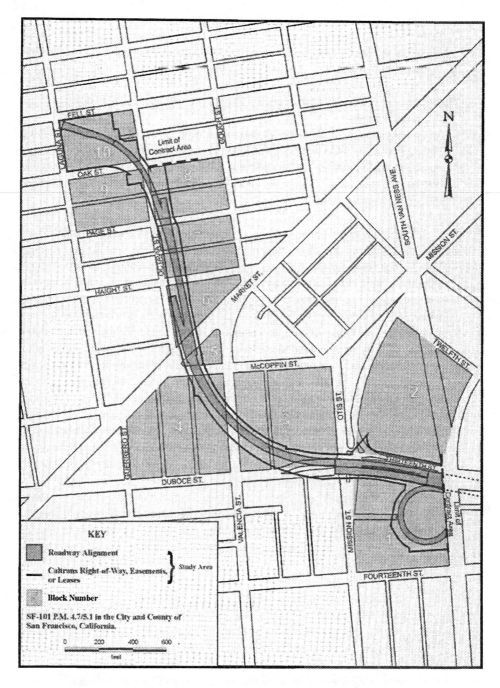

**Figure 8.1**  Central Freeway Replacement Project area, showing blocks included in research design.

ologists delicately sift through the soil. Archaeologists thus often have a finite—and, in truth, usually too-limited—time to complete all their fieldwork. If an archaeologist knows that only fifty-two weeks are available to complete an entire project, it does not make sense to plan fifty weeks of fieldwork and only two weeks for analysis and report writing. Officials at the agency sponsoring the research expect to receive the final report on deadline, so that they can continue with their work.

The implementation phase should include weeks and months when the investigators complete their background research. This research includes a great deal of reading, both archaeological and archival. Any oral interviewing and architectural analysis (Chapter 7) may have begun or even been completed before the excavation starts.

*Fieldwork.*   The time spent in the field varies infinitely with the research design and funding. A complete excavation of a large colonial fortification might require a huge crew and months of careful investigation of its foundation trenches, post holes, standing walls, to say nothing of village layouts both inside and outside. The investigation of a tiny lot in a small town may only take the archaeologist a day to investigate. At the fort, the archaeologist may opt for block excavation—where the crew exposes a large area of the site—and in the city block, they may use only a series of well-placed 8-inch (20.3 cm) diameter post holes. Several equally valid ways exist to excavate an archaeological site.

Every excavation, however modest, requires meticulous records, careful handling of all excavated material, and a place to store both. To create a place to compile their notes and records, many fieldworkers construct on-site facilities, sometimes as simple as a tarpaulin strung between trees. Other excavators use on-site trailers or they rent nearby houses. Archaeologists use these facilities to wash and inventory their artifact finds. They may also use the temporary lab for emergency conservation work, and as a place to complete computer entries and inventories. In-field processing is preliminary to the permanent, more thorough laboratory analysis that follows any archaeological excavation. On-site processing has the advantage of allowing the archaeologists to examine the objects as they are discovered, and enables them to adjust their research design while the excavation is still in progress.

*Analysis.*   Most excavators say that one month in the field requires at least three months in the laboratory. This estimate may be conservative because special circumstances may prolong the analysis for many months, and even for years. These are the months when the researchers process all the information they collected during the fieldwork. An archaeological lab usually has large, long tables for cleaning, marking, and analyzing artifacts. The laboratory workers have access to precise measuring tools (such as digital calipers), scales, and microscopes, while they enter their information directly into their computer databases. Some excavators use bar codes to mark bags of artifacts. Most field laboratories also have small libraries and artifact reference collections for comparison with excavated pieces. The field team must process and accession all the artifacts in a consistent format for future identification and for long-term storage.

A flurry of activity begins once the materials are back at the home lab. Transcribers type the oral interviews from audio cassettes, draftspeople clean and redraft architectural plans and maps of archaeological features, photo processors develop, print, and catalog the photographic record, and the archaeologists redraw their plans and maps as they make them ready for publication.

When all the finds are properly accessioned, the research team examines each one, describes it, and prepares inventories and tables showing the kinds and quantities of artifacts they found at the site. This research can be detailed and revealing. In their analysis of nineteenth- and twentieth-century Inuit sites on the coast of Labrador, Canada, Melanie Cabak and Stephen Loring specifically examined a kind of European ceramic called "stamped earthenware." This term refers to an inexpensive and rapidly applied decorative technique that potters put on their ceramic vessels. They would cut a design into a sponge and then dip the sponge into pigment. They would then press the sponge against the surface of an unglazed ceramic, leaving the imprint of the design. They would perform this operation until they had the desired pattern. The motifs they used were often geometric or floral, but they could also use unique designs. Cabak and Loring examined a collection from a site called Nain that yielded 115 stamped sherds. They divided the types in the sample (the 7 different motifs) into the 5 colors present: purple, green, blue, red/green, and polychrome (many colors). Archaeologists usually present this material in table form for the sake of convenience and ease in interpretation (Table 8.1).

Food remains, such as animal bones and plants, require not only preliminary sorting on site, but careful analysis by specialists. Such finds are vitally important, because they enable excavators to reconstruct the dietary habits of past households, neighborhoods, and communities.

Zooarchaeologists specialize in the study of animal bones of all kinds. Most are trained in both archaeology and biology because their research goes far beyond the mere identification of animals once consumed for food. They separate

**Table 8.1** *Tabular Presentation of Stamped Sherds from Nain Site, Labrador*

| Motif | Purple | Green | Blue | Red/Green | Polychrome | Total |
|-------|--------|-------|------|-----------|------------|-------|
| fleur-de-lis | 33 | 2 | - | - | - | 35 |
| cross | 2 | - | - | - | 1 | 3 |
| leaf | - | - | 3 | - | 4 | 7 |
| floral | - | 11 | - | 10 | 10 | 31 |
| geometric | - | - | 23 | - | 4 | 27 |
| flag | - | - | - | 2 | - | 2 |
| unknown | 3 | 2 | - | 3 | 2 | 10 |
| **Total** | **38** | **15** | **26** | **15** | **21** | **115** |

domestic animals like cattle and sheep from game like deer and rabbits. They calculate the minimum number of individuals in a collection as a way of establishing the amount of meat represented by the bones. Many bones exhibit revealing evidence of old butchering techniques—knife cut marks, saw marks, and other kinds of human activity. These small signs can sometimes provide fascinating insights on the distinct ways in which a various ethnic or social groups used animals for food.

Zooarchaeologist Diana Crader successfully studied the faunal remains excavated from one of the slave buildings at Jefferson's Monticello (Figure 8.2). She discovered that the bones told a different story than the historical documents. The textual sources indicated that pork was a staple of the slaves' diet. The archaeologists did, in fact, discover that pig bones outnumbered cow bones in the archaeological deposits, but as Crader stated, "beef seems to play a very large role in the diet based on estimates of pounds (kg) of available meat." Overall, she expected the quality of the meat at the slave building to be low, but she learned from the bones that Jefferson's enslaved ate both high-quality limbs and low-quality heads and feet. At another slave dwelling at Monticello, however, Crader learned that the slaves did not eat high-quality meats. This evidence led her to believe that Jefferson may have arranged his slaves in a social hierarchy, in which some had a better diet than others. Proof of the social hierarchy among Monticello's enslaved community may thus only be detected in the archaeological record.

Ethnobotanists, sometimes called "archaeobotanists," are specialists in plant remains. These specialists have both archaeological and botanical training. They

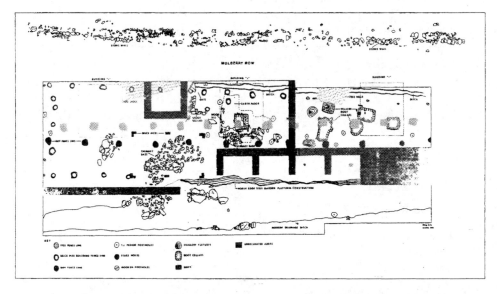

**Figure 8.2**   Mulberry Row slave quarters, Monticello, Virginia, as excavated in 1983–1984.

study both direct evidence for the human use of plants—seeds, nutshells, corn cobs—and indirect evidence—leaves, bulbs, rinds, pollen. Like zooarchaeologists, their research goes far beyond the mere identification of domesticated and wild species. They generally face more difficulties than zooarchaeologists in presenting exact species counts, however, because larger seeds like peach pits may be underrepresented as opposed to smaller ones, such as grape pips.

In her research on the subsistence patterns of the colonial Spanish in Florida, Georgia, and South Carolina, ethnobotanist Margaret Scarry found evidence for a wide variety of plants at Spanish forts and town sites. These included Old World cultigens (watermelon, cantaloupe, peach, grape, olive), indigenous, New World species (squash/pumpkin, bean, maize), and exotic, New World plants (lima bean, chili pepper). This evidence thus shows that Spanish settlers adopted a diverse strategy to ensure their survival. They introduced their own plants to the New World, they accepted many that the Native Americans grew locally, and they imported still others from colonial outposts in the Caribbean, Mesoamerica, and South America. Spanish colonists accepted many plant foods from the local native peoples, but their food habits seem to have maintained many Spanish characteristics. Such important insights would be impossible without the evidence provided by historical archaeology.

*Interpretation.*   Interpretation tests an archaeologist's skills, creativity, and understanding to the maximum; it is the process of making sense of all the accumulated data, of judging it against theoretical formulations. Historical archaeologists use a wide range of theories from anthropology and other social sciences, including history, for this purpose. The importance of such skills are amply demonstrated by the analysis of colonial Spanish subsistence strategies in the southeastern United States. Scarry, working closely with zooarchaeologist Elizabeth Reitz, conducted a thorough analysis of the plant and animal remains found at several colonial sites. Their research allowed them to understand the natural world the Spanish encountered in what was for them a New World. They explored the Spanish response to their new environment in light of such anthropological issues as adaptation—how the Spanish learned to live in the new environment—and acculturation—how the Spanish and the coastal Native Americans learned from one another and adopted elements of one another's culture.

Historical archaeologists, like all archaeologists, often decide that their interpretations can be strengthened by reference to broad frameworks devised by scholars outside archaeology. Some historical archaeologists, for example, have adopted a framework introduced by French historian, Fernand Braudel. According to Braudel, the past can be viewed as consisting of three scales: individual time, social time, and geographical time, or long-term history. Individual time is the history of people "in reference to the environment within which they are encompassed." Social time is the history of "groups and groupings," and long-term history is "traditional history," the history of "oscillations" and trends. In archaeology, the individual scale consists of studies of artifact styles and particular sites.

These are elements of the past that are influenced by specific events and by the actions of individuals. The social scale involves the study of social groups and the larger circumstances that affect families, kin networks, economic classes, and other groupings of people. In modern history, this scale is likely to involve the large trends that exist across national and even international boundaries. Long-term history concerns the unfolding of history over several generations.

Historical archaeologist Paul Shackel used Braudel's framework in his study of the development of personal discipline in Annapolis, Maryland, between the years 1695 and 1870. For him, individual time was the archaeology conducted at individual house lots, with the primary data being the artifacts collected from each site. He specifically wrote about the ways in which ceramics and toothbrushes (both of which were found during excavation) were used to create a sense of individuality in the home. In interpreting Braudel's middle scale of history, social time, Shackel concentrated on what was happening throughout Annapolis from the late seventeenth to the late nineteenth century. His sources for this analysis were contemporary newspapers, personal letters, travelers' guides, and probate lists. To examine long-term history and its relation both to the individual house lots and the city as a whole, Shackel drew back even further to study the history and social impacts of etiquette. His goal at this scale was to understand why people in Annapolis cared about whether they were using the "right" kind of plate or whether they "appropriately" managed their time. Shackel's use of Braudel's three scales allowed him to offer many significant insights that he may otherwise have overlooked had he concentrated only on the individual house lots.

The interpretations that historical archaeologists offer about the sites they study are varied and sometimes even controversial. No formula can be presented to show precisely how archaeologists frame their interpretations. Ideas about the past ultimately spring partly from each individual's attitudes, perceptions, and educational experiences. Interpretations also tend to be like fashion: They come into style, and after a while they go out of vogue and are discarded. Attempts to disprove the myth of the Mound Builders (Chapter 1) helped transform North American archaeology from a hobby of the idle rich into a serious scientific pursuit. Today, we shudder to think that many nineteenth-century archaeologists once thought that the Lost Tribes of Israel, the Vikings, or some other Indo-European peoples built the mounds that dot eastern North America. Thankfully, the Mound Builder myth is today confined to the dustbin of outmoded ideas.

*Publication.*    No archaeological project is truly complete until the results are published. Without some dissemination of their findings and interpretations, the excavators have done nothing more than wrest artifacts from the ground. The act of recovery can be meaningful when a site is threatened with imminent destruction, but unless the results of an excavation are widely available, then the archaeological information is effectively lost and the site is destroyed forever.

Specialist archaeological site reports are usually highly technical and are published in sources not readily accessible to nonarchaeologists. The report on the San Francisco freeway mentioned above was submitted to the California Department of Transportation. This report is a highly professional account of the research, with a great deal of important information, but it is unlikely that nonarchaeologists are even aware that this report exists. Professional historical archaeologists know about it, but it is largely inaccessible to a wider audience.

To counteract the problem of making archaeological material available to a broad audience, some historical archaeologists write popular accounts of their research in addition to their highly technical site reports. Ivor Noël Hume is well known for his ability to make dense, complex archaeological information accessible to the public. *Martin's Hundred: The Discovery of a Lost Colonial Virginia Settlement*, detailing the excavations at Wolstenholme Towne, Virginia, stands as one of the great popular accounts of historical archaeology. His book *If These Pots Could Talk: Collecting 2,000 Years of British Household Pottery* is a masterwork that recounts forty years of knowledge about everyday British ceramics. Noël Hume wrote it for everyone interested in ceramics: collectors, archaeologists, amateur historians, and others.

### Excavation

The thrill of archaeological discovery is very real, but extreme caution is the watchword. British excavator Sir Mortimer Wheeler, one of the finest excavators in archaeological history, said that "It is essential to check any sort of excitement instantly, and to insist firmly on quiet routine." Modern excavation is as much science as a carefully controlled experiment in a chemistry lab, even though the conditions may be far different. When Noël Hume excavated at Martin's Hundred, his excavators found an early-seventeenth-century close helmet, the first ever found in North America. A close helmet has a heavy visor that can be closed to cover and protect the entire head and face. The much-corroded find took many hours to remove in one piece from the ground (see below), but the entire removal took place under controlled conditions. Everyone knew that undue haste could break the helmet into tiny pieces and it would be lost forever. Only complete patience and the utmost care could save the specimen.

*Contexts of Space and Time.*   All excavation is based on the contexts of space and time. As a result, excavators must record data in two dimensions—horizontal and vertical. The horizontal dimension is maintained with the use of a site grid, a checkerboard of standard-sized squares placed across the entire site. There is nothing magical about the size of square chosen. Archaeologists decide in their research design which size will meet their needs for the particular site being excavated. Historical archaeologists sometimes disagree over the use of meters and centimeters or feet and inches, but regardless of the measurement scale used, each square in the grid receives a unique designation based on its distance from a datum point, or main point of reference, keyed into a local map. Field archaeologists can distinguish all the material from every excavation unit from all other finds, structures, and features by reference to the square's designation.

The use of a reference point allows archaeologists to keep accurate records on horizontal location year after year, and even permits someone else to excavate the same site and to use the identical grid years later. For example, when Samuel Smith, a historical archaeologist with the State of Tennessee's Division of Archaeology, excavated Fort Southwest Point, a late-eighteenth- and early-nineteenth-century American military post in eastern Tennessee, he used a grid of 10-foot (3.1 m) squares. When he started, he thought the grid covered the entire site. But when he revisited the site two years later, he found that he had to expand the grid to conduct further excavations on one end of the site. Because he used a uniform grid in the first place, it was no problem at all to expand it later. Also, because of the grid's regularity, he was easily able to correlate the information from the new part of the grid with the material found earlier. The grid allowed Smith to keep track of the horizontal location of the 34,666 artifacts he found at the fort.

Space is horizontal; time is usually vertical. As we saw in Chapter 5, the context of time is based on the Law of Superposition, on stratified layers identified during excavation. At Fort Southwest Point, Smith divided the history of post into five stages, based on historical documents: 1779–1796, 1797–1800, 1801–1807, 1808–1811, and 1812–present. He would have preferred to isolate each historical stage in distinct, easily distinguishable soil layers, but the correlation between the historical phases and the soil layers was not so clear-cut. When he excavated a 40-foot (12.2 m) long trench through a depression in the soil, he not only discovered two parallel stone walls from a barracks building; he also found no less than eleven separate soil layers.

Soil and artifacts are deposited in layers, so archaeologists like to excavate each layer separately. Historic sites can be particularly challenging in this regard, not only because they may have been occupied for only a few generations, or at most for a few centuries, but also because the occupation layers can be extremely thin. Consider a major city, like London, where generation after generation has repeatedly rebuilt on the same spot. When contractors clear away the earlier buildings and their foundations, all that is left for the archaeologist are small lenses of soil and datable artifacts that can take months to analyze and interpret. Thin soils also appear at sites inhabited for brief periods.

*Methods.*    Like all archaeologists, historical archaeologists conduct both vertical and horizontal excavations, depending on their research design. *Vertical excavation* is used at small sites or in situations where the archaeological team has limited time and funds. This kind of investigation is intended to provide as much information as possible without excavating a large portion of a site. In vertical excavation, only small parts of a site are excavated with trenches and small excavations usually measuring less than 10 feet (3.1 m) square. Archaeologists refer to the smallest vertical excavations as "tests" or "test excavations."

Archaeologists at Fort Southwest Point, Tennessee, initially used vertical excavation as a quick and relatively easy way to locate old building foundations. They used a mechanical backhoe to cut two long, perpendicular trenches through the center of the site (Figure 8.3). One trench, running southeast to

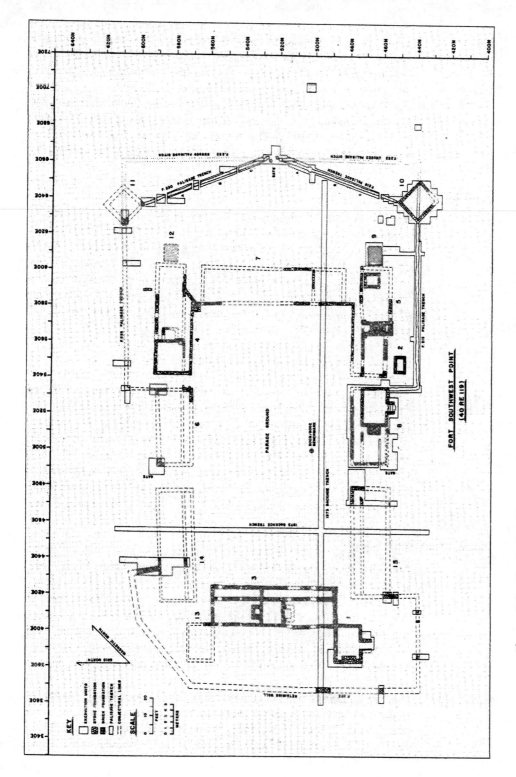

**Figure 8.3** Vertical and horizontal excavations at Fort Southwest Point, Tennessee, 1973–1986.

northwest, was 185 feet (56.4 m) long; the other, running southwest to northeast, extended for 300 feet (91.5 m). The second trench crossed six different walls. In the second season of research at the site, the crew excavated a number of 10-foot-squares (3.1 59 m). These excavations gave them more control than the mechanical excavation, but at the cost of much slower progress. The use of the smaller test excavations meant, however, that they could locate buried features more carefully. They could also simultaneously investigate several areas. They knew they could wait to conduct complete excavation of features until more funds became available.

Ten years passed before the State of Tennessee developed plans to reconstruct Fort Southwest Point. The archaeologists then had to alter their research design from merely locating foundations and other features to large-scale archaeological investigation planning to provide information that could be employed in the reconstruction. They continued to use limited vertical excavation to relocate the buried walls found earlier and to find still-undiscovered foundations, but their new research design called mostly for horizontal excavation.

Archaeologists use *horizontal excavation*, also called "area" or "block" excavation, to expose entire building foundations and large areas of sites. By exposing entire buildings, excavators can study the architecture, as well as the spatial relationships between wells, outbuildings, houses, dumps, and other features, to say nothing of the internal alterations made to a building over long periods.

**Figure 8.4**　Vertical trench excavation in the west wall of Southwest Point, Tennessee.

Horizontal excavation worked well at Fort Southwest Point, because the archaeologists wanted to expose entire building foundations. Before horizontal excavation, a probable building called Structure 8 appeared merely as a large depression on the northeast side of the fort. Excavation over this depression measured roughly 30 by 46 feet (9.2 by 14.0 m) in size (Figure 8.5). The archaeologists perfectly planned their excavation strategy because the building's foundation was only 22 feet wide and 43 feet long (6.7 by 13.1 m). The builders had positioned Structure 8 directly in front of the fort's front wall so that anyone approaching the fort would have encountered it rather than the exterior wall itself (Figure 8.6). Careful excavation of Structure 8 allowed archaeologists to envision how it had been built: "This 43 by 22 ft. building was almost certainly constructed of logs (but with plank floors) with a central chimney and a full-length front porch . . . it would have been two stories in height. . . . Windows were probably present on the side of the building facing the fort's interior but not on the exterior side. On the first floor, the central chimney no doubt had fireboxes on its east and west sides."

Archaeologists found three clay stairs at Structure 8 leading down to the building's cellar. This find caused them to wonder whether the fort's residents had used this building for storing valuable goods while the fort functioned as the Cherokee Indian Agency in the early nineteenth century. Local Native Americans were able to receive ploughs, spinning wheels, and other "civilizing" items from the U.S. government at Fort Southwest Point during this period. The fort's designers may have constructed the steps into the cellar so that Native Americans could receive their objects without actually entering the fort itself.

*Tools.*   Archaeological excavation is a deliberate, slow-moving process that requires infinite patience. Patience pays off, however, because, as excavations at Fort Southwest Point show, much can be revealed through painstaking excavation (Figure 8.7). The spade and the diamond-shaped "pointing trowel" constitute the symbols of archaeological excavation. Today's archaeologists can use everything from bulldozers to the finest brushes and dental picks. Any digging tool, even the bulldozer, can be useful in the hands of an expert. Archaeologists only use bulldozers and other pieces of heavy equipment when absolutely necessary, and for the most part, they prefer to rely on trowels and shovels.

The archaeologist's trowel is a remarkable implement, used both for straightening the edges of excavations and smoothing stratigraphic profiles, and for fine-grained digging of house foundations, hearths, and other features. It is most efficient when its long edges scrape delicately across damp soil, delineating the boundary between a dark, inconspicuous soil stain (like a posthole) and the surrounding lighter soil. No fieldworker ever walks without a trowel in hand, for it is the archaeologist's Swiss Army knife.

Archaeologists sometimes discover, however, that a trowel is simply too coarse a tool for the job at hand. Cleaning burials, exposing waterlogged plant remains, removing the soil from a decaying adobe wall—these tasks are the

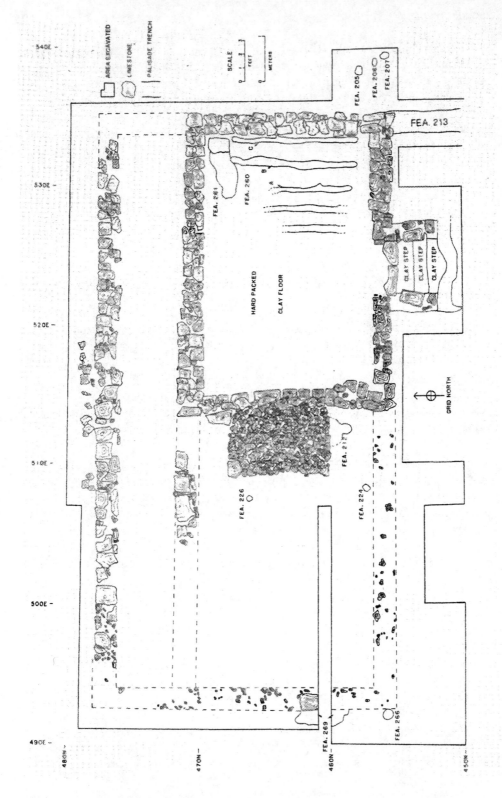

**Figure 8.5** Map of horizontal excavation of Structure 8, Fort Southwest Point, Tennessee.

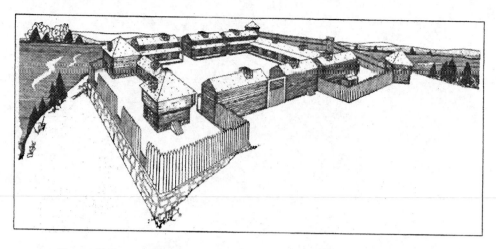

**Figure 8.6** Artist's reconstruction of Fort Southwest Point, Tennessee, based on archaeological findings. Structure 8 is to the right of the main gate. The entrance to the cellar appears in front.

"watchmaker's tasks" of archaeology, as Mortimer Wheeler once called them. The archaeologist hunched over an excavation carefully removing tiny grains of soil does bear a striking similarity to a watchmaker bent over the tiniest screws, springs, and gears. Both jobs require patience and skill. Dust pans, whisk brooms, paint brushes, dental picks, and even sharpened pieces of bamboo come into play at critical moments. Dental picks are especially useful when cleaning bones because their varied working edges allow archaeologists to scoop and scrape, lever, or dig tiny holes, just as your neighborhood dentist does on your teeth. Many archaeologists make friends with their dentists just to acquire their worn-out tools for the field!

Archaeologists regularly screen all, or in some cases a sizable portion, of the soil they excavate. This procedure is especially important in historical archaeology because the screens catch the smallest artifacts—straight pins, glass beads, buttons—that were used in homes across the world in modern times. The size of the screen mesh varies with the problem at hand, but most historical archaeologists prefer quarter-inch (6.35 mm) or even eight-inch (5.08 mm) mesh to recover glass beads and other tiny objects. Such tiny objects can offer great insights on the past, and so it is necessary that historical archaeologists do everything in their power to find them.

*Field Recording.* "Excavation, no matter how skillfully conducted, is sheer wasted effort unless the results are properly recorded." These words of Ivor Noël Hume's emphasize the need for careful record keeping in archaeological

**Figure 8.7**    Structure 8, Fort Southwest Point, Tennessee, before and after horizonital excavation.

research. Without accurate records, even the best excavation is an exercise in destruction. In the final analysis, every archaeological dig is only as good as the records that survive from it. Here are some of the day-to-day records kept on a well-organized excavation.

- *Field Notes.* Notes compiled during the progress of the fieldwork are the diary of the excavation. Their authors meticulously and thoroughly describe the daily activities on site. Field notes are the synthesis of the excavation and are the place where stratigraphy is initially analyzed and unfolding interpretations of the site are jotted down. They provide a record of the locations of structures and major finds. Field notes are compiled not only for the excavator's use, but also as a permanent record for posterity. Keepers of field notes should err on the side of overcoverage. Nothing is worse than inadequate notes that omit critical stratigraphic information or architectural data. The great Mesopotamian archaeologist Leonard Woolley used to inspect his assistants' field notes every evening. He was right, for these notes constitute our only insights into his most important excavations.

- *Site Maps and Plans.* This body of data from an excavation includes a detailed, scale map of the entire site, drawings of each excavation unit with stratigraphic profiles, a complete stratigraphic sequence of the entire site, plans of all human-built features, and architectural drawings if appropriate. Being made in the field, they constitute a directly observed record of the archaeological contexts that have been destroyed by excavation.

- *Artifact and Finds Inventory.* The inventory includes a complete list of all finds. Today, this list is most often stored on a computer, with specific find information entered into a database that can be accessed using any number of search commands.

- *Photographic Record.* The photographic record accompanies the maps, plans, and field notes as primary documentation of the excavation. The photo record is generally composed of black and white prints, color slides, and digital images. When compiled, the images show the progress of the entire excavation from start to finish. The photos are also necessary for the published report of the excavation because they depict important finds and architectural elements as they appeared during excavation.

- *Administrative Records and Accounts.* These records contain the practical aspect of the archaeological fieldwork. They include information about the crew's labor: when each person worked and how many hours they spent in the field. They also include a running total of the project's expenses so that the chief archaeologist can keep track of the day-to-day costs of the excavation. These records collectively provide an irreplaceable archive of the project. Even after the archaeologists have published their final report of the excavation, the administrative records are a vital part of the archaeological record and should be preserved as archival records.

## Conservation

The soil is often the archaeologist's worst enemy, for the vagaries of preservation play havoc on the archaeological record. Miracles of survival sometimes come to light, like the marvelous wooden artifacts and jewelry from Egyptian pharaoh Tutankhamun's tomb, or the Bronze Age wooden planks a foot wide and up to 8 feet long (0.3 to 2.4 m) from the waterlogged Bronze Age village at Flag Fen, England. Most often, however, natural soil chemicals cause both perishable wood and other organic artifacts and food remains to deteriorate and often to disappear completely. When Kenneth Kidd discovered the post holes at the Sainte Marie I site, all that remained were dark soil stains where the posts had once stood. The wood itself had long since rotted away because of the chemicals in the soil.

Luckily, not all objects disappear completely, even in the harshest of conditions. Ceramics, glass, and stone objects typically survive, even under the worst natural conditions. Objects of iron, lead, pewter, copper, gold, and silver can endure with the proper soil and climatic conditions, but they will probably vanish in time. Leather, wood, and even paper sometimes remain over short periods or in waterlogged or very dry conditions. When excavating Fort Bowie, a nineteenth-century U.S. Army post at Apache Pass, Arizona, archaeologists from the University of Arizona found soda pop bottles that still had remnants of the labels adhering to them. These bottles show that the soldiers at the fort drank strawberry soda, sarsaparilla with iron, and orange cider. When archaeologists examined the remains of the Missouri River steamer *Bertrand*, which hit a snag in the river and sank on April 1, 1865, they found several bottles and jars with their labels still intact. They also found numerous boxes stamped with the products' names, the wholesalers' names, their places of origin, and their final destinations in the American West.

Artifact conservation is a serious and difficult task, and conservator Per Guldbeck's description is appropriate: "sometimes likened to the dramatic stories of surgeons saving people from the consequences of disease or accident." Like surgeons, artifact conservators must be highly and intensively educated with equal doses of common sense, knowledge of chemistry, and patience. Laboratory conservation is rarely dramatic. It is typically a slow process that involves weeks, even months, of delicate renovation, soaking organic materials in chemicals, and devising ingenious restoration techniques. The procedures are largely routine and well established, the hardest part being to judge when the expense of permanent conservation is justified. Complete conservation is usually reserved only for artifacts destined for museum display or for unusually important and unique finds.

Some of the most dramatic conservation efforts come in the field, as archaeologists struggle to save a unique, delicate artifact from destruction. Ivor Noël Hume's discovery of an early seventeenth-century close helmet at Wolstenholme Towne is a perfect example.

The excavators there faced a challenging problem: how to remove the helmet so that conservators could stabilize it for study and museum display? When first unearthed, the helmet was no longer actually iron; it had been reduced to a rusty ferrous shell encased in clay. If its discoverers attempted to remove the shell like any other artifact, they would have utterly destroyed it. The conservators devised a simple scheme to remove the helmet from the surrounding soil. They built a steel box frame around it, then poured a silicone molding compound into the box. The 200-pound (91 kg) load was then winched out of the ground and taken to the laboratory for further conservation. The removal of the boxed helmet from the field took two full days. By the time the excavators found a second helmet close by, the conservators had devised a new system of recovery. The steel box and molding compound were replaced with strips of fiberglass screen softened with glue. The conservators carefully placed these strips over the helmet's shell, and applied wet paper and plaster-of-paris to the screen. The conservators used this method to remove the entire compound in an old tire. The second helmet was thus much lighter and easier to transport.

The second phase of the conservation process took place in the laboratory. Colonial Williamsburg conservator Gary McQuillen used small tools to remove the dirt from the inside of the helmet. He pried off the plaster and dissolved the screen and the glue. He next used a tiny air-blasting gun to remove the surface of the rust, often leaving the helmet only a millimeter thick in places. McQuillen's dedication and delicate work of conservation brought the helmet back to life, and it now serves as a triumphant centerpiece in The Winthrop Rockefeller Archaeology Museum at the Wolstenholme Towne site in Williamsburg.

Conservation can reveal information that may remain hidden on a poorly preserved artifact. A skilled conservator can reveal corroded design features, discover identifying makers' marks, and make otherwise deteriorated artifacts easier to identify and study.

Conservation has been highly successful at Fort Michilimackinac, Michigan. Decades of excavation have yielded thousands of metal objects, including knives, forks and spoons, flintlock gun parts, and tools of all sorts. Most of these objects required conservation treatment before archaeologists could study them. Conserved military buttons have helped to identify the individual regiments that served in the fort. Records say that the British Tenth Regiment served at Michilimackinac between 1772 and 1774. Many pewter buttons, emblazoned with a large "10," confirm the official documents. Other buttons, marked with a raised "RI 18," belonged to the British Eighteenth, or Royal Irish, Regiment. This unit is known to have served in the American Revolution in 1777, but records do not indicate that any of its members were garrisoned at Fort Michilimackinac. Only the buttons tell this tiny piece of history.

## BACK TO THE LABORATORY

For all the glamour of excavation, most research time is spent back in the laboratory, working on artifacts and other finds in far more detail than is possible in the field. It is here, in much greater comfort and with better facilities, that the long process of classifying artifacts unfolds.

## Classifying and Grouping Historical Artifacts

Everyone arranges objects as part of day-to-day living. We classify eating utensils—knives, forks, and spoons—because each one looks unique and has a different use. Many of us even keep each utensil in a separate compartment in the drawer. We classify roads according to their surface finishes and distinguish minivans from trucks. We group lifestyles, artifacts, even cultures, and make choices between them. By the same token, archaeologists arrange artifacts, not in the same way we do in everyday life, but as a means of ordering their excavated data. Without some form of ordering system, the past would appear as chaos, a jumble of artifacts with no apparent similarities.

Archaeological arrangements are artificial formulations based on criteria devised by archaeologists. Archaeological arrangement is a way of imparting meaning to artifacts. The classificatory systems do not necessarily coincide with those used by the people who made and used the original artifacts. Ordering is a process that creates units that can have meaning based on function (knives, forks, spoons), shape (round buttons, square buttons), style (red glass beads, blue glass beads, white glass beads with blue and red stripes), and material of manufacture (copper pots, brass pots, iron pots).

The arrangement of artifacts has four main objectives:

1. *To organize data into manageable units.* This means separating ceramic sherds from metal objects, bone tools from leather garments—preliminary data processing.
2. *To describe units.* By identifying the individual characteristics (or attributes) of hundreds of artifacts, or clusters of artifacts, archaeologists can arrange them in terms of their attributes into relatively few units. Such units are economical ways of comparing large numbers of artifacts.
3. *To provide a hierarchy of units, which orders the relationships between them.* The units stem, in part, from the use of a variety of raw materials, manufacturing techniques, and functions.
4. *To study artifact variability.* Arrangement provides an easy way to compare different artifact assemblages, and to study the differences and similarities between them.

Archaeologists engage in two kinds of artifact arrangement: *classification and grouping*. In classification, the archaeologist uses units of arrangement that exist prior to the excavation. Each category is mutually exclusive, so when archaeologists sort the excavated artifacts, they know immediately into which category a particular artifact belongs. Suppose we plan to excavate a site that we know from historical records was inhabited from 1750–1830. Before beginning our excavation, we may decide to sort the artifacts into six categories: ceramics, glass, iron, nonferrous metal, bone, and other materials. Our central rule of classification is thus "material of manufacture." But we could also choose to sort the artifacts into only two units: ceramics and non-ceramics, or we could use three units: glass, bone, and neither glass nor bone. The point is that the units exist before the excavation, and the archaeologist, after excavation, must sort the recovered artifacts into the preexisting units.

No prearranged units exist in grouping. In this method of division, the archaeologist permits the artifacts to establish the units. A category called "iron" would not exist in a collection that contains no iron objects.

The arrangement of artifacts into classes and groups is a difficult process. Historical archaeologists, however, are often aided by the presence of systems of *folk classification*, or arrangements created by the people who made and used the excavated artifacts. Historical archaeologists can often learn the past systems from textual sources, like potters' records, newspaper ads, and public notices. The original system employed by the artifact makers and users makes the task of ordering immeasurably more straightforward, because the units formulated by archaeologists coincide with those used in the past. Ceramics are perhaps the most common body of artifacts from modern-era sites, and luckily for historical archaeologists, many of their mass-produced forms are well documented in contemporary records.

Between 1640 and 1680, English artist Randle Holme tried to record and draw the objects, including ceramics, with which he was familiar. Holme was in the process of researching the symbols of English heraldry for a book published in 1688. He showed that the terms used for ceramics could be confusing. For instance, the following terms could all be used to describe a "dish": platter, dish, midleing dish, broth dish, bason [basin], sallet dish, trencher plate or plate, and saucer. Later, the anonymous author of *The Complete Appraiser* (1770) was more precise than Holme. He used measurements to distinguish between the different kinds of ceramic vessels. He said that "plates" were between $7\frac{3}{4}$ inches (19.7 cm) and $9\frac{3}{4}$ inches (24.8 cm) in diameter, whereas "dishes" ranged from $10\frac{3}{4}$ inches (27.3 cm) to 28 inches (71.1 cm) across.

The arrangements presented by Randle Holme and by the author of *The Complete Appraiser* are folk classifications. Each sorted material culture—in this case, ceramic dishes—in a way that made sense to the people who used it. Folk ordering systems are important to historical archaeologists, because they provide a foundation for understanding how people in the past used and thought about their material culture. As is true of all classifications, they exist independent of any excavated sample of artifacts.

Mary Beaudry of Boston University and five colleagues used folk classifications to develop an ordering system for colonial ceramics from domestic sites in the Chesapeake region of Maryland and Virginia. Their Potomac Typological System, or POTS, was based on the work of Randle Holme, the author of *The Complete Appraiser*, and several probate inventories. They used the probate lists to understand the range of vessels present in the colonial Chesapeake, and to give them insight into the terms used to describe them. For example, the inventory of Francis Lewis, who died in 1677, lists "2 pewter dishes, 3 plates, 2 porringers"; the inventory of Robert Slye's slave quarters, for the year 1671, includes "1 iron bottle, 1 iron pot, 1 frying pan."

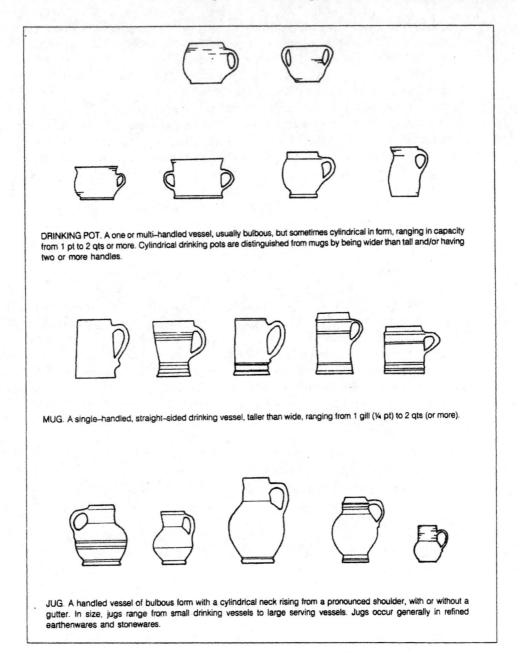

DRINKING POT. A one or multi–handled vessel, usually bulbous, but sometimes cylindrical in form, ranging in capacity from 1 pt to 2 qts or more. Cylindrical drinking pots are distinguished from mugs by being wider than tall and/or having two or more handles.

MUG. A single–handled, straight-sided drinking vessel, taller than wide, ranging from 1 gill (¼ pt) to 2 qts (or more).

JUG. A handled vessel of bulbous form with a cylindrical neck rising from a pronounced shoulder, with or without a gutter. In size, jugs range from small drinking vessels to large serving vessels. Jugs occur generally in refined earthenwares and stonewares.

**Figure 8.8**   Seventeenth-century ceramic vessel forms in the Chesapeake.

POTS is an elaborate, widely used system with a basis in solid historical fact. Beaudry and her colleagues defined twenty-eight separate types of ceramics used in the seventeenth century (Figure 8.8). Their system includes vessel forms recognized today: cups, saucers, jugs, and candlesticks. But many of the forms are no longer used today and so may strike us as curious. For instance, a "costrel" is a jug or bottle with two handles. Travelers and field laborers used these vessels as drink containers, much like canteens. A "sillabub pot" was a short, squat pot with two handles and a spout like a tea kettle. It was used for serving sillabub (wine or liquor mixed with sweetened milk or cream), posset (hot, sweetened milk curdled with wine or ale), and wassail (ale or wine spiced with roasted apples and sugar).

The ordering system POTS is a good example of how historical archaeologists can use textual sources and archaeological finds to create a useful analytical tool. Systems like POTS order the artifacts but retain the historical integrity of the folk classification.

All archaeological interpretation is rooted in theory. It is to this topic that we must now turn.

## TIME TRAVEL

### Fresh Water Pond, New York City, 1810–1834

In its earliest years, the City of New York was largely restricted to the southern tip of Manhattan. As the area's population grew, the city expanded up Manhattan into a region of pastures and unimproved, simple roadways. A major geographic feature of this area was a large, circular body of water known as the "Collect Pond" or the "Fresh Water Pond." The availability of useful water had encouraged several industries, including tanneries, to locate near the pond. From this rural location they could make their products unhindered, and then transport them for sale to the city at relatively little expense. Late-eighteenth-century tanneries, however, were not environmentally friendly, and they quickly polluted the pond. With the expansion of the city, the city leaders realized that the industries occupied increasingly valuable land. Thus, seeking to integrate this area into the fabric of the city, they order the pond filled and a new street, Anthony Street, to be constructed across its southwestern edge. By 1814, the Fresh Water Pond had disappeared. Some of the industrialist sued the city for forcing them to uproot their businesses, but other owners saw a bright future in renting space to newly arrived households and shopkeepers. The area just south of the Fresh Water Pond came to be called the Five Points, because of the five corners created by the intersection of Anthony, Cross, and Orange streets.

Many of the men and women who moved into the working-class neighborhood near the old Collect Pond were free African Americans. They came as a result of emancipation and because of earlier migrations of other African American families. They also believed that they could live in the burgeoning city relatively anonymously and also find work with little

*(continued)*

*Source:* Claudia Milne. 2002. "On the Grounds of the Fresh Water Pond: The Free-Black Community at Five Points, 1810–1834." *International Journal of Historical Archaeology* 6:127–142.

problem. Early-nineteenth-century census records reveal that this area had the highest percentage of free black households in lower Manhattan. The heads of these households were artisans—shoemakers, carpenters, and laborers—or seamstresses and domestics.

Between 1810 and 1820, many free blacks in the city lived with white families. New York state law decreed that all children born into slavery after July 4, 1799, were legally free. Even so, the law also said that females were required to be "in service" until age twenty-five; males until twenty-eight. The "in service" requirement effectively meant that many legally free men and women were essentially enslaved within white households. Some of these individuals were able to negotiate the terms of their indenture and to make cash payments to ensure their freedom. When freed of their indenture commitments, if they had them, many African Americans choose to move to the Five Points area. Some support groups, such as the African Mutual Relief Society, offered assistance and aid to in-migrating African Americans.

New York's African American community also established numerous cultural institutions in the area, including several churches of different denominations and schools. These centers had many functions, including providing the community's civic leadership and offering the nucleus for political activities. The community also started a newspaper called *Freedom's Journal* that argued against slavery, oppressive anti-black legislation, and colonization.

The African American community was understandably opposed to the continuation of enslavement, and they accordingly staged anti-slavery protests in 1810, 1819, 1826, and 1832. Human bondage was *the* controversial issue of the nineteenth century, and debate over it threatened to destroy the United States. The waves of European immigrants who settled in New York in the early decades of the nineteenth century did not necessarily share the African American community's views on slavery, and conflicts erupted as both views were given voice and put in print.

Working-class people from both the African American and the European immigrant communities also tended to view each other as possible competitors for jobs. Many Europeans had moved into the cheap accommodations of the Five Points area as well, and the proximity of individuals with widely differing viewpoints fostered conflict and disagreement. Public meetings were organized to promote both abolition and anti-abolition perspectives, and violent mobs often surged through the city's streets. Conflict culminated with five nights' of violence during the summer of 1834, with pro-slavery supporters attacking the homes of prominent non–African American merchants and ministers who argued for abolition. Vandalism soon spread beyond their homes and even the African Mutual Relief Society was attacked. Windows were smashed, and several residences and businesses were burned to the ground. Such racism and hostility, coupled with rising rents and competition over jobs convinced many of the neighborhood's African Americans to seek employment and residence elsewhere.

# Chapter 9

# Interpreting the Historical Past

*"Look not mournfully into the past."*

Henry Wadsworth Longfellow, 1839

Of all the many subfields of archaeology, none is more multidisciplinary in its perspective than historical archaeology. Historical archaeologists draw on ideas and concepts from many disciplines, including anthropology, history, geography, sociology, and landscape architecture. In this chapter, we discuss some of the theoretical approaches that form the basis for the interpretation of the archaeological record from historic sites.

Many students tend to shy away from the more theoretical aspects of archaeology. This is unfortunate because theory forms the discipline's core. No one should be afraid of theory; it simply constitutes the ways in which various archaeologists think the past should be interpreted. Each archaeologist brings to the field his or her own preconceptions, outlooks, and experience and, as archaeologists struggle to make sense of the past, they tend to present it in different ways. They emphasize certain elements of the past and downplay others. Human history represents a complex interconnected series of personal interactions, motivations, and actions, and deciphering them with archaeological information is difficult. The only reasonable place to begin is with one's understanding of "how the world works": what is important to emphasize and what we can afford to ignore.

Archaeologists can disagree about one another's interpretations, and sometimes these arguments can be quite heated. Individual archaeologists believe in their interpretations and the vast majority of archaeologists offer views of the past that they believe are as correct as the information will permit. Archaeologists accordingly tend to stand by their interpretations. But disagreements about theory are honest differences of opinion. They are not setbacks, but collective achievements in interpretation. Theory thus presents a rich area of study for all archaeologists, including those examining modern history.

In this book, we can only present three broad theoretical approaches in historical archaeology: humanistic, scientific, and humanistic science. Students must understand that these are not the only approaches possible. Individual archaeologists are constantly working to present new theoretical approaches that have the potential to provide greater insights about the past.

## HUMANISTIC HISTORICAL ARCHAEOLOGY

Humanism is a philosophy that focuses on the inherent dignity of humanity, on the potentials, sensibilities, and actions of real men and women. The humanistic approach is expressed well by historical reconstructions that attempt to put today's visitors in touch with their historical counterparts by showing how people in the past lived. Historical reconstructions at "living museums" that seek to place the modern visitor "inside" the past are humanistic in their basic framework. As we have seen at Colonial Williamsburg, Virginia, and Greenfield Village, Michigan (Chapter 3), the act of taking visitors back in time usually involves not only documents, but also artifacts and buildings. The material remains of the past—chairs, glass tumblers, knives and forks—can create powerful impressions in the minds of onlookers. Museum reconstructions are vivid ways of bringing the past alive by using both commonplace and more exotic artifacts to recreate the human dimension of a once-bustling building or community.

Humanistic historical archaeology is often associated with the physical reconstruction of buildings, but not invariably. In a classic study of the late 1960s, Robert Ascher and Charles Fairbanks provided a compelling picture of slavery by adopting a humanistic approach. They excavated the ruins of a slave cabin on Rayfield Plantation on Cumberland Island, directly off the coast of Georgia. Some of the largest and richest estates in the hemisphere were located in this region. Ascher and Fairbanks estimated that enslaved men and women had lived in the cabin from about 1834, when Robert Stafford bought Rayfield, until the end of the American Civil War in 1865. A brick chimney was all that remained of the cabin a century later. Ascher and Fairbanks said their goal in excavating was "to discover and convey a sense of daily life as it might have been experienced by the people who lived in the cabin." They adopted a unique approach to help bring enslavement to life. They interspersed their archaeological report—the basic stratigraphic drawings and excavation photographs—with a literary "soundtrack" taken from primary documentary sources. They quoted the great African American orator Frederick Douglass speaking about what it was like to be considered property: "I had now a new conception of my degraded condition. Prior to this, I had become, if not insensible to my lot, at least partly so." Ascher and Fairbanks also found a list of enslaved people in an archive, men and women who had been sold to Stafford as part of the plantation in April, 1834. This simple list, when united with the physical remains of the cabin, offered a profoundly human portrait of life in bondage. Such a picture adds depth to their archaeological finding that "Life inside the cabin produced an ash layer that eventually spilled out of the fireplace and onto the floor where the sand turned a darker color through time and use." Through their masterful combination of historical and archaeological source materials, Ascher and Fairbanks linked the differences they observed in the soil layers at the cabin site with the lives of once-living, real men and women. They created a human picture of slave life and placed us in the slave cabin without actually building a physical replica. Their illustration of a tiny, blue-glass bead found inside the cabin remains makes us wonder who had worn this bead and what was it like living in lifelong bondage? Slavery was not an abstraction to Ascher and Fairbanks; it was the deeply personal experience of real men and women.

The roots of humanism in historical archaeology go back to the field's earliest days, to the time when historical archaeology was associated almost totally with the discipline of history. When John Cotter excavated Jamestown in the 1950s, one of his primary goals was to summarize the archaeological findings "so as to indicate the way of life which was developing in Virginia during the 17th century." When Kenneth Kidd studied the mission of Sainte Marie I in Ontario, Canada, in the 1940s, his intention was to provide information about "the activities of the Jesuit Fathers in the decade of their residence among the Huron Indians." These archaeologists viewed their research as part of the study of history as a humanistic discipline. In 1964, Ivor Noël Hume described the fledgling field of historical archaeology as the "handmaiden to history." He meant this colorful phrase to suggest that historical archaeologists complement the humanistic side of historical study.

The humanistic approach remains a pervasive and fruitful thread through historical archaeology to this day, even though many archaeologists have adopted a more overtly scientific approach. The more scientific approaches, however, do not diminish the importance of the humanistic approaches, and both are able to exist side by side in today's historical archaeology.

### Humanistic Archaeology at Kingsmill

A model example of humanistic historical archaeology is William Kelso's 1984 study of seven plantations at Kingsmill, near Williamsburg, Virginia. Kelso, Director of Archaeology for the Association for the Preservation of Virginia Antiquities, is a social historian who has considerable experience and expertise using historical archaeology as a tool for understanding colonial Virginia.

The subtitle of his book *Kingsmill Plantations, 1619–1800: Archaeology of Country Life in Colonial Virginia*, aptly summarizes Kelso's perspective, for he was interested in presenting a well-developed picture of past seventeenth- and eighteenth-century life in Virginia. Kelso accordingly concentrated on three central elements of the past: history, things, and people. He reconstructed the historical context of colonial Virginia from primary documents, and recounted the rise of the tobacco economy, the incidents of Bacon's Rebellion in 1676, and the steady advance of the Virginian frontier as it moved inland from the coast. Kelso realized that historical events are situated within a physical environment that is partly composed of things: "colonial Virginians surrounded themselves with an evolving material culture that from documents alone is difficult to reconstruct."

Housing constitutes a central feature of material culture, and one of Kelso's goals was to explain the changes in housing styles in colonial Virginia. History shows that many English men and women in colonial Virginia ceased living in small "earthfast" homes—with dirt floors and upright support posts buried in the ground—and began to inhabit brick homes built as a result of the plantation economy. Kelso's research with estate records showed that "what people furnished their houses with varied considerably, so much so that it is difficult to generalize for any one period or class." An individual family's dishes, their wine bottles, and their furniture can thus only be reconstructed from archaeological finds.

Without people, none of the historical events of the Kingsmill area (recounted in historical records), and not one material object (illuminated from the archaeological research) could exist. To help bring the historical actors into focus, Kelso concentrated on the area's elites because they were the people who wrote about themselves and who, in turn, were written about by others. Enslaved men and women were seldom written about in any great detail.

Kelso introduced us to individuals such as Humphrey Higginson, who "arrived in Virginia in 1635, soon married into the 700-acre [283 ha] Tuttey's Neck land and, with the rank of captain, soon added the 320-acre [130 ha] Harrop tract to his growing Kingsmill estate." We also learned of George Percy, Jamestown's "lieutenant governor," who described the Kingsmill area in 1607 as a bountiful paradise: "The soil was good and fruitful, with excellent good timber. There are also great stores of vines in bigness of a man's thigh, running up to the tops of trees in great abundance. We also did see many squirrels, conies, blackbirds."

Kelso's archaeological research at the seven Kingsmill sites encompassed the full range of colonial society, including the excavation of planter's mansions and slave quarters. His strategy relied on horizontal excavation, so he was able to provide maximum information about housing conditions and site layout (Figure 9.1). We can thus easily see the social distinctions between the owners and the enslaved men and women. As Kelso noted, "Certain reasonably clear patterns emerge from the comparison of the Kingsmill archaeological remains. The reasons for the similarities and their cultural meaning are not so easy to grasp. There are definite settlement patterns, certain architectural traditions, an evolving landscape architecture, and consistency in certain aspects of slave life." Large-scale, eighteenth-century planters chose prominent locations for their mansions and built impressive, formal gardens. Slaves constructed root cellars in their homes, possibly without their masters' knowledge, and made do (Figure 9.2). These images emerge from Kelso's humanistic perspective. From him we learn to "reconstruct the setting within which landlords and laborers went about their lives within Virginia's tobacco empire."

**Figure 9.1** Horizontal excavation of Burwell mansion and kitchen, Kingsmill, Virginia, 1975.

## SCIENTIFIC HISTORICAL ARCHAEOLOGY

When American archaeologists "discovered" anthropology in the 1960s (Chapter 2), they also embraced the scientific method. In their attempts to make anthropological archaeology more rigorous, a number of excavators urged their colleagues to conduct research that was explicitly scientific. They argued that archaeologists should be able to meet the highest scientific standards in their research, and that they should devise intricate models of past societies that could be tested with carefully designed hypotheses. Archaeologists should strive, they said, to contribute to knowledge of human life by discovering general laws of behavior. In their view, the final goal for scientific archaeologists should be to explain the complex cultural processes that govern human life throughout history.

Interest in scientific archaeology exploded in archaeology in the late 1960s and 1970s. The leading proponent of an explicitly scientific perspective in historical archaeology was Stanley South from the University of South Carolina. His

**Figure 9.2** Excavated root cellar of a slave cabin, Kingsmill, Virginia.

book *Method and Theory in Historical Archaeology*, first published in 1977, was a clarion call for historical archaeologists to be overtly scientific in their research.

South believed that the route toward a scientific historical archaeology must start with archaeologists being able to recognize patterns among the artifacts they excavate. He argued that men and women living within a cultural tradition should have left the same kinds of artifacts, in roughly similar percentages, in the soils of their past residences. Sites inhabited by peoples from different cultural traditions should present artifact patterns that are distinct. How can archaeologists discover the patterns? According to South, the answer rested in quantifying the artifacts into categories. The categories he used were: Kitchen, Bone, Architectural, Furniture, Arms, Clothing, Personal, Tobacco Pipe, and Activities. South devised these general classes of artifacts during his study of several colonial sites—from dwellings to forts—in the Carolinas. To discern the pattern represented in any artifact collection, an archaeologist must compute the percentage of each class. Some sites are characterized by large numbers of architectural artifacts (like nails) and almost no tobacco pipes, while others have high percentages of kitchen (dishes and bottles) and architectural artifacts and almost no furniture objects.

Once computed, South's patterns could be used to construct theories of behavior that could be tested at new sites. If an archaeologist discovered a new pattern, then the people who lived at that site could be assumed to have been culturally different from the people who created the already identified patterns. South believed that the continuing process of site excavation, pattern recognition, and site testing would lead to a truly scientific archaeology that could be as rigorous as chemistry or physics (Figure 9.3). He also thought that historical

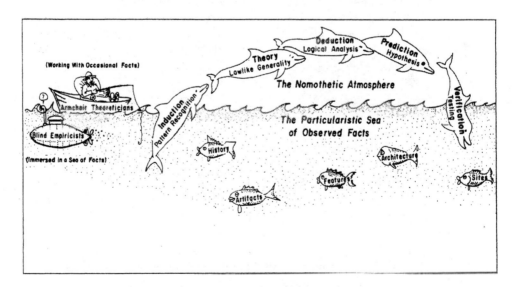

**Figure 9.3** South's flowchart showing the scientific method. The archaeologist should follow the path of the dolphin.

archaeology could only receive the attention and respect it deserves by using rigorous scientific methods.

Many archaeologists immediately found South's ideas appealing. It presented a straightforward way to analyze the mass of archaeological finds from the smallest to the largest site. Simple artifact identification and comparison was all that was required to determine whether the newly excavated site was just like any of the others for which a pattern had already had been calculated.

### Scientific Historical Archaeology at Camden

Archaeologist Kenneth Lewis conducted a study explicitly following the scientific methodology outlined by South. Lewis, now at Michigan State University, focused on a town called Camden, in north-central South Carolina.

During the height of the American Revolution in 1780, British soldiers built Camden in the South Carolina backcountry. They originally intended it as one of a chain of posts across the state that would secure the region for the British. Camden's geographical position made it a perfect communication hub for the frontier, and the British soon used it as a central redistribution point for war munitions coming inland from Charleston. They fortified the town (Figure 9.4), and two battles were fought nearby. Camden continued to function as a frontier center after the war, and it rapidly grew in importance. As the town prospered, new residents moved to the town's north side, and by 1812, they had abandoned much of the old town.

In the mid-1970s, Lewis was given the opportunity to excavate part of the old town. The Camden Historical Commission wished to develop the site, and they needed specific architectural information that only archaeology could supply. Lewis excavated along the southwest palisade of the town and on a small part of its interior. Rather than offer a humanistic portrait of daily life in Camden, Lewis chose an overtly scientific research plan that focused on the town's place in the South Carolina frontier.

Lewis began by constructing a frontier model that emphasized "primarily cultural change among intrusive cultures faced with adaptation to a frontier situation." He built the model using a number of generalizations drawn from anthropological and historical literature. His first generalization was that "complexly organized intrusive societies react or adapt in a patterned way to the conditions imposed by a frontier situation." This means that settlers in a new environment will react to a frontier situation in a nonrandom, or patterned, way. This patterned reaction will be cultural, based on the people's traditional concepts of what is important, how they should act, and so forth. Another generalization was that "as the colony moves through time it also travels through space, expanding with the influx of new settlers." Lewis devised eleven hypotheses from these generalizations "around which new data may be organized and analyzed." One such hypothesis was that "the colonial settlement tended to lie adjacent to the significant routes of transportation and communication connecting Camden with the outside world."

**Figure 9.4** 1781 map of Camden, South Carolina.

Lewis used vertical excavations—small trenches and test units—to evaluate his hypotheses (Figure 9.5). For example, the spatial distribution of architectural artifacts—nails and bricks—convinced him that seventeen buildings had indeed been built next to the roads that ran through old Camden. This finding lead him to conclude that his hypothesis about the settlement pattern was confirmed: "the general form of the colonial occupation at Camden is basically that of an English two-row settlement, with a single main street and 2 cross-streets."

Lewis's study of Camden is scientific in tone and scope. He included no artifact photographs or drawings, and he did not focus on important individuals or interpret how significant historical events affected the townspeople. His focus was on the process of frontier settlement: how the settlement pattern of the town changed over time, how Camden fitted into the frontier economy as a

**Figure 9.5**   Row of bricks in excavation unit at Camden, South
Carolina, 1975.

communication center, and how Native American villages were not a barrier to
the expansion of the frontier. He provided a picture of how Camden, as a frontier
town, was part of a larger process of European settlement and life in the New
World. The Camden study brings science to the core of historical archaeology and
opts for scientific precision as a way of examining changes in a historic community over time.

## HUMANISTIC SCIENCE IN HISTORICAL ARCHAEOLOGY

Interest in scientific historical archaeology peaked in the 1970s, and since then
most historical archaeologists have pursued a perspective that is not easily characterized simply as either humanistic or scientific. Perhaps the best term for this
varied perspective is "humanistic science," because most practitioners have
adopted something from both humanism and science. Many historical archaeologists seek to contribute something meaningful to knowledge about past daily life,
as would the humanist, but as anthropologists, most would also not wish to leave

social science behind. Most historical archaeologists therefore adopt a middle course and blend the humanistic and scientific perspectives.

The union of science and humanism has bred many innovative perspectives and has given a dynamic excitement to the field. Historical archaeologists are actively pushing the boundaries of knowledge by presenting and exploring new approaches and interpretations. Here we focus only on the work of two major theorists, James Deetz and Mark Leone, both of whom have a considerable following in historical archaeology.

### Historical Structuralism

The approach used by the late James Deetz may best be described as *historical structuralism*. Deetz, a former professor of anthropology at the University of Virginia, began by studying the late prehistoric and early historic Arikaras, village-dwelling, horticultural Native Americans who lived along the Missouri River in today's South Dakota. His doctoral dissertation, published in 1965, was part of the movement to test the waters of process-oriented, scientific archaeology. Using archaeological information collected from Arikara sites, Deetz sought to determine whether he could observe a correlation between the pottery they made and the dramatic social transformations they experienced after contact with Europeans. Their numbers dropped precipitously as they suffered from new diseases, they steadily moved their villages further and further up the Missouri River, and they changed their ideas about where newly married couples should live. The Arikaras traditionally had a residence pattern with a rule that newly married couples should live in the villages of the bride's family. They moved their villages north as deadly epidemics spread and as hostile neighbors encroached on their lands. They abandoned the custom of matrilocality for a more liberal one that was not so strict about post-marriage residence. Deetz wondered whether these significant cultural changes could be observed in their pottery. Women made the pots of the Arikaras, and girls learned the craft of pottery manufacture from their mothers or grandmothers. Deetz wanted to know whether the movement of girls away from their maternal kin had any affect on their pottery.

When Deetz studied the pottery excavated from a number of village sites along the Missouri River, he observed that over time the pottery did indeed show an increased irregularity of design elements. He expected that with the decline of matrilocality, female potters moved away from the villages of their birth and maternal kin. In the new arrangement, any single village could contain female potters originally from several, once widely spaced villages. The mixing of women from different maternal lineages meant that several styles of pottery could appear within the same village, as women continued to make the kind of pottery with which they were familiar. Deetz's research suggested that the maximum stress among the Arikaras occurred between 1720 and 1750, the time of greatest variability in their pottery.

Deetz's study, though criticized by many other archaeologists, quickly became a classic because his method was scientific and his perspective was anthropological. Over the next several years, however, Deetz turned away from the study of historic Native Americans to investigate America's earliest colonial English settlers. It was as part of this effort that he developed his structuralist approach.

Structuralism is a perspective that aims to discover the hidden themes and relations in a culture. It has a complex history as a major theoretical approach in anthropology, beginning with the work of a number of French scholars, most notably sociologist, Emile Durkheim, and cultural anthropologist, Claude Levi-Strauss. They and their followers developed structuralism partly in reaction to another pervasive theoretical perspective, *functionalism*. Functionalists are interested in learning how cultural institutions fit together and work in conjunction to maintain a culture. Proponents of functionalism tend to see culture as composed of several individual institutions that, like the pieces of a jigsaw puzzle, can be assembled and understood in their totality. The job of the functionalist anthropologist is to study cultural institutions—marriage, kinship, cosmology—and to determine how they fit together. Structuralists found the functional view inadequate because it never explained a culture's deeper structures. How did the social institutions actually work? Instead of being interested in the pieces of the puzzle—as are functionalists—structuralists are interested in the driveshaft that causes the machine to cut the pieces into their individual shapes. Their interest lies in the deep structures of culture.

Deetz was strongly drawn to structuralism, but only when combined "with a strong dose of old fashioned historiography." He drew much of his intellectual inspiration from the research of folklorist Henry Glassie. In his widely read *Folk Housing in Middle Virginia*, published in 1975, Glassie presented a structuralist interpretation of vernacular architecture in two Virginia counties. His goal was to write a "grammar" of vernacular architecture that would show the choices individual builders had available to them when they raised a new house. When it came to deciding the location of house's various features—fireplace, stairway, hall, porch—builders faced almost countless options. They could locate a stairway in a public or a private space, enclose a porch to make an artificial climate or leave it off entirely, cluster their outbuildings in one spot or scatter them across the backyard. That vernacular builders consistently choose certain options meant that they were all following some deep structure, some patterned logic of the culture. Structuralists tend to believe that this logic is like the grammar of a language.

Glassie focused specifically on standing buildings, but Deetz chose several kinds of material culture in his effort to study the deep structure of the colonial mind. Arguing that material culture is "the track of our collective existence," Deetz examined tombstones, house designs, ceramic colors, customs of eating, and music, and he discerned significant changes over time. For example, eighteenth-century tombstones underwent a dramatic change. In the early years of the century, craftsmen put images of skulls on gravestones, but in the later years they carved angelic cherubs on them (Figure 9.6). During the same period, butchers

**Figure 9.6**   Colonial gravestone in New England.

changed from hacking cuts of meat from the carcass with chopping tools to removing them carefully with saws. Deetz also noticed that ceramics also underwent a transformation. By the late eighteenth century, bone white dishes had
replaced the once-fashionable browns, greens, and yellows.

Deetz perceived these dramatic changes in material culture as purposeful
and interconnected. Tombstone carvers simply did not grow tired of the death-
head patterns, just as ceramic makers did not stop making earth-tone vessels on
a whim. Deetz argued instead that all of the changes he observed in material

culture—from houses to cuts of meat—represented what he called the "Georgian mind set." This term referred to the way Englishmen and women saw the world during the reigns of the English kings George—I, II, and III (1714–1820). A series of structural rules—the grammar—operated behind this mind set to arrange culture, to order things in a certain way. Deetz believed that each culture has these rules and, even though their members may not be aware of them, archaeologists can observe them in material culture. The death's head on a tombstone is a powerful emotional device connoting Puritan orthodoxy, whereas the angel suggests a liberalization of Puritanism and the rise of an intellectual belief system. The use of a saw to remove meat from a carcass denotes the rise of individualism through the use of "portion control." Hacked cuts were imprecise and impersonal; sawn portions were neat and individualized. The popularity of white dishes symbolized a movement away from nature and toward artificiality. The change in dish color did not merely represent a technological innovation; it hid a deep meaning, a structure that the entirety of a culture's material objects represent.

Many of Deetz's colleagues and students have followed his theoretical lead. These archaeologists have for the most part sought to use his ideas and general approach as a starting point for their own research. One such archaeologist is Martin Hall, a professor of historical archaeology at the University of Cape Town, South Africa. In a paper published in 1992, Hall built on Deetz's historical structuralism by adding the idea of "discourse." A "discourse" is created by the interaction, the "conversation," among material objects, written texts, and spoken words. The "conversation" of things takes place within a specific historical context. No formal laws of the human mind exist in such settings, only discourses that make their own rules as they develop. The rules make sense within the cultural tradition, and much of the discourse is symbolic.

Hall used Westover Plantation, the colonial estate owned by the powerful Byrds of Virginia, to illustrate his point. A purely structural analysis of the plantation would tend to push the Byrds, as historical actors, into the background. The way they built their mansion, the position of their slave quarters, the very dishes from which they ate, would all be structured by the Enlightenment Mind, a frame of thought that also includes "the Georgian mansions of England, Mozart's music, Jane Austen's novels, and formal gardens." In Hall's discursive analysis, the Byrds move to center stage as members of the ruling elite. He believed that their architecture and displays of public wealth were really symbolic reminders of their supreme social power. When considered in its totality, "the material world of Westover and the actions of patriarch, family, and slave would be statements in a discourse."

Hall perceived the world of artifacts to be a uniquely powerful realm, a place in which individual men and women used material things to resist the influence of domination and to redefine themselves within the changing social order. Moving to Cape Town (Figure 9.7), Hall demonstrated how Europeans at the Cape of Good Hope used colonial ceramics in this manner. The Dutch East India Company adopted a three-tiered hierarchy of ceramics. They put common,

**Figure 9.7** A View of the Cape of Good Hope from on board the 'Resoution' by William Hodges, 1772.

cheaply made redwares decorated with bright green and yellow glazes on the lowest level. Above them they placed coarse porcelains brought to the Cape from Indonesia. They regarded the rare, fine porcelains imported from the royal kilns of China as the finest of ceramics (Figure 9.8). But Chinese porcelain vessels were far more than mere elegant, domestic wares. They were also important in an elaborate ceremony of display that included drinking tea and holding formal dinner parties. Elite families proudly displayed their fine porcelains as symbolic reminders of their social power and importance. Not surprisingly, sherds of such delicate wares occur frequently in the archaeological sites once inhabited by members of the Dutch colonial elite. But surprisingly, Hall also found fragments of fine porcelains in the homes of the enslaved, together with the coarse redwares common among the lower levels of society. Coarse porcelains, the domestic wares most common in the deposits left by Dutch soldiers, however, were absent from the slaves' houses.

Enslaved men and women conceivably could have been issued ceramics different from those commonly used by Dutch soldiers. But how can we explain the fine porcelains in the slave quarters? Hall believed that the slaves stole fine dishes as a gesture of symbolic defiance. On a deeper level, these same fine porcelains symbolically "turned the world upside down, allowing the repressed victims of a patriarchal world to reconstitute daily a 'space' for themselves." The fine porcelains had a meaning for the slaves that was quite distinct from that of their Dutch masters.

Hall expanded the boundaries of historical structuralism, and his approach is innovative and interesting. He and Deetz, however, are not the only historical archaeologists who have combined science and humanism in an effort to understand the historical past. Another approach espouses what can be called "critical materialism."

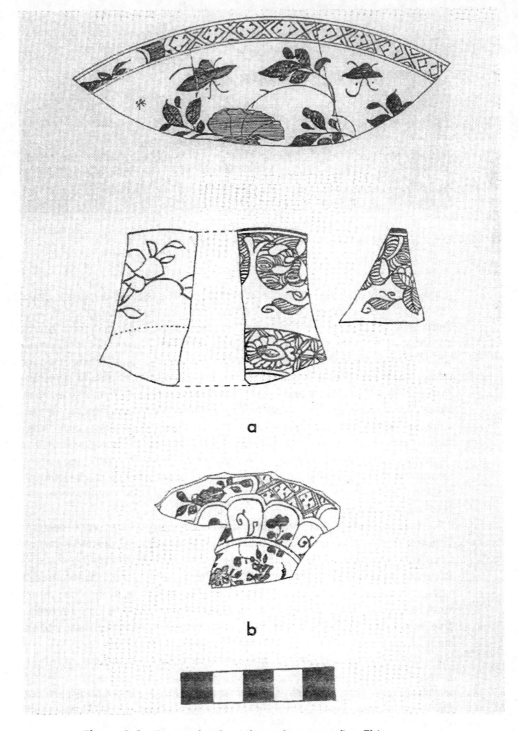

**Figure 9.8**   Pieces of early-eighteenth-century fine Chinese porcelain dinner plates from Cape Town, South Africa.

### Critical Materialism

*Critical materialism* is our term for an approach that combines "critical theory" with "materialism." Materialism is an ancient perspective in which the reality of physical matter generally takes precedence over ideas and thought processes. Critical theory, a twentieth-century refinement of the nineteenth-century ideas of Karl Marx, was proposed by scholars of the Frankfort School of sociology in the 1920s, among them Theodor Adorno, Max Horkheimer, and Herbert Marcuse. These scholars argued that knowledge is never truly neutral, because it is affected by the investigator's class interests. The affect can be intended, but it is usually unconscious. Rather than to pretend that research is unbiased and free of judgment, critical theorists argue that we should recognize the hidden prejudices inherent in our research. We should understand that our research is "reflexive"; it reflects back on itself. Critical theorists argue that research is never passionless, never atheoretical.

Mark Leone of the University of Maryland has developed an approach that links materialism with "critical theory." He concentrates on the close relationship between the class structure in a society and its technology.

Leone began his career like Deetz in process-oriented archaeology. In a study of Mormon fences published in 1973, Leone emphasized a perspective that considered archaeology as a science of technology. The anthropologist in Leone was interested in "how technology affects culture and how technology is manipulated by culture." As a historical archaeologist, he was equally concerned with technology's historical aspects.

Nineteenth-century Mormons built fences and walls, and they continue to build them today. A traditional historical explanation for the Mormon use of fences held that the use of this technology was merely a throwback to their days in New England. When the Mormons traveled west through Illinois and the Great Plains, finally settling in Utah, they took the idea of fences with them. Fences thus simply seemed to represent something the Mormons knew from the past. But Leone was dissatisfied with this simplistic explanation, so he asked a perceptive question: Why did the same settlers not bring other elements of New England material culture with them? Why just fences, and why do Mormon farmers continue to build similar fences today? Leone believed that the Mormons used fences to divide their space in ways that made sense within the context of their religious beliefs. Technology, as represented by fences, was embedded in Mormon life at every level. The use of space, their subsistence strategies, and their ways of interacting socially were all tied to technology in some way. As Leone said, "It is not just that Mormons and their religion created settlements and spatial subdivisions and made life work: Mormonism could not exist without the spatial representations and technological devices that allowed its population to exist." In other words, the fences and the religion tended to reinforce one another.

A strong thread of mental process ran through Leone's Mormon study, in that a relationship existed between fence technology and the ideas that caused

Mormons to build them. Leone also argued that even though archaeology is about the past, it is conducted in the present. As he put it, "Archaeology is a product of the present; it is used by the present."

His examination of Mormon culture soon led Leone to consider "critical theory" as a framework to understand the linked relationship between class position, ideological belief, and the modern uses of archaeology. Critical theory has a wide following outside archaeology, in legal scholarship, history, geography, and several other disciplines. Archaeologists espousing this approach argue that the scientific objectivity sought by process-oriented archaeologists like Stanley South is not really possible. Artifacts do not "speak" for themselves; archaeologists are not mere translators. Artifacts are not value-free even when they are quantified and expressed as frequencies and percentages. Archaeologists, in fact, create artificial categories when sorting artifacts, and the very act of creating these categories is a biased process. Why, for example, did South have a separate category "Smoking pipes" rather than just including them under "Activities"? Why was "Kitchen" a category instead of "Food Preparation"? Critical theorists believe that archaeologists give artifacts meaning; they are interpreters rather than translators. That these meanings sometimes may have importance outside archaeology should be celebrated as a way for archaeology to develop a greater sense of relevance within modern society. As Leone said, "an exploration of the political function of archaeology may produce both a consciousness of the social function of archaeology as well as a set of questions for archaeology to address that may be of greater social benefit." To give only one example, the complex relationship between politics and archaeology has surfaced in the many controversies over the excavation and reburial of Native American skeletal remains and grave goods. Archaeologists may perceive the excavation of Native American graves to constitute an important avenue for learning about the past, but many Native Americans view excavation as desecration. The excavation, though clearly "about" the past, takes place in the present and affects living people.

Leone has focused much of his attention on a major historical phenomenon of the modern era—the growth of capitalism—as it was played out in Annapolis, Maryland. He views capitalism as a way of organizing life, as a way of setting up social categories. For Leone, capitalism is not merely an economic system, something removed from social analysis. Capitalism is part and parcel of each and every segment of life, a culture in and of itself. All activity in Annapolis—past and present—had an umbrella of capitalism spread over it. But making this claim is not enough because an important question for Leone is: "How did capitalism actually operate on the ground—that is, in people's daily lives?" Or: "How can historical archaeologists study capitalism?"

Annapolis has a rich historical tradition, and Leone was able to begin his study with probate inventories. From these lists of property he constructed four wealth-holding groups for the years from 1690–1775. Though probate records were seldom kept for enslaved African Americans, poor whites, most women, and free African Americans, they nonetheless include a major segment of the historical population. Historians have shown that capitalism had an increasing influence on life in Annapolis throughout the eighteenth century. When they compared the early years of the century with later decades, they discovered that, with time, more people worked for wages, merchants made more money, and more consumer goods entered the city. Leone took these facts as a starting point and combined them with his ideas about the importance of class.

Working closely with colleagues Parker Potter and Paul Shackel, Leone showed how people's lives became more standardized over time and how there existed an "increasing interchangeability of things, acts, and persons." In the early seventeenth century, men and women often acted communally. They slept in the same rooms, they ate their meals from one or two bowls, and they did not use personalized silverware. With the rising influence of capitalism, however, people's lives became more regulated and consequently more interchangeable with everyone else's. Men and women now paid attention to clocks, they had a certain time for lunch, and they each had their own dishes and forks during dinner. It was at this time that potters developed the various kinds of ceramic vessels mentioned in the POTS program (Chapter 8).

Leone and his colleagues excavated three domestic household sites in Annapolis to study the important social changes that occurred between the late-seventeenth and the mid-eighteenth centuries. One site each represented the upper-wealth group, the middle-wealth group, and a household whose members had climbed from the lowest wealth group in the 1740s to the highest group over the next several years. To measure social change using glazed ceramics, Leone, Potter, and Shackel devised a clever formula. Their idea was that an increase in ceramic variation would signal the increasing impact of capitalism on the daily lives of ordinary men and women. Greater ceramic variability meant greater and more diverse purchasing from an ever-increasing stock of potential objects. Leone and his colleagues took the number of types of ceramics in a sample, combined it with the number of plate sizes—the "type-sizes"—and divided it by the number of types present. They then multiplied the quotient by the number of plate sizes to produce an index number. The index number of a soil layer that contained five type-sizes, three different ceramic types (porcelain, pearlware, whiteware), and four different sizes of plates, would be calculated as: $(5/3)(4) = 6.67$ (Table 9.1). The higher the value, the greater the variation. When they computed the index value for the three sites at Annapolis, they saw that the values indeed increased over time. For example, at the Hammond-Harwood House, belonging to the upper-wealth household, the value increased from 2.0 in the mid- to late-eighteenth century to 27.0 in the late-eigthteenth to early-nineteenth century. At the Thomas Hyde House site—where the household moved from the lowest wealth group to the highest—the index values started at 1.0 in the early-eighteenth century. By the mid- to late-eighteenth century the

**Table 9.1**  *Ceramic Index for Annapolis, Maryland*

| | Plate Diameter (Inches) | | | | | |
| Ceramic Type | 4 | 5 | 6 | 7 | 8 | 9 |
| --- | --- | --- | --- | --- | --- | --- |
| Porcelain | — | — | — | — | x | — |
| Pearlware | — | — | — | x | — | x |
| Whiteware | x | — | — | — | — | x |

*Source:* Mark P. Leone, Parker B. Potter, Jr., and Paul A. Shackel, 1987. "Toward a Critical Archaeology," *Current Anthropology* [28: 288].

index value was 2.0, and by the late-eighteenth to early-nineteenth century, it was 24.5. The value was 73.1 for the mid-nineteenth century. The message from these values was inescapable for Leone and his associates: "The greater variety of dish sizes and wares in the archaeological record reflects a new etiquette, and increasing segmentation at the table that served both as a training ground for the new order and as reinforcement for it."

The research of Leone and his colleagues indicates that the changes in material culture that archaeologists can observe between the seventeenth and the nineteenth centuries do not simply reflect transformations of some deep mental construct. They represent wholesale social changes brought about because of, and through, human experiences within capitalism.

A good analogy for thinking about theory in historical archaeology is to envision a music store where the CDs are arranged in neat rows by category. Some people will find the jazz section appealing, but others will be drawn to rock and roll. Still others will go directly to the classical section. Many people will make their way through several categories, finding something they like about each one of them. Archaeological theories come and go like trends in music. The music store of 1980 did not look like the music store of 2000, and the store of 2001 was not an exact duplicate of the store in 2000. Scholars pick and choose theories something like fussy CD shoppers. Some archaeologists are drawn to class analysis, some to the mental constructs that underlie the creation of bottles, dishes, and houses. Still others find value in the scientific perspectives developed in the 1960s. Individual archaeologists tend to defend their own way of looking at the past, but in the final analysis most experts are willing to accept that several equally valid perspectives can be used to interpret the past.

Whatever their theoretical perspective, archaeologists are engaged in the study not of individuals, but of groups. Even on historic sites, the archaeological record only rarely allows us to associate artifacts or structures with actual known individuals. Most archaeologists usually study the actions of people organized into social groups, many of whom lacked significant historical voices because they were ignored. It is to the study of such groups that we must now turn.

# TIME TRAVEL

## Ross Female Factory, Tasmania, 1848–1855

Van Diemen's Land (or Tasmania, as it was renamed in 1855) is an island off the southeastern tip of Australia. Between 1803 and 1854, the British government shipped seventy-four thousand convicted felons to the penal colony on Van Diemen's Land. Roughly twelve thousand of these prisoners (about 16 percent) were women.

The British built a network of female prisons on Van Diemen's Land, and they named one of them the Ross Female Factory. "Factory" was short for "manufactory," because the theory behind such institutions was that the imprisoned women would learn to better themselves through productive labor. Most prisoners were assigned to work for non-convict settlers, for local merchants, or on public works projects.

The Ross Female Factory began as a male-only institution, but in 1847 a plan was formulated to convert the prison into a facility that could house women and their children. As a male prison, the Ross institution was initially (in 1833) composed of four brick huts with thatched roofs. In 1834, the prison authorities decided to modify the living arrangements and built a long brick building with a thatched roof. They also added a mess room, a cookhouse, houses for an overseer and a constable, two sheds, and a muster yard. The structures were arranged in a neat square with the muster yard in the center. The prison underwent significant physical alteration after the women arrived. New fences were built and some stone floors were replaced with wooden floors. Six solitary confinement cells were constructed, and a bakehouse was among the new facilities. Window panes were in-stalled, and all wards received a coat of whitewash. The women usually slept in hammocks, but thirty iron bedsteads were ordered for the hospital. A boundary fence was later built to prevent convicts from engaging in unauthorized communication.

The women prisoners at the Ross Female Factory were usually sent there as a secondary measure. Most had originally been transported to Van Diemen's Land from Britain because they had been convicted of petty theft or of a crime against property. They could also be sent there for illegitimate pregnancy, public drunkenness, or homosexuality.

Once at the institution, the superintendent divided the women into three groups. They were assigned to the "crime class" upon arrival. This designation meant that they had to work in the prison laundry or to perform sewing under contract for local settlers. After a period of good behavior, a woman could be assigned to the "hiring class." Members of this group were assigned domestic duties on nearby farms, or else they worked in the hospital, nursery, or held semi-supervisory roles. The third division, the "punishment class," was composed of women who flaunted the rules, disobeyed the jailers, or were caught in possession of forbidden objects. These women were confined to solitary cells, usually with decreased food rations. They could also have their heads shaved and be made to wear iron collars as further signs of humiliation. The solitary cells were separated from the main prison compound by 9-foot (2.7-m) high wooden fences.

*(continued)*

Source: Eleanor Conlin Casella. 2001. To Watch or Restrain: Female Convict Prisons in 19th-Century Tasmania, *International Journal of Historical Archaeology* 5:45–72; Eleanor Conlin Casella, *Archaeology of the Ross Female Factory: Female Incarceration in Van Diemen's Land, Australia.* (Launceston: Queen Victoria Museum and Art Gallery, 2002).

The women's solitary cells measured only about 4 by 6 feet (1.2 by 1.8 m), making them smaller than the men's cells. Their walls were made of rough, cut sandstone rubble, and were about 20 inches (50 cm) thick. They had earthen floors situated below the level of their doors, giving the cells a dark, dungeon-like quality.

The solitary conditions faced by the women from the "punishment class" were harsh and brutal, but this does not mean that the women were completely broken. It is likely that while in solitary confinement, the women participated in an underground trade network using the occasional piece of coinage or buttons as monetary tokens. They probably used this currency to obtain objects not allowed in solitary, like tobacco and alcohol. Once they had gotten such items, they hid them under the cells' earthen floors. They also dug pits into the floors to store bottles, foodstuffs, white clay tobacco pipes, and other banned objects. Prison authorities must have discovered both the secret exchange network and the way in which the women hid the contraband, because they had new floors of hard clayey-silt installed in the cells. The clay surfaces were both easier to inspect and considerably more difficult to excavate surreptitiously. The laying of the clay floors had a detrimental impact on the secret trade, but it did not completely curtail it.

# Chapter 10

# The Archaeology of Groups

*"The adequate treatment of the disenfrancished groups in America's past, excluded from historical sources because of race, religion, isolation, or poverty, is an important function of contemporary historical archaeology and one that cannot be ignored."*

Kathleen Deagan, 1982

In the late 1980s, archaeologist Mary Beaudry and her colleagues at Boston University set about studying the nineteenth-century Boott Cotton Mills in Lowell, Massachusetts. They learned several things from historical documents: that wealthy entrepreneurs from Boston incorporated the mill on March 22, 1835; that they had named it after Kirk Boott, their agent; and that two other agents were named Benjamin French and Linus Child. The documents revealed much about the prominent men of Boott Mills, but it said little about all the others. What about them?

More than 1,000 mill workers, 950 women and 120 men, produced about nine million yards of cloth annually. These now largely forgotten men and women made it possible for the well-documented Boston entrepreneurs to grow rich. Mill workers, and other industrial workers, are for the most part an anonymous labor force, mentioned only rarely in factory records. We know some of the Boott Mills workers' names. In 1860, thirty-two-year-old James Stoddard was a mill hand; thirty-four-year-old Mary Hanscom was a seamstress, and twenty-four-year-old Charles E. Dodge a beltmaker. The mill records tell us little else, and only historical archaeology has the potential to give voice to these now-silenced men and women. In this chapter, we discusses some ways in which historical archaeologists can illuminate the lives of anonymous social groups within increasingly complex, modern societies.

Account books compiled by mill officials provide the formal version of the mill hands' diet. A report published in 1886 listed the food provided for sixty-six men and eleven women for one month (Figure 10.1). It included 400 pounds (149.2 kg) of roast beef, 272 pounds (101.5 kg) of beef steak, 160 pounds (59.7 kg) of ham, and 70 pounds (26.1 kg) of salt pork. The workers also consumed mackerel, cod, and other fish, as well as an assortment of beans, rice, squash, and cheese.

The account books initially appear to present a thorough and complete understanding of the mill hands' diet, but archaeological research provides another perspective. Animal bones and plant remains excavated from the boarding house site offered fresh insights. The published lists provided for "the demands for nutrients to 75 laboring men at moderate work for 30 days, or 1 man for 2,250 days." The faunal remains suggested, however, that the people in the mill found it desirable, and perhaps even necessary, to supplement their diet with other foodstuffs. Zooarchaeologist David Landon's analysis reveals that the families at Boott Mills also ate turkey, chicken, and mutton, even though these foods are not mentioned in the records. Sheep bones in the archaeological collection proved that the workers ate the least expensive shank cuts and forequarters. The workers probably purchased these foods on their own, and this explains the absence of these foods in the historical sources. Ethnobotanist Gerald Kelso discovered that in addition to undocumented cuts of meat, the mill hands also ate grains, grapes, and blackberries or raspberries. The archaeological remains cannot tell us which employees ate the grapes, grains, and mutton, but their presence at the boarding house provides a more complete picture of the diet of the workers as a group.

One great strength of historical archaeology is that it can sometimes flesh out the more commonplace details of the lives of society's anonymous working people, men and women like Stoddard, Hanscom, Dodge, and the hundreds of others who toiled alongside them every day at the Boott Mills. More often, however, individuals are blurred in the archaeological record with other individuals. Their names are lost to history, and so they come down to us through their artifacts and food remains, as members of once well-defined social and economic classes, as males and females, as ethnic groups. How do archaeologists study such complicated groups?

As may be supposed from the previous chapter, no one answer is possible. Different archaeologists will approach the study of social groups in different ways. In this chapter, we only present a few options.

## CULTURAL COMPLEXITY AND SOCIAL STRATIFICATION

Historical archaeologists investigate complex, socially stratified societies, with people living in literate, pre-industrial, or industrial civilizations. *Social stratification* means that a society is divided into two or more groups that are ranked relative to one another in terms of economic, social, or other criteria. Many years ago, anthropologist Elman Service divided human societies into pre-state and state-organized societies. Pre-state societies consisted of hunting bands and simple horticultural societies. These social organizations were either egalitarian in

| Kinds. | FOOD-MATERIALS. | | | NUTRIENTS. | | |
|---|---|---|---|---|---|---|
| | Prices per lb. | Quanti- ties. | Costs. | Protein. | Fats. | Carbohy- drates. |
| | cents. | lbs. | | lbs. | lbs. | lbs. |
| Beef, . . . . . | 10 | 425 | $42 50 | 57.4 | 106.3 | - |
| Beef steak, . . . . | 16 | 250 | 40 00 | 36.3 | 39.0 | - |
| Beef, corned, . . . . | 7 | 300 | 21 00 | 34.5 | 85.5 | - |
| Beef stew, . . . . | 5 | 100 | 5 00 | 14.0 | 31.3 | - |
| Pork, roast, . . . . | 10 | 100 | 10 00 | 11.4 | 36.2 | - |
| Ham, . . . . . | 12 | 150 | 18 00 | 21.9 | 51.5 | - |
| Salt pork, . . . . | 10 | 25 | 2 50 | 0.7 | 19.1 | - |
| Lard, . . . . . | 8 | 150 | 12 00 | - | 146.5 | - |
| Cod and haddock . . . | 7 | 150 | 10 50 | 14.6 | 0.3 | - |
| Halibut, . . . . | 14 | 50 | 7 00 | 7.6 | 2.1 | - |
| Total meats, fish, etc., . . | | 1,700 | $168 50 | 196.4 | 519.8 | - |
| Butter, . . . . | 20 | 150 | $30 00 | 1.5 | 131.3 | 0.7 |
| Cheese, . . . . . | 10 | 30 | 3 00 | 3.1 | 10.7 | 0.7 |
| Milk, . . . . . | 2 | 2,000 | 40 00 | 68.0 | 74.0 | 96.0 |
| Eggs, . . . . . | 16 | 69 | 11 00 | 8.0 | 7.0 | 0.4 |
| Total dairy products and eggs, . | | 2,249 | $84 00 | 85.6 | 223.0 | 97.8 |
| Flour, . . . . . | 3¼ | 1,372 | $44 59 | 152.3 | 15.1 | 1,034.5 |
| Rice, . . . . . | 8 | 15 | 1 20 | 1.1 | - | 11.9 |
| Corn starch, . . . . | 9 | 10 | 90 | - | - | 8.3 |
| Crackers, . . . . | 5 | 48 | 2 40 | 5.1 | 4.5 | 83.0 |
| Sugar, . . . . . | 7 | 400 | 28 00 | - | - | 386.8 |
| Molasses, . . . . | 4½ | 77 | 3 50 | - | - | 54.7 |
| Potatoes, . . . . | 1 1-12 | 1,800 | 19 50 | 34.2 | 3.6 | 331.2 |
| Beans, . . . . | 4¾ | 95 | 4 50 | 22.0 | 2.0 | 51.0 |
| Pease, . . . . . | 1¾ | 30 | 50 | 6.9 | 0.5 | 15.7 |
| Turnips, . . . . | 5-6 | 90 | 75 | 0.8 | 0.2 | 4.5 |
| Beets, . . . . . | ¾ | 60 | 38 | 1.1 | 0.1 | 6.0 |
| Cabbage, . . . . | 1½ | 36 | 48 | 0.6 | 0.1 | 1.6 |
| Apples, . . . . | 1½ | 600 | 8 00 | 1.8 | - | 85.4 |
| Raisins, . . . . | 13 | 10 | 1 30 | 0.3 | - | 8.3 |
| Total vegetable food, . . | | 4,643 | $116 00 | 226.2 | 26.4 | 2,011.0 |
| Total animal food, . . | | 3,949 | 252 50 | 284.0 | 742.8 | 97.8 |
| Total food, . . . | | 8,592 | $368 50 | 510.2 | 769.2 | 2,108.8 |
| Meats, fish, etc., per man per day, . . . . . | | .96 | $0 10 | .11 | .30 | - |
| Dairy products and eggs, per man per day, . . . . | | 1.29 | 05 | .05 | .13 | .06 |
| Animal food, per man per day, | | 2.27 | $0 15 | .16 | .43 | .06 |
| Vegetable food, " " . | | 2.66 | 07 | .13 | .01 | 1.15 |
| Total food, " " . | | 4.93 | $0 22 | .29 | .44 | 1.21 |

**Figure 10.1** Account book of food for millworkers, Lowell, Massachusetts, published in 1886.

organization, or incorporated minor social differences based on sex, lineage, or some other factor. State-organized societies—Sumerians, ancient Egyptians, Aztecs—were marked by a highly stratified social organization, headed by a small class of (often-heredity-based) rulers and nobles. Aztec society, for example, was composed of nobles, commoners, and slaves, but within these broad social groupings were numerous important economic classes, like merchants, priests, and warriors. Early pre-industrial civilizations depended not on fossil fuels, but on simple technologies and the labor of human hands, as well as highly centralized governments. Many of their institutions persisted for long periods, right through Roman times and into the so-called European Age of Discovery. Each of these societies comprised numerous, often competing social groups.

Such cultures, even though stratified, did not have capitalistic—or profit-motivated—economies that were intended to be global. The Europeans who traveled to other lands planned to find great sources of wealth. When Prince Henry the Navigator of Portugal sent his ships southward around the western bulge of Africa in the 1420s, his captains sailed in the service of the Crown, as did Christopher Columbus seventy years later. Explorers like Hernán Cortes sailed in service to a state-sponsored monarchy. When he discovered the Aztec capital of Tenochtitlán in 1521, it was proclaimed that he was to remit to the Spanish monarch a fifth of all the Aztec gold he could find. The conquistadors were members of complex, highly stratified societies. Individuals were members of distinct social classes, and everyone had a well-defined place in society: some were soldiers, some priests, others blacksmiths. Contemporary documents tell us, however, that many Spanish immigrants to New Spain were also poor men from rural farming villages. They came without wives and often married into Indian families, creating the mestizo class of today.

Faced with this historical reality, the problem for historical archaeologists is simply stated: historical records report the names of monarchs, captains, and generals, even of some priests and merchants. They also refer to humbler folk in general terms. How, then, do we identify such groups in the archaeological record—from their artifacts, food remains, structures, and burials? Available historical records may indicate that certain groups of people—enslaved Africans, Native American women, European immigrant laborers—once lived at a particular site. The archaeological problem in such cases is not simply to identify these groups from the remains they left behind, but to try to understand how the people used their material culture to indicate and to symbolize their identity. Identifying social identity is a difficult task, but it is one that makes historical archaeology an important social science. But because historical archaeology is a relatively new field of study, a body of sophisticated work on the deeper issues involving the identification of past social groups is just now being developed. Many historical archaeologists have had to be content with first being certain that they can actually identify past groups from their archaeological remains.

Associating collections of artifacts with, say, blacksmiths is difficult at the best of times, especially in domestic situations, where people lived in families, distant from their place of work. Only rarely does an excavator find an artifact that belongs to a historically identifiable individual. For example, while excavating the overseer's cabin at Cannon's Point Plantation, Georgia, archaeologist John Otto found a glass disk engraved "Hugh F. Grant" and "1829." This disk, possibly a lens of some sort, was undoubtedly owned by Hugh Fraser Grant, the son of a wealthy planter who lived in the area. Records show that Grant was eighteen years old in 1829. Wealthy planters' sons often worked as overseers to learn the business of running a large plantation before they acquired their own, so it is possible that Grant served as the Cannon's Point overseer before his marriage in 1831. The etched inscription allows us to state with confidence that the lens was once his property. This kind of association between a specific historical personage and an artifact is rare even in historical archaeology.

Any study of social groups requires meticulous historical research because the amassed evidence will help provide the context for the specific archaeological questions that may be posed. For instance, in 1085, William the Conqueror dispatched census takers throughout England to take stock of all that he had conquered nineteen years earlier. He was in search of statistical information to keep at his fingertips, and the information he received is today known as the celebrated Domesday Book. When recorders compiled the Book the following year, they filled it with names and numbers—of those who paid their taxes and tithes. The names of elites are frequently noted: "The King has 18 burgesses. . . . The Bishop of Chester has 14 dwellings. . . . Earl Roger has 3 dwellings. . . . Robert of Stafford has 3 dwellings." Despite this careful record keeping, expert R. Welldon Finn said that the Domesday Book "does not enable us to arrive at a really close estimate of the total population of 11th-century England." Why? Because commoners—the "lesser" folk—are mentioned, not by name, but only in reference to some larger group. For instance, Totmonslow Hundred contains "1 free man and 10 villagers who have 5 ploughs"; at Pirehill Hundred are "4 villagers, 8 smallholders and 4 slaves who have 2 ploughs." The census takers did not consider these people important enough to record their names.

Cemeteries, although controversial to excavate, often provide important clues about social stratification. Archaeologists generally assume that in death men and women tend to reflect the social standing they held in life. They therefore consider clothing, ornaments, and grave objects to be good indicators of the deceased's social position. One reason for the association between grave appearance and past social standing rests on the simple fact that different burials in the same cemetery can be quite distinctive. A brief example will demonstrate the differences.

In her examination of a seventeenth-century cemetery used by the Narragansetts in Rhode Island, archaeologist Patricia Rubertone investigated fifty-six burials. Included in the sample were fifteen males, twenty-eight females, and thirteen unknown individuals. As a group, the burials contained a wide variety of European materials—glass wine bottles, brass kettles, lead shot, buttons—and Native American objects—pottery vessels, textiles, shell beads. But the distribution of the objects in the graves was not equal. A burial of a three-year-old contained a bracelet made of glass and brass, a glass medicine bottle, an iron hoe, and a metal spoon, while the burial of a fifteen-year-old female contained only a single shell. Some burials had finger rings, others did not. Three adult women's burials contained hoes, whereas only one adult male had a hoe.

Archaeologists have to assume that differences in artifact association must mean something, but what? How do archaeologists unravel the meaning of such obvious differences? One way to attempt to learn something about social stratification in the complex societies of historical archaeology is through a focus on social class.

## Social Class

"Class" is a difficult concept, and social scientists disagree about its precise definition. Some say that a person's social class membership has to do with his or her "life's chances," the opportunity to acquire property, education, and material things. Others contend that class membership, and even life chances for that matter, have more to do with a person's relationship to production. Some people own factories and agricultural land, other people work in them. People are thus either owners (haves) or workers (have-nots). Many people equate class with income. In short, definitions of class abound. In one well-known definition, anthropologist Marvin Harris defined a class as a group of people who have a similar relationship to the structure of social control in a society and who possess similar amounts of power over the allocation of wealth, privilege, resources, and technology. An important point about classes is that an individual's membership in a particular class can change as that person acquires (or loses) something of value in the society, such as wealth, power, position, or education. Furthermore, men and women in a class system only know their position in a relative way. We may all have some idea as to whether we stand in the upper, middle, or lower class, but we generally do not concern ourselves with whether we are part of the upper middle class or the lower upper class.

The difficulty of reaching an agreement in existing class systems makes it incredibly difficult for historical archaeologists to understand past class organizations. What is important in historical archaeology is the correlation of specific pieces or groups of material culture with particular social classes.

Historical archaeologist Steven Shephard studied the relationship between material culture and class membership in Alexandria, Virginia. Alexandria began as a small trading post primarily for tobacco in the early 1730s, but soon grew into a major mercantile center. At its height, the city boasted a population stratified into classes that extended from enslaved African Americans on the bottom to wealthy planters and merchants on the top. Shephard examined three early-nineteenth-century sites in the city in the hopes of finding material evidence of class membership. City records indicated that two sites could be classified as having been within the middle class (based on income and occupation). The third was in the much poorer lower class. From the thousands of artifacts excavated by the city's archaeological staff, Shephard decided to focus on glazed ceramics because archaeologists can study them in terms of quantity, quality, and variety. Alexandrian families usually purchased large quantities of ceramics during the course of their lives. These pieces could be of vastly different quality, from fine imported wares to everyday kitchen pieces, in well-defined shapes and sizes. Shephard examined a sample of about thirteen hundred bowls, cups, saucers, and plates from different neighborhoods, and noticed that the middle-class households had a greater quantity and variety of dishes than did the lower-class household. Middle-class families also had more matched pieces than the poorer household, and of the matched pieces, the middle class had a greater variety of pieces.

Shephard's findings may appear somewhat obvious. Given our own personal knowledge of class differences, we can well imagine that men and women in higher social positions will have a greater variety of dishes than someone lower down the social ladder. Shephard's conclusion, however, that "the quantity and quality variables are the strongest correlates of class membership," provides an avenue of inquiry for others to follow. Historical archaeologists can easily document the quantities and qualities of the artifacts they find at archaeological sites.

One obvious factor that influences the ability of class members to acquire certain dishes, or anything else, hinges on whether they can obtain them. We cannot buy what is not available, no matter how much we can afford it. We can expect the upper class to have a greater ability to obtain the goods they want. After all, they are generally "in control" (or at least know who is). But if elites wish to live off the beaten path, far from highways or railroads, we may be willing to concede that they could have trouble obtaining some artifacts and commodities. But is this true?

Sherene Baugher and Robert Venables decided to test this idea by examining ceramic artifacts excavated at seven eighteenth-century sites in New York State. They chose two sites in the country, and five sites in New York City—two on Staten Island, three on Manhattan. They used historical records to establish that each site was inhabited by upper- or middle-class households. One site was inhabited by Sir William Johnson, the famous Englishmen who was the liaison between the British government and the powerful Iroquois. Less well-known people, but no less wealthy, lived at the other sites. Having used documents to establish the class affiliation of the sites' residents, Baugher and Venables compared the artifacts from each location. They also focused on ceramics, but they found few differences between them. Each site contained the expensive, imported porcelains and finely made white tablewares that are usually associated with eighteenth-century wealth. Baugher and Venables did observe a difference in the inexpensive tablewares: kitchen pieces made locally and directly purchased from their producers. Their finding seems to suggest that the household members probably saw no reason to spend money importing mixing bowls, churns, and jars when they were easily available for less cost locally. These pieces were for use in the kitchen, out of the public eye. It seems, therefore, that a household's location played some role in artifact acquisition. Even elites in the backwoods could buy the exotic things they wanted, but they also made conscious decisions about their purchases. Then as now, class helps shape what can be bought. Upper-crust, colonial New Yorkers, regardless of address, could easily mimic the fashions of London and other European capitals.

In a provocative and important essay published in 1988 and entitled "Steps to an Archaeology of Capitalism," archaeologist Robert Paynter stated that historical archaeologists can do much more than simply identify the presence of classes at past archaeological sites. He proposed that historical archaeologists can make strong contributions to the very understanding of class. The potential to make this contribution exists because material culture plays such a large part in many theories of class.

Paynter's ideas are extremely intriguing. In discussing glass bottles—objects frequently found by historical archaeologists—Paynter stated that the transition from mouth blowing to machine manufacture was more than simply a technological innovation. The development of bottle-making machines came about because labor strikes and work stoppages by glass blowers made the industry a risky proposition for factory owners. Bottle manufacturers sought to circumvent work-stopping labor problems by decreasing the number of "troublesome" employees. An automatic bottle maker was one obvious way to do this. When put in this light, the bottle fragments found by historical archaeologists during excavation represent much more than a mere technological improvement; they symbolize the way one class—glass factory owners—reacted to the protests of another class—glass blowers.

A new generation of historical archaeologists are investigating class with great vigor. Much more remains to be done on the subject of class identification and meaning, but current research points in new and interesting directions. Today's historical archaeologists are busy examining the ways in which social classes were created and maintained, the ways in which class members used material objects to identify themselves, and the ways in which various social classes struggled for control, power, and dignity.

### Gender

Men and women constitute the two most basic groups in the vast panorama of human history. Archaeologists for years found it easy to speak of these two groups in simplistic terms. Prehistoric men hunted, so all stone arrowheads and spear points were "male" objects; women cooked, so all potsherds were "female" objects. Scholars usually assumed that a society's "movers and shakers" were men; they were responsible for cultural change and technological advancement. Women stood behind the scenes: homemaking, weaving, and cooking.

Western convention recognizes only two sexes. We imagine sex to be based on physiology rather than on behavior. Not every culture, however, makes this assumption. The eighteenth-century Tahitians of the south Pacific recognized three sexes: male, female, and mahu. The mahu were permanent transvestites who were not regarded as oddities. Neither were they considered to be males or females. Visiting Europeans were horrified by the mahu. John Turnbull described them in 1813 as "a set of men . . . whose open profession is of such abomination that the laudable delicacy of our language will not admit it to be mentioned." The famed William Bligh, captain of *H.M.S. Bounty*, later set adrift by his mutinous crew in 1788, said of one particular mahu, "The Women treat him as one of their Sex, and he observes every restriction that they do, and is equally respected and esteemed." Many Native American societies also recognized three sexes. Among the Crow of Montana, for instance, the berdache was the equivalent of the Tahitian mahu. Finds-Them-and-Kills-Them, a Crow berdache, dressed like a woman and performed the domestic chores of a woman. Other Crows saw him not as a deviant male, but as a member of a third sex.

Westerners also tend to equate sex with gender. But gender refers to culturally prescribed behavior. Among the Tahitians and the Crows, we Westerners would see two sexes and two gender roles: males and females. The mahu and berdache would constitute deviant males. The Tahitians and the Crows, however, would perceive two sexes and three gender roles: males and females; and male, female, and transvestite behavior.

Numerous archaeologists, some working in collaboration with ethnographers, are working to dispel the Western perception of equating gender with sex. They propose that archaeologists must learn to evaluate the many roles, systems, and ideologies that involve gender. As historical archaeologist Donna Seifert said, "women are not defective men; pregnancy, childbearing, and nursing are not necessarily disabilities; women's behavior, experience, and history is not deviant behavior because it is not the same as men's." The study of gender is not just about women; it is about women and men interacting to create and maintain society. When we learn about women's roles in the past, we automatically also learn something about men's roles. Giving women a voice in the past empowers us to develop a deeper, realistic understanding of history and culture.

Consider, for example, Seifert's 1991 study of "Hooker's Division," the nineteenth-century red light section of Washington, D.C. Hooker's Division was named for Major General Joseph Hooker, who, as commander of the Army of the Potomac in 1863, ordered the concentration of the city's prostitutes in one part of town. The city council forced Hooker to take this drastic step because they were growing increasingly concerned about the burgeoning number of off-duty soldiers flooding the nation's capital. Many of these troopers, fresh from Midwestern farms and probably away from home for the first time, went looking for fully stocked saloons and fast women. History tells us that many of them found both in Hooker's Division.

Remarkably, even though prostitution is considered to be "the world's oldest profession," archaeologists before Seifert had not studied it in great detail. Rather than seeking to examine Hooker's Division as a way to learn about one particular group of women, Seifert chose to envision prostitution as a kind of gender relationship. Serving as a sexual partner in this situation represented a necessary job rather than an expectation of marriage. Gender relationships and expectations within society permit prostitution to flourish.

When Seifert examined the materials excavated from Washington's red light district, she found artifacts associated with clothing present in much greater quantity in Hooker's Division than at other, more purely residential parts of the city. The buttons came from a variety of garments, ranging from fancy ladies' robes to everyday men's and women's shirts and coats. The excavators unearthed several men's trouser buttons, perhaps lost by the brothel porters, or by the young men who ventured into Hooker's Division.

The archaeologists also discovered that objects of personal hygiene and adornment (mirrors, combs, and jewelry) occurred more often in the red light district than at other, nearby residences. A jar of "Valentine's Meat Juice," for the cure of "social diseases," also says something about the health and concerns of the ladies in Hooker's Division and the realities of their occupation.

Seifert's findings are important because they provide a voice for women too long absent from the archaeological story of the past. Her wider objective is perhaps more important, however, because she studied a gender relationship. Prostitutes worked to support themselves and their families as part of this relationship. Prostitution is not simply an aberrant whim that "just happens" to some women; it has economic and social roots that relate to gender roles in society.

In some cases, simply the act of demonstrating the presence of women at a site is enough to shake forever the foundations of once-cherished androcentric, or male-focused, interpretations. Archaeologists have recently done a superb job of placing women at sites where they have long been invisible. Logging camps, like military forts, are usually seen as bastions of manhood. We imagine that lumberjacks, cut in the image of Paul Bunyan, went into virgin forests like soldiers and did battle with nature. They turned trees into usable lumber using only their brute strength and force of will. When women are mentioned in the historical records of the lumber industry, they are usually "in town." Written histories thus tend to project only one image of logging: that it was a male-only activity.

But the reality of logging was far different than the image. Archaeologist Janet Brashler concretely proved that women were involved in logging. She examined historic photographs and read numerous historical reports, and learned that women lived in logging camps. They were an integral part of the timber industry. Brashler rooted her research in the idea that gender is an organizing principle of group relations. This perspective allowed her to look beyond the all-male shanty camp that forms the basis for most of our modern images of logging. She discovered the widespread use among loggers of family shanty camps. These settlements were different-sized communities in which families lived together in the forests. Dogway, West Virginia, for example, was a temporary logging town established by the Cherry River Boom and Lumber Company. Residents lived there from about 1910–1915 to 1927. Brashler made numerous surface finds at this abandoned town site: intricately decorated transfer-printed dishes, cast iron stove parts, rusted barrel hoops and springs, and different-colored glass fragments. She also saw crumbled brick chimneys, caved-in root cellars, old railway grades, and the location of sixty old railroad cars that had been converted into housing.

Brashler gave women a voice within the sphere of the Cherry River Boom and Lumber Company. Archaeologists interested in the gender relations of the logging industry face a challenge as they attempt, in Brashler's words, "to define more clearly the artifact assemblages found in family camps, single-gender camps, family shanty camps, camps with red-light districts, and camps where one or two women might have been present as the wives of the foreman or cook." How can the artifacts unearthed from logging sites be used to give voice to the women of the logging industry? How do the rusty tin cans, bent metal plates and cups, broken glass bottles, and iron pot fragments represent logging-oriented gender roles?

Circumstances prevented Brashler from excavating any of the logging camps she found during her surveys, so she was forced to work entirely with materials collected from the surface. Her research nonetheless challenges us to look for women where our preconceived notions may suggest they were absent.

We often assume that the earliest colonists and explorers from Europe were men. After all, no women accompanied Columbus on his first or second voyages to the New World. But several archaeologists are rapidly changing this male-only view of colonialism. History records that Spanish women engaged in numerous trades, from folk medicine to textile production, but that women were generally expected to be homemakers. In the sixteenth and seventeenth centuries, Spanish women generally came to the New World as the wives of wealthy aristocrats. The main responsibility of these women was to maintain the Spanish colonial household.

Authors of colonial Spanish documents usually ignored the typical Spanish wife. Luckily, however, archaeologists can unearth evidence of their presence. At Puerto Real, Haiti, Charles Ewen found material evidence for the presence of women in the deposits of the sixteenth-century townsite. At one high-status residence, Ewen found a lace bobbin made of bone, a number of glass beads, a ring fashioned from jet (a dense, black coal), and a pendant in the shape of a unicorn. Nothing else is known of the woman, or women, who used the bobbin or wore the ring, pendant, and beads, but now that their presence is acknowledged, archaeologists can continue to search for them. At a seventeenth-century Spanish mission site in Tallahassee, Florida, Bonnie McEwan has excavated objects similar to those found in Haiti: jet rings, metal sequins or beads, small brass rings, a quartz pendant in a teardrop shape.

McEwan's research demonstrates that women lived in colonial Spanish communities and that Spanish wives had a dramatic role in shaping colonial society. Colonial Spanish wives made their impact felt by interacting with the female Native American and African American domestics who worked alongside them in their homes. According to McEwan, Spanish women integrated domestic workers "into their culture through language instruction, religious indoctrination, and training in European traditions and mores." The continuity with Spain that women sought in their colonial homes was impressed upon their domestic servants because Spanish wives were ultimately responsible for seeing that the home conformed to the Spanish ideal. Spanish women were thus on the front line of cultural change, bringing Spanish culture to non-Spaniards, and deciding which elements of non-Spanish culture to adopt in their homes. Spanish women were not only present in colonial New Spain, they also played an important role in bringing Spanish culture to the continent they had only just discovered.

Historical archaeologists investigating gender roles and, indeed, other social elements of daily life, have tended to envision the household as a unified body composed of individuals who all work together toward the common good of the group. Conflicts, though we may imagine them to have occurred, are largely left unnoticed in the background. In an intriguing and creative article, however, archaeologist Hadley Kruczek-Aaron challenged this perspective and in the process provided a more sophisticated view of gender roles.

Kruczek-Aaron focused on the estate of Gerrit Smith (1797–1874), a famous politician and reformer, who lived in New York state. Historical records report that the Smith household was the scene of two interpersonal struggles: one occurred between the household's elite women and their working-class, female housekeeper and nanny, and the second conflict occurred between Gerrit Smith and his wife Ann and daughter Elizabeth. One of the conflicts that existed between Smith and his daughter Elizabeth concerned the latter's interest in fashionable things. Smith's personal philosophy was built around the notion of simple living, while Elizabeth wanted to live her life surrounded by the amenities of high living. Documentary sources indicate that Smith won many of the contests over fashion because their home was described as decorated in a minimalist fashion, with simple furnishings and no mirrors, expensive carpets, or heavy drapery. Excavations revealed, however, that Smith did not win every battle. The archaeological discovery of intricately decorated, transfer-printed dishes proves that the Smith women asserted their control over at least one domain of material culture, their dinner wares. The women could use these decorative pieces as display items within their otherwise simple surroundings to impress their friends and visitors. The romantic patterns on the dishes led Kruczek-Aaron to conclude that the designs "challenge the notion that the Smiths led a thoroughly Spartan existence."

The importance of Kruczek-Aaron's article stems from her interest in depicting gender roles as social factors that must be negotiated by women and men. Her perspective is insightful because she understands that gender roles are not static through time. The study of gender and gender roles offers great promise to historical archaeology by helping to overturn long-held stereotypes about men and women, while at the same time demonstrating the interpretive potential of historical archaeology.

### *Ethnicity*

Historical archaeologists investigated ethnicity before they began to study class membership or gender relations. Ethnicity was historical archaeology's first foray into the sociology of the past.

Experts disagree on a precise definition of ethnicity, but in general they consider an ethnic group to be an assemblage of people who share enough physical and cultural characteristics to define themselves as "us," and to define everyone else as "them." Ethnicity refers to the characteristics a group accepts as pertinent to them. Ethnic groups can be "nationalities," such as the Croats and Serbs in Bosnia-Hercegovina, or "people," such as the Gypsies of Europe. Historical archaeologists in the United States have focused most of their attention on African, Hispanic, and Asian ethnic groups, although they have also examined several European groups as well.

For all its study by historical archaeologists, the correlation between ethnicity and material culture remains poorly understood. Sherene Baugher and Robert Venables had explicit historical information concerning the ethnicity of the people who lived at four of the seven sites they studied in New York state. Sir William Johnson, who lived on the Mohawk River, was Irish; Robert Livingston, who lived on the Hudson River between Albany and New York City, was of Scottish and Dutch ancestry; Jacob Rezeau, who lived in the center of Staten Island, was French; and Christopher Billopp, who lived on the southern tip of Staten Island, was English. Even with this knowledge, Baugher and Venables were unable to observe any clear evidence of ethnic difference among the archaeological remains at the sites.

Lu Ann De Cunzo of the University of Delaware drew the same conclusion in her study of Paterson, New Jersey. De Cunzo examined the artifacts from six nineteenth-century privies. Paterson was founded in 1791 by the Society for the Establishment of Useful Manufacture. The town was the first planned manufacturing community in America and, even though the town was not a great success at first, it soon became the destination of several immigrant groups, including people from the islands of western Europe.

The six privies De Cunzo studied were associated with Irish and English settlers. She scrutinized the artifact collections from each privy, but found no clear evidence of Irish or English identity. She found no clay pipes with Irish slogans imprinted on them, no insignia related to Irish independence, nothing symbolizing pride in the British Empire. She saw no differences in the quantity and diversity of ceramic and glass objects in the privies. The medicine bottles, ceramic plates and cups, and liquor bottles indicated nothing particularly suggestive of ethnicity. In short, De Cunzo was unable to distinguish any material differences between historically documented Irish and English households. As she wrote, "The English and especially the Irish, maintained their ethnic identity through family and church ties and participation in voluntary ethnic associations, but like the Americans they strove for upward mobility and displayed the American 'ethic' of conspicuous consumption." In other words, both Irish and English immigrants strove to be "American" at the expense of any clear material expression of their individual ethnic identities.

The New York and New Jersey examples show just how hard it is to distinguish ethnic groups from household artifacts alone. Many researchers for this reason turned to the study of "ethnic markers." Ethnic markers are individual artifacts or groups of artifacts that can undeniably indicate the presence of certain ethnic groups at archaeological sites. The opium smoking pipe brought to the United States by nineteenth-century Chinese immigrants is a classic example of an ethnic marker. Opium pipe bowls have a distinctive appearance, and historical archaeologists can easily identify them once they know their characteristics. Made of either pottery or stone (such as jade), the bowls resemble fancy doorknobs that have a hole, the "smoking hole," running downward through their center. This bowl was attached to a long pipestem and completed the opium pipe, or "pistol" (Figure 10.2).

When Roberta Greenwood, then an archaeologist with the Los Angeles County Museum of Natural History, conducted research on Main Street in Ventura, California, in the 1970s, she used opium pipes as ethnic markers. She found small glass medicinal vials and opium pipe bowls in a mix of aboriginal and nineteenth-century artifacts. These objects immediately signaled the presence of Chinese residents in the area. Greenwood's general expectation was that in a community that contained men and women of both Chinese and non-Chinese heritage, some artifacts could be singled out to represent each group. Her reasoning on the surface, and given the time she proposed it, seemed to make great sense.

Greenwood found a well and a trash pit that she specifically identified with the Chinese. Well over half of the artifacts from these features were of Chinese origin, including rice bowls, tea cups, ginger jars, and soy bottles. She identified other ceramic cups, plates, bowls, and chamber pots as non-Chinese artifacts.

Greenwood argued that several kinds of artifacts, in addition to opium pipes, could be viewed as ethnic markers. Her pioneering research followed conventional wisdom and her assumptions are difficult to criticize. Greenwood was following a new line of research, and she had no body of comparative information to consult. We must not criticize her too strongly because some objects truly may be uniquely associated with Chinese people. Greenwood no longer holds the views she published in the 1970s, and she, like all historical archaeologists, realizes that easy interpretations rest too strongly on ethnic stereotypes. How can we ever assume that a porcelain tea cup or a soy bottle was only used by Chinese men and women? Could no one else ever use a soy bottle? The problem of association is perhaps most extremely expressed by the opium pipe bowl. Many people associate opium smoking only with Chinese immigrants to North America, and pictures of Chinese men smoking opium are legion. But was opium smoking strictly a Chinese habit?

In a study published in 1993, anthropologist Ruth Ann Sando and archaeologist David Felton reported on their examination of the store records of the

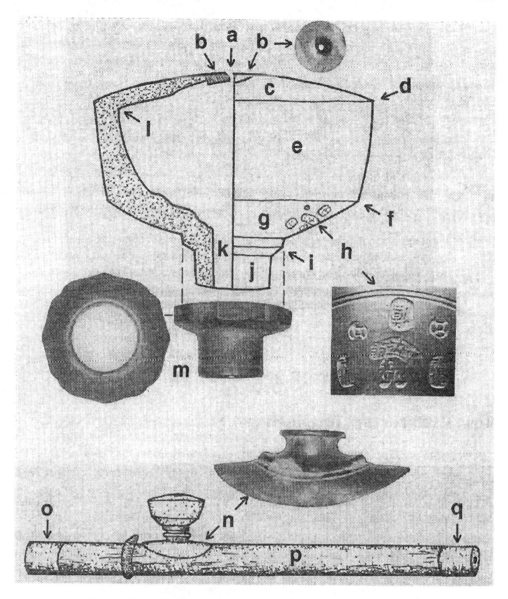

**Figure 10.2** Parts of an opium pipe: a. smoking hole, b. insert, c. smoking surface, d. rim, e. side, f. shoulder, g. base, h. stamps, i. flange, j. stem, k. basal hole, l. rim joint, m. metal connector, n. saddle, o. end piece, p. pipe stem, q. mouthpiece.

Kwong Tai Wo Company for the years 1871–1883. The store was located in northern California, but precisely where is unknown. The 160 pages of records ended up in the Bancroft Library at the University of California, Berkeley. The purpose of Sando and Felton's study was to provide archaeologists with a more comprehensive view of the kinds of material objects Chinese residents had available to them. The Kwong Tai Wo records offer information about the kinds of ceramic tablewares Chinese people bought and used, and they offer a rare commentary on where the main profits of the business lay. For the twelve years covered by the account books, the total value of the ceramics mentioned is only $266.80. For the ten years from 1873–1883, the total value of the opium sold exceeded $2,850.

The Kwong Tai Wo store sold at least ten different kinds of opium, some with exotic names meaning "Abundant Luck," "Abundant Memory," and "Everlasting Peace." Archaeologists throughout the American West have found can lids bearing the names of these varieties. One thing Sando and Felton learned in their research was that "Widespread use of opium was a prominent feature of life in America throughout the late 19th century, among both Chinese and non-Chinese alike." Although it is true that Chinese people generally took their opium by smoking, and that non-Chinese ingested theirs in medicines, many non-Chinese also smoked the substance. This evidence shows that it is far too simplistic to argue that finding part of an opium pipe at an archaeological site means that Chinese people once lived there.

Possible ethnic markers abound in the archaeological record. Mark Leone and his colleagues unearthed a steel comb at a site known as Gott's Court in Annapolis, Maryland. Gott's Court was an apartment house that from 1906 until the mid-1930s was home to about twenty-five African American households. Leone and his team excavated the site as part of their interpretive project to understand and interpret the history and culture of historic Annapolis (Chapter 12). The enigmatic comb was one of the most intriguing finds they made at Gott's Court. Not knowing the past function of the comb, they began their inquiry by searching old catalogs and scouring archaeological site reports. Their hope was that someone else had found a similar comb and knew its function, but they had no success. No other archaeological specimens were known to exist. When a photograph of the comb appeared in the *Washington Post*, an African American housekeeper visited the archaeological lab and told the archaeologists that their mystery object was a hot comb used by African Americans to straighten their hair. The archaeologists were excited that their mystery artifact had been identified, but they still had much to learn about its past function. They initially interpreted the comb as a way by which African Americans could strive to integrate themselves into the job market. Straighter hair might be a feature that potential, non-African American employers would view as a positive sign of personal attitude. African Americans with whom the research team spoke, however, said that this was not the case at all. The hot comb was used, they said, not as a tool of assimilation into white society, but rather as a way to ensure their cultural survival. African Americans could use the hot comb to make it appear as if they had been assimilated, when, in fact, this was not true. The use of the hot comb was simply a prudent way of negotiating the rules of white society. The hot comb is clearly an ethnic marker, but one that once had a profound symbolic meaning.

Do white clay smoking pipes proclaiming "Erin Go Bragh" (Ireland For Ever) symbolize Irish ethnicity? Does a blue bead found in the remains of a plantation cabin mean that it was worn by an enslaved African American? Do the brightly colored yellow and red majolica ceramics from the Iberian Peninsula always signal the presence of Spanish or Portuguese colonialists? Historical reality is much more complicated than any stereotype would admit. As Lu Ann De Cunzo's research in New Jersey demonstrated so well, ethnicity can be hidden and difficult to discover at archaeological sites. Even when census rolls, personal letters, and land deeds allow historical archaeologists to determine the ethnicity of the people who once lived at a particular property, the artifacts are rarely equally forthcoming about their past owners' ethnicity.

## Race

Ethnicity and race are closely intertwined, and both present formidable challenges for historical archaeologists. Both social elements are difficult, and sometimes well nigh impossible, to identify in the archaeological record.

Most people tend to confuse race and ethnicity, so much so that the two have become practically synonymous in everyday speech. Even experts can sometimes make the mistake of confusing the two concepts. V. Gordon Childe, one of history's greatest, although eccentric, archaeological thinkers, said in 1926 that "The correlation of cultural with racial groups is generally hazardous and speculative." Childe actually meant "ethnic" groups, and his wording was unfortunate because he made this statement in his widely read *The Aryans: A Study of Indo-European Origins.* The book was so well known that it was eagerly read by the Nazis who generally approved of the way he depicted the Aryans. Childe, a lifelong socialist, was never able to forget that they had misused his serious work of archaeological interpretation to justify their own pernicious deeds.

People in one group often use race to designate people in another group. People use ethnic terms to identify themselves because of some shared or perceived identity. Race is usually narrowly defined on the basis of an outward characteristic, most notably physical appearance. Anthropologists today completely reject the term "race" as a valid human category, preferring instead to see human physical diversity simply as variety. In 1945, British anthropologist M. F. Ashley Montagu referred to race as humanity's "most dangerous myth."

Showing the fallacy of racial categories does not necessarily mean that historical archaeologists can afford to ignore race, or that the impact of racial identification is negligible on living men, women, and children, past and present. Some people in the past did use racial categories to designate certain human groups, and we know that social behavior was affected by their usage. We know that ideas of racial inequality were common in world history (and still are), but can they be shown archaeologically?

A number of historical archaeologists are diligently working to unravel the archaeological mysteries of race. Paul Mullins, an archaeologist at Indiana University-Purdue University Indianapolis, is a leading figure in this effort. In a boldly innovative paper presented in 1993, Mullins proposed that African

Americans, as part of the wider American consumer society, faced special challenges because of racism. African Americans used mass-produced objects in certain
unique ways. As he said, "In the face of racism, the ability to conduct, represent,
and veil their communities was crucial to African America's cultural integrity and
very survival." The purchase and use of material things by men and women of
African descent was accordingly always "constrained by racism's myriad social
discriminations, legal codes, informal barriers, and economic boundaries."

To support his ideas, Mullins used his excavations at the Maynard-Burgess
House in Annapolis, Maryland. This property was occupied by two African
American families—first by the Maynards and then by the Burgesses—from
1847 until 1980. Mullins discovered that fish and other seafoods were important
ways for African Americans to circumvent the normal marketplace. The faunal
remains also show that after the mid-nineteenth century, the Maynards relied
more on store-bought foods. By the beginning of the twentieth century, the
household relied almost exclusively on professionally butchered meats. The excavated bottles from the house also show that by 1890, the Maynards purchased
brand-name foods and canned very little of their own food. Hundreds of fragments of tin cans and a large collection of bottles from professionally packaged
foods—coupled with only two canning jars and one ceramic crock—combine to
show that the Maynards had fully bought into the American national market.
Like most urban dwellers, they no longer preserved their own foods. They preferred instead to go to the store and buy them. Also, bottles from twenty-six na-
tionally advertised brands of medicinal products—like mineral water and
Bromo Seltzer—show that the Maynards relied on over-the-counter products
rather than on home remedies.

Several pieces of ceramic tablewares lay amongst the glass bottles,
butchered animal bones, and medicine bottles. These dishes resembled those excavated at Gott's Court, mentioned above: They were mismatched. Mullins believed the African Americans in Annapolis used a specific strategy to obtain their
ceramics. They may have purchased a few new vessels, but they probably obtained much of their tableware through barter and informal exchange. As one
woman told the research team in 1991: "I don't remember us having any good
china sets, you know . . . I think a lot of stuff was passed down from grandparents
to parents." Mullins believed that the mix of ceramics found in the excavations at
the Maynard-Burgess House "argues that everyday dining was a context in
which the Maynard household felt little compulsion to aspire to dominant styles
or project the appearance of assimilation." What this means is that African Americans did not feel the need to appear to be a part of white society when they were
at home and out of the public eye. Mullins believed that African Americans
bought into the American consumer society along with everyone else, but they
were more likely to hide their affluence because of racist attitudes in society. As a
result, the consumerism of African Americans was more tactical, "a richly tex-
tured effort to negotiate the contradictions of a society structured by racism and
socioeconomic marginalization."

Mullins's study of the Maynard-Burgess House demonstrates the difficulty inherent in the archaeological study of racism. Straightforward interpretations are impossible. The Maynards, like the men and women at Gott's Court, negotiated within white society in subtle ways that did not compromise their integrity. Hardly surprisingly, their methods of negotiation are difficult to identify today, for they were both complex and clandestine. We can only identify them from the dispassionate evidence of distinctive artifacts, which the negotiators bought, used, and threw away.

In another study of race, this one from Virginia and Jamaica, Ywone Edwards-Ingram demonstrated the often subtle character of racial negotiation. She examined the role that medicine could play in the social relations created between enslaved African Americans and their Anglo-American masters. Her specific interest was in the use of plants for medicinal purposes. She discovered that enslaved men and women were often able—sometimes on the sly, sometimes openly—to visit their own doctors and healers, men and women who, like them, were held in lifelong bondage on the same plantation. Enslaved Africans may have felt a sense of personal power when visiting these traditional healers. They also probably appreciated the cultural aspects of using African doctors: in doing so, they were preserving something of their traditional way of life.

Most of us today probably do not think of medicine as cultural, but we can clearly see this character in Edward-Ingram's study. African Americans relied on cures that had African roots, those that employed charms, specific colors, and certain materials, and which involved an established ritual behavior from Africa. Enslaved African Americans could use plants for food, but they could also employ them for curing in situations where their owner purposefully withheld medical care. African American women could also use plants to induce abortion. The use of plants to end pregnancy was another act of personal power because slaves could consciously choose whether to increase the slave owner's supply of human chattel by bringing another life into enslavement.

White slave owners generally used their conceptions of race to attempt to instill a sense of inferiority on enslaved men and women. Slave owners could force their power and authority over their work force by withholding food and other supplies, including medicine. The gathering of plants, for various purposes, was one way in which enslaved people could negotiate the racial hierarchy in which they found themselves. They could use their knowledge of plants as a form of social power. This knowledge today indicates the complex nature of racial negotiation, as African Americans sought to deal with the racism they encountered on a daily basis.

### Social Class, Gender, Ethnicity, and Race

We have explored social class, gender, ethnicity, and race as if they are all separate concepts. We have possibly implied that archaeologists and other social scientists can deftly extract these complex subjects from society and put them each under a microscope of interpretation. But the separation of class, ethnicity, gender, and race is only a convenience; in society, the separation has no grounding in reality. Social scientists (including archaeologists) considering such complex social variables must guard against "essentialism," the idea that some categories are inherently correct and exist in all times and places. We must remember that all notions of social class, ethnicity, gender, and race exist within particular social settings. Ideas about each is free to vary with time and place, and meaning in one culture would not necessarily have meaning in another.

We would all agree that no single individual is just an African American, just a member of the middle class, or just a woman. A person can be an African American woman who belongs to the middle class, but she cannot occupy only one category. Why? Because in complex, highly stratified social organizations, any single individual is simultaneously a member of many groups. Historical archaeologists know this and so they are constantly trying to decide how best to study the social complexities of past societies. In Steven Shephard's study of classes in Alexandria, Virginia, mentioned above, middle-class households were headed by men who were of European-American descent. They were often owners of a small number of enslaved men and women. The nearby lower-class neighborhood was inhabited by free African American unskilled laborers. The prostitutes in Hooker's Division researched by Donna Seifert were working-class women who were trying to feed their families; they were not simply women who had gone astray. The people in the Gerrit Smith house were not just women, they were women of European descent and members of the elite and the working classes.

Class membership, gender role, ethnic affiliation, and race are like the strings of a net; they are interconnected and inseparable. The groups we have illustrated nonetheless do provide historical archaeologists with a means for organizing their analyses and framing their interpretations. But as the analyses and perspectives of historical archaeology have grown more sophisticated, a number of archaeologists have consciously sought to study social groups as intertwined, complex networks of social actors. One of the first studies of this sort, even though it is far from perfect, concentrated on a slave plantation in the American South.

John Otto, who excavated at Cannon's Point Plantation in Georgia, was one of the first historical archaeologists to attempt to study an antebellum slave plantation as if it were composed of men and women who were not just slaves or slave owners, but who were members of several social groups at the same time.

Otto used his knowledge of history, historical sociology, and anthropology to construct a model of plantation society in the antebellum South. Social groups formed a central feature of his model, and he proposed that the plantation's inhabitants were simultaneously members of at least three social groups, which he termed "statuses." A "racial/legal status" created two groups of people: free (white planters and overseers) and unfree (black slaves). Three groups existed as a "social status": managers (planters), supervisors (overseers), and slaves (workers). An "elite/subordinate status" created two more groups: elites (planters) and subordinates (overseers and slaves). The groups existed side by side, and each individual on the plantation belonged to all three of them. An African American field hand would belong to the unfree racial/legal group, the worker group, and the subordinate group. A German overseer would share the "free" group with the planter family and the "subordinate" group with the enslaved men and women.

The spatial arrangement of Cannon's Point Plantation meant that it was an easy matter to link distinct sites with planters, slaves, and overseers. The planter's house was located on the extreme northern end of the island, overlooking the salt marsh. As was typical of the slave-owning South, the planter's part of the site contained several buildings: his house, a detached kitchen, a few small sheds and outbuildings, and some small slave cabins, reserved for the enslaved men, women, and children who labored inside the master's house. The cabins of the field slaves were located farther away and close to the agricultural fields. The overseer's cabin was situated between the field slaves' homes and those of the house servants, probably to increase surveillance over the enslaved work force (Figure 10.3).

Having associated specific sites with slaves, overseers, and planters, Otto believed it would be possible to examine the artifacts unearthed from each site to learn how they reflected the three different "statuses" that existed within his model of plantation society. To learn the differences between his "racial/legal status" groups, he grouped together the artifacts found at the planter site and at the overseer site (because both were free whites). He then compared them with those unearthed at the slave site (because they were unfree blacks). To study the "social status" groups, he compared the three sites individually, and to investigate the "elite/subordinate status," he grouped the overseer and slave artifacts (the subordinates) and compared them with those from the planter site (the elites).

Otto's comparisons did show differences. His examination revealed that the liquor bottles from the three sites represented the racial/legal status. The planter and the overseer sites contained more gin bottles than the slave quarters, but the latter contained more ale, port, and wine bottles. Food remains reflected both the racial/legal status and the elite/subordinate status. The animal bones proved that slaves were more dependent on wild animals than were either the white planter or the overseer households. Wild species such as deer composed a full 45 percent of the slaves' meat diet. The planter family ate fewer wild animals, but the number of species in the bone sample from their house site was larger than that from either the overseer or the slave sites. Ceramic vessel forms reflected social status because each plantation group used a different variety of forms. In the planter deposits, flat wares—plates, deep soup plates, and platters—constituted more than 80 percent of the ceramic collection. Excavations in the overseer's site yielded only 28 percent flat vessels, and in the slave area only 19 percent of the excavated ceramic vessels were in these forms. But, over 40 percent of the vessels in the slave cabins were bowls; in the overseer deposits, 25 percent of the ceramics were bowls. Ceramic decoration seemed to reflect the elite/subordinate status

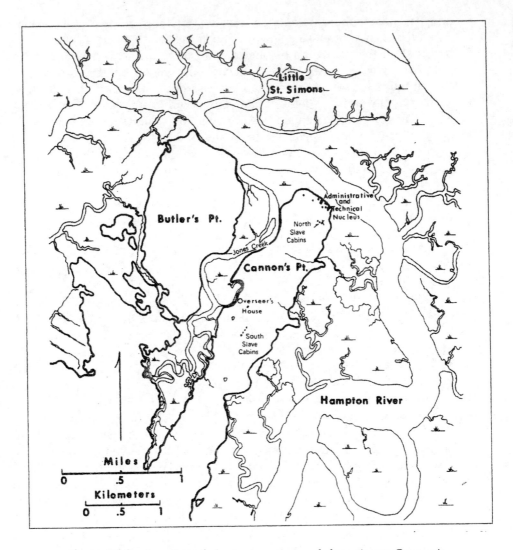

**Figure 10.3**   Location of planter, overseer, and slave sites at Cannon's Point Plantation, St. Simons Island, Georgia, 1794–1860.

because the planter site had many more transfer-printed vessels than either the overseer or the slave sites. Otto used these complex artifact comparisons to conclude that the three statues can be identified in the archaeological deposits at Cannon's Point Plantation. But he cautioned that some artifacts may signal different things and that diversity existed because plantation society was complex.

Archaeologist Lynn Clark provided another important study that demonstrated the interconnections between various social groups. Clark was also interested in how archaeologists can learn about the interactions between ethnicity and class. Rather than excavate, as Otto had done, she choose to study a common kind of material culture readily available above the ground: gravestones. Clark was interested in seeing whether ethnic symbols on tombstones could be associated with lower-class standing, and she selected over one thousand gravestones in Broome County, New York, to test her idea. The ethnic groups who lived in Broome County were German-Jewish, Italian, Irish, and Slovak immigrants. Her reasoning was that as immigrant men and women climbed the social ladder in late-nineteenth- and early-twentieth-century America, they had to appear to surrender their ethnicity. They had to assimilate into mainstream American society and downplay their distinct European heritages. She thought that people in the lower class would have been less likely to have given up their ethnic symbols, because they would not be trying to assimilate. They could continue to use gravestone symbolism to stress their ethnic uniqueness. She also thought that gravestones should become more alike in the middle class because these people would have been compelled to leave their ethnic symbols behind.

Clark's survey of the gravestones showed that ethnic groups and social classes had a wide variety of available options. Upper-class, white-collar workers traditionally established their place in the social order by demonstrating their wealth and power. The greatest display of wealth in any cemetery is a mausoleum, and before 1940, all mausoleums in the cemeteries Clark studied were built by upper-class professionals or administrators. These people were either assimilated Americans or Irish in heritage. After the 1920s, however, upper-class Americans, Irish, and German Jews displayed their wealth less frequently on their gravestones, but after about 1940, blue-collar Italians began to build mausoleums. By the 1950s and 1960s, Italians often built large mausoleums, but the upper class had stopped doing so. Jewish graves were distinct by their widespread use of epitaphs, but particularly so after the 1930s.

Clark's work in "above-ground archaeology" shows how ethnicity and class are intertwined into a complex bundle that archaeologists can unravel only with the greatest difficulty. Today's archaeologists often find it impossible to decide whether a people's actions were guided by their class position, ethnic affiliation, or some complex combination of both. Archaeological solutions to the puzzles of past society become even more elusive when gender and concepts of race are thrown into the mix. The creative research projects mentioned throughout this chapter—and a growing number of archaeologists are conducting these important studies in many places around the world—show how difficult it is for archaeologists to attempt social analyses. Even historical archaeologists, scholars who often have the benefit of highly useful texts, cannot count on making easy social interpretations. Archaeologists who try to assign people from the past to groups is sure to encounter pitfalls. Class, gender, ethnicity, and race are important issues that will challenge historical archaeologists for many years to come. They represent cutting-edge issues in the field for the foreseeable future.

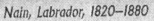

## TIME TRAVEL

### Nain, Labrador, 1820–1880

The Inuit of Labrador had encountered European visitors for at least 250 years before the Moravians established a mission there in the mid-eighteenth century. First the Vikings had come, and then European fishermen had realized in the sixteenth century that the bountiful waters of the north Atlantic was a rich source of cod and other northern fish species. Before long, vessels manned by French, Basque, and Portuguese crews plied the coasts of Inuit territory. The Inuit were not always pleased to find European foreigners in their territory and they often staged raids against them. British entrepreneurs quickly understood that these raids were bad for business, and their government urged the Moravian Brethren—organized in 1457 in what is today the Czech Republic—to establish a Christianizing mission among them.

The Moravians accepted the challenge, believing that they could serve several important functions. They could bring Christianity to the Inuit, act as a buffer between them and the incoming Europeans, and keep the Inuit away from the vices of the European sailors. Their first mission, in 1752, ended quickly, however, when the Inuit murdered five of its members. Undaunted, they tried again in 1771 and established a mission settlement at Nain. They followed this success with two other missions, one north of Nain in 1776 and one south in 1782.

Missions have obvious religious goals, and the Moravians made it clear that they wanted to convert the Inuit. But the impact of missions is never only religious, because missionaries also impart their views on morality, law, and economics to their native audience. The natives who frequently visit or live around missions may slowly acquire the foreigners' atti-

tudes as well as their religious beliefs. One implication of missionary work, particularly in the eighteenth and nineteenth centuries, was that part of the Christianizing process involved accepting foreign material culture. As the Inuit on the coast of Labrador learned about Christianity and the European way of doing things, they also developed an interest in possessing products manufactured in Europe. The desired objects were initially related to survival, with steel fish hooks and hunting gear being much sought after. But by the mid-nineteenth century, the Inuit had become dependent on European foods, and regularly consumed biscuits, dried peas, bread, and tea. In the mission's early years, the Inuit would barter their seal skins, caribou hides, and fish for the desired European goods, but over time, they began to work for the missionaries for wages. They would then use these wages to purchase items directly from the mission store.

The Labrador Inuit, like many native peoples around the world, were drawn to European glazed ceramics. A particular kind of ware traded to the Inuit, and readily accepted by them, is called "stamped earthenware." Ceramists also refer to it as "sponge-decorated" or "cut sponge-decorated," because the decoration is put onto the white-bodied vessel using the root of a sponge into which a design has been cut. The sponge is dipped in pigment and pressed onto the vessel. A light glaze and firing fixes the image to the vessel. The stamped decorations could be either monochrome or polychrome, but the pigments used were typically vibrant blues, pinks, greens, browns, reds, purples, and yellows. The designs could take many

*(continued)*

*Source*: Melanie Cabak and Stephen Loring, 2000. "A Set of Very Fair Cups and Saucers: Stamped Ceramics as an Example of Inuit Incorporation." *International Journal of Historical Archaeology*, 4 1–34.

forms with floral and geometric motifs being especially common.

Cut sponge-decorated wares were generally inexpensive to purchase, and so they were often used by people on the lower end of the socioeconomic spectrum. They became popular in the 1840s and were made until the 1930s, with their peak of popularity being in the 1880–1910 period.

The Inuit at Nain had at least thirty-seven different stamped vessels. The majority were small hollow vessels (either saucers, cups, or mugs), followed closely by bowls. Most of the vessels had monochrome decorations in purple, green, or blue, in six decorative motifs: fleur-de-lis, stylized cross, leaf, floral, geometric, and flag.

The presence of the stamped earthenware ceramics at the Nain mission indicates that the Inuit in the settlement experienced a significant shift in their dietary habits during the nineteenth century. Before the missionaries had arrived, their food consisted of whale, seal, walrus, and polar bear, supplemented with wild berries, shellfish, and waterfowl. The presence of the missionaries altered their traditional pattern to be sure, but the Inuit were not totally changed. For example, they tended to use small-to medium-sized bowls rather than plates. In addition to using the bowls to serve and eat their traditional stews, they also filled them with oil for dipping their meat. The also used bowls as blubber lamps, and they regularly used teacups for many different sorts of beverages including tea.

# Chapter 11

# GLOBAL HISTORICAL ARCHAEOLOGY

*"Everything that has happened since the marvelous discovery of the Americas—from the short-lived initial attempts of the Spanish to settle there, right down to the present day—has been so extraordinary that the whole story remains quite incredible to anyone who has not experienced it at first hand."*

Bartolomé de Las Casas, 1542

In Chapter 1, we remarked that the modern world was shaped by compelling historical forces. The European Age of Discovery, the trade in enslaved Africans, the development of capitalism, and the Industrial Revolution all played major roles in forging nation-states and in mixing and mingling Western and non-Western cultures in every corner of the world. Anthropologist Eric Wolf described this centuries-long process of globalization in his modern classic, *Europe and the People Without History,* published in 1982. He made the point that every human society was affected in one way or another by the expansion of Western civilization into the remotest corners of the globe. The past five centuries have seen the development of what historical sociologist Immanuel Wallerstein termed the "modern world system." French historian Fernand Braudel described the "capitalist world-economy" that developed after about A.D. 1415 as "a fragment of the world, an economically autonomous section of the planet able to provide for most of its own needs." Braudel felt that the "links and exchanges" between the different parts of the world economy created a certain global unity.

Since the late 1970s, experts have created a vast historical literature with an explicitly global perspective. Much of this writing is dense and specific to one tiny region of the globe, and a student can quickly get lost in the complications of these ideas and drown in an ocean of scholarly jargon and historical fact. For the purposes of this book, we prefer to think of the contacts and associations maintained by Europeans in the world as "networks." Our inspiration comes from Eric Wolf, who defined modern world history as composed of "chains of causes and effects at work in the lives of particular populations." As Wolf aptly remarked: "The world of 1400 was already burgeoning with regional linkages and connections; but the subsequent spread of Europeans across the oceans brought the regional networks into worldwide orchestration, and subjected them to a rhythm of global scope." Men and women who, through their relations and contacts, interact as if in a web, can be said to constitute a "network."

Network theorists work in many social sciences because networks involve people, places, and things. Telephone cables, sewer pipelines, and highways can all be described as networks, and we are all familiar with the concept of the computer network. Social network theorists study people and their interrelationships, while geographic network theories study places and their distributions across landscapes. In social network analysis, individuals and groups can be imagined as nodes or points with their relations being represented as lines. A mother and daughter, for example, would be represented as two points with a line connecting them. The same can be imagined for places. Two archaeological sites can be represented as dots on a map with a road or path connecting them. Historical archaeologists must understand both social and geographic connections, because a social connection between groups may also be geographically expressed. A connection between a mother and her daughter may be geographic as well as social: They may live in different villages but still remain personally "close." We can easily imagine that the more complex a society, the more frequent and diverse the social and geographic interconnections between people and places. The use of a network model helps us understand these connections in a visual way.

After about 1415, and increasingly so up until the present day, many networks were global in scope. Many connections were created by trade. Artifacts were bartered for raw materials and food, and commodities could move hundreds or thousands of miles between ports. Our goal in this chapter is to use one modern-era network to explain one of the most exciting areas within today's historical archaeology: the study of colonialism and culture contact. Our focus is on the Dutch Empire, which developed in the seventeenth century.

Dutch explorers, traders, and colonists built an extensive network of villages, forts, and cities around the world. In this chapter, we take you on a brief tour of a few of their settlements to illustrate the richness of research in historical archaeology. We focus on sites that tell us something about contacts between Europeans and non-Europeans. Of all the historical processes that have occurred since 1415, none have been more dramatic and more significant than the multicultural contacts that developed as a result of Western exploration and colonization.

## CULTURAL CONTACTS

The so-called European Age of Discovery had a profound and often catastrophic impact on indigenous peoples around the world. Cultural anthropologists have long been intrigued by this "clash of cultures," and in their research, they have proven that the interactions were never one-sided. Two cultures in contact learn from one another. Indigenous peoples across the globe were impressed by the durability of the Europeans' iron axes and the way their brass kettles could withstand intense heat without cracking like clay pots. Many peoples thus rapidly incorporated foreign objects into their daily lives. Many Mesoamerican peoples adopted Old World cereal crops, cattle, goats, and sheep without hesitation, because they understood their advantages for survival. But the same societies were not simply users of foreign objects, they were also donors. Native American farmers were the most expert agriculturalists of the sixteenth century, and Europeans soon carried amaranth, potatoes, tomatoes, and tobacco back to the Old World. These crops had major impacts on European life. To cite only one example, the potato of South America rapidly became a staple of the Irish diet, so much so that when the crop was struck by a devastating fungus in 1845, people referred to the starvation that followed as "The Irish Potato Famine."

The process of cultural and social interaction was extremely complex and often quite subtle. The history of the process varied with location. Many cultural changes resulting from decisions made in good faith by one generation could have dramatic and dangerous effects on their descendants. The Khoi Khoi herders of the Cape of Good Hope at the southern tip of Africa were under such pressure to trade their cattle to beef-hungry Dutch visitors that they bartered away not only their surplus bulls, but also their cows. Many Khoi Khoi were thus without cattle a generation later, because they had no breeding stock.

A culture in contact tends to view the other culture through a well-defined cultural lens. Some Maori of New Zealand considered Captain Cook and his men gods who came from across the horizon. On the other hand, Cook and his crew were horrified to find freshly butchered human bones in abandoned Maori camps. Europeans for generations considered the Maori fierce cannibals, to the point that passing ships hesitated to land among them. Multicultural contacts of all sorts created what anthropologist Nicholas Thomas referred to as "mutual entanglements" and "shared histories." Generations of increasingly complex transactions contributed to a tangled history.

French historian Fernand Braudel said that indigenous peoples around the world were affected by "the mighty shadow cast" over them by Western Europe. But they were not necessarily destroyed by this shadow. What many Europeans took to be submission and acquiescence were in fact complex strategies for survival. Many Aztec communities in Mexico sought to minimize their contacts with their new colonial Spanish masters. The Aztecs' conversion to Catholicism was actually a careful blending of cultural elements. They adapted their traditional religious beliefs and close social ties to the realities of a new society, one wherein they were economically marginal and on the bottom of the social ladder.

Blendings of European and indigenous cultures are reflected not only in surviving native belief systems and oral traditions, but also in subtle changes in artifacts of every kind. It is here that the historical archaeologist enters, for judicious excavation and survey can often reveal fascinating information about contacts between local groups and an expanding European-centered world system.

The examples that follow provide instances in which archaeology has cast significant new light on complex cultural interactions in the past five hundred years. For convenience, we focus specifically on the Dutch world empire.

## THE DUTCH EMPIRE

In July 1581, the northern provinces of what is today the Netherlands declared their independence from Spain. About seventy-five years earlier, the Netherlands, then called "The Low Countries," came under Spanish rule when Charles V inherited it from the dukes of Burgundy. The Dutch fought for their freedom until 1648, when the King of Spain finally agreed to recognize their independence.

The Dutch became major players in world history during the seventeenth century. This so-called "Golden Age" saw Dutch sailors establish a maritime empire that at its height accounted for one-half of the world's shipping. Amsterdam grew to become the world's most active commercial city, and the Dutch enjoyed the highest standard of living in Europe. The national wealth enjoyed by the Dutch was built upon a foundation of colonialism.

Europeans became increasingly convinced, during the fifteenth century, that great wealth could be made outside Europe. The brutal conquests of the Spanish in Mexico had brought vast amounts of gold back to Madrid and helped them to create an impressive empire. Other Europeans desperately wanted their share of these riches, and so each nation-state devised its own strategy for moving into the burgeoning global market.

Seeking to create their niche, Dutch entrepreneurs in 1602 combined to form the Dutch East India Company, known as VOC (Verenigde Oostindische Compagnie). The agents of this company created a vast trading network that lasted until 1795. They drove English and Portuguese merchant ships from Indonesia, which they named the "Netherlands Indies." They built a capitol in the region and named it Batavia (today's Jakarta).

The success of the Dutch East India Company encouraged other entrepreneurs to develop the Dutch West India Company. The focus of this enterprise rested on the riches of the New World and Africa. In today's United States, the Dutch built a city called New Amsterdam (now New York) in 1623. They colonized much of the area around the city, and also captured islands in the Caribbean from the Spanish.

The vast Dutch Empire went into steady decline beginning in the 1670s. France and England, both searching for greater control of the world's wealth, formed a secret alliance against the Netherlands and attacked it in 1672. The Dutch survived this assault and, after a period of peace, the English once again declared war on the Netherlands in 1780, because the Dutch had supported the American Revolution. The English defeated the Dutch in 1784, and only eleven years later, the French occupied the country and renamed it the Batavian Republic. The occupation spelled the end of the once-powerful Dutch Empire.

The story of the Dutch Empire has been repeated by many other nations who have sought to control the world's economy. But during its heyday, the Dutch built settlements in places across the globe. Historical archaeologists have been able to investigate several of these colonial outposts in Africa, North America, the Caribbean and South America, and Asia.

### Africa

European contacts with African cultures were as complex as similar contacts throughout the world. The Portuguese were attracted to the African coasts by gold and slaves, by trading ventures so profitable that they sought to control access to the interior by fortifying strategic locations. In 1482, a full decade before Columbus set foot in the Americas, the Portuguese Crown authorized the building of an imposing fort on the coast of modern Ghana in West Africa. This fort, named the Castle São Jorge da Mina, lies on a rocky headland, built to protect what the Portuguese hoped would be a lucrative gold trade with the interior (Figure 11.1). A small African community called Elmina was soon built under the castle walls, for it was Africans who actually controlled the trade with the gold-mining peoples far inland. The Portuguese held the castle for 155 years, and

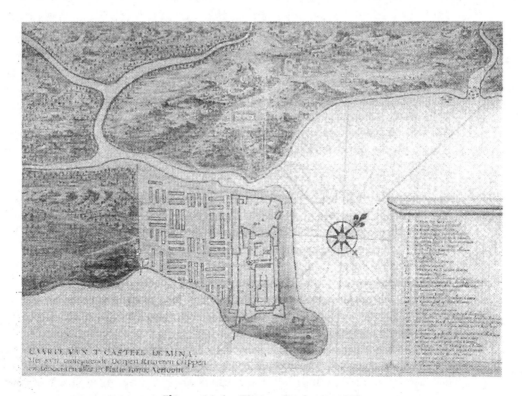

**Figure 11.1**　Elmina Castle, ca. 1637.

maintained an evermore precarious control over the "gold coast" trade as the Dutch rose to power. In 1637, the Dutch succeeded in capturing the castle. It proved a profitable investment for them for over two centuries, until the Gold Coast was ceded to the British in 1872.

Fante people inhabited the area around Elmina before the Portuguese arrived, but other indigenous groups soon moved in, realizing the material advantage of living near an important European trading post. The size of the African community quickly swelled. By 1700, it had more than one thousand stone houses and a population of perhaps as many as fifteen thousand. The townspeople, although culturally Fante, actually regarded themselves as a politically and even culturally distinct people. After a series of conflicts with these folk, the British bombarded Elmina both from land and sea, destroying it on June 13, 1873. They leveled the town's ruins and used the site for a parade ground.

Happily for archaeologists, the site has remained undeveloped and available for excavation. Elmina offers a unique opportunity to examine the ways some Africans learned from and taught the Europeans who lived alongside them. Archaeologist Christopher DeCorse, from Syracuse University, has probed the settlement for several years. He has excavated 3,011 square feet (271 sq m) and has exposed another 600 square feet (54 sq m). These excavations yielded more than 100,000 artifacts. His research has permitted an intimate look into African-European interaction along the Gold Coast.

Most of the artifacts DeCorse excavated date to the eighteenth and nineteenth centuries. Many document connections between Elmina and the rest of the world. White clay tobacco pipes came from England and the Netherlands, porcelain was made in Chinese factories, and glass bottles once held American patent medicines. An almost whole, gray stoneware jug from Germany was brilliantly decorated with blue rosettes and ribbons. In its center the letters "A R," refer to Queen Anne ("Anne Regina"), the English monarch from 1702–1714.

DeCorse's important research also documents cultural change in the cosmopolitan community beneath Elmina's walls. Many Africans and Europeans visited the fort, not only from overseas but also from far in the interior. During some periods of the fort's history, Mande traders and Asante people from the interior were active participants in the town's daily life. At other times, European slavers brought Africans from far inland both to labor locally and for export to Brazil and other parts of the New World. The Dutch were also active slave traders during their time at Elmina, transporting thousands of captive Africans to their plantations in the Netherlands Antilles.

Archaeology shows that the people of Elmina were selective in the cultural changes they were willing to accept. For example, the presence of buttons and buckles within the artifact collection attests to changes in dress styles. Slate pencils and writing slates show that at least some of the townspeople were literate. In contrast, European burial customs and cemeteries—including one reserved for the Dutch—did not come into general use before 1873. People buried their dead under the floors of their houses. Burials were found beneath all the house floors

DeCorse excavated, even those having less than twelve inches (thirty cm) of soil above bedrock.

DeCorse's excavations provide a unique picture of cultural continuity within an environment of continual economic and political change. Local Africans were indeed changed by regular contact with Europeans, but they also were not overwhelmed. They simply adapted to new circumstances in a purposeful way, adopted new artifacts and new customs when it was to their perceived advantage to do so.

It is a truism to say that the world of the early twenty-first century is forged from deep historical roots. Nowhere is this sentiment truer than South Africa, where the complex politics of today result from centuries of interaction and misunderstanding between indigenous African peoples and foreign Europeans, including the Dutch. Historical documents and oral traditions reveal a great deal about the interactions between these different peoples, but historical archaeology is rapidly filling in many gaps in the story and providing fresh insights.

When Portuguese captain Bartolemeu Diaz anchored in Mossel Bay, east of the Cape of Good Hope, South Africa, in 1488, he found himself in a peaceful and beautiful bay surrounded by green hills. Skin-clad herdsmen grazing large cattle on the lush grass, soon fled at the sight of Diaz's ships. These people were Khoi Khoi, nomadic cattle herders and foragers, people with the simplest of possessions, but a highly sophisticated adaptation to the unpredictable semitropical environment of the Cape. The Portuguese, and the Dutch who followed them, considered the Khoi Khoi little more than animals, people without an intelligible language or any recognizable religion. Sailors' tales recounted how they smeared themselves with rancid butter and how they could smell them from thirty paces. The Europeans called them by the derogatory name "Hottentots."

The Khoi Khoi, however, were vital to the passing ships of Europe because they supplied fresh meat to crews wrestling with scurvy. These visitors generally left the Khoi Khoi alone. With no reports of gold being found in their territory, the Europeans had no interest in their land. The policy of non-involvement changed in 1652, when the Dutch East India Company built a small fort at the Cape. The dynamics of cultural interaction changed at once, because the European newcomers were colonists, farmers in search of land and grass for grazing. Seeking pasture land rather than gold, they soon encroached on the territory of the Khoi Khoi and restricted their movements. The Dutch also forced them to trade their cattle, even their much-needed breeding stock. VOC agents told the colonists to "tolerate, negotiate, manipulate" the local people. Most followed this advice to such a devastating effect that the traditional culture of the Cape Khoi Khoi vanished within a century. The survivors eked out a living as ranch hands or domestic servants, or moved far inland to escape the Dutch.

The outlines of this story are well known, but many details remain a mystery. In 1984, Carmel Schrire, an archaeologist at Rutgers University, embarked on a study of Oudepost I, "Old Post," a small, stone fort the Dutch built in 1669 to show the increasingly aggressive French that they "owned" the Cape. The French soon lost interest in the area, so the four to ten Dutchmen who lived at the post until 1732 spent their days trading with the neighboring Khoi Khoi. Schrire's work included a major excavation of buildings associated with Oudepost. The area around the post had not seen much settlement after 1732, so the sites were pristine.

Historical records report the construction of the VOC outpost, but only archaeological research can provide more precise details. No map or plan of the remote post is known to exist. Schrire's excavations revealed that the Dutch built three small buildings on the beach at Oudepost I (Figure 11.2). One was an irregularly shaped fort that encompassed over 4,400 square feet (400 sq. m). The second building, placed to the northwest, was a long, rectangular structure that

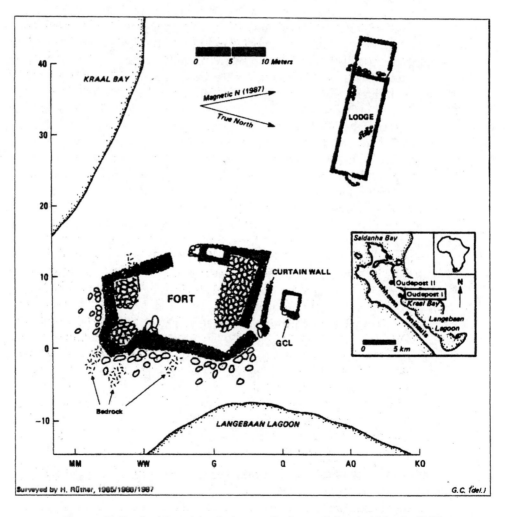

**Figure 11.2**   Building foundations at Oudepost I, South Africa in 1987.

measured 18.5 by 65.1 feet (5.6 by 19.8 m). This building may have served as the garrison's barracks, because Schrire found domestic artifacts and food remains associated with it. The third structure, whose function is unknown, was located directly north of the fort and measured only 9.3 by 10.6 feet (2.8 by 3.2 m).

Archaeology revealed that the Dutch settlers constructed the buildings of rocks collected from the shore. Schrire learned that the garrison did not deposit their refuse in one particular dump, but tossed it everywhere, leaving a broad layer of seventeenth-century glass, ceramics, gunflints, and metal across the site. The presence of Khoi Khoi pottery, stone tools, and bone spear points in the midden deposits attest to their connection with the outpost as well.

Historical accounts provide abundant evidence for interaction between Khoi Khoi inhabitants and Dutch settlers. For example, in 1670, the fort's commandant reported that a small band of Khoi Khoi arrived to offer their services in fighting the French. In 1726, another post commandant wrote: "The said Hottentot, having some cattle of his own, I hired for two years to take care of our sheep, on condition that he would be properly supplied with liquor and tobacco." The important issue that interested Schrire was thus not *whether* the Khoi Khoi and the Dutch interacted at Oudepost, but rather *how* they interacted.

The faunal remains tell part of the story. The authors of historical texts dwell on the importance the Dutch placed on the cattle trade. Their relentless demand for meat, gained either by trade or theft, is thought to have put tremendous pressure on local Khoi Khoi groups. Cattle bones are indeed commonplace in the archaeological deposits at Oudepost I. But the archaeological remains also provide a much more complete picture of Dutch subsistence. Instead of relying completely on sheep and cattle, the Europeans also adopted something of the Khoi Khoi's traditional subsistence strategy. The Dutch settlers partly followed the hunter-gatherer lifestyle the Khoi Khoi had practiced for generations. Schrire's findings provided irrefutable proof of this Dutch strategy, as large numbers of fish, mammal, and bird bones were excavated in the fort's middens. Domesticated species accounted for only about 28 percent of the animal bones found at the site.

Oudepost I offers insights into Dutch/Khoi Khoi interaction, and also a brief, albeit telling, glimpse into the thoughts of at least one Dutch member of the garrison. This unknown soldier has left us a tantalizing clue of his service at the post by etching a simple palm tree onto an ostrich egg shell (Figure 11.3). Palms did not grow at the Cape then, so Schrire imagined that a lonely soldier who pined for his days in warmer, more hospitable southeast Asia had created the image: "he embellished an ostrich egg with memories—his dreams mingling with reality, here, on the far African shore."

The Cape Khoi Khoi did not survive permanent European settlement in their homeland. Oudepost I flourished at a time when Dutch farmers were staking out ranches deep inside Khoi Khoi territory, disrupting centuries-old seasonal movements that prevented the herders from overgrazing their large territories in

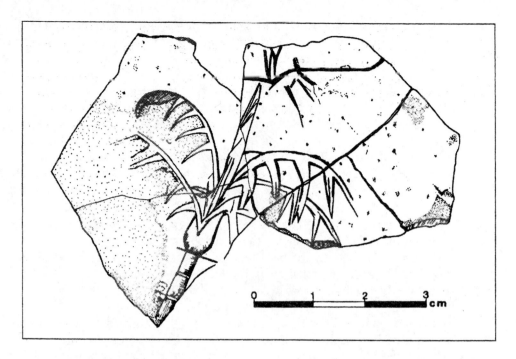

**Figure 11.3**   Etched ostrich shell found at Oudepost I, South Africa.

the interior. By the late eighteenth century, the Cape Khoi Khoi were effectively extinct, with only a few survivors living on the margin of colonial society. Early European records chronicle their fate, and researchers like Schrire fill in many details of their day-to-day existence, the mundane events that never appear in documents.

Research by Stacey Jordan, a student of Schrire's, has given us an excellent view of how Dutch settlers at the Cape sought to create a way of life that was similar to what they had known at home. When Dutch settlers first went to the Cape, they took with them pewter plates and cups and wooden vessels. These were the containers used on Dutch ships at the time. After 1666, they increasingly used Asian porcelains, but they did not have their traditional, and most familiar, coarse red earthenwares. Dutch potters had made coarse earthenware vessels since the fourteenth century. Coarse earthenware was a common kind of ceramic produced in Europe during the Middle Ages, and it is still made today. Coarse earthenware is low-fired and usually glazed—on the inside only, the outside only, or both—in earth-tone colors. Today's terra cotta flower pots, usually unglazed, are red coarse earthenwares.

In the absence of their familiar dishes, Dutch settlers at the Cape were forced to eat with their hands out of large pots. Some of the men even used shells as spoons, in a method that would have appeared barbaric to members of the

Dutch culture. In 1663, the commander at the Cape sought to change this behavior by requesting that the VOC send him potters from home. They approved his request, and the first coarse earthenware pottery was established at the Cape two years later. The commander was so happy that he wrote in his diary: "This morning, for the first time, diverse kinds of baked and glazed earthenware were taken from the oven in the new pottery and found to be very good. Some were sold this afternoon on the public market, and a considerable quantity kept back for the next market day."

Jordan's analysis of the coarse earthenwares excavated from the Cape shows that Dutch potters made different vessels for different purposes. They made pots of various sizes for storage, and pots, pans, skillets, pot lids, and drainers for food preparation. They also produced saucers, plates, bowls, and pitchers for serving food, and special vessels for heating and lighting their homes. But Jordan believed that these European-style ceramic vessels were more than simply functional. She believed that in addition to having specific uses, the ceramics were also an attempt by the Dutch East India Company to maintain a sense of Dutch identity. Jordan also thought that the Company's representatives in the Cape—the elite officers and administrators—sought to use these ceramics as a way to maintain the class structure of the Netherlands. Settlers who used ceramics that were familiar to them, even though they had been made in Africa, reinforced the idea that they were neither the wealthy entrepreneurs who ran the VOC nor the indigenous Khoi Khoi. They were simply working people.

Traveling to the Cape of Good Hope was not without risk and the Dutch East India Company lost many ships to storms, reefs, and bad judgment. One such ship, the *Oosterland*, was found by sport divers off the Cape in 1988 and investigated by archaeologists in the early 1990s. Dutch shipwrights built the ship in the Netherlands in 1684, and it became an important part of the Company's trading fleet, making three successful voyages to Asia. But, it also had a checkered history. Its sailors had to turn back on her maiden voyage after only two weeks because of bad weather, and in 1697, eleven people on board died from the drinking water and at least thirty-five others were taken ill. While waiting in 1697 at the Cape to rendezvous with other ships for the long journey home, a northwesterly gale caused another ship to crash into the *Oosterland*. The wind shifted the following day, causing the ship to go adrift and to strike the sea bed. On hitting the bottom, the ship's mast splintered and the hull broke apart. Only two people survived out of the three hundred on board.

The wreck lay only about 918 feet (280 m) offshore, under only about 20 feet (6 m) of water. The archaeologists used sonar (Chapter 6) to chart the wreck's precise location on the sea floor. Their excavations—the first systematic maritime field school in South Africa's history—revealed the kinds of objects the ships of the VOC transported: stoneware jugs of German manufacture, clay pipes from the Netherlands, porcelain vessels made in China, spices, porcelain statuettes in the shape of ducks, eagles, and Buddhist lions, and wicker baskets containing blue dye.

### North America

Giovanni da Verazzano is the first recorded European to visit the area that would later become New Amsterdam and then New York. Sailing along the coast in 1524, Verazzano encountered a native people dressed in multicolored birds' feathers who greeted them with great joy. Verazzano sailed under the French flag, and it was not long before Portuguese and Spanish cartographers were showing the location on their maps and charts.

The rise of the Dutch Empire meant that they would be looking for places around the world to settle, and the region observed by Verazzano appeared to offer a fertile opportunity. In 1609, Henry Hudson set sail from the Netherlands to explore this region, arriving in September. Hudson and his crew discovered that while some Native Americans were happy to see them, others were not so impressed, and one attack resulted in the death of one of his men. Still, most of the indigenous inhabitants of the area were willing to interact peacefully with the Dutch, and trading partnerships were soon arranged.

As part of their North American empire, the Dutch West India Company built an outpost, called Fort Orange, on the Hudson River at the site of today's Albany, New York. Constructed in 1624, this wooden outpost was about 150 miles (241 km) from the Atlantic. The Dutch held the fort, rebuilt in stone, until 1664, when the English captured it. The Dutch retook the fort in 1672, but they returned it to the English only two years later, and their North American empire was largely finished.

Archaeologists first conducted excavations at the site of Fort Orange in 1970 and 1971. These initial excavations were intended to salvage important information before the site was disturbed by the construction of a highway. The preservation at the site was unexpectedly good, and the archaeologists were able to investigate portions of the fort as well as the remains for four houses located inside its walls. These excavations provided a wealth of information about the material culture of daily Dutch life in the colonies (Figure 11.4). A curious group of artifacts was composed of over thirty white clay smoking pipe stems with notches cut into them. These stems came from the kind of pipes discussed in Chapter 5 (see Figure 5.6). Paul Huey, the archaeologist who studied the pipes knew that several interpretations were possible to explain their odd appearance. Perhaps the pipes were notched as part of a process of making beads from them. This explanation seemed unlikely, because the pipe stems are extremely brittle and cutting a notch into them was unnecessary; they would break easily without the notch. Another explanation might be that smokers cut the notches to allow more air into the pipe. This practice is unknown, so it remains a remote possibility. Huey, however, discovered that when one blows through these stems they produce a soft, high-pitched whistle. Anthropologists and archaeologists have shown that Native Americans in New York State commonly used whistles made of reeds and other materials. Perhaps Native Americans had fashioned the whistles from pipes. Equally interesting is a painting, dating to the same time as Fort

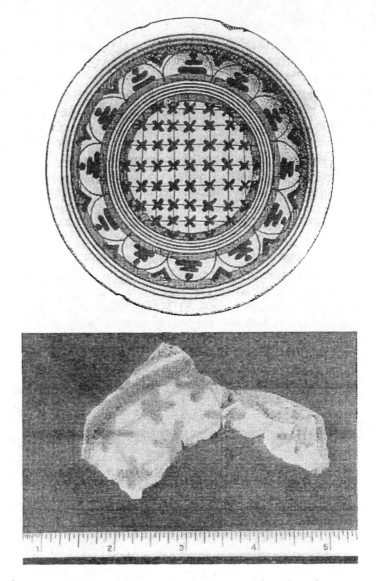

**Figure 11.4**   Dutch majolica sherds excavated from Fort Orange, ca. 1648–1657.

Orange, showing European peasants using simple flutes that look much like a white clay pipe stem. If the notched pipes were indeed used as whistles, then it means that Dutch colonists in the New World, who found themselves far from home, may have created the pipe flutes for their own sense of well-being. The sound of a traditional Dutch air may have calmed the homesickness of the colonists.

In addition to investigating the remains of Fort Orange itself, historical archaeologists have also been able to conduct some excavations at the site of Beverwyck, the town Dutch settlers built around the fort. Others have performed excavations in New Amsterdam, today's New York City.

Archaeologist Meta Janowitz examined the nature of the colonial Dutch diet in New Amsterdam. Textual information suggested that the preparation of Dutch food was relatively uncomplicated. Cooks fried pancakes and waffles, and boiled porridge. Common foods like bread, cheese, and smoked meat did not require additional cooking. Other foodstuffs, like fish and meat, required processing before cooking.

Janowitz pointed out that the archaeologist's ability to locate evidence of much colonial Dutch food is questionable. Porridge, waffles, and cheese leave no archaeological traces. As a result, the best routes toward understanding Dutch eating habits is indirectly through their ceramics and animal bone refuse.

The seventeenth-century Dutch commonly used vessels called *grapen* for cooking and food consumption. *Grapen* were bulbous, glazed coarse earthenware pots that had three little feet and one or two handles. Dutch households also used a skillet that also had three squat feet. Janowitz was able to examine archaeological examples of these vessels and, even more intriguing, was able to see them being used in contemporary paintings by Dutch masters.

Records indicate that the residents of New Amsterdam obtained foodstuffs from many sources. They received beef, wheat, pork, and butter from Dutch and English farmers on Long Island; beef, sheep, and cider apples from New England; and beef, pork, and fruit from Virginia. Native American traders also bartered their maize and pumpkins in the city.

The diet of the colonial Dutch in New Amsterdam was generally European in character. The colonists may not have had all the same foods they had available at home, but they did have the same kinds of food: meats, grains, and fish. Their main concession to North America was the adoption of eating maize, one of the most important staples of the Native American diet. Archaeological evidence from seven sites, dating from about 1650–1720, indicates that the residents' diets did not change much after the English assumed control of New Amsterdam and renamed it New York (1664).

In their book *Unearthing Gotham: The Archaeology of New York City*, archaeologists Anne-Marie Cantwell and Diana diZerega Wall explain how Dutch colonists appropriated the wampum of the Native Americans who lived in the region of today's New York City. Native Americans made tiny beads from shells they found along the coast. The beads were tubular in shape, and white or purplish-black in color (Figure 11.5). They made the white beads from the central column of the whelk shell and the dark beads from the purple spots on hard-shell clamshells.

The use of wampum by Native Americans was complex and firmly embedded within their culture. They strung the beads together in long strands or wove them into belts, and gave them away at important times. They considered the

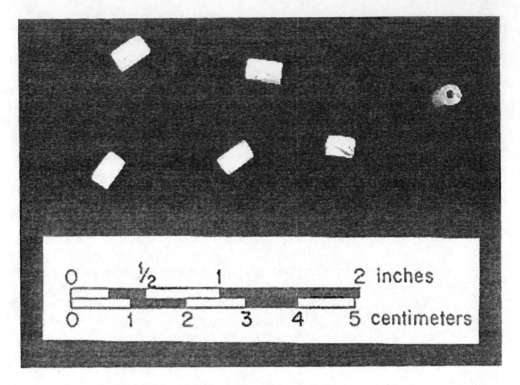

**Figure 11.5**   Wampum beads.

beads to be valuable, highly significant objects. They could give the beads away as ceremonial gifts, use them in gambling, or bury them with the dead. Traditional healers could use the beads in their rituals, and entire groups could give wampum belts to Europeans as proof of their commitment to a new treaty. When woven into patterns, wampum belts could also be used as historical records of important events.

The cultural significance of wampum was largely lost on the Dutch. They called it *sewant* and simply used it as money. Agents from the Dutch West India Company amassed large amounts of wampum and used it in their dealings with Native Americans during the height of the fur trade. Before long, European settlers throughout New York and New England used wampum as their sole currency. Dutch settlers used it to pay their rents, make good on a fine, or purchase much-needed foodstuffs. They could even buy property with the tiny shell beads.

Archaeologists working in New Amsterdam have discovered evidence of wampum manufacture. At a small outpost called Fort Massapeag, archaeologists discovered a large midden filled with shell beads in various states of manufacture. Unfortunately, this site has suffered from years of thoughtless looting and other forms of destruction, so the evidence from it is not as good as it could be. Even so, the discovery of the wampum indicates that the manufacture of the shell beads began as an important cultural event that, with the advent of Dutch involvement, became an economic tool of exchange. As the demand for wampum grew, Native Americans and European colonists spent an increasing amount of their time making the beads. Fort Massapeag became a combination Fort Knox and mint, a place were wampum could be made, stored, and collected.

Wampum, though tiny and seemingly insignificant, is actually central to understanding the interactions between Native Americans and Dutch settlers in colonial North America. Any archaeologists who, for whatever reason, misses the beads during their excavations, necessarily does a serious disservice to history. Wampum provides an excellent example that the smallest artifacts can have the greatest importance to understanding the past.

### The Caribbean and South America

The historical archaeologists working in the Caribbean are making significant contributions to knowledge. Archaeologist Norman Barka has conducted several years of excavation on the island of St. Eustatius, where the Dutch settled in 1636 and built Fort Oranje. St. Eustatius is part of the Netherlands Antilles, which includes the islands of Curaçao, Bonaire, Saba, and St. Maarten. Barka and his teams have investigated a number of lots in the only town on the island of St. Eustatius, called Oranjestad, also known as Upper Town. Oranjestad was composed of 44 blocks that contained dwellings, stores, governmental buildings, and chapels. Barka and his students recorded 397 buildings during an architectural survey of Upper Town. Their excavations in various parts of the settlement retrieved an assortment of Dutch material items, including wine and water bottles and glazed ceramics.

Barka's archaeologists also investigated "Concordia," the country estate of Governor Johannes de Graaff. De Graaff was born on St. Eustatius and served as its commander, or governor, from 1776–1781. The island's merchants grew wealthy during these years by supplying arms, ammunition, and other commodities to the rebel forces of the American Continental Army. De Graaff and many of his contemporaries used their newfound riches to purchase land for the cultivation of sugar and enslaved Africans to produce it. Excavations at the estate in the late 1990s discovered a number of building foundations, including a sugar boiling house, a section of brick pavement, and a duck pond. Barka believed that his excavations at Concordia provided evidence of both the lives of the Dutch colonial elite and the many enslaved men and women who worked for them.

Historical archaeologists have also been researching the Dutch habitation of the islands of Curaçao and St. Maarten. The islands' Dutch settlers followed a pattern established throughout the Caribbean, and in the seventeenth century began growing sugar cane and producing sugar using enslaved African labor.

Dutch explorers and colonists moved into northeast Brazil in 1630 and quickly began to challenge the Portuguese Empire there. They built forts and fortified outposts throughout the lands they held. In 1631, they built yet another Fort Orange (Forte Orange), a classic four-bastioned fort in Pernambuco.

The colonial forces of the Dutch were intent on keeping their foothold in South America, and they sent regular armed parties to investigate the settlements of both Native South Americans and their Portuguese rivals. The early Portuguese Empire in Brazil was based on the labor of enslaved Africans to cultivate and produce sugar. They stretched their plantations out along the picturesque Brazilian coast, leaving the interior to the indigenous cultures. Enslaved men and women, however, frequently escaped the inhuman slave regime and trekked into the interior in search of freedom. The settlements these fugitive slaves established were called "quilombos" or "maroon communities." One of the largest and most famous quilombos in world history was called Palmares.

At its height, Palmares was reported to have as many as twenty thousand residents living in ten separate villages. Contemporary reports indicate that the villages were surrounded by stockades and that the houses were made in an African style. The people of Palmares constructed a political system similar to what they had known in Africa, most likely the region of today's Angola. A king ruled the settlements, supported by a number of lesser leaders. Palmares was geographically situated between the towns and plantations of the Portuguese on the coast, the villages of Native South Americans in the interior, and the Dutch outposts to the north (Figure 11.6).

The Dutch feared the power of Palmares and sent almost yearly raids against it beginning in 1640. The accounts kept by Dutch raiders provide our earliest descriptions of the maroon kingdom. The only known contemporary image was made by a Dutch observer in 1647. By 1670, the Portuguese had expelled the Dutch from Brazil, leaving the king in Lisbon to decide what to do about Palmares.

Archaeological research at Palmares as been minimal, but it has revealed artifacts that may be Dutch in origin. Archaeologists working at the Sierra da Barriga, the site of Macaco, the capitol of Palmares, retrieved several coarse earthenware sherds that may be Dutch or Portuguese in origin. Much more research is required before archaeologists will obtain a clear understanding of the history and culture of the great maroon kingdom of Palmares. Research there, however, amply demonstrates the importance of historical archaeology.

### Asia

Historical archaeologists have yet to devote intensive interest in the archaeology of Dutch colonialism in Asia, though interest is growing. Some of the reasons for the lack of study are purely practical, but others involve political and economic factors. One great source of information about the Dutch in this region, however, are Dutch East India Company (VOC) shipwrecks. Underwater archaeologists have explored sunken VOC ships in the waters around the Netherlands, southern Africa, India, and Australia. Maritime historians estimate that the Company lost somewhere around 250 ships in the 200 years of its existence, many of them in Asian waters.

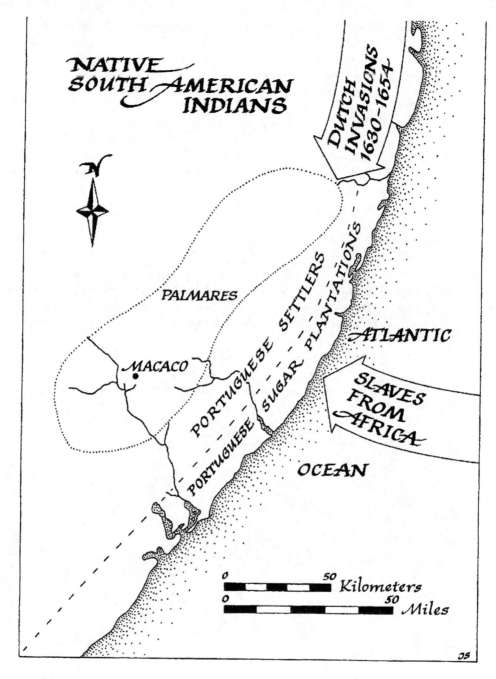

**Figure 11.6** Location of Palmares.

One of the most famous, and perhaps infamous, VOC wrecks is the *Gelder-malsen*. The wreck of the *Geldermalsen* occurred in 1752, when it struck a reef off the Riau Archipelago in Indonesia. The ship broke apart and sank, taking eighty of its men down with it. The cargo of the *Geldermalsen* provided a glimpse at the nature of the trade that the VOC carried on between the Netherlands and its 250 outposts in Asia.

The wreck site contained copper alloy candlesticks, glass stemware, 24 iron cannon, an abundance of German stoneware, and glass bottles of different sizes. The most amazing find by far was 150,000 pieces of fine, blue and white Chinese porcelain. Originally packed into 203 crates, the collection included complete dinner sets (plates, serving dishes, butter dishes, sauce boats, salad bowls), tea cups and saucers, chocolate cups and saucers, tea pots, and milk bowls (Figure 11.7). Also included were soup bowls, cuspidors, and vomit pots. All the pieces were delicately shaped and beautifully decorated. The cargo of the *Geldermalsen* is most definitely a treasure.

But controversy over the *Geldermalsen's* cargo arose precisely because it *was* a treasure. The finds were extremely valuable, and the site was not carefully excavated by trained archaeologists. Instead, an English treasure hunter named Michael Hatcher salvaged the collection from the sea bottom in 1985 and, realizing its value, promptly shipped it to Christie's auction house in Amsterdam.

**Figure 11.7**   Porcelain from the *Geldermalsen* lying on the sea floor.

Hatcher had earlier retrieved twenty-three thousand pieces of Chinese porcelain from a sunken Chinese junk dating to around 1640. The auction of these pieces had netted him approximately $2 million. The cargo of the *Geldermalsen* did not disappoint him; he made about $15 million from it.

The mining of archaeological sites, on both land and underwater, raises significant ethical problems for professional archaeologists. First, simply removing objects from a wrecksite (or a terrestrial site) destroys the archaeological context. As we noted earlier, archaeologists use the soil and an artifact's associations to help tell them about that artifact. Archaeologists cannot wrest much information from artifacts without knowing their contexts. But Hatcher's salvors payed no attention to context during their "excavation" of the *Geldermalsen*. In fact, they merely used a big nozzle to suck the debris from the artifacts. Archaeological contexts were not their concern; they were after valuable artifacts. Second, Hatcher and his crew were only interested in objects they could auction. Professional archaeologists know that sometimes the most important objects are those that have little or no monetary value. Half of a Ming dynasty plate, for instance, has as much archaeological importance as a whole plate, but the broken specimen has no resale value. Collectors want whole vessels for their china cabinets.

Salvaging wrecks like the *Geldermalsen* raises profound, far-reaching questions for archaeologists. The International Congress of Maritime Museums condemned the salvage of the *Geldermalsen* in 1986. We deal with many of the ethical issues now facing historical archaeology, and in fact all archaeology, in both the next and the final chapter.

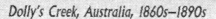

## TIME TRAVEL

### Dolly's Creek, Australia, 1860s–1890s

The rush for gold has inspired unbounded hope and depressed madness throughout the world, as eager prospectors have sought their fortunes from the earth. History shows that Europeans have pursued gold both in their settled colonies and in lands fabled for the supposed richness of their untapped deposits. In the 1850s, the Moorabool goldfield of southeastern Australia, located about 38.5 miles (62 km) west of Melbourne, was known as a gold-rich area just waiting to be exploited by eager miners.

Industrial mining involves the studied research of geologists and engi-neers, with discovered veins being worked by waged miners in the employ of large companies. Such capitalist concerns are usually interested in making a big strike, exhausting it, and then moving to the next deposit-rich area. This may be the general view of mining today, but many individual prospectors in the mid-nineteenth century were not employed as paid miners; they were subsistence miners who often took their families into the frontier to work "poor man's diggings."

*(continued)*

Source: Susan Lawrence, *Dolly's Creek: An Archaeology of a Victorian Goldfields Community.* (Melbourne: Melbourne University Press, 2000).

Subsistence miners established communities, often composed of entire families, who mined for precious metals with the goal of providing a sustainable living. Most really did not expect to strike it rich. They would have willingly accepted the "big strike" if it came, but most understood that they would never be truly *nouveau riche*; they were simply miners making a living. One community of subsistence miners in Australia was called Dolly's Creek.

In the late 1850s, a group of anonymous miners traveled north up the Moorabool River in search of unexplored gold fields. Near the settlement of a squatter named Morrison they found, to their excitement, gold-bearing gravels. They decided to establish a camp on the spot, and they promptly named it Dolly's (or Dolly) Creek after a prospecting technique. At the time, a "dolly" was an instrument miners used to divide and mix stiff clay or cement with water in a tub.

At the height of its settlement, over six hundred people lived at Dolly's Creek in over two hundred houses. Most of their homes were of simple construction, with canvas roofs and bark or timber walls. A few houses were more substantial, being made of stone or wood. The canvas houses usually had one room, and measured only about 6.5 by 11.5 feet (2 by 3.5 m) in size. Other houses in the camp could be as large as 11.5 by 16 feet (3.5 by 5 m) in size. The miners equipped their homes with fireplaces built of roughly hewn blocks of quartzite held together with mortar made mostly of mud. These fireplaces required almost constant maintenance, because if left untended, they would collapse when the mud washed out. The chimneys above the fireplaces were built of wood, sheets of iron, or even animal hides. Most of the houses had glass windows, and at night the people used candles stuck in empty bottles or kerosene lamps for light. At least one house in the village, perhaps used as a store or pub, was built more solidly than the rest. Its walls were composed of a number of layers that served to make it watertight and relatively secure. Its canvas inner surface was strengthened by several additional layers of newspaper, heavy cardboard, and tin.

The residents of Dolly's Creek had the usual complement of consumer goods available during the period. People usually think that late-nineteenth-century miners, loggers, and other extractive industry workers used only tin dishes. Tin wares were more durable than ceramics; when dropped they would bend but not break. The men and women at Dolly's Creek may have used tin dishes, but they also used a wide variety of glazed earthenwares. The members of the individual households owned a number of transfer-printed dinner plates, teacups, saucers, and other vessels decorated in blue, mulberry, green, red, black, and brown. They made no attempt to use matching sets, but they were not immune to adding a few amenities: Some of the houses had wallpaper decorated with floral designs.

The Dolly's Creek villagers probably selected their personal possessions with one eye on their transportability. They undoubtedly realized that they might need to relocate to another gold field and that it would be a huge inconvenience to carry cartloads of objects along with them. But people in the settlement did have some treasured objects. One notable piece was a brass mantle clock. When the owner of the clock left the village—perhaps hoping to return—he or she took out the working mechanism and left the case behind.

The diet at Dolly's Creek was simple but varied. They drank beer and wine, champagne, gin, whiskey, as well as other drinks. They made stews, soups, and roasts with chicken, beef, pork, mutton, and rabbit. They purchased this meat from butchers who commonly lived in mining camps. For their health, they relied on patent medicines, just like thousands of other men, women, and children who lived during the late nineteenth century.

# Chapter 12

# HISTORICAL ARCHAEOLOGY AND CULTURAL RESOURCE MANAGEMENT

*"I think good CRM is about people with conflicting views sitting down and reasoning with each other, seeking mutually agreeable solutions."*

Thomas F. King, 2002

Students of historical archaeology will encounter cultural resource management (CRM) at some point during their careers. The growth in CRM research has been partly responsible for the rapidly increased interest in historical archaeology around the world. CRM research has also done much to promote archaeology to the public. We present in this chapter some basic information about cultural resource management that will explain the nature and importance of this activity to historical archaeology.

## THE CHANGING FACE OF HISTORICAL ARCHAEOLOGY

Historical archaeology as practiced at the beginning of the twenty-first century is different from much of the historical archaeology that was practiced before the mid-1970s. Not only have theoretical and methodological emphases changed over time, but the very nature of the workforce has also undergone a transformation. Only a few years ago, the vast majority of professional archaeologists were teaching in academic departments or building educational exhibits for museums. Archaeologists were largely engaged in pure research that would promote knowledge and education. The basic idea was that their books and museum exhibits would serve the public good by providing information about the latest advances in knowledge about human history and culture. The situation is vastly different today, because most archaeologists work as professionals within a business-oriented, cultural resource management environment. This cohort of archaeologists includes a huge number of historical archaeologists as well. CRM archaeologists may be employed by governmental agencies responsible for protecting a nation's cultural heritage, by engineering companies engaged in large construction projects, or by privately owned firms dedicated solely to archaeological consulting. A few universities also maintain CRM research units.

A membership survey conducted by the Society for Historical Archaeology revealed that most practicing historical archaeologists are engaged in CRM research in some fashion. Fully 71 percent of the respondents to the survey reported that they had completed a cultural resource management study during the 1993–1998 period. Only 29 percent of the responding members said they had engaged in any teaching during the same period. These employment figures represent a major shift in the practice of historical archaeology. More individuals are now fully employed in historical archaeology than ever before, but their main activities occur in cultural resource management rather than in universities or museums (Figure 12.1). What has brought about the shift from educational instruction to sponsored research conducted under contract?

Perhaps ironically, part of what caused the expanded employment opportunities for historical archaeologists was the economic expansion that occurred

**Figure 12.1**   Double fireplace foundation discovered at Ashland-Belle Helene Plantation, Louisiana, as part of a project conducted for the Shell Chemical Company by archaeologists from Earth Search Inc.

throughout the world following the Second World War. Over the past few decades, the expansion of cities, the construction of strip malls in once-empty fields, and the unrelenting use of agricultural land for the building of new homes, small businesses, and industries has meant that archaeological sites were being destroyed at an ever-increasing rate. As the dual process of construction (of the new)/destruction (of the old) was advertised and explained to growing numbers of concerned citizens, individuals committed to saving the past began to stress the need for increased preservation and protection.

Some concerned individuals developed organizations dedicated to preservation and protection, but these groups were usually concerned only with the homes of prominent members of history or with fairly small geographical areas. What was needed was governmentally imposed regulations that would set limits on the destruction of important archaeological sites and historic properties.

Many countries had enacted laws to protect their nation's antiquities before 1945. In the United States, for example, Congress passed an antiquities act in 1906 and added to it in 1935. Though these acts protected archaeological and historic properties on government land, it was all too clear that much of the new construction was taking place outside government-controlled areas. The legislation was tightened in 1966 and again in 1971 to mandate the archaeological assessment of all construction projects that used federal funding or were federally assisted, whether or not the work was conducted on federal property. The new emphasis on federal funding and assistance, as opposed solely to location on federal land, appeared in Section 106 of the National Historic Preservation Act of 1966. For this reason, archaeologists and cultural resource managers usually refer to the archaeological study of potentially important sites and properties as "the Section 106 process." The terms of this process were fine-tuned in 1979, 1986, and again in 1999.

CRM archaeology is designed differently from the pure research efforts of academic archaeologists. Archaeologists whose main responsibilities rest with providing instruction in colleges and universities can spend years, or even decades, studying one topic before they feel fully qualified to write about it. CRM archaeologists are under much tighter constraints.

Unlike purely academic archaeologists, CRM archaeologists conduct research for a specific sponsor who requires clearance for a construction project or other landscape-modifying endeavor. Cultural resource archaeologists are sometimes referred to as "contract" archaeologists to indicate that they work under the terms of legal contacts that specify the precise work they will perform for their client, who is paying the bill. Archaeologists working in CRM may be under contract to survey the right-of-way for a new highway or they may conduct limited excavations on a town lot slated for the location of new apartment buildings. They may also perform extensive excavations at sites deemed especially significant within an area to be disturbed by large-scale construction (Figure 12.2). The archaeologists' clients can range from a small, local water district to a huge

**Figure 12.2**   Excavation of the Paddy's Alley site in north Boston, Massachusetts, found as part of the massive Central Artery Project.

federal agency, with their fees reflecting the amount and level of research to be performed.

CRM archaeologists are required, as part of their contracts, to complete detailed, fully professional reports of their investigations. These reports are typically thorough and detailed because the archaeologists must strive to fulfill the terms of the contract. These reports usually include a complete history of the region under study, a detailed explanation of the methods (survey or excavation) they used to examine the area to be modified, a thorough statement of their findings, and their recommendations about each individual site they discovered or examined. Some of the questions they will address are: Did they find anything during their field survey? If so, what? Did they discover anything that could be deemed "significant," or important enough for further study? Should the construction project proceed without further archaeological study of the area?

In addition to the client, governmental archaeologists constitute the primary audience for CRM reports of investigations. These men and women are trained archaeologists who are charged by their government to ensure that all archaeological and historical contract work has been done professionally and thoroughly. They are the individuals who are ultimately responsible for ensuring the protection of sites within their jurisdictions, and they make the final decisions about which sites to protect based on the CRM archaeologists' findings and recommendations.

The reports of CRM archaeologists are invaluable sources of information about the archaeological history of an area. The archival and field research they conduct under the terms of their contracts make them experts on those places they have studied. One problem with these reports, however, is that they are seldom widely distributed. Part of the restriction on distribution is purely practical, because CRM reports contain the precise locations of archaeological sites. Site location information must be kept away from looters and others who would thoughtlessly destroy precious archaeological sites if they knew where to find them. The sensitive nature of the information contained in most contract reports is the reason that governmental agencies are their primary repositories. The governmental archaeologist's office is usually the first stop when CRM archaeologists are contracted to survey a particular area. They need to check the federal site databases and examine all previous reports completed for the area to be studied. Access to the materials is usually readily given, but not always. Access to some reports may be restricted to professional archaeologists, but in some cases, even professionals may have difficulty gaining access to sensitive archaeological information. The proprietary rights of the sponsors who originally paid for the research may be at issue, and we may expect that increased security may also inhibit access to some archaeological material. For example, archaeological surveys conducted for federal agencies on the grounds of nuclear power plants may be much more difficult to obtain in the future, because of governmental concerns about terrorism. The often-limited distribution of CRM reports has lead many archaeologists to refer to them as a "gray literature": They exist, but in a shadowy and often inaccessible way.

As noted above, cultural resource professionals must concern themselves with the issue of "significance." This concept, though easy to understand in principle, is not as straightforward as one may think. Archaeologists working in cultural resource management spend a good deal of their time thinking about significance, because it is the cornerstone of the preservation legislation.

The basic idea behind significance is practical. Faced with expanding economic growth (what its supporters call "progress"), even the most die-hard preservationists must admit that some archaeological and historical sites will be destroyed by new construction. The destruction of old buildings and sites has occurred in one form or another for centuries, and we must accept this reality to some degree. Not everything can realistically be saved. As a result, preservationists realized that they had to devise measures that would permit someone to decide which sites and properties are especially important and must be saved at all costs if possible. This plan of action was quite reasonable, but how could anyone decide what sites from the past are important enough to preserve? Someone interested in the ancient Maya in Mexico may not attach much importance to a nineteenth-century shipwreck off the coast of Italy. A maritime archaeologist, however, may view the Italian wreck site as tremendously significant.

As may be expected, different nations have various ideas about what is significant. In the United States, the issue of significance was written into the preservation legislation. Under guidelines prepared by the U.S. Department of the Interior, a site is deemed significant if it is eligible to be listed in the National Register of Historic Places (created in the 1966 act). The National Register is a federally sponsored database of sites judged important to some aspect of American history. To be registered, an archaeological site or historic property must be deemed significant in at least one of the following areas: integrity; importance at the local, state, or national level; appropriate age (over fifty years); and exhibit exceptional value if not meeting any of the other requirements. When assessing a site's suitability, archaeologists should consider the site's association with important events and people, its architecture, and the cultural and historical information the site has the potential to contribute. Contract archaeologists must fully understand these criteria to enable them to make informed recommendations about specific sites. Since 1966, over seventy-six thousand sites and properties have been listed on the National Register, and the governmental database has information on over one million individual properties.

How do CRM archaeologists acquire the information that allows them to make informed recommendations about important sites and properties? They use the same methods used by all archaeologists. They conduct background research by reading the reports of other archaeologists, and they perform field surveys and excavations (Figure 12.3). Historical archaeologists conducting CRM research also use abundant amounts of documentary and often even oral evidence to support their recommendations. Only by conducting thorough research will they be able to make a case for preservation, protection, and study.

The enactment of the preservation laws in the United States has had a tremendous affect on historical archaeology. Once this legislation was in place, field archaeologists engaged in CRM research could no longer ignore modern-period sites. They realized that they were required to locate and identify sites that could be as little as fifty years old. When CRM archaeologists walked down the right-of-way of a future highway and searched for evidence of archaeological sites, they knew that modern-period sites were included within their mandate. In the year 2000, for example, archaeologists who discovered the remains of a 1930s logging camp had to decide whether it could be judged significant because it satisfied the fifty-year cut-off date. The requirements of the legislation meant that archaeologists who only had training or interest in Native American prehistory either had to learn about historical archaeology or they had to hire qualified historical archaeologists on their permanent staffs. They would violate the terms of the law and their contracts if they ignored historical archaeology. In their important guide to archaeological significance, historical archaeologists Donald Hardesty and Barbara Little present a case study of the Iron and Steel resources of Pennsylvania for the years 1716–1945. The archaeological examination of their

**Figure 12.3**  The floor of a Chinese business in Sacramento, California, excavated by historical archaeologists from Sonoma State University under contract with the U.S. General Services Administration.

last two periods, covering the years 1867–1901 and 1902–45, would have been largely impossible, within a CRM environment, without the requirements of the legislation.

Many countries are still wrestling with the idea of preserving and protecting modern-period sites. This debate rages everywhere, including in countries that, unlike the United States, have a long tradition of literacy, or in other words, a long tradition of "history." In the Republic of Ireland, for instance, the National Monuments Act, first passed in 1930 and amended in 1954 and 1987, states that to be protected a site must predate A.D. 1700. Documented Irish history begins several centuries earlier, so the period of "history" covered by the act is actually quite long. The wording of the legislation means, however, that a site dating after 1700 is not automatically covered by the legislation. This restriction leaves out many sites that have major importance to modern Irish history. Several sites that historical archaeologists would consider important have possibly been ignored by Ireland's contract archaeologists. They are not professionally obligated to examine them if they are not considered to constitute archaeological sites. The omission of post-1700 sites constitutes a significant problem in Irish preservation law. In all fairness, the federal archaeologists who work for the National Museum of Ireland and for Dúchas, the Irish Heritage Service, understand the limitations of the legislation, and they are working to expand it. Their action is extremely positive, because some day people may look back and wonder why no one did anything to protect eighteenth- and nineteenth-century sites in the Irish countryside. Nations across the globe are deciding with increasing frequency that modern-period sites are a legitimate focus for archaeological research.

## SOME PROS AND CONS OF CRM ARCHAEOLOGY

Cultural resource management, like any profession, has pros and cons. Not everyone agrees about these, because individuals have different views and attitudes. People can tolerate some conditions better than others. My comments about the pros and cons of CRM research derive from my own experience and observation. As is true of most professional historical archaeologists working today, I have been involved in CRM research in many different capacities. I have witnessed CRM archaeology from the small survey to the governmental office.

There is no question that all students of archaeology will benefit from having some experience in CRM archaeology. They will acquire a vast range of experience as they work in what is usually a fast-paced and rapidly changing environment. They will conduct primary research on a huge number of wildly different archaeological sites and historic properties, and they will gain abundant personal experience in diverse areas. In the course of a single day, a CRM archaeologist conducting a survey in the western United States may examine a prehistoric Native American encampment, an early-twentieth-century mining settlement, and a nineteenth-century battlefield. Contract archaeologists in Europe may be called upon to investigate a prehistoric megalithic monument and a fourteenth-century castle all in the same field trip. Their contracts will require them to research each site fully, and to comprehend each site's history, cultural importance, current condition, and ultimate significance. They will be required to draw maps of the sites and to collect artifacts that lie on the surface. They will have to recognize prehistoric and modern-period artifacts, to understand the fine points of ancient flint scrapers and modern, machine-cut nails. Extensive experience can be quickly gained in cultural resource management.

Travel is another significant advantage to CRM archaeology. Archaeologists under contract are often required to travel great distances and to stay in various locations for long periods of time. Archaeological travel is a wonderful learning experience, both in terms of the historical and cultural knowledge one can gain and the personal growth that is acquired. Widening our experience helps us all to become better citizens of the world, as we learn that all peoples share many of our concerns, wishes, and hopes for the future. CRM archaeology provides an excellent way for archaeologists to immerse themselves in the life of a place that they may have otherwise have never had occasion to visit. And, because they may stay in one location for several weeks, they can make new, lasting friends and learn new cultural and regional traditions.

Archaeologists working in CRM environments also have the opportunity to sharpen their research, writing, and critical thinking skills. Cultural resource archaeologists must write fully competitive, professional proposals that outline their qualifications and their precise plans for meeting the terms specified in the request for proposals. They know, because they work in the business world, that other archaeologists are bidding on the same contract. As a result, they must make their proposals as good as possible. They must demonstrate their knowledge of archaeological methods and their familiarity with the region in question. They must show that they are qualified and eager to do the research. They must also submit a detailed budget, along with a schedule to show that they can complete the research on time and under budget. Contract archaeologists are seldom able to petition for an extension of time or for more funding, because their research is conducted to satisfy the construction schedules of their sponsors. They are usually tied to the terms they outlined in their proposal.

Writing a proposal forces archaeologists to organize their thoughts and to sharpen their abilities to work within a specified time frame. These are skills that all archaeologists should acquire regardless of their work environment, and experience in cultural resource management provides these skills in abundance.

For projects involving historical archaeology, contract archaeologists must know where to find the most appropriate archival repositories. They will have to conduct their background historical research in the most efficient way possible, and they must learn how to work quickly and efficiently. They must learn how to extract the most pertinent information from the most important sources and not allow themselves to get sidetracked. Old newspapers can be a tremendous source of information about modern-period archaeological sites and the people who once lived in them. Most nineteenth-century newspapers, however, included large sections of product ads, many of which were printed on the front page. These old ads make fascinating reading, and it is easy to become enthralled by their wild claims and unique ways of promoting their products. But unless the CRM archaeologist has a specific, contract-related reason for studying these ads, the time spent reading them may be difficult to justify to his or her sponsor. That is not to say that the reader will not have acquired a great deal of interesting and potentially important information. But it may be difficult to make the highway engineer understand why the report is late because the archaeologist became interested in ads for nineteenth-century patent medicines!

Some people may find the traveling to get tiring after awhile. A great deal of relocating can accompany CRM archaeology, because archaeologists must go the projects' locations. They cannot conduct field surveys from the library! Much of the traveling is seasonal and hectic. Fieldwork is not possible in environments with cold winters and deep snowfalls, and it is during this period that contract archaeologists would prefer to write their final reports and plan for future work. One problem, however, is that some CRM firms must reduce their staffs during non-fieldwork periods. Not everyone needed to excavate a site can play a role in preparing the final report. As a result, employment in CRM research can be seasonal and short-term. Many CRM firms will hire field workers only for specific projects and then be forced to let them go when the project is completed. Long-term employment may be difficult to obtain with the smallest CRM companies, because the managers of those firms must work diligently to maintain their payrolls. Most managers strive to keep a core of highly qualified staff members, but in the worst economic times, even this may not be possible. The larger firms can often employ their field workers as lab technicians when the weather precludes fieldwork.

Another problem with cultural resource management can involve the work load itself. Contract archaeologists obtain a great deal of extremely valuable experience, but often because they are working on several projects at once. The reality of time sometimes means that research may be hurried to meet a deadline. CRM archaeologists have deadlines set as part of their contracts. These dates can seldom be renegotiated to any significant extent. Construction engineers and real estate developers fully expect to receive clearance for their projects on time so that they can begin construction. CRM projects thus run for a set period of time and no more. A project effectively disappears when the deadline comes and the final report is submitted. Once that happens, another project must immediately begin. The reality of CRM archaeology is that the members of a firm must be working on proposals for new projects while they are completing the research and report preparation for their current projects. The managers of cultural resource firms must worry about cash flow just like any other business person. They cannot afford to overextend themselves with too many employees, and they cannot afford to miss deadlines.

CRM archaeologists do not have the ability to control the extent of their research, and they cannot always focus on specific research topics that interest them. What is eligible for study by the cultural resources management team is specified by the terms of the contract, and archaeologists who go beyond these specifications are liable to find themselves outside the limits of the contract.

In Chapter 8, we mentioned research conducted under the direction of Adrian and Mary Praetzellis in San Francisco, California. They performed this CRM research project in the route of the San Francisco Central Freeway under contract with the City and County of San Francisco. The Praetzellises and their team of archaeologists at Sonoma State University are some of the most qualified CRM historical archaeologists in the world, and their work stands as models for those wishing to learn the proper way to approach contract archaeology. Their summary for the San Francisco Central Freeway project provides an excellent overview of the restrictions that CRM archaeologists can face in their research:

> The Central Freeway Replacement Project will involve the retrofitting and widening of the existing elevated structure between South Van Ness Avenue and Fell Street. Ten city blocks will be affected by the Central Freeway Replacement Project. Subsurface impacts associated with the retrofit phase are currently anticipated on only four of the project blocks, but project plans for the widening of the freeway have not yet been finalized, so the entire right-of-way requires careful study for archaeological potential.

What this means is that the archaeological research team was restricted to the ten blocks that would be affected by the highway work. They would essentially be outside the limits of the contract if they chose to conduct research on properties and sites outside the right-of-way. Their map of the project area shows that Block 3 is bounded by Otis Street on the east, Duboce Street on the south, Valencia Street on the west, and McCoppin Street on the north. The projected path of the freeway cuts through the southern part of the block and swings up through its western half (Figure 12.4). Archaeological and historical sites in the path of the freeway in Block 3 are eligible for study under the terms of the contract, but any sites south of Duboce Street are not eligible (at least under the terms of the contract). Such limitations are common in CRM research, and contract archaeologists have learned to live with them.

## SOME ETHICAL ISSUES IN CRM ARCHAEOLOGY

Archaeologists often confront ethical challenges. These challenges can involve the way they interact with indigenous peoples, their willingness to conduct research on artifact collections they think may have been looted, and the conduct of archaeological excavation at sites some people may judge to be sacred. A host of other possible situations cannot even be guessed in advance.

CRM archaeologists also face ethical issues in the course of their research, some of which are entirely unique to their environment. Because they operate in the competitive business world, CRM archaeologists are usually engaged in a delicate balancing act between their desire to perform good archaeology and the practical requirement to maintain the financial viability of their consulting

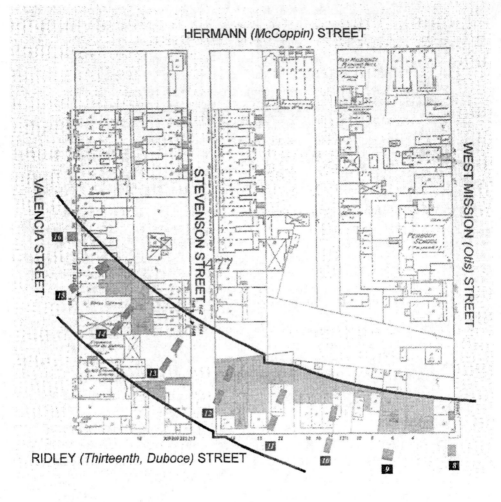

**Figure 12.4**   Highway right-of-way for the San Francisco Central
Freeway Project.

companies. Contract archaeologists cannot simply choose what to study and ignore the rest. They are required to acquire consulting contracts and to meet their
legal obligations once they have the contract. Any contract archaeologist who decided that he or she would only take contracts restricted to a narrow research
topic would not be in business for long.

Cultural resource professionals are often called upon to make choices that
defy easy resolution. They must often make decisions within a rapidly changing
environment and collaborate with a constantly changing set of clients' representatives. Some of the clients and their agents may even be hostile to the archaeology. They may see it as an unnecessary burden, something designed only to

waste their time and consume their financial resources. They may even believe that the CRM archaeologists have a vested interest in prolonging the work to maintain their employment. Some people are simply opposed to archaeology because they mistakenly think it is "anti-progress." Part of the problem involves the archaeology profession's general lack of public education (a trend that is quickly changing), but much of the problem is also ingrained in the culture of capitalism.

In their essay "Cultural Resource Management and the Business of Archaeology," archaeologists Christopher Bergman and John Doershuk state that the CRM professional must understand many different things, including:

- all regulations concerning CRM legislation;
- all permit requirements of the agencies involved in the contract;
- the specifics of the client's industry, financing, and construction schedule;
- the project's guidelines;
- the limits of their professional capabilities to meet the terms of the contract;
- ways to adapt their archaeological methods to the needs of the client;
- how to identify and document all possible archaeological and historic sites that may be found in the area specified by the contract; and
- how to negotiate the various differences of opinion that may arise.

This list aptly demonstrates the difficulty of conducting good CRM archaeology. Public relations skills exist outside the demands of the archaeology itself. Cultural resource specialists must be good field archaeologists, expert researchers, good writers, and skilled at personal relations.

In the worst possible situations, cultural resource archaeologists may find themselves in conflict with their sponsor. Unscrupulous real estate developers may ask the archaeologists they have hired to "forget" that they saw an archaeological site or to make recommendations that serve the sponsor's needs but which will forever damage the integrity of an archaeological site. In the legislation passed in the United States, three "phases" of archaeological research are defined. Phase I usually refers to a pedestrian, or walk-over, survey, and Phase II usually means limited excavation used to judge the subsurface integrity of a site. Phase III typically refers to more complete excavation. Thomas King, long-time expert on American CRM archaeology, refers to this three phase system as "find it/assess it/dig it up (Phase I-II-III)." Let's suppose that an archaeologist is under contract to conduct a Phase I survey of a piece of ground, located near a white sandy beach, that is slated to become the site of a luxury apartment complex. In the course of the survey, the archaeologists discover what might be the encampment of individuals engaged in a local eighteenth-century, anti-tax revolt. A single document found in the local archives mentions this site in the vicinity, but does not provide a precise location. The field archaeologists cannot determine whether this is the site from the surface features and artifacts alone. They also cannot access the extent of the site or even learn whether the soil conditions have preserved anything without further exploration at the Phase II or possibly even Phase III level. The problem is that the developer is eager to get his buildings up before the summer so that he can start renting out the apartments to work-weary vacationers. He does not want to pay for further archaeological research, and he wonders why "his" archaeologists are doing this to "him." He asks them to forget about the site, and if they cannot do that, perhaps they can downplay its importance in their report. What do the archaeologists do? Do they report the developer to the authorities and possibly lose future contracts in the area? Do they agree to the developer's demands and ignore their professional ethics?

Fortunately, CRM archaeologists seldom encounter such crass behavior during the course of their work. Most developers understand the need to preserve and protect a nation's heritage, if sometimes only reluctantly. But CRM archaeologists must be aware that such encounters do occur, and they must think how they will respond to such challenges.

CRM archaeology is a major element of today's historical archaeology. Like anything else, it has its good points and its bad. Generally, however, all students of historical archaeology will benefit from some exposure to the world of contract research. Cultural resource management is not the only complex issue facing modern historical archaeology. In the final chapter, we consider some of the other major issues confronting the field in the twenty-first century.

## TIME TRAVEL

### Hacienda Tabi, Yucatan, Mexico, 1876–1911

With the independence of Mexico from Spain, the jewel in its one-time colonial crown, a small class of landowners, mostly of European descent, exerted their authority within the emerging sociopolitical system. One arm of their effort to gain control was economic. With the cessation of colonial control from Iberia, several members of the European elite increased the size of their landholdings. Needing laborers to work their fields and so produce an income from their vast estates, these landowners established ways to dominate the indigenous Mayas. One place that experienced the changes wrought in the late nineteenth century was Hacienda San Juan Bautista Tabi, a prominent sugar estate in the Yucatan peninsula.

Haciendas were large estates worked by indigenous villagers who were held in a state of debt peonage. Like the classic New World slave plantation, hacienda workers (literally, peons) were held in a kind of legal bondage. The owners did not actually own their laborers' bodies, as in slavery, but their workers were hopelessly in debt to them. Workers in debt were legally bound to their estates until they repaid what they owed. Debts were amassed through a series of well-crafted schemes, including allowing workers to purchase on credit vastly overpriced commodities at the hacienda store. Because workers seldom made enough money to

*(continued)*

Source: Allan D. Meyers and David L. Carlson, 2002. "Peonage, Power Relations, and the Built Environment at Hacienda Tabi, Yucatan, Mexico." *International Journal of Historical Archaeology* 6:225–252.

pay off their debts, they were required to continue to live (and to work) on the estate they owed. Such practices perpetuated the presence of poverty-stricken workers on estates year after year.

The practice of debt peonage in Mexico was always oppressive, but it became even more so during the rule of President Porfirio Díaz (1876–1911). During this period, many haciendas, including Hacienda Tabi, established categories of debt that set the amount of work for individual peons. Individuals with less than 100 pesos of debt, "temporary workers," usually only had to work during harvest. People with over 200 pesos of debt had to work every day except Sunday. They also could not leave the estate without their supervisor's consent.

Given the nature of hacienda labor, it was inevitable that conflicts would arise between owners and workers. Part of the ongoing struggle was reflected in the physical construction of the haciendas themselves. The physical layout of Hacienda Tabi had two main elements: a large, open "great yard" around which were situated the owner's estate house, surrounded by the church, sugar mill, and stables. The second structural element was the workers' village. It was designed on a grid of fourteen square-to-rectangular residential blocks that were arranged around two sides of the owner's complex. Two open plazas were included within the village grid, and four streets ran out of the settlement in the cardinal directions.

The first hacienda zone, with the estate's principal buildings, was intended to express the power and dominance of the hacienda owner. His house was a long, spacious, two-story building, with elaborate staircases, numerous decorative arches, and massive windows. Its two floors contained about 27,770 square feet (2,580 square meters) of floor area. The proximity of the house to the stables and the sugar mill were designed to indicate that the owner controlled these economic realms. The nearness of the church reinforced the idea that the economic and political order was upheld by the religious order. People from the village wishing to enter the church had first to walk into the "great yard" in front of the owner's elaborate house. This path reminded them of the power that the owner's family (and his entire class) held over people like them. But the effect of viewing the huge landowner's house was more than merely symbolic. The estate's workers also knew that it housed two, tiny confinement cells on the west end of its lower floor. These cells measured only 8 feet (2.5 meters) square. Hacienda workers could be confined at any time in these cells for disobeying the rules or for exhibiting some forbidden behavior. They were also whipped as part of their punishment.

The houses of the hacienda workers were rectangular in design with rounded corners. They had only about 344 square feet (32 square meters) of floor space. They were built either of perishable materials or more durable stone blocks. The quality and size of the houses varied with the labor position of their occupants. Salaried workers on fixed wages had higher prestige than workers paid only by the amount of work they performed. Salaried workers thus lived in more substantial and slightly larger houses than task laborers. Four qualities of workers' houses at the hacienda tended to reflect the estate's hierarchy of work.

# Chapter 13

# THE PAST
# IN THE PRESENT

*"The absence of romance in my history will, I fear, detract somewhat from its interest; but
I shall be content if it is judged useful by those inquirers who desire an exact knowledge
of the past as an aid to the interpretation of the future."*

Thucydides, 431–413 B.C.

Historical archaeology is the archaeology of ourselves, a field of research that
spans many centuries. We use methods that can be applied with equal facility to
medieval villages or today's landfills. Historical archaeology serves as a mirror
into our own lives, and of those of people living only a few generations ago. The
innovative research of archaeologist William Rathje has attracted wide attention
for his examination of modern-day urban landfills and trash dumps. He refers to
his field as "garbalogy." Rathje has calculated that the Fresh Kills landfill on
Staten Island, New York, is twenty-five times the size of the Great Pyramid of
Khufu at Giza, Egypt, and forty times the size of the Temple of the Sun at Teotihuacán, Mexico. He has recovered fresh hot dogs, guacamole, and other foodstuffs from landfills that date to the 1950s and he has discovered that newspaper
almost never deteriorates when stuffed into a landfill's air-starved environment.
Rathje's excavations have an important bearing on many of today's most serious
issues, including recycling and refuse management.

In light of Rathje's research, can we easily draw a line between past and present? When the U.S. Congress enacted legislation establishing the National Register of Historic Places in 1976, it defined "antiquity" as fifty years from the
present. In the year 2000, artifacts and buildings manufactured in 1950 were officially "ancient." The fifty-year interval is purely arbitrary and effectively mean-
ingless except within a narrow legal context. The past is, as we all know, a
seamless continuum that is cultural and social, political and economic, techno-
logic and environmental. When archaeologist Jane Busch wrote that "The tin can

has played a significant role in American history and can play a significant role in archaeology," she was absolutely correct. She envisions tin cans as vehicles of history, easily dated by telltale technological improvements in seals and seams. It is no coincidence that her study incorporated the "modern sanitary can," the kind we all bring home from the grocery store. Whether we think about it or not, we are all actors in history.

We explore in this chapter some of historical archaeology's roles in today's world. We also suggest some ways that you can become involved in this exciting and rapidly changing field.

## LIVING ARCHAEOLOGY

Each of us is an actor in the unfolding sweep of history. We are thus repositories of "living history," archives crammed with memories of past events and current experiences. Our daily comings and goings, the people we meet, and the objects with which we surround ourselves all constitute history being lived in a very real way. It follows from this simple reality that historical archaeologists are part of the history they study. Ivor Noël Hume is a modern actor in the ongoing history of Colonial Williamsburg (Chapter 6), just as Mark Leone is part of the history of Annapolis (Chapter 10). The line between past and present is blurred in historical archaeology, and archaeologists of modern history cannot truly separate themselves from it. As anthropologist David Pilbeam observed in the *Washington Post* in 1983, "We do not see things as they are, we see things as we are."

Nowhere is this statement truer than at living history exhibits, such as Plimouth Plantation, Massachusetts, which are popular, often international, tourist attractions. Historical archaeologist James Deetz played a leading role at Plimouth in developing accurate plans for the reconstructed buildings. The settlement is today "inhabited" by men and women wearing period costumes. These "residents" shoe horses, card and dye wool, cook over large iron cauldrons, and fashion delicate glass vases and bowls using time-tested methods. The visitor to this "colonial" town experiences living history—a modern vision of life centuries ago reconstructed from historical documents and archaeological research.

Living museums can be found all over the world. Henry Ford's Greenfield Village (Chapter 3) is a well-known example. So is the Yorvik Viking Centre in York, England, where the daily life of a Anglo-Scandinavian town dating to A.D. 850–1050 has been recreated so vividly that even voices and smells are piped in. Visitors descend underground in a small car, and pass through the centuries until they emerge on a Viking street. The car travels through the excavations that reconstructed the town, into the archaeological laboratory that contains a small display of important finds. Tourists can even visit the "touching wall" of potsherds. Everything is calculated to entertain and enlighten, to make history come alive. Each of the over one million people who visit Yorvik each year becomes part of the history of the site.

One of the most intriguing living museums in the United States is the slave quarters constructed at Colonial Williamsburg's eighteenth-century Carter's Grove Plantation. The Carter's Grove house, built between 1750 and 1755, is a huge brick mansion with a beautifully restored central stairway and baronial gardens. The slave cabins tell a story quite different than that of the mansion. They are located about 800 feet (244 m) northwest of the mansion, partially screened by a row of trees. They consist of a cluster of four reconstructed wooden cabins with accompanying yards (Figure 13.1). Their designs are based on archaeological evidence. The largest building belonged to the enslaved foreman and his family. At the quarters today, African American men and women, dressed as slaves and "living" in the cabins, explain to modern visitors, in deeply personal terms, what it must have been like to have been enslaved at Carter's Grove. The actors play their parts with passion, and develop their stories using the slave remembrances collected during the 1930s.

**Figure 13.1**  Reconstruction of the slave quarters at Carter's Grove Plantation, Virginia.

Even as evocative as the cabins are to modern visitors, can we ever truly say that the cabins of the enslaved are *only* about the past? The actors undoubtedly put much of themselves into their historical performances. As actors in our contemporary world, they use history to help us better understand enslavement, racism, and discrimination. Their stories are powerful history lessons that take much of their power from the reconstructed cabins. When faced with the cabins' physical reality, visitors are unavoidably forced to confront the reality of America's slave past.

Another perspective on living history comes from an innovative series of archaeological projects conducted in Annapolis, Maryland, under the general direction of Mark Leone, of the University of Maryland. Using several eighteenth- and nineteenth-century sites as a focus, Leone and his co-workers have developed a program that uses archaeological fieldwork to engage visitors to the city. Leone even hired a media consultant to help his team develop the best site tour possible. Their consultant, Philip Arnoult, the director of a theater project, first queried the archaeologists on what sorts of questions visitors typically ask them: How do archaeologists know where to look for sites? How do they date objects, and how do they interpret what they learn? Armed with these questions, Arnoult worked with Leone and his team on the tour itself. Before long, more than one hundred people a day were visiting the Annapolis archaeological project. In the summer and fall of 1982, seven thousand people toured the Victualling Warehouse Site alone. This warehouse, built sometime before 1747, was used to handle supplies for the Continental Army during the American Revolution.

The archaeologists at Annapolis learned three important elements of a successful tour. First, they discovered that the educational aspects of the projects must have as high a priority as the research itself. By educating the public, they could help eliminate two commonly held misconceptions about archaeology: that it is conducted by stuffy old men in pith helmets who are completely oblivious to the world around them, and that it is determined to stop all construction projects in the name of science. Second, Leone and his team learned that the tours had to be structured. Both the visitors' path across the site and the information their guides told them had to be consistent. The archaeologists giving the tour must be willing to adjust their narratives in light of new finds and to accommodate visitors' questions. Archaeology conducted with these ideas in mind becomes an interactive enterprise, with excavators and visitors almost equally engaged in the research. And finally, the Annapolis archaeologists found that archaeological research must not be presented as if it is only about the past. In Leone's words, "there must be a convincing tie to the present drawn out of the material from the past." The archaeologists at the Victualling Warehouse told the visitors of the site's history. They also made certain that the visitors understood that many of Annapolis' business owners saw the archaeology as creating a tangible link between them and the city's historic business owners. The warehouse is undeniably an important component of the city's commercial history.

The Annapolis archaeologists used their site-tour approach to draw visitors into the town's history. Each visitor's place in history is in some ways as important as was that of Daniel Dulany, the owner of the Victualling Warehouse, whose property was seized in 1781 because of his loyalist sympathies.

## POLITICS AND HISTORICAL ARCHAEOLOGY

The idea that the past studied by historical archaeologists exists independently of the present raises a controversial albeit significant question: do contemporary politics ever exert a force on historical archaeological research? The subjects we address in Chapter 9—social class, ethnicity, race, and gender—are all emotional, contemporary issues. Archaeologists who explore them must understand that they may sometimes tread on potentially slippery political ground.

Governments and emerging states have long used archaeological research for various ends. The Nazis unashamedly used archaeology for political ends in the 1930s and early 1940s. Their program was dramatized in somewhat exaggerated form in the popular movie *Indiana Jones and the Raiders of the Lost Ark*. Indiana Jones thwarts the evil Nazi archaeologists who are attempting to locate the all-powerful Ark of the Covenant so that they can use it in their plans for world domination. The Nazis in this movie were fanciful depictions, but the story itself has a historical basis. In 1935, Heinrich Himmler, the head of Hitler's dreaded S.S., created a research organization called Ahnenerbe, or "Ancestral Heritage." Much of this organization's "research" was more laughable than dangerous. They really did try to find the Holy Grail (like *Indiana Jones and the Last Crusade*), they searched for Atlantis, they studied the history of German bread, and they believed that their early Germanic ancestors had learned to harness the energy of lightning and had used it as a weapon! The "scientists" of Ahnenerbe also used their often-fudged archaeological findings to support their ideas of ethnic inferiority. They altered the cultural chronologies of Eastern Europe to fit their theories of Nordic superiority. Archaeology as practiced by the Nazis had a well-defined political agenda.

Historical archaeologist Robert Paynter once noted that "History is written by the winners." The conquistadors' version of the Conquest of Mexico is the story that dominates the history books, while the histories and fates of the conquered Aztecs and other Native American peoples are often ignored. We are now witnessing a profound change in our visions of history. New perspectives are growing in part by an expanding interest in non-Western cultures, and indigenous scholars are actively seeking to reclaim their heritage for themselves and their children. Indigenous peoples are using archaeology to regain control over their histories and to educate their young people about the resilience of their traditional cultures. Australian Aborigine groups are using archaeology to tell their side of the continent's history. The Maori of New Zealand are aggressively reclaiming their history, both to foster their cultural identity and to support their land claims. Such efforts on the part of indigenous people permit us to develop more sophisticated, multifaceted views of history.

Several Native American groups are pursuing active programs of heritage restitution, and many of their projects involve historical archaeology. One such project, sponsored by the Northern Cheyenne of southeastern Montana, was designed to study the Outbreak of 1879.

The Outbreak came about as the result of a series of contacts between the U.S. government and the Northern Cheyenne, who lived in the southern Montana–northern Wyoming area. Cheyenne leaders agreed to the Medicine Lodge Treaty of 1867, but they did not understand that this meant they would be moved south to "Indian Territory," today's Oklahoma. Several prominent Cheyenne leaders protested the move, and in fact some of them went to Washington in 1872 to plead with President Grant to allow them to stay in their traditional homeland. Grant agreed to let them stay, but with Custer's defeat at the Little Bighorn, the Northern Cheyenne began to fear reprisals, even though they were not involved in the battle. Under the leadership of Dull Knife and Little Wolf, the Northern Cheyenne sought a safe haven in the Big Horn Mountains. Their peace was short-lived because they were soon discovered and attacked by the U.S. cavalry. Faced with extreme hardship on the open plains if they fled, the Northern Cheyenne surrendered to the military at Fort Robinson, Nebraska, in April 1877. Tired of trying to feed themselves on a landscape that was becoming increasingly barren of bison—their main food source—the Northern Cheyenne agreed to try life in Indian Territory. They moved there a couple of months later, but it was not long before more than two-thirds of their people were racked with fever and disease in the unfamiliar environment. Desperate for relief, Dull Knife and Little Wolf led a group of their followers out of Oklahoma and toward their homeland in September 1878. The 353 Northern Cheyenne who fled, weak from sickness, knew that they would be pursued and killed or captured by the cavalry. Splitting into two groups, they maintained a running battle with the soldiers for several days. Little Wolf's band established a camp for the winter in northwestern Nebraska. Dull Knife's people, however, were persuaded to surrender to the cavalry at Fort Robinson. The conditions Dull Knife's band faced at the fort were little better than those in Oklahoma, and on the night of January 9, 1879, he led the famed Outbreak from the fort. Having taken with them only five rifles and several old pistols, Dull Knife's people could not offer much resistance to the cavalry, and sixty-four of them were killed. The military sent most of the captured male leaders of the Outbreak to Dodge City, Kansas, for trial; they sent the rest of the Cheyenne to the Pine Ridge Agency in southwestern South Dakota. Dull Knife and his family escaped capture by hiding in a cave, but they were eventually also taken to Pine Ridge. Dull Knife's people finally settled on the Tongue River Reservation in Montana, where they remain today.

The Northern Cheyenne have always told a different story of the break-out than that presented by military historians. Official accounts state that the Cheyenne used a northern route to escape. The Cheyenne, relying on oral accounts passed from generation to generation, have always argued for a more southerly route. The routes are actually close to one another, and the controversy is seemingly unimportant—unless you are a Northern Cheyenne wanting to reclaim your heritage. Their hope is to build a commemorative path along the escape route and a visitors' center to tell their side of the break-out. Movies like *Cheyenne Autumn* for too long have presented the story of the Cheyenne from a non-native perspective. Many Cheyenne believe that now is the time for them to present their own history. Establishing the route of the escape is one way to begin this storytelling.

In 1987, Northern Cheyenne from Dull Knife College in Montana teamed up with archaeologist Larry Zimmerman—a leader in promoting relations of understanding between Native Americans and archaeologists—to use archaeology to find evidence of the escape route. The Native American crew members provided geographical guidance and incorporated their traditional prayers and storytelling into the fieldwork. The archaeologists surveyed both routes for lead pistol balls, rifle bullets, and other telltale clues of the pursuit. They found several lead pistol balls and rifle bullets along the southern route, but none along the officially sanctioned northern path. The Cheyenne were vindicated. In the words of project leader, J. Douglas McDonald, they "came to understand that their long-felt mistrust of archaeology might no longer be necessary. Both the archaeologists and the Northern Cheyenne learned that they can be natural allies, sometimes each possessing what the other needs."

Joe Watkins, a member of the Choctaw tribe and the holder of a doctorate degree in archaeology, has asked the important question: "Why don't more American Indians get involved in archaeology?" Some Native American scholars, such as Vine Deloria Jr, author of the widely read *Custer Died for Your Sins* (1969), have taken a strong stand against archaeology, and have even espoused pseudo-archaeological interpretations that no professional archaeologist today takes seriously. An association with fringe archaeology—dealing with space aliens, lost worlds, and fantastic histories—merely drives a wedge between archaeologists and indigenous peoples and makes cooperation even more difficult. Watkins has adopted a more measured and sensible approach, and has sought to discover the common ground that indigenous peoples and archaeologists share. Differences of opinion will arise between indigenous peoples and professional archaeologists, just as individual archaeologists disagree. Such disagreements are inevitable. But we must remember that archaeologists do not own the past; it is not theirs and theirs alone to interpret. It is far more productive to realize that we should all view ourselves, regardless of our profession, as stewards and guardians of the past.

## PLUNDERED HISTORY

Archaeology is sadly under siege all over the world. Deep plowing, industrial development, mining, and runaway urban sprawl, to say nothing of looters and vandals, are decimating the archaeological record everywhere. The past vanishes before our eyes with bewildering, often tragic speed, to the point where one wonders if archaeology will survive the onslaught. As we have emphasized, the archaeological record is a finite resource. Once disturbed or destroyed, it is gone forever. The battle for the past is serious. At stake is the very survival of humankind's priceless cultural heritage.

National Geographic Society archaeologist George E. Stuart gave his assessment of the problem in 1989: "To me it is a miracle that any remnant of the human past has survived, for it seems that both nature and man are constantly engaged in the processes of obliteration." Stuart was talking both in general and specific terms. The battle for the past is joined in urban building lots, along the rights-of-way of expanding freeways, in lush valleys about to be flooded by hydroelectric dams, and in hundreds of other locales across the globe. Apart from industrial activity, mechanized agriculture, and destruction caused by the population explosion, plain human greed is always at work. Some people have a powerful, illogical urge to collect and own the artifacts of the past and to display them on their mantles or in their cabinets. Everything from the past is grist to the fanatical collector: beer cans, barbed wire, firearms—and other artifacts.

Just south of the hustle and bustle of Dublin, Ireland, sits a castle known as Carrickmines, the site of a medieval and post-medieval garrison settlement. Anglo-Norman colonists used the castle for over four hundred years, from 1200–1642, as a base from which they could attack the Irish chiefdoms of the Wicklow Mountains, just south of Dublin. The castle was destroyed in 1642 when Irish rebels were massacred there by English soldiers.

Archaeologists were familiar with the site for many reasons, not the least of which is that one of the largest collections of medieval rural pottery ever made in Ireland came from this site. The site has the potential to shed new insights on the complex relations between Anglo-Norman settlers and indigenous Irish tribesmen and women during a period of intense culture change. But in late 2001, the site of Carrickmines Castle was in danger of being destroyed forever.

The traffic in Dublin is horrendous and growing worse every year. The number of cars in the city has increased dramatically, and all highways and thoroughfares are clogged most of the day. To solve the burgeoning problem of urban congestion, the Irish National Roads Authority began constructing a large motorway designed to ring the city center. The idea was that drivers could visit the outskirts of the city without first having to travel into the city itself. During the construction of the southern route of the motorway, however, it was clear that Carrickmines Castle stood directly in the highway's path. If the road was to be built, the castle site would have to be destroyed. But first, the government spent millions on an archaeological study of the site.

The funds spent on the archaeological study of Carrickmines was vast, but a number of committed activists believed that it was still not adequate, and they mounted a protest to save it. Some people, called the "Carrickminders," set up an occupation to block heavy equipment from endangering the site. The protesters said they were not opposed to the highway—its need is quite obvious—but they did not believe that destroying their heritage was the proper way forward. In September 2002, the Irish Minister of Transport stated that 40 percent of the site would be lost to the road, but that construction had to continue. He also noted that archaeologists had worked at the site for two years at a cost of €2 million (about $2.3 million). He said that the government had decided they would move the castle's remaining defensive wall and preserve it for future generations. The protestors condemned this action, stating that it would effectively destroy the integrity of the site. In October 2002, an organization called The Friends of Medieval Dublin, an advocacy group that had mobilized over the destruction of Wood Quay (the site of Dublin's original Viking town) in the 1970s, held "The Carrickmines Forum." A number of Ireland's most important medieval scholars delivered papers on the significance of the site to Irish history.

The situation at Carrickmines Castle is, as of this writing, unresolved. But similar situations are unfortunately being played out across the globe as the needs of heritage conflict with upgrades and additions to a nation's infrastructure. Archaeologists and developers simply must find ways to cooperate for the good of all. Once an archaeological site is destroyed, it is gone forever.

### The Antiquities Market

The conflict over Carrickmines, and the looting of the wreck of the *Geldermalsen* (mentioned in the previous chapter), raises an important ethical question: Who owns the past? Is the answer humanity as a whole, the owners of a site or a collection of artifacts, their descendants, the current land owner, or the government? No easy answers exist, and different nations have devised various solutions. In the United States, for example, people place a high premium on private property, and the destruction of a site on someone's land generally cannot be stopped. In other countries, such as Ireland, all archaeological artifacts belong to the government, as the custodian for the people of the nation.

Antiquities can bring big money in the marketplace. In 1991, a *Time* magazine article cited some glaring examples. On the night of February 2, 1990, masked gunmen attacked a storeroom housing artifacts from Herculaneum, the Roman town buried along with Pompeii by the eruption of Mount Vesuvius in A.D. 79. The robbers carefully selected 223 of the most precious artifacts from the Herculaneum collection. The items they stole were worth an estimated $18 million. In Amsterdam the following year, criminals stole twenty paintings from the Van Gogh Museum. These bandits were caught when their car got a flat tire, but the value of their heist was estimated at about $500 million. In Cambodia, the heads of Buddhist and Hindu statues in the magnificent twelfth-century capital of Angkor have been sawn off their bodies for sale to collectors. And the thefts have not stopped. The English newspaper *The Guardian* reported in March 2003 that the Art Loss Register, a database of stolen objects, lists 126,000 pieces!

Art theft and artifact looting raise basic ethical questions for professional archaeologists. Should they ever study looted collections? The artifacts of gold and copper as well as sculpted pottery made by the Moche culture of the northern coast of Peru (A.D. 100–800) fetch thousands of dollars on the open market. A major controversy swirled around archaeologist Christopher Donnan when he studied and published information on looted objects made by the Moche. Some experts thought that Donnan had made a serious error in professional judgment by appearing to condone looting and private collecting. But Donnan told a different story. As a scientist, and probably the leading authority on the Moche people, he defended his action by stating that he was merely seeking to document ancient Moche art and society. The stealing of artifacts is lamentable, but should archaeologists ignore the opportunity to learn from well-preserved, looted artifacts? As Donnan wrote in 1991, "It is tragic that looting takes place, and I know of no archaeologist who does not decry the loss of critical information that results. But to stand by when it is possible to make at least some record of whatever information can still be salvaged simply compounds the loss."

Looting is also a serious problem at historic sites. Developers seek to build rows of identical houses on revered sites, and hobbyists destroy archaeological deposits with their thoughtless diggings. Many amateur archaeologists might throw up their hands in horror at the destruction of Carrickmines Castle, but they may believe that no harm results from running metal detectors over historic sites in search of coins, buttons, bullets, and other collectibles. After all, they argue, are there not historical documents, photographs, and even living people who remember historic sites?

Many military encampments and battlefields are especially plagued with collectors who have a passionate urge to acquire and sell spent bullets, brass buttons, and other military objects. Bottle hunters tunnel into nineteenth-century trash heaps for patent medicine bottles, old milk and beer bottles, and colorful glass flasks that will fetch money at antique shows. Bottle hunters know that privies are prime spots to find complete specimens, and many avidly seek them. They use long, T-shaped metal probes to search for the buried soft fill of an abandoned privy, then dig into it feverishly, destroying layer after layer of stratified information in quest of a discarded, whole bottle. A collectibles market that pays hundreds, even thousands, of dollars for a single specimen fuels their search. These so-called "bottle diggers" know that money is to be made in selling archaeological finds.

Many well-respected and expert historical archaeologists maintain large, personal artifact collections, usually acquired by purchase. These collections are used to train students in artifact identification and for comparative and dating purposes. These "type" or "reference" collections are valuable sources of information when they are composed of non-looted objects. Random collections lacking all archaeological context are merely objects, with little but artistic merit.

Archaeology began as treasure hunting, and many of the world's great museums acquired collections through excavations that were little more than glorified exercises in looting. Much was undoubtedly saved for posterity because of the acquisitive policies of early museum curators and wealthy collectors, at a time when archaeologists were few and far between and antiquities departments were nonexistent in most countries. Today's collectors and antiquities dealers still argue passionately that they are saving the past by collecting it and preserving it for future generations. These are specious arguments in today's world. Now we have thousands of professional archaeologists, numerous museums, and a clear understanding of the importance of artifacts and their archaeological contexts. Most major museums have adopted tough acquisition policies that demand contextual information that is designed to discourage looting. But the antiquities traffic continues unabated and will flourish as long as unscrupulous, unthinking people believe that personal ownership is more important than historical knowledge. Their philosophy is easily set down: I have taste, I have the money to indulge it, and as a tasteful, wealthy person, I have the individual right to own any part of the past I wish. Or do I?

## Who Owns the Past?

Should archaeological sites and artifacts be in private or public hands? Do any of us have the right to say that we own the past?

Many governments have enacted legislation that makes all archaeological sites, whether on private or public land, the property of the state. In the United States, the law effectively offers no protection to sites on privately owned land. Americans place an enormous premium on personal rights and on individual ownership. Many of the most important archaeological sites in North America— for example, Chaco Canyon and Mesa Verde in the Southwest—are under public ownership, but hundreds of lesser sites rest on private land. The fur traders' post in South Dakota, the silver miner's cabin in Nevada, the tiny British outpost in Australia, all are as vital a part of the archaeological record as Mesa Verde. The right to ownership of land carries with it important responsibilities, not only for conserving soil and water, but also for protecting historic sites. Many land owners properly recognize and accept these responsibilities, especially when they feel a strong historical identification with a site. In the American West, many ranchers may protect a nineteenth-century barn because their grandfather built it. In such cases, the interests of the landowner and the historical archaeologist coincide.

In the late 1980s the author was involved in a project just like this in south Louisiana. He was contacted by the owners of the McIlhenny Company, the manufacturers since 1868 of Tabasco Brand Pepper Sauce at Avery Island, Louisiana. The owners of the island had transformed it over the years from a sugar plantation to the production site of the world-famous hot sauce. Avery Island had been a typical sugar plantation. Enslaved families lived in small duplex cabins and labored in the cane fields or worked in the master's kitchen. The planters oversaw the slaves' labor, marketed the sugar they produced, and lived in Marsh House, the oldest house on the island. No one knows precisely when the house was built, but it was a functioning residence by 1818. Marsh House was eventually converted into a guest house and conference center for the McIlhenny Company. In the mid-1980s, the house sustained a devastating fire that destroyed much of its superstructure.

The McIlhenny Company has a long and admirable history of promoting environmental and historical preservation, and so, when they planned to restore and renovate the house, they contacted the author to conduct an archaeological testing program there. The company wanted to ensure that they did not destroy or damage any artifacts or earlier structural remains during the renovation process.

The archaeological project was a complete success. The McIlhenny Company was true to its dedication to preservation. They did nothing that would compromise the integrity of the archaeological remains on their island. If academic research goals and corporate requirements could always be so closely linked, many of the problems faced by archaeologists could be avoided. Developers would also learn that archaeology is not a danger to them. As of this writing, a team from the University of Alabama continues an active research program at Avery Island with the sponsorship of the McIlhenny Company.

The Avery Island case is still more of an exception than the rule. The battle for the past is far from over. Public attitudes toward the past are more often than not couched in terms of financial value and economic gain rather than responsibility for the history of our forebears. Archaeologists must strive to change the modern-day mind set that is willing to sacrifice the past for financial gain. What will future generations think of us if we do not protect the past for them?

## THE FUTURE OF HISTORICAL ARCHAEOLOGY

Where does the future of historical archaeology lie? Much depends on our success in saving the past for coming generations, on developing working partnerships with land owners and entrepreneurs, and in learning to respect the views of the world's indigenous peoples. Creative partnerships will probably become more common in the future, as all segments of society find it easier to join hands to protect the environment and the remains of those who inhabited it before us.

Historical archaeology is today exploding around the world. The field has the very real potential to add new theoretical approaches to social science regardless of its emphasis. Many of the theoretical perspectives will involve fundamental issues in historic and modern society—in the spheres of cultural interaction, ethnic diversity, the creation of race, and changing gender roles. Archaeology is unique in its ability to chronicle processes of cultural change over centuries, and even over decades and years. The social and cultural changes of the past appear to us in material terms, in architectural modifications and ever-shifting fashions of style and design.

The archaeological record is usually anonymous, a chronicle of working men and women going about their business day after day, year after year, leaving no record behind except the most prosaic of artifacts and food remains. Such finds are the heart and soul of historical archaeology because they offer a unique searchlight into the dark recesses of history. Archaeological evidence allows us to discover the lives of the humble folk "without history," and to learn the intricate relationships between men and women, conquerors and conquered, oppressors and oppressed.

Historical archaeologists will continue to rewrite important chapters of history. They will document the complex relations between enslaved African Americans and plantation owners, between Spanish friars and Native Americans living in the shadow of mission walls, between Dutch colonists and indigenous peoples across Asia. As increasing numbers of scholars choose to examine history from a global perspective, we will come to see the European Age of Discovery and the Industrial Revolution as complicated developments that involved ever-changing relationships between European nations and myriad human societies in every corner of the world. Unraveling the complexities of these relationships will require multidisciplinary research—conventional archival work and oral histories, as well as linguistic inquiries, ethnographic investigations, and a truly global form of historical archaeology. Historical archaeology is already a multidisciplinary enterprise, but it will become even more so as multicultural perspectives on recent history assume ever-greater importance. Future definitions of history cannot be confined to the narrow universe of documents alone. We must envision the study of history as encompassing a broad range of disciplines, each with its own contribution to make to a multicultural past. Historical archaeology will most certainly be one of these disciplines.

## HISTORICAL ARCHAEOLOGY AND THE LOCAL HISTORICAL SOCIETY

Historical societies are the backbone of local history in many countries. Some are humble organizations, mainly devoted to local genealogical research. Others support museums and archives, and maintain active publication programs, lecture series, and diverse member services. The larger societies employ professional administrators and historians and maintain active connections with local universities and colleges. Many of them have adult education programs. Most historical societies are invaluable resources for both archaeologists and students, especially individuals who are deeply engaged in historic preservation and research into local history. Historical societies often realize the general importance of historical archaeology and understand its relevance to their community's history. They sometimes sponsor archaeological digs, often working in close collaboration with professional archaeologists from a local university or college. These projects are especially rewarding because they acquaint nonarchaeologists with the profession in a very real way.

A perfect example of this kind of project occurred in 1992 in Bloomington, Illinois. Historical archaeologists Mark Groover, Melanie Cabak, and David Babson, then with Illinois State University, worked closely with members of the Bloomington-Normal Black History Group on the excavation of the Wayman African Methodist Episcopal Church and Parsonage. The Bloomington-Normal

Black History Group is an organization of local citizens interested in promoting an understanding of African American history in these two Midwestern towns. The group is sponsored by the McLean County Historical Society in Bloomington. Organized in 1843, the Wayman A.M.E. Church has long been a focal point of local African American religious expression. Groover, Cabak, and Babson organized excavations on the historic church site with the help of twenty-one volunteers. Some of the excavators were adolescent members of the black history club.

The Wayman excavation was spectacularly successful, recovering hundreds of artifacts used at the church. Some of the most interesting artifacts relate to health. Medicine bottles found at the site convinced the archaeologists that the church was used as a place to dispense medicines to the parishioners. Historical records even showed that a doctor once lived in the church's residence. The church was apparently an important provider of health care to the nineteenth-century African American community, and the backyard of the church was the scene of many social gatherings. The limited excavations conducted with the assistance of the historical society did much to confirm ideas about the changing role of the church in local African American life.

Historical societies can be a vital resource for historical archaeology, with open-ended potential for all kinds of exciting research and preservation projects that can be used to train competent fieldworkers and sustain popular enthusiasm about the past. All archaeology, by its very nature, seems a luxury in a world beset by catastrophic social problems, nationalist rivalries, terrorism, and war. Yet it most emphatically is not a luxury, because it offers a superb avenue for studying and understanding human cultural diversity over long periods.

Most of you will never become professional archaeologists, nor should you. This book, however, hopefully sparks your commitment to the past, something that you can enjoy for the rest of your life. All of us enjoy a magnificent cultural legacy from the remote and not-so-remote past, a past that each generation must preserve for their children and grandchildren. So, please, whatever your interest in archaeology and history, please do all you can to save the past for the future. Generations to come will censure us if we do not.

Here are some guidelines:

- Treat every archaeological site and artifact as a finite resource that, once destroyed, can never be replaced.
- Report all archaeological discoveries to responsible archaeological authorities (archaeological surveys, museums, university or college departments, government agencies).
- Obey all laws relating to archaeological sites.
- Never dig at a site without proper training or supervision, even if you think it is a harmless place to find bottles or other artifacts.
- Never collect archaeological finds from any country for your private collection or for profit.

- Respect all burial grounds because most have profound spiritual significance.

## BEING EDUCATED IN HISTORICAL ARCHAEOLOGY

How can a person embark on a career in historical archaeology, a rapidly burgeoning field? A growing number of universities around the world are beginning to offer professional training in the subject, and the number grows almost yearly. The lack of programs dedicated to historical archaeology only relates to the relative newness of the field. But historical archaeology is a field in which career opportunities will open up in coming years, especially as multidisciplinary curricula gain increased popularity.

To become a professional archaeologist requires a minimum of a master's degree, and to do serious research and teach at the university level, a doctorate degree. Even at a university that does not offer a specific degree in historical archaeology, undergraduate students can still learn enough to obtain admission into a good master's or doctoral program. Our advice is to declare a major in anthropology or in social history, then design your curriculum, as much as you can, around courses in anthropology, archaeology, history, and geography. Enroll in as much cultural anthropology as possible, because courses in this field will give you a grounding in cultural diversity on a global scale and help you to develop an anthropological perspective and a background in theories of culture.

In terms of archaeology itself, you should focus on method and theory. The more you can learn about excavation methods and past archaeologists' theories, the better prepared you will be for future graduate work. Courses in historiography, archival research methods, and oral history, as well as surveys in regional and world history, will stand you in good stead as you develop your skills in historical research methods. Your studies in geography should include courses in cultural geography, landscape design, settlement analysis, and even cartography. Geographers can teach you about vernacular architecture, about analyzing spatial arrangements of people and settlements, and how to read a landscape.

If you are seriously interested in applying to graduate school, you should plan to attend an archaeological field school. The archaeological site is the classroom for these courses, and the pens and papers are trowels and shovels. Field schools in prehistoric archaeology have been offered since at least the 1930s, but the number of field schools in historical archaeology is growing yearly. Both the Society for Historical Archaeology (SHA) and the Archaeological Institute of America (AIA) maintain lists of field schools, and *Archaeology* magazine regularly publishes information about archaeological field schools. Some websites also contain information about how to apply to a field school. You can also consult your archaeology professors. They may know of local field schools or be able to steer you toward information sent to their departmental office. A field school is a wonderful opportunity to gain practical field experience and also to find out whether you have an aptitude for fieldwork. It is far better to test yourself in the field before you invest in graduate school. Archaeological excavation and survey can be tough, demanding, and dirty work, and it is not for everyone, even many people with an honest love of history.

Professional training in historical archaeology, or in any kind of archaeology for that matter, comes from master's and doctoral programs at major universities. Anyone seeking to become a professional researcher and university professor must obtain a doctorate degree. This process takes several years and involves completing a major piece of original research. Increasing numbers of people are electing to take a master's in archaeology, frequently specializing in conservation, cultural resource management, and other topics that have a strong resource management emphasis. Many of these graduates find jobs in government agencies or in the environmental impact assessment industry.

The choice of a graduate program depends on many variables, including the quality and interests of the faculty, the kind of historical archaeology you wish to pursue, and your methodological and theoretical interests. You will be best served by studying with a professional engaged in research that interests you. Your archaeology professors will have contacts in the field and will probably know which departments best suit your interests. If you are not enrolled at a university or college that offers archaeology courses, do not be afraid to e-mail or write nearby professional archaeologists. In most cases, they will be happy to assist you.

Finally, and most important: Do not contemplate a career in historical archaeology unless you have a passionate interest in the subject and a real commitment to the past. Archaeology is not a field for the lukewarm enthusiast, or for those who seek undemanding job security. All archaeological jobs require unlimited enthusiasm, a willingness to relocate, abundant energy, the ability to tolerate discomfort and low salaries, and, above all, passion and a sense of humor. For those who meet these criteria, archaeology is one of the most satisfying jobs on earth.

Professional archaeological societies promote the highest standards of archaeological research. Most of them have created rigid sets of guidelines to judge the qualifications of archaeologists. The guidelines are usually tough for good reason. Archaeological sites are a nonrenewable resource; once they are destroyed, they are gone forever. They deserve nothing but the best professional attention.

## JOBS IN HISTORICAL ARCHAEOLOGY

Archaeologists generally outnumber paying jobs in the field, so the employment picture is always tight, especially at colleges and universities during times of declining resources. Until very recently, archaeologists only worked in universities and colleges, teaching during the academic year, and perhaps conducting field schools or doing research during the summers. Some archaeologists also found positions in museums. The employment picture has changed dramatically over the past couple of decades, as more and more professional opportunities for archaeologists have opened up in government, in nonprofit organizations, and in private consulting companies conducting environmental research and cultural resource management. Many archaeologists have administrative positions in their country's agencies that protect cultural history. Most of these bodies require the contribution of trained historical archaeologists because of their broad, multidisciplinary training: in archaeology, historiography, historic preservation, anthropology, and geography. Museums and historical societies also offer opportunities to acquire on-the-job training, and sometimes paid internships.

## USEFUL ADDRESSES

A good place to find resources about historical archaeology are the websites of the major societies that have been created specifically for historical archaeology. We have included their addresses below. These sites are all active as of this writing, but should you have difficulties, simply search under the organization's name.

> The Society for Historical Archaeology: www.sha.org/
>
> The Society for Post-Medieval Archaeology: www.spma.org.uk/
>
> The Australasian Society for Historical Archaeology: www.asha.org.au/

Other countries may be creating similar societies. For example, Italy has a post-medieval archaeology website: www.archeologiapostmedievale.it. Readers should repeatedly check various websites.

In this brief introduction to historical archaeology, we have tried to communicate the excitement of this emerging field. We showed in Chapter 2 that historical archaeology is not a discipline with a long and venerable history. Compared with other kinds of archaeology, it is only an infant. Historical archaeology's youth gives it vitality. The field is exciting, and historical archaeologists are pushing current knowledge to the limit, challenging old interpretations and creating bold, new ones. The rapid accumulation of knowledge in a field as new as historical archaeology is inevitable. We are not troubled that some of what we have written here will be corrected by our colleagues or even replaced with better and more complex examples. On the contrary, we are excited by the prospect. Even in the social sciences, knowledge is a process of researching, writing, researching anew, and writing again. Change is occurring quickly in historical archaeology. New sites are being excavated all the time, and increasing numbers of students are being introduced to our field. Historical archaeologists are exploring parts of the globe that only recently were blank territories on the map of archaeological knowledge. If you are fascinated by the archaeology of recent history and are enthused by its promise, then we welcome you to historical archaeology with open arms.

# TIME TRAVEL

## John Russell Cutlery Company, Massachusetts, 1833–1933

Industrialization appears, to many of us, as a nameless, faceless monolith. Objects get produced in factories and are shipped to stores where we purchase them. Part of the apparent anonymity of industrialism undoubtedly stems from the mass of often poorly documented workers who actually perform the labor. At its heart, however, the urge to produce mass quantities of commodities for sale and profit is generally begun by a single person who perceives an opportunity and who is socially well-positioned enough to take advantage of it. Such was the case with the establishment of the John Russell Cutlery Company in northern Massachusetts.

John Russell, born in 1797, was the son of a jeweler and silversmith who lived in Greenfield, Massachusetts, not far from the border with Vermont. As a young man, Russell was a speculator in southern cotton, and after making a bit of money in this endeavor, he decided to return to Massachusetts to develop a cutlery industry. His plan was to compete with the highly successful Sheffield, England, cutlery industry, a name that was synonymous with quality. In partnership with his brother, Russell began producing chisels in the early 1830s. Their firm became widely known for their innovative production methods, and they even won an award for their chisels in 1834. The company had branched out into cutlery by the 1840s, and produced the famous Green River knife. This knife became *the* tool used by fur trappers throughout the American west. A trapper without a Green River knife was not considered much of a frontiersman. The Russell company continued to prosper throughout the late nineteenth century, but by 1900, only

about 11 percent of knives produced in the United States came from companies in Massachusetts. In 1933, the Harrington Cutlery Company, in southern Massachusetts near Connecticut, purchased the Russell company, making Russell-Harrington Cutlery.

The nature of modern industrialism is such that the owners of capitalist industries must constantly strive to stay profitable and efficient. In their drive for profitability, factory administrators must repeatedly upgrade the production process by buying new equipment or inventing innovative techniques. The productive process at the Russell factory changed from simple hammering to mechanical stamping. Stamping was a speedier manufacturing process that could be accomplished by workers who had a minimum of skill and training.

The transformation of the labor process was accompanied by a modification of the physical structure of the Russell factory. Workers engaged in hammering could be stationed around the factory and conceivably could manufacture an entire knife at their workbench. With increasing mechanization, however, the arrangement of workers on the shop floor became segmented and ordered. Workers engaged in monotonous work, such as grinding and polishing knife blades, were organized in neat rows. Their tasks were as interchangeable as they themselves appeared to be. Piece-workers of this sort were not even able to stand up and get a new knife because young boys would bring the unfinished knives to them. Workers with the most tedious jobs

*(continued)*

Source: Michael S. Nassaney and Marjorie R. Abel, "Urban Spaces, Labor Organization, and Social Control: Lessons from New England's Nineteenth-Century Cutlery Industry." In *Lines That Divide: Historical Archaeologies of Race, Class, and Gender*, James A. Delle, Stephen A. Mrozowski, and Robert Paynter, Eds. (Knoxville: University of Tennessee Press, 2000), pp. 239–275.

thus continuously labored. Their work was semi-skilled, so if one worker tired out or was sick for the day, another worker could simply be slotted into his place.

Factories in production during the late nineteenth century were more than simply places of work; they also incorporated tenements as workers' quarters. These living spaces were usually planned to be as monotonous and interchangeable as the workers themselves. The Russell Company tenements were composed of long rows of brick apartments with three stories. The company owned both the factory and the tenements, and the loss of a job also meant the loss of a place to live.

The linkage between workplace and home had the effect of uniting the processes of living and working. Laboring in the factory for wages, under the demands of a foreman, was made to seem as natural as living day to day. The connection between work and home was made even clearer when families were compelled to take in boarders in an effort to make ends meet. Wives of Russell factory workers used the backyards of their apartments for gardening and raising animals for subsistence, and for washing their family's clothes and possibly even the clothes of nearby elites. Some women even worked in the cutlery factory, but they earned less money than their male counterparts.

# GUIDE TO FURTHER READING

The references that follow, though selective, will give you access to the more technical literature of historical archaeology. Any one of several comprehensive method and theory texts on the market will provide you with excellent background to the general principles of archaeology. Much of the literature of historical archaeology appears in professional journals or in reports of limited distribution. We recommend you consult an expert before attacking the more specialist literature. For your convenience, however, we include the archaeological works used to prepare each chapter, as well as a few more general background readings.

Students may wish to read works exploring the humorous side of archaeology. Three excellent, fun books are Paul Bahn's, *Bluff Your Way in Archaeology* (Partridge Green, Horsham: Ravette, 1989), and Paul Bahn's and Bill Tidy's, *Disgraceful Archaeology, or Things You Shouldn't Know About the History of Mankind!* (Stroud, Gloucestershire: Tempus, 1999). A classic is David Macaulay's, *Motel of the Mysteries* (Boston: Houghton Mifflin, 1979).

Professional archaeologists are even beginning to write theory-based novels and even comic books. Interested students should see Adrian Praetzellis's *Death By Theory: A Tale of Mystery and Archaeological Theory* (Walnut Creek, California: AltaMira, 2000), his *Dug to Death: A Tale of Archaeological Method and Mayhem* (Walnut Creek, California: AltaMira, 2003), and Johannes H. N. Loubser's, *Archaeology: The Comic* (Walnut Creek, California: AltaMira, 2003).

## GENERAL WORKS ON HISTORICAL ARCHAEOLOGY

The best short account of historical archaeology is James Deetz's widely read *In Small Things Forgotten: The Archaeology of Early American Life* (revised and expanded ed., Garden City, NY: Anchor Press/Doubleday, 1996). Ivor Noël Hume's, *Historical Archaeology* (New York: Alfred A. Knopf, 1972) is a somewhat outdated, but still elegant work focusing on European American sites in North America. The same author's *The Virginia Adventure* (New York: Alfred A. Knopf, 1994) is a fascinating account of historical archaeology at Roanoke and Jamestown, Virginia. Abundant information about the field also appears in *The Encyclopedia of Historical Archaeology*, Charles E. Orser Jr., Ed (London: Routledge, 2002).

More specialized edited volumes include Geoff Egan and R. L. Michael (Eds.), *Old and New Worlds* (Oxford: Oxbow, 1999); Lisa Falk (Ed.), *Historical Archaeology in Global Perspective* (Washington D.C.: Smithsonian Institution Press, 1991); Pedro P. A. Funari, Martin Hall, and Siân Jones (Eds.), *Historical Archaeology: Back from the Edge* (London: Routledge, 1999); Mark P. Leone and Parker Potter, Jr. (Eds.), *The Recovery of Meaning: Historical Archaeology in the Eastern United*

*States* (Washington D.C.: Smithsonian Institution Press, 1988); Randall H. McGuire and Robert Paynter (Eds.), *The Archaeology of Inequality* (Oxford: Basil Blackwell, 1991); Robert L. Schuyler (Ed.), *Historical Archaeology: A Guide to Substantive and Theoretical Contributions* (Farmingdale, NY: Baywood, 1978). Stanley South, *Method and Theory in Historical Archaeology* (New York: Academic Press, 1977); and Stanley South (Ed.), *Research Strategies in Historical Archaeology* (New York: Academic Press, 1977).

Students interested in post-medieval archaeology in Great Britain should consult David Crossley, *Post-Medieval Archaeology in Britain* (Leicester: Leicester University Press, 1990) and Richard Newman, *The Historical Archaeology of Britain, c. 1540–1900* (Stroud, Gloucestershire: Sutton, 2001).

Historical archaeologists are now writing useful case studies of modern-period sites. Three excellent studies are: Kenneth L. Feder, *A Village of Outcasts: Historical Archaeology and Documentary Research at the Lighthouse Site* (Mountain View, CA: Mayfield, 1994), Janet D. Spector, *What This Awl Means: Feminist Archaeology at a Wahpeton Dakota Village* (St. Paul: Minnesota Historical Society Press, 1993), and David Starbuck, *The Great Warpath: British Military Sites from Albany to Crown Point* (Hanover, NH: University Press of New England, 1999). A workbook for historical archaeology students has been published: *Doing Historical Archaeology: Exercises Using Documentary, Oral, and Material Evidence* by Russell J. Barber (Englewood Cliffs, NJ: Prentice-Hall, 1994).

## MAJOR JOURNALS COVERING HISTORICAL ARCHAEOLOGY

The major English-language journals dealing solely with historical archaeology are *Historical Archaeology* (published in the United States by the Society for Historical Archaeology), *Post-Medieval Archaeology* (published in England by the Society for Post-Medieval Archaeology), *The International Journal of Historical Archaeology* (published in the United States by Kluwer Academic/Plenum), and *The Australasian Journal of Historical Archaeology* (published by The Australasian Society for Historical Archaeology). The major archaeological journals concentrating on prehistory have traditionally not published articles about historical archaeology, but articles by historical archaeologists are beginning to appear with more regularity. Students should occasionally check these journals for important information about archaeology: *American Antiquity, Latin American Antiquity, Antiquity,* and *Journal of Field Archaeology*.

## CHAPTER 1: WHAT IS HISTORICAL ARCHAEOLOGY?

The topics explored in this chapter are discussed, usually superficially, in most of the books mentioned above. For the use of written records in historical archaeology consult Mary C. Beaudry (Ed.), *Documentary Archaeology in the New World* (Cambridge: Cambridge University Press, 1988) and Barbara J. Little (Ed.), *Text-Aided Archaeology* (Boca Raton, FL: CRC Press, 1992).

Historiography has generated an enormous literature and students should consult their library's database for the most recent titles. Two classics are Marc Bloch, *The Historian's Craft*, trans. Peter Putnam (New York, Vintage, 1953) and Edward H. Carr, *What Is History?* (New York: Alfred A. Knopf, 1961). A similar work, written by a respected archaeologist, is V. Gordon Childe, *History* (London: Cobbett Press, 1947). More recent essays include: R. F. Atkinson, *Knowledge and Explanation in History: An Introduction in the Philosophy of History* (London: Macmillan, 1978); Daniel J. Boorstin, *Hidden History* (New York: Harper and Row, 1987) and David Hackett Fischer, *Historians' Fallacies: Toward a Logic of Historical Thought* (New York: Harper and Row, 1970). A wonderful book by a historian that makes explicit use of historical archaeology is T. H. Breen, *Imagining the Past: East Hampton Histories* (Reading, MA: Addison-Wesley, 1989). Students wishing to learn how the presentation of history can be skewed should begin with Michael Parenti, *History as Mystery* (San Francisco: City Lights Books, 1999) and Michel-Rolph Trouillot, *Silencing the Past: Power and the Production of History* (Boston: Beacon, 1995).

Eric Wolf, *Europe and the People Without History* (Berkeley: University of California Press, 1984) is indispensable on the European Age of Discovery and issues of interconnectedness. Another superb source is Thomas C. Patterson, *Inventing Western Civilization* (New York: Monthly Review Press, 1997).

### Specialist Literature

Adams, William H., *Silcott, Washington: Ethnoarchaeology of a Rural American Community*. Reports of Investigation 54. (Pullman: Laboratory of Anthropology, Washington State University, 1977).

Armstrong, Douglas V., *The Old Village and the Great House: An Archaeological and Historical Examination of Drax Hall Plantation, St. Ann's Bay, Jamaica*. (Urbana: University of Illinois Press, 1990).

Hagget, Peter, *The Geographer's Art*. (Oxford: Basil Blackwell, 1990).

Hogarth, David G., *Authority and Archaeology: Sacred and Profane*. (London: John Murray, 1899).

Schmidt, Peter R., *Historical Archaeology: A Structural Approach in an African Culture*. (Westport, CT: Greenwood, 1978).

Schuyler, Robert L., Historical Archaeology and Historic Sites Archaeology as Anthropology: Basic Definitions and Relationships. *Historical Archaeology* 4(1970):83–89.

———Parallels in the Rise of the Various Subfields of Historical Archaeology. *Conference on Historic Site Archaeology Papers* 10 (1977):2–10.

## CHAPTER 2: A BRIEF HISTORY OF HISTORICAL ARCHAEOLOGY

Father Martin's excavations at Sainte Marie appear in Kenneth E. Kidd's *The Excavation of Ste. Marie I* (Toronto: University of Toronto Press, 1949), and mention of Hall's excavations can be found in Deetz's "Late Man in North America:

Archaeology of European Americans," in *Anthropological Archaeology in the Americas* (Washington, D.C.: Anthropological Society of Washington, 1968) pp. 121–130. In addition to Leone and Potter's *The Recovery of Meaning*, and McGuire and Paynter's *The Archaeology of Inequality*, already mentioned, case studies in contemporary historical archaeology can be found in the special issue of *Historical Archaeology* "Meanings and Uses of Material Culture," Barbara J. Little and Paul A. Shackel (Eds.), 26(1992) 26:3.

### *Specialist Literature*

Baker, Vernon G., *Historical Archaeology at Black Lucy's Garden, Andover, Massachusetts: Ceramics from the Site of a Nineteenth Century Afro-American* (Andover, MA: Philips Academy, 1978).

Beaudry, Mary C. and Stephen A. Mrozowski (Eds.), *Interdisciplinary Investigations of the Boott Mills, Lowell, Massachusetts, Volume I: Life at the Boarding Houses, A Preliminary Report.* (Boston: National Park Service, 1987).

Binford, Lewis R., Archaeology as Anthropology. *American Antiquity* 28(1962):217–225.

Cohn, Bernard S., An Anthropologist Among the Historians: A Field Study. *The South Atlantic Quarterly* 61(1962):13–28.

Deagan, Kathleen, Avenues of Inquiry in Historical Archaeology. In *Advances in Archaeological Method and Theory*, vol. 5, Michael B. Schiffer (Ed.), pp. 151–177. (New York: Academic Press, 1982).

Delle, James A., *An Archaeology of Social Space: Analyzing Coffee Plantations in Jamaica's Blue Mountains.* (New York: Plenum, 1998).

Fish, Carl Russell, Relation of Archaeology and History. *Proceedings of the State Historical Society of Wisconsin at the Fifty-Eighth Annual Meeting Held October 20, 1910*, pp. 146–152. (Madison: State Historical Society of Wisconsin, 1911).

Fontana, Bernard L., On the Meaning of Historic Sites Archaeology. *American Antiquity* 31(1965):61–65.

Greenman, Emerson F., *Old Birch Island Cemetery and the Early Historic Trade Route, Georgian Bay, Ontario.* (Ann Arbor: University of Michigan Press, 1951).

Hagen, Richard S., Back-Yard Archaeology at Lincoln's Home. *Journal of the Illinois State Historical Society* 44 (1951):340–348.

Hardesty, Donald C., *The Archaeology of Mining and Miners: A View from the Silver State* (Tucson, AZ: Society for Historical Archaeology, 1988).

Harrington, J. C., Archaeology as an Auxiliary Science of American History. *American Anthropologist* 7 (1955):1121–1130.

———*New Light on Washington's Fort Necessity.* (Richmond, VA: Eastern National Park and Monument Association, 1957).

Hodder, Ian, *Reading the Past: Current Approaches to Interpretation in Archaeology.* (Cambridge: Cambridge University Press, 1986).

Isaac, Rhys, *The Transformation of Virginia, 1740–1790.* (Chapel Hill: University of North Carolina Press, 1982).

Jelks, Edward B., Archaeological Explorations at Signal Hill, Newfoundland, 1965–1966. *Canadian Historic Sites: Occasional Papers in Archaeology and History,* no. 7 (Ottawa: National Historic Sites Service, 1973).

Kidd, Kenneth E., *The Excavation of Ste. Marie I* (Toronto: University of Toronto Press, 1949).

Leone, Mark P., Interpreting Ideology in Historical Archaeology: Using the Rules of Perspective in the William Paca Garden in Annapolis, Maryland. In *Ideology, Power, and Prehistory,* Daniel Miller and Christopher Tilley (Eds.), pp. 25–35. (Cambridge: Cambridge University Press, 1984).

Mouer, L. Daniel, Cheasapeake Creoles: The Creation of Folk Culture in Colonial Virginia. In *The Archaeology of 17th-Century Virginia,* T. R. Reinhart and D. J. Pogue, (Eds.), pp. 105–166. (Courtland: Archaeological Society of Virginia, 1993.)

Paynter, Robert. Historical and Anthropological Archaeology: Forging Alliances. *Journal of Archaeological Research* 8 (2000):1–37.

——Historical Archaeology and the Post-Columbian World of North America. *Journal of Archaeological Research* 8 (2000):169–217.

Shackel, Paul A. and Barbara J. Little, (Eds.), *Historical Archaeology of the Chesapeake.* (Washington, D.C.: Smithsonian Institution Press, 1994).

South, Stanley, *Method and Theory in Historical Archaeology.* (New York: Academic Press, 1977).

Wheaton, Thomas R. and Patrick W. Garrow, Acculturation and the Archaeological Record in the Carolina Lowcountry. In *Archaeology of Slavery and Plantation Life,* Theresa A. Singleton (Ed.), pp. 239–259. (Orlando: Academic Press, 1985).

Woolworth, Alan and Raymond Wood, The Archaeology of a Small Trading Post. *River Basin Survey Papers, Bulletin 176* (Washington, D.C.: U.S. Government Printing Office, 1960)

Yentsch, Anne, Chesapeake Artefacts and Their Cultural Context: Pottery and the Food Domain. *Post-Medieval Archaeology* 25(1991):25–72.

## CHAPTER 3: HISTORICAL CULTURE, SOCIETY, AND HISTORICAL SITES

Anthropologists have written numerous books about the history, nature, and future directions of their discipline. An excellent and very readable history of anthropology is Annemarie de Waal Malfefijt, *Images of Man: A History of Anthropological Thought* (New York: Alfred A. Knopf, 1974). For a more complete synthesis see Fred W. Voget, *A History of Ethnology* (New York: Holt, Rinehart, and Winston, 1975). Good collections of readings in anthropology are Paul Bohannan and Mark Glazer (Eds.), *High Points in Anthropology* (2nd ed., New York: Alfred A. Knopf, 1988) and Johnnetta B. Cole (Ed.), *Anthropology for the Nineties: Introductory Readings* (New York: The Free Press, 1988).

For archaeology as anthropology see Guy Gibbon *Anthropological Archaeology* (New York: Columbia University Press, 1984). An older source is Mark P.

Leone (Ed.), *Contemporary Archaeology: A Guide to Theory and Contributions* (Carbondale: Southern Illinois University Press, 1972).

Classic articles on ethnographic analogy and the direct historical approach include: Robert Ascher, "Analogy in Archaeological Interpretation," *Southwestern Journal of Anthropology* 17(1961):317–325; and Julian H. Steward, "The Direct Historical Approach to Archaeology," *American Antiquity* 7(1942):337–343. The use of analogy in historical archaeology: Charles E. Orser, Jr., "Ethnohistory, Analogy, and Historical Archaeology," *Conference on Historic Site Archaeology Papers* 13 (1979):1–24; and Robert L. Schuyler, "The Use of Historic Analogs in Archaeology," *American Antiquity* 33(1968):390–392. For analogical reasoning in archaeology, see P. Nick Kardulias. "Estimating Population at Ancient Military Sites: The Use of Historical and Contemporary Analogy," *American Antiquity* 57(1992): 276–287.

Research designs and sampling are controversial issues. Research designs are discussed in Lewis R. Binford, "A Consideration of Archaeological Research Design," *American Antiquity* 29(1963):425–441. For sampling see James W. Mueller (Ed.), *Sampling in Archaeology* (Tucson: University of Arizona Press, 1975). Another good source is Stephen Plog, Fred Plog, and Walter Wait, "Decision Making in Modern Surveys," in *Advances in Archaeological Method and Theory, Vol. 1*, Michael B. Schiffer (Ed.), pp. 383–421, (New York: Academic Press, 1976).

Many books and articles discuss historic preservation. Books heavily slanted toward archaeology are Thomas F. King, Patricia Parker Hickman, and Gary Berg (Eds.), *Anthropology in Historic Preservation: Caring for a Culture's Clutter* (New York: Academic Press, 1977), and Thomas F. King, *Cultural Resource Laws and Practice: An Introductory Guide* (Walnut Creek, California: AltaMira, 1998). Two good books about the preservation of historical buildings, towns, and environments: Antoinette J. Lee (Ed.), *Past Meets Future: Saving America's Historic Environments* (Washington, D.C.: Preservation Press, 1992); and Arthur P. Ziegler, Jr. and Walter C. Kidney, *Historic Preservation in Small Towns: A Manual of Practice* (Nashville: American Association for State and Local History, 1980).

### Specialist Literature

Beattie, Owen and John Geiger, *Frozen in Time: Unlocking the Secrets of the Doomed 1845 Arctic Expedition* (New York: Penguin, 1987).

Binford, Lewis R., Smudge Pits and Hide Smoking: The Use of Analogy in Archaeological Reasoning. *American Antiquity* 32(1967):1–12.

Boorstin, Daniel, *Hidden History* (New York: Harper and Row, 1987).

de Barros, P. L., The Effect of the Slave Trade on the Bassar Ironworking Society, Togo. In *West Africa During the Atlantic Slave Trade: Archaeological Perspectives*, C. R. DeCorse, (Ed.), pp. 59–80. (London: Leicester University Press, 2001).

Fox, Richard Allan, Jr., *Archaeology, History, and Custer's Last Battle: The Little Bighorn Reexamined* (Norman: University of Oklahoma Press, 1993).

Handler, Jerome S. and Frederick W. Lange, *Plantation Slavery in Barbados: An Archaeological and Historical Investigation* (Cambridge: Harvard University Press, 1978).

Harrington, Spencer P. M., Bones and Bureaucrats: New York's Great Cemetery Imbroglio. *Archaeology* 46, 2 (1993):28–38.

Heite, Edward F., *Archaeological Data Recovery on the Collins, Geddes Cannery Site, Road 356A, Lebanon North Murderkill Hundred, Kent County, Delaware.* (Wilmington: Delaware Department of Transportation, 1990).

Kelly, Roger E. and Marsha C. S. Kelly, Arrastras: Unique Western Historic Milling Sites. *Historical Archaeology* 17, 1 (1983):85–95.

Kidder, A. V., *An Introduction to the Study of Southwestern Archaeology, with a Preliminary Account of the Excavations at Pecos.* (New Haven: Yale University Press, 1924).

Lamb, Teresia A., *Preliminary Archaeological Reconnaissance and Assessment of Destrehan Plantation, St. Charles Parish, Louisiana.* (New Orleans: Archaeological and Cultural Research Program, University of New Orleans, 1983).

Lewis, Kenneth E. and Helen W. Haskell, *The Middleton Place Privy: A Study of Discard Behavior and the Archaeological Record.* Research Manuscript 174. (Columbia: South Carolina Institute for Archaeology and Anthropology, 1981).

Linebaugh, D. W., Forging a Career: Roland W. Robbins and Iron Industry Sites in the Northeastern U. S. *Industrial Archaeology* 26(2000):5–36.

Mrozowski, Stephen A., "Historical Archaeology as Anthropology." *Historical Archaeology* 22 (1988) 1:18–24.

Munson, Patrick J., Comments on Binford's "Smudge Pits and Hide Smoking: The Use of Analogy in Archaeological Reasoning." *American Antiquity* 34(1969):83–85.

Murray, Jeffrey S., The Mounties of Cypress Hill. *Archaeology* 41, 1(1988):32–38.

Pastron, Allen G., William C. Hoff's Gold Rush Emporium: Bonanza from Old San Francisco. *Archaeology* 41, 4 (1988):32–39.

———On Golden Mountain. *Archaeology* 42, 4 (1989):48–53.

Pearce, J., A Late 18th-Century Inn Clearance Assemblage from Uxbridge, Middlesex. *Post-Medieval Archaeology* 34(2000):144–186.

Reinhart, Theodore R. (Ed.), *The Archaeology of Shirley Plantation.* (Charlottesville: University Press of Virginia, 1984).

Scott, Douglas D., Richard A. Fox, Jr., Melissa A. Connor, and Dick Harmon, *Archaeological Perspectives on the Battle of the Little Bighorn* (Norman: University of Oklahoma Press, 1989).

Starbuck, David R., *Massacre at Fort William Henry.* (Hanover: University Press of New England, 2002).

Starbuck, David R., and Mary Bentley Dupré, Production Continuity and Obolescence of Traditional Red Earthenwares in Concord, New Hampshire. In *Domestic Pottery of the Northeastern United States, 1625–1850,* Sarah Peabody Turnbaugh (Ed.), pp. 133–152. (Orlando: Academic Press, 1985).

Tuck, James, A Sixteenth-Century Whaling Station at Red Bay, Labrador. In *Early European Settlement and Exploration in Atlantic Canada,* G. M. Story (Ed.), pp. 41–52. (St. John's: Memorial University of Newfoundland, 1982).

Tylor, Edward Burnett, *The Origins of Culture, Part I of "Primitive Culture."* (New York: Harper and Row, 1958).

Upward, Geoffrey C., *A Home for Our Heritage: The Building and Growth of Green-field Village and Henry Ford Museum, 1929–1979*. (Dearborn, MI: Henry Ford Museum Press, 1979).

## CHAPTER 4: HISTORICAL ARTIFACTS

Many authors have discussed material culture. Some relevant studies and essays include: Leland Ferguson (Ed.), *Historical Archaeology and the Importance of Material Things* (California, PA: Society for Historical Archaeology, 1977); Ian M. G. Quimby (Ed.), *Material Culture and the Study of American Life* (New York: W. W. Norton, 1978); and Thomas J. Schlereth (Ed.), *Material Culture Studies in America* (Nashville: American Association for State and Local History, 1982). See also: Arthur Asa Berger, *Reading Matter: Multidisciplinary Perspectives on Material Culture* (New Brunswick, NJ: Transaction, 1992); Mihaly Csikszentmihalyi and Eugene Rochberg-Halton, *The Meaning of Things: Domestic Symbols and the Self* (Cambridge: Cambridge University Press, 1981); Chandra Mukerji, *From Graven Images: Patterns of Modern Materialism* (New York: Columbia University Press, 1983); Robert Blair St. George (Ed.), *Material Life in America, 1600–1860* (Boston: Northeastern University Press, 1988); and Thomas J. Schlereth, *Artifacts and the American Past* (Nashville: American Association for State and Local History, 1980) and *Cultural History and Material Culture: Everyday Life, Landscapes, Museums* (Ann Arbor, MI: UMI Research, 1990). Two wonderful anthropological studies of material objects are Mary Douglas and Baron Isherwood, *The World of Goods* (New York: Basic, 1979) and Nicholas Thomas, *Entangled Objects: Exchange, Material Culture, and Colonialism in the Pacific* (Cambridge: Harvard University Press, 1991).

Interesting books about historical artifacts in Europe, written by non-archaeologists, include Lisa Jardine, *Worldly Goods: A New History of the Renaissance* (New York: W. W. Norton, 1998), Sarah Richards, *Eighteenth-Century Ceramics: Products for a Civilised Society* (Manchester: Manchester University Press, 1999), Daniel Roche, *A History of Everyday Things: The Birth of Consumption in France, 1600–1800* (Cambridge: Cambridge University Press, 2000), and Raffaella Sarti, *Europe at Home: Family and Material Culture, 1500–1800* (New Haven: Yale University Press, 2002).

The study of artifacts in historical archaeology is a huge topic. A good starting point is Ivor Noël Hume's *A Guide to Artifacts of Colonial America* (New York: Alfred A. Knopf, 1969). The complexities of the subject are well covered in Richard A. Gould and Michael B. Schiffer's (Eds.), *Modern Material Culture: The Archaeology of Us* (New York: Academic, 1981); Daniel Miller's *Material Culture and Mass Consumption* (Oxford, England: Basil Blackwell, 1987) and Suzanne Spencer-Wood's edited volume *Consumer Choice in Historical Archaeology* (New York: Plenum, 1987).

Makers' marks on ceramics and glass: Geoffrey A. Godden, *Encyclopaedia of British Pottery and Porcelain Marks* (New York: Bonanza, 1964) and Julian Harrison

Toulouse, *Bottle Makers and Their Marks* (New York: Thomas Nelson, 1971). American pottery marks: William C. Gates and Dana E. Ormerod, "The East Liverpool Pottery District: Identification of Manufacturers and Marks," *Historical Archaeology* 16 (1982) 1–2; and Ralph M. and Terry H. Kovel, *Dictionary of Marks. Pottery and Porcelain* (New York: Crown, 1953). Books on makers' marks exist for many different classes of artifacts, many of them from small presses, often geared to antique collectors. One example is Malcolm A. Rogers, *American Pewterers and Their Marks* (Southampton, NY: Cracker Barrel Press, 1968).

### Specialist literature

Allen, J. and J. Barber, A Seventeenth-Century Pottery Group from Kitto Institute, Plymouth. In *Everyday and Exotic Pottery from Europe, c. 650–1900: Studies in Honour of John G. Hurst*, D. Gaimster and M. Redknap, (Eds.), pp. 225–254. (Oxford: Oxbow, 1992.)

Becker, Carl L., What Are Historical Facts? *Western Political Quarterly* 7(1955):327–340.

Cotter, John, *Archaeological Excavations at Jamestown Colonial National Historical Park* (Washington, D.C.: National Park Service, 1958).

Deagan, Kathleen, *Spanish St. Augustine: The Archaeology of a Colonial Creole Community.* (New York: Academic Press, 1983).

Deetz, James F., Scientific Humanism and Humanistic Science: A Plea for Paradigmatic Pluralism in Historical Archaeology. *Geoscience and Man* 23(1983):27–34.

Gradwohl, David M. and Nancy M. Osborn, *Exploring Buried Buxton: Archaeology of an Abandoned Iowa Coal Mining Town with a Large Black Population.* (Ames: Iowa State University Press, 1984).

Lehmer, Donald J., *Introduction to Middle Missouri Archaeology.* (Washington, D.C.: National Park Service, 1971).

Lief, Alfred, *A Close-Up of Closures: History and Progress.* (New York: Glass Container Manufacturers Institute, 1965).

Martin, Ann Smart, The Role of Pewter as Missing Artifact: Consumer Attitudes Toward Tablewares in Late 18th Century Virginia. *Historical Archaeology* 23, 2(1989):1–27.

Monks, Gregory G., Architectural Symbolism and Non-Verbal Communication at Upper Fort Garry. *Historical Archaeology* 26, 2(1992):37–57.

Orser, Charles E., Jr., *The Material Basis of the Postbellum Tenant Plantation: Historical Archaeology in the South Carolina Piedmont.* (Athens: University of Georgia Press, 1988).

Pendergrast, Mark. *For God, Country, and Coca-Cola: The Unauthorized History of the Great American Soft Drink and the Company that Makes it.* (New York: Scribner's, 1993).

Schlereth, Thomas J., Material Culture Studies in America, 1876–1976. In *Material Culture Studies in America*, Thomas J. Schlereth (Ed.), pp. 1–75. (Nashville: American Association for State and Local History, 1982).

Shackel, Paul A., *Personal Discipline and Material Culture: An Archaeology of Annapolis, Maryland, 1695–1870* (Knoxville: University of Tennesee Press, 1993).

Stewart-Abernathy, Leslie C., *The Moser Farmstead* (Fayetteville, AR: Arkansas Archaeological Survey, 1986).

Thomas, David Hurst, Saints and Soldiers at Santa Catalina: Hispanic Designs for Colonial America. In *The Recovery of Meaning: Historical Archaeology in the Eastern United States*, Mark P. Leone and Parker B. Potter Jr. (Eds.), pp. 73–140. (Washington, D.C.: Smithsonian Institution Press, 1988).

## CHAPTER 5: TIME AND SPACE

Context, time, and space are central concepts discussed by any basic archaeological method and theory textbook. David Lowenthal's *The Past is a Foreign Country* (Cambridge: Cambridge University Press, 1985) offers a fascinating commentary on the meaning of time to modern society.

For information about association, superposition, relative chronology, and dating methods in archaeology consult any basic text for up-to-date descriptions of the various methods. The basics of site formation processes appears in Michael B. Schiffer *Formation Processes of the Archaeological Record* (Albuquerque: University of New Mexico Press, 1987).

Space and settlement archaeology continue to be major topics in archaeology. Three older, but still very good, studies are K. C. Chang (Ed.), *Settlement Archaeology* (Palo Alto, CA.: National Press, 1968); David L. Clarke (Ed.), *Spatial Archaeology* (London: Academic Press, 1977); and Ian Hodder and Clive Orton, *Spatial Analysis in Archaeology* (Cambridge: Cambridge University Press, 1976). A good settlement study in historical archaeology: Michael J. O'Brien, *Grassland, Forest, and Historical Settlement: An Analysis of Dynamics in Northeast Missouri* (Lincoln: University of Nebraska Press, 1984).

For proxemics see Edward T. Hall, *The Hidden Dimension* (Garden City, NY: Doubleday, 1966). An archaeological discussion of how humans learn about space is Thomas Wynn, *The Evolution of Spatial Competence* (Urbana: University of Illinois, 1989). An archaeological treatment of proxemics is Ruth Tringham (Ed.), *Territoriality and Proxemics: Archaeological and Ethnographic Evidence for the Use and Organization of Space* (Andover, MA: Warner Modular, 1973).

### Specialist literature

Biddle, Martin, The Rose Revisited: A Comedy (?) of Errors. *Antiquity* 63(1989):753–760.

Binford, Lewis R., A New Method of Calculating Dates from Kaolin Pipe Stem Fragments. *Southeastern Archaeological Conference Newsletter* 9, 1(1962):19–21.

Burke, Heather, *Meaning and Ideology in Historical Archaeology: Style, Social Identity, and Capitalism in an Australian Town.* (New York: Kluwer Academic/Plenum, 1999).

Catts, Wade P. and Jay F. Custer, *Tenant Farmers, Stone Masons, and Black Laborers: Final Archaeological Investigations of the Thomas Williams Site, Glasgow, New Castle Country, Delaware.* (Wilmington: Delaware Department of Transportation, 1990).

Cotter, John L., Daniel G. Roberts, and Michael Parrington, *The Buried Past. An Archaeological History of Philadelphia* (Philadelphia: University of Pennsylvania Press, 1992).

Hamilton, Scott, Over-Hunting and Local Extinctions: Socio-Economic Implications of Fur Trade Subsistence. In *Images of the Recent Past: Readings in Historical Archaeology*, Charles Edward Orser, Jr., (Ed.), pp. 416–436. (Walnut Creek, California: AltaMira, 1996).

Harrington, J. C., Dating Stem Fragments of Seventeenth and Eighteenth Century Clay Tobacco Pipes. *Quarterly Bulletin of the Archaeological Society of Virginia 9*, 1(1954):10–14.

Harris, Edward C., *Principles of Archaeological Stratigraphy.* (New York: Academic Press, 1979).

Heighton, Robert F. and Kathleen A. Deagan, A New Formula for Dating Kaolin Clay Pipestems. *Conference on Historic Site Archaeology Papers* 6(1972):220–229.

Kent, Susan, *Analyzing Activity Areas: An Ethnoarchaeological Study of the Use of Space.* (Albuquerque: University of New Mexico Press, 1984).

Lawrence, Susan, *Dolly's Creek: An Archaeology of a Victorian Goldfields Community.* (Melbourne: Melbourne University Press, 2000).

Noël Hume, Ivor, *Martin's Hundred: The Discovery of a Lost Colonial Virginia Settlement* (New York: Delta, 1983)

Orrell, John and Andrew Gurr. What the Rose Can Tell Us. *Antiquity* 63(1989): 421–429.

Praetzellis, Mary and Adrian Praetzellis, *The Mary Collins Assemblage: Mass Marketing and the Archaeology of a Sacramento Family.* (Rohnert Park, CA: Anthropological Studies Center, Sonoma State University, 1990).

———*"For a Good Boy": Victorians on Sacramento's J Street.* (Rohnert Park, CA: Anthropological Studies Center, Sonoma State University, 1990).

Robinson, William J., Tree-Ring Studies of the Pueblo de Acoma. *Historical Archaeology* 24, 3(1990):99–106.

South, Stanley, Evolution and Horizon as Revealed in Ceramic Analysis in Historical Archaeology. *Conference on Historic Site Archaeology Papers* 6(1972):71–116.

## CHAPTER 6: HISTORICAL SITE SURVEY AND LOCATION

Much of the information covered in this chapter can be found in Noël Hume's *Historical Archaeology*. The application of subsurface surveying techniques in archaeology is covered in Don H. Heimmer, *Near-Surface, High Resolution: Geophysical Methods for Cultural Resource Management and Archaeological Investigations* (Denver: Interagency Archaeological Services, National Park Service, 1992). Although much of the presentation is technical, this book has a comprehensive bibliography with many sources directly related to historical archaeology. Another extremely useful source is E. B. Banning, *Archaeological Survey* (New York: Kluwer Academic/Plenum, 2002).

Classic works on reading the landscape are W. G. Hoskins, *The Making of the English Landscape* (New York: Penguin, 1970), E. Sloane, *Our Vanishing Landscape* (New York: Ballantine, 1974), and M. T. Watts, *Reading the Landscape of America.* (New York: Macmillan, 1957).

General books about subsurface surveying in archaeology include Anthony Clark's *Seeing Beneath the Soil: Prospecting Methods in Archaeology* (London: Batsford, 1990) and Irwin Scollar's *Archaeological Prospecting, Image Processing, and Remote Sensing* (Cambridge: Cambridge University Press, 1989). Also useful is the British journal *Archaeometry.*

Classic sources on the earliest efforts to use aerial surveying in archaeology are both by O. G. S. Crawford: *Air Survey and Archaeology* (Southampton: His Majesty's Stationery Office, 1924) and *Air-Photography for Archaeologists.* (London: His Majesty's Stationery Office, 1929).

## Specialist Literature

Arnold, J. Barto III, Marine Magnetometer Survey of Archaeological Materials near Galveston, Texas. *Historical Archaeology* 21, 1(1987):18–47.

Arnold, J. Barto III, G. Michael Fleshman, Curtiss E. Peterson, W. Kenneth Stewart, Gordon P. Watts, Jr., and Clark P. Weldon, USS *Monitor:* Results from the 1987 Season. *Historical Archaeology* 26, 4(1992):47–57.

Bailey, Richard N., Eric Cambridge, and H. Denis Briggs, *Dowsing and Church Archaeology* (Wimborne, Dorset: Intercept, 1988).

Benn, David W. (Ed.), *Big Sioux River Archaeological and Historical Resources Survey, Lyon County, Iowa: Volume I.* (Springfield: Center for Archaeological Research, Southwest Missouri State University, 1987).

Bevan, Bruce W., David G. Orr, and Brooke S. Blades, The Discovery of the Taylor House at the Petersburg National Battlefield. *Historical Archaeology* 18, 2(1984):64–74.

Clapp, N., *The Road to Ubar: Finding the Atlantis of the Sands.* (Boston: Houghton Mifflin, 1998).

Connor, Melissa, and Douglas D. Scott, Metal Detector Use in Archaeology: An Introduction. *Historical Archaeology* 32, 4(1998):76–85.

Costello, Julia G. and Phillip L. Walker, Burials from the Santa Barbara Presidio Chapel. *Historical Archaeology* 21, 1(1987):3–17.

Ellwood, Brooks B., Electrical Resistivity Surveys in Two Historical Cemeteries in Northeast Texas: A Method for Delineating Burial Shafts. *Historical Archaeology* 24, 3(1990):91–98.

Gasco, Janine, Survey and Excavation of Invisible Sites in the Mesoamerican Lowlands. In *Approaches to the Historical Archaeology of Mexico, Central and South America*, J. Gasco, G. C. Smith, and P. Fournier-Garcia, (Eds.), pp. 41–48. (Los Angeles: Institute of Archaeology, 1997).

Kenyon, Jeff L. and Bruce Bevan, Ground-Penetrating Radar and Its Application to a Historical Archaeological Site. *Historical Archaeology* 11(1977):48–55.

Mason, Randall J., An Unorthodox Magnetic Survey of a Large Forested Historic Site. *Historical Archaeology* 18, 2(1984):54–63.

Noël Hume, Ivor, *Archaeology and Wetherburn's Tavern* (Williamsburg: Colonial Williamsburg Foundation, 1969).

Randi, James, The Matter of Dowsing. *Skeptic* 6, 4 (1998):6–7.

Sonderman, Robert C., Looking for a Needle in a Haystack: Developing Closer Relationships between Law Enforcement Specialists and Archaeology. *Historical Archaeology* 35, 1 (2001):70–78.

Synenki, Alan T. (Ed.), *Archaeological Investigations of Minute Man National Historical Park, Volume I: Farmers and Artisans of the Historical Period.* (Boston: National Park Service, 1990).

von Frese, Ralph R. B., Archaeomagnetic Anomalies of Midcontinental North American Archaeological Sites. *Historical Archaeology* 18, 2(1984):4–19.

von Frese, Ralph R. B., and Vergil E. Noble, Magnetometry for Archaeological Exploration of Historical Sites. *Historical Archaeology* 18, 2(1984):38–53.

Weymouth, John W. and William I. Woods, Combined Magnetic and Chemical Surveys of Forts Kaskaskia and de Chartres Number 1, Illinois. *Historical Archaeology* 18, 2(1984):20–37.

## CHAPTER 7: PRE-EXCAVATION FIELDWORK: DOCUMENTS, INTERVIEWS, BUILDINGS

Several good books on historical methods have been written by trained historians. Older examples include Mary Sheldon Barnes, *Studies in Historical Method* (Boston: D.C. Heath, 1896); Gilbert J. Garraghan, *A Guide to Historical Method* (New York: Fordham University Press, 1946). A more recent manual is Robert Jones Shafer (Ed.), *A Guide to Historical Method*, 3rd ed. (Homewood, IL: Dorsey, 1974). Also of use is the undergraduate manual, Norman F. Cantor and Richard I. Schneider, *How to Study History* (New York: Thomas J. Crowell, 1967). For general comments, you may wish to consult Jacques Barzun and Henry F. Graff, *The Modern Researcher*, 4th ed. (San Diego: Harcourt Brace Jovanovich, 1985). The journal *Historical Methods* is also a useful source.

For oral history see Willa K. Baum's *Oral History for the Local Historical Society*, 3rd ed. (Nashville: American Association for State and Local History, 1987). This book includes step-by-step instructions by someone who knows a great deal about conducting oral interviews. Transcribing techniques are explained in Willa K. Baum, *Transcribing and Editing Oral History* (Nashville: American Association for State and Local History, 1977) and Mary Jo Deering, *Transcribing Without Tears: A Guide to Transcribing and Editing Oral History Interviews* (Washington, D.C.: George Washington University Library, 1976). Louis Gottschalk, Clyde Kluckhohn, and Robert Angell, *The Use of Personal Documents in History, Anthropology, and Sociology* (New York: Social Science Research Council, 1945), and Jan Vansina,

*Oral Tradition as History* (Madison: University of Wisconsin Press, 1985) provide important information as well.

The definitive source on HABS/HAER documentation and surveying is John A. Burns (Ed.), *Recording Historic Structures* (Washington, D.C.: American Institute of Architects Press, 1989). An excellent source for learning how to assess standing structures as archaeological sites is Richard K. Morriss, *The Archaeology of Buildings* (Stroud, Gloucestershire: Tempus, 2000). Another superb source is Matthew Johnson, *Housing Culture: Traditional Architecture in an English Landscape* (Washington, D.C.: Smithsonian Institution Press, 1993).

### Specialist Literature

Baker, T. Lindsay and Billy R. Harrison, *Adobe Walls: The History and Archaeology of the 1874 Trading Post.* (College Station: Texas A & M University Press, 1986).

Breen, T. H., *Imagining the Past: East Hampton Histories* (Reading, MA: Addison-Wesley, 1989).

Davidson, James West and Mark Hamilton Lytle, *After the Fact: The Art of Historical Detection.* (New York: Alfred A. Knopf, 1982).

Jurney, David H. and Randall W. Moir (Eds.), *Historic Buildings, Material Culture, and the People of the Prairie Margin.* (Dallas: Archaeology Research Program, Southern Methodist University, 1987).

Landers, Jane, *Fort Mose, Gracia Real de Santa Teresa de Mose: A Free Black Town in Spanish Colonial Florida.* (St. Augustine: St. Augustine Historical Society, 1992).

Worthy, Linda H., *All That Remains: The Traditional Architecture and Historic Engineering Structures, Richard B. Russell Multiple Resource Area, Georgia and South Carolina.* (Atlanta: National Park Service, 1983).

## CHAPTER 8: ARCHAEOLOGICAL FIELDWORK: FIELD AND LABORATORY

Two good sources to begin with are Philip Barker's *Techniques of Archaeological Excavation,* 2nd ed. (New York: Universe, 1982), and Martha Joukowsky's *A Complete Field Manual of Field Archaeology: Tools and Techniques of Field Work for Archaeologists* (Englewood Cliffs, NJ: Prentice-Hall, 1980). Ivor Noël Hume's *Historical Archaeology,* already cited, is a classic, though somewhat outdated, source on fieldwork for historical archaeologists. The field report for Fort Southwest Point: Samuel D. Smith (Ed.), *Fort Southwest Point Archaeological Site, Kingston, Tennessee: A Multidisciplinary Interpretation* (Nashville: Tennessee Department of Environment and Conservation, Division of Archaeology, 1993).

An excellent, easy-to-read book about simple artifact conservation is Per E. Guldbeck's *The Care of Historical Collections: A Conservation Handbook for the Nonspecialist* (Nashville: American Association for State and Local History, 1972). For information about the Wolstenholme Towne helmets see Ivor Noël Hume, "First Look at a Lost Virginia Settlement," *National Geographic* 155, 6(1979):734–767; and his "New Clues to an Old Mystery," *National Geographic* 161, 1(1982):52–77. Wolstenholme Towne is described in the same author's *Martin's Hundred* mentioned above.

For the basics of archaeological typology, you should consult widely available texts. The Potomac Typological System, POTS, appeared in Mary C. Beaudry, Janet Long, Henry M. Miller, Fraser D. Neiman, and Garry Wheeler Stone, "A Vessel Typology for Early Chesapeake Ceramics: The Potomac Typological System," *Historical Archaeology* 17, 1(1983):18–43.

### Specialist Literature

Crader, Diana C., The Zooarchaeology of the Storehouse and the Dry Well at Monticello. *American Antiquity* 49(1984):542–558.
———Slave Diet at Monticello. *American Antiquity* 55(1990):690–717.
Herskovitz, Robert M., *Fort Bowie Material Culture* (Tucson: University of Arizona Press, 1978).
Noël Hume, Ivor, *If These Pots Could Talk: Collecting 2,000 Years of British Household Pottery.* (Milwaukee: Chipstone Foundation, 2001).
Reitz, Elizabeth J. and C. Margaret Scarry, *Reconstructing Historic Subsistence with an Example from Sixteenth-Century Spanish Florida.* (Tucson, AZ: Society for Historical Archaeology, 1985).
Stone, Lyle M., *Fort Michilimackinac, 1715–1781: An Archaeological Perspective on the Revolutionary Frontier* (East Lansing: The Museum, Michigan State University, 1974).
Switzer, R. R., *The Bertrand Bottles: A Study of 19th-Century Glass and Ceramic Containers.* (Washington, D.C.: National Park Service, 1974).

## CHAPTER 9: INTERPRETING THE HISTORICAL PAST

Articles dealing with the development of historical archaeology up to 1978 can be found in Schuyler's *Historical Archaeology*, mentioned above. Humanistic studies are Robert Ascher and Charles H. Fairbanks, "Excavation of a Slave Cabin: Georgia, U.S.A.," *Historical Archaeology* 5 (1971):3–17; William M. Kelso, *Kingsmill Plantations, 1619–1800: Archaeology of Country Life in Colonial Virginia* (Orlando: Academic Press, 1984). More scientific studies include Stanley South, *Method and Theory in Historical Archaeology*; Kenneth E. Lewis, *Camden: A Frontier Town in Eighteenth-Century South Carolina* (Columbia: South Carolina Institute of Archaeology and Anthropology, 1976). Studies by Deetz are "Material Culture and Worldview in Colonial Anglo-America," in Leone and Potter's *The Recovery of Meaning*, pp. 219–233, and his *In Small Things Forgotten*. His much less structuralist book is *Flowerdew Hundred: The Archaeology of a Virginia Plantation, 1619–1864* (Charlottesville: University Press of Virginia, 1993). Henry Glassie's book is *Folk Housing in Middle Virginia: A Structural Analysis of Historic Artifacts* (Knoxville: University of Tennessee Press, 1975). Martin Hall's paper on Cape Town, South Africa, appears as "Small Things and the Mobile, Conflictual Fusion of Power,

Fear, and Desire," in *The Art and Mystery of Historical Archaeology: Essays in Honor of James Deetz*, Anne Elizabeth Yentsch and Mary C. Beaudry (Eds.), pp. 373–399. (Boca Raton, FL: CRC Press, 1992). Mark Leone's principal paper is: "The Georgian Order as the Order of Merchant Capitalism in Annapolis, Maryland," in Leone and Potter's *The Recovery of Meaning*, pp. 235–261. His paper on Mormon fences is "Archaeology as the Science of Technology: Mormon Town Plans and Fences," in *Research and Theory in Current Archaeology*, Charles Redman (Ed.), pp. 125–150. (New York: John Wiley and Sons, 1973). Also extremely useful is Paul A. Shackel's, *Personal Discipline and Material Culture* mentioned above. An important statement on critical theory as it can be applied to historical archaeology is: Mark P. Leone, Parker B. Potter, Jr., and Paul A. Shackel, "Toward a Critical Archaeology," *Current Anthropology* 28(1987):283–302.

## CHAPTER 10: THE ARCHAEOLOGY OF GROUPS

Class, ethnicity, gender, and race have generated a vast literature. The following are useful for our purposes: William C. McCready, *Culture, Ethnicity, and Identity: Current Issues in Research* (New York: Academic Press, 1983); H. Edward Ransford, *Race and Class in American Society: Black, Chicano, Anglo* (Cambridge, MA.: Schenkman, 1977); Peter I. Rose, *They and We: Racial and Ethnic Relations in the United States* (New York: Random House, 1981); and Stephen Steinberg's *The Ethnic Myth: Race, Ethnicity, and Class in America* (Boston: Beacon Press, 1989). These books, and the sources they cite, give an ample introduction to the topic of social groups. Marvin Harris's definition comes from his introductory textbook *Culture, People, and Nature: An Introduction to General Anthropology*, 4th ed., (New York: Harper and Row, 1985).

Archaeological studies of gender can be found in Dale Walde and Noreen D. Willows (Eds.), *The Archaeology of Gender: Proceedings of the Twenty-Second Annual Conference of the Archaeological Association of the University of Calgary*, (Calgary: University of Calgary, 1991), and in Cheryl Claasen (Ed.), *Exploring Gender Through Archaeology: Selected Papers from the 1991 Boone Conference* (Madison, WI: Prehistory Press, 1992). Archaeologists examining gender are making great strides, and students are encouraged to search their library databases for the most recent books.

### *Specialist Literature*

Baugher, Sherene and Robert W. Venables, Ceramics as Indicators of Status and Class in Eighteenth-Century New York. In *Consumer Choice in Historical Archaeology*, Suzanne M. Spencer-Wood (Ed.), pp. 31–53. (New York: Plenum Press, 1987).

Brashler, Janet G., When Daddy was a Shanty Boy: The Role of Gender in the Organization of the Logging Industry in Highland West Virginia. *Historical Archaeology* 26, 4(1991):54–68.

Clark, Lynn, Gravestones: Reflections of Ethnicity or Class? In *Consumer Choice in Historical Archaeology*, Suzanne M. Spencer-Wood (Ed.), pp. 383–395. (New York: Plenum Press, 1987).

De Cunzo, Lu Ann, *Economics and Ethnicity: An Archaeological Perspective on Nineteenth Century Paterson, New Jersey*. Ph.D. dissertation, University of Pennsylvania, Philadelphia.

Edwards-Ingram, Y., African American Medicine and the Social Relations of Slavery. In *Race and the Archaeology of Identity*, Charles Edward Orser, Jr. (Ed.), pp. 34–53. (Salt Lake City: University of Utah Press, 2001).

Greenwood, Roberta S., The Chinese on Main Street. In *Archaeological Perspectives on Ethnicity in America: Afro-American and Asian American Culture History*, Robert L. Schuyler (Ed.), pp. 113–123. (Farmingdale, NY: Baywood, 1980).

Kruczek-Aaron, H., Choice Flowers and Well-Ordered Tables: Struggling over Gender in a Nineteenth-Century Household. *International Journal of Historical Archaeology* 6(2002): 173–185.

McEwan, Bonnie G., The Archaeology of Women in the Spanish New World. *Historical Archaeology* 26, 4(1991):33–41.

Mullins, Paul R., *Race and Affluence: An Archaeology of African America and Consumer Culture*. (New York: Kluwer Academic/Plenum, 1999).

Orser, Charles E., Jr., Ed., *Race and the Archaeology of Identity*. (Salt Lake City: University of Utah Press, 2001).

————*Race and Practice in Archaeological Interpretation*. (Philadelphia: University of Pennsylvania Press, 2003).

Otto, John Solomon, Race and Class on Antebellum Plantations. In *Archaeological Perspectives on Ethnicity in America: Afro-American and Asian American Culture History*, Robert L. Schuyler (Ed.), pp. 3–13. (Farmingdale, NY: Baywood, 1980).

Paynter, Robert, Steps to an Archaeology of Capitalism: Material Change and Class Analysis. In *The Recovery of Meaning: Historical Archaeology in the Eastern United States*, Mark P. Leone and Parker B. Potter, Jr. (Eds.), pp. 407–433. (Washington, D.C.: Smithsonian Institution Press, 1988).

Rubertone, Patricia E., *Grave Undertakings: An Archaeology of Roger Williams and the Narragansett Indians*. (Washington, D.C.: Smithsonian Institution Press, 2001).

Sando, Ruth Ann and David L. Felton, Inventory Records of Ceramics and Opium from a Nineteenth-Century Chinese Store in California. In *Hidden Heritage: Historical Archaeology of the Overseas Chinese*, Priscilla Wegars (Ed.), pp. 151–176. (Amityville, NY: Baywood, 1993).

Seifert, Donna J., Within Sight of the White House: The Archaeology of Working Women. *Historical Archaeology* 26, 4(1991):82–108.

Shepherd, Steven J., Status Variation in Antbellum Alexandria: An Archaeological Study of Ceramic Tableware. In *Consumer Choice in Historical Archaeology*, Suzanne M. Spencer-Wood (Ed.), pp. 163–198. (New York: Plenum Press, 1987).

Wurst, Lu Ann and Robert K. Fitts, Ed., Confronting Class. *Historical Archaeology* 33, 1 (1999):1–195.

Wylie, Jerry and Richard E. Fike, Chinese Opium Smoking Techniques and Paraphernalia. In *Hidden Heritage: Historical Archaeology of the Oversees Chinese*, Priscilla Wegars (Ed.), pp. 255–303. (Amityville, NY: Baywood, 1993)

## CHAPTER 11: GLOBAL HISTORICAL ARCHAEOLOGY

*Europe and the People without History* by famed anthropologist Eric Wolf (Berkeley: University of California Press, 1982) is a fundamental source for this chapter. A more popular account focusing on a variety of groups is Brian Fagan, *Clash of Cultures* (New York: W. H. Freeman, 1984). The sources used in preparing this chapter are:

### Africa

DeCorse, Christopher R., *An Archaeology of Elmina: Africans and Europeans on the Gold Coast, 1400–1900.* (Washington, D.C.: Smithsonian Institution Press, 2001).

Hall, Martin, *Archaeology and the Modern World: Colonial Transcripts in South Africa and the Chesapeake.* (London: Routledge, 2000).

Jordan, Stacey C., Coarse Earthenware at the Dutch Colonial Cape of Good Hope, South Africa: A History of Local Production and Typology of Products. *International Journal of Historical Archaeology* 4(2000):113–143.

Jordan, Stacey C. and Carmel Schrire, Material Culture and the Roots of Colonial Society at the South African Cape of Good Hope. In *The Archaeology of Colonialism*, C. L. Lyons and J. K. Papadopoulos (Eds.), pp. 241–272. (Los Angeles: Getty Research Institute, 2002).

Schrire, Carmel, The Historical Archaeology of the Impact of Colonialism in Seventeenth-Century South Africa. In *Historical Archaeology in Global Perspective*, Lisa Falk (Ed.), pp. 69–96. (Washington, D.C.: Smithsonian Institution Press, 1991).

——Digging Archives at Oudepost I, Cape, South Africa. In *The Art and Mystery of Historical Archaeology*, Anne Elizabeth Yentsch and Mary C. Beaudry (Eds.), pp. 361–372. (Boca Raton, FL: CRC Press, 1992).

——*Digging Through Darkness: Chronicles of an Archaeologist.* (Charlottesville: University Press of Virginia, 1995).

Schrire, Carmel and D. Merwick, Dutch-Indigenous Relations in New Netherland and the Cape in the Seventeenth Century. In *Historical Archaeology in Global Perspective*, L. Falk (Ed.), pp. 11–20. (Washington, D.C.: Smithsonian Institution Press, 1991).

Schrire, Carmel, K. Cruz-Uribe, and J. Klose, The Site History of the Historical Site of Oudepost I, Cape. In *South African Archaeological Society Goodwin Series* 7(1993):21–32.

Werz, B. E. J. S., Maritime Archaeological Project Table Bay: Aspects of the First Field Season. In *South African Archaeological Society Goodwin Series* 7(1993):33–39.

### North America

Cantwell, Ann-Marie and Diana diZ. Wall, *Unearthing Gotham: The Archaeology of New York City.* (New Haven: Yale University Press, 2001).

Gilbert, A. S., G. Harbottle, D. DeNoyelles, A Ceramic Chemistry Archive for New Netherland/New York. *Historical Archaeology* 27, 3(1993):17–56.

Huey, Paul R., Reworked Pipe Stems: A 17th Century Phenomenon from the Site of Fort Orange, Albany, New York. *Historical Archaeology* 8(1974):105–111.

——The Dutch at Fort Orange. In *Historical Archaeology in Global Perspective*, L. Falk (Ed.), pp. 21–67. (Washington, D.C.: Smithsonian Institution Press, 1991).

Janowitz, Meta F., Indian Corn and Dutch Pots: Seventeenth-Century Foodways in New Amsterdam/New York. *Historical Archaeology* 27, 2(1993):6–24.

Peña, Elizabeth S., The Role of Wampum Production at the Albany Almshouse. *International Journal of Historical Archaeology* 5 (2001):155–174.

### The Caribbean and South America

Huey, Paul R., Dutch Colonialism. In *The Encyclopedia of Historical Archaeology*, Charles E. Orser, Jr. (Ed.), pp. 161–164. (London: Routledge, 2002).

Menezes, J. L., M. and J. R. R. Rodrigues, *Fortificações Portuguesas no Nordeste do Brasil: Séculos XVI, XVII, e XVIII.* (Recife: Pool Editorial, 1986).

Orser, Charles E., Jr., Toward a Global Historical Archaeology: An Example from Brazil. *Historical Archaeology* 28, 1(1994):5–22.

Orser, Charles E., Jr. and Pedro Paulo A. Funari, Archaeology and Slave Resistance and Rebellion. *World Archaeology* 33 (2001):61–72.

### Asia

Gawronski, Jerz., VOC Shipwrecks. In *The Encyclopedia of Historical Archaeology*, Charles E. Orser, Jr. (Ed.), pp. 563–566. (London: Routledge, 2002).

Kist, J. B., Integrating Archaeological and Historical Records in Dutch East India Company Research. In *Maritime Archaeology: A Reader of Substantive and Theoretical Contributions*, L. E. Babits and H. Van Tilburg (Eds.), pp. 39–45. (New York: Plenum, 1998).

Jörg, C. J. A., *The Geldermalsen: History and Porcelain.* (Groningen: Kemper, 1986).

Miller, George L., The Second Destruction of the *Geldermalsen. Historical Archaeology* 26, 4(1992): 124–131.

## CHAPTER 12: HISTORICAL ARCHAEOLOGY AND CULTURAL RESOURCE MANAGEMENT

United States legislation appears in King, Hickman, and Berg's *Anthropology in Historic Preservation*, already cited, pp. 199–302, and in Philip Speser and Kathleen Reinburg, *Federal Archaeology Legislation: A Compendium, Vol. 4* (Washington: Foresight Science and Technology, 1986).

Other important books about CRM archaeology and ethics are: Hardesty, Donald L. and Barbara J. Little, *Assessing Site Significance: A Guide for Archaeologists and Historians* (Walnut Creek, CA: AltaMira, 2000); Thomas F. King, *Thinking about Cultural Resource Management: Essays from the Edge* (Walnut Creek, CA:

AltaMira, 2002); Thomas F. King, *Federal Planning and Historic Places: The Section 106 Process.* (Walnut Creek, CA: AltaMira, 2000); Robin Skeates, *Debating the Archaeological Heritage* (London: Duckworth, 2000); Karen D. Vitelli (Ed.), *Archaeological Ethics* (Walnut Creek, CA: AltaMira, 1996); and Larry J. Zimmerman, Karen D. Vitelli, and Julie Hollowell-Zimmer (Eds.), *Ethical Issues in Archaeology* (Walnut Creek, CA: AltaMira, 2003).


## CHAPTER 13: THE PAST IN THE PRESENT

Site visitation at Annapolis is covered in Mark Leone "Method as Message: Interpreting the Past with the Public," *Museum News* 62, 1(1983):34–41, and in Parker B. Potter, Jr., *Public Archaeology in Annapolis: A Critical Approach to History in Maryland's Ancient City.* (Washington, D.C.: Smithsonian Institution Press, 1994). An important statement of the program appears, with the comments of critics and supporters, in Leone, Potter, and Shackel, "Toward a Critical Archaeology," mentioned above. A critique of the Carter's Grove slave quarters appears in Terrence W. Epperson's "Race and the Disciplines of the Plantation," *Historical Archaeology* 24, 4(1990):29–36.

An excellent starting point for learning about the political uses of archaeology is Peter Gathercole and David Lowenthal (Eds.), *The Politics of the Past*, (London: Unwin Hyman, 1990). This book contains information about the Nazis' program of "archaeology," as well as information about the efforts of several indigenous groups to reclaim their histories.

Site destruction, vandalism, and looting continue to constitute major problems for archaeology. For a starting point, see Ian Graham, "Looters Rob Graves and History," *National Geographic* 169, 4(1986):452–461; George E. Stuart, "The Battle to Save Our Past," *National Geographic* 175, 3(1989):392–393; Brian Alexander, "Archaeology and Looting Make a Volatile Mix," *Science*, 250(1990): 1074–1075; James Walsh, "It's a Steal," *Time* 138, 21(1991):86–88; Christopher B. Donnan, "Archaeology and Looting: Preserving the Record," *Science* 251(1991): 498; Colin Renfrew, *Loot, Legitimacy, and Ownership: The Ethical Crisis in Archaeology* (London: Duckworth, 2000).

For controversies over artifact collecting, see Gillett B. Griffen, "In Defense of the Collector," *National Geographic* 169, 4(1986):462–465; and Colin Renfrew, "Collectors are the Real Looters," *Archaeology* 46, 3(1993):16–17.

For discussions of the relations between archaeologists and indigenous peoples, see Joe Watkins, *Indigenous Archaeology: American Indian Values and Scientific Practice.* (Walnut Creek, CA: Altamira Press, 2000).

For job opportunities and training in historical archaeology, your best source is a professional archaeologist, but a short booklet, *Opportunities in Historical Archaeology*, is available from the Society for Historical Archaeology. A careful check of their website will also provide useful information for students wishing to pursue a career in historical archaeology.

Other sources used in preparing this chapter are Jane Busch, "An Introduction to the Tin Can," *Historical Archaeology* 15, 1(1981):95–104; J. Douglas McDonald, Larry J. Zimmerman, A. L. McDonald, William Tall Bull, and Ted Rising Sun, "The Northern Cheyenne Outbreak of 1879: Using Oral History and Archaeology as Tools of Resistance." In *The Archaeology of Inequality*, Randall H. McGuire and Robert Paynter (Eds.), pp. 64–78. (Oxford: Basil Blackwell, 1991); and Charles E. Orser, Jr., *Historical Archaeology at Marsh House (Residence Hill Site, 16IB130), Avery Island, Louisiana.* (Avery Island: Avery Island, Inc., 1987).

# GLOSSARY

This glossary gives informal definitions of key words and ideas in the text. It is not a comprehensive dictionary of historical archaeology. Jargon is kept to a minimum, but a few technical expressions are inevitable. Some terms commonly used in archaeology but not specifically described in this book are also included for convenience.

**absolute dating:** Dating in calendar years before the present; see chronometric dating.

**activity area:** A spatial patterning of artifacts indicating that a specific activity, such as bone button making, once took place there.

**Age of Discovery:** The period of Western global expansion, c. A.D. 1415 to about 1800.

**analogy:** A process of reasoning whereby two entities that share some similarities are assumed to share others.

**analysis:** A stage of archaeological research that involves describing, classifying, and interpreting artifactual and nonartifactual data.

**anthropology:** The study of humanity in the widest possible sense, from the earliest times to the present; includes cultural and physical anthropology, anthropological linguistics, and anthropological archaeology.

**anthropological archaeology:** A form of anthropology studying extinct human societies or extinct phases of surviving cultures using material remains; its objectives are to construct culture history, reconstruct past lifeways, study cultural process, and understand the social aspects of daily life.

**antiquarian:** Someone interested in the past who studies, collects, and perhaps even excavates antiquities in an uncontrolled manner; contrasts with today's professional archaeologist.

**archaeological context:** See **context.**

**archaeological culture:** A group of assemblages representing the remains of a cultural expression that no longer exists either at all or in the same way today.

**archaeological data:** Material recognized as significant by an archaeologist and collected and recorded as part of his or her research; the four main classes are: artifacts, features, structures, and food remains.

**archaeological reconnaissance:** Systematic attempts to locate, identify, and record the distribution of archaeological sites on the ground and against the natural geographic and environmental background.

**archaeological theory:** A body of theoretical concepts providing both a framework and a means for archaeologists to look beyond the material objects for explanations and interpretations of the past.

**archaeological unit:** Arbitrary unit of classification established by archaeologists to separate one collection of artifacts in time and space from another for the purpose of analysis.

**archaeologist:** Someone who studies the past using controlled, systematic methods, with the motive of recording and interpreting past cultures; does not collect artifacts for profit or personal display.

**archaeomagnetic dating:** Chronometric dating using magnetic alignments from buried features, such as ceramic kilns, that can be compared with known fluctuations in the earth's magnetic field; produces a date in years.

**area excavation:** Excavation of a large, horizontal area, usually intended to uncover houses and village settlement patterns.

**artifact:** Any object manufactured or modified by human beings.

**assemblage:** All the artifacts found at a site, including the sum of all sub-assemblages.

**association:** The relationship between an artifact and other archaeological finds and features at a site.

**attribute:** A well-defined feature of an artifact that cannot be further subdivided; archaeologists identify types of attributes, including form, style, and technology, to interpret artifacts.

**attribute analysis:** Analyzing artifacts using many of their features; the features, or attributes, are studied statistically to produce clusters of characteristics that can be used to identity statistical classes of artifacts.

**burial site:** An archaeological site once used for burying the dead, especially cemeteries.

**ceramics:** Objects of fired clay; historical archaeologists usually use the term to refer only to glazed sherds; see **pottery**

**chronological types:** Types defined by form that are time markers.

**chronometric dating:** Dating in years before the present; absolute dating.

**class:** Two definitions: In archaeology, the name for a idealized kind of artifact, like "bottles," that can be broken down into specific types, like "wine bottles" and so on; unlike groups, classes exist independently of specific collections of artifacts. In a wider context, a group of people who have a similar relationship to the structure of social control in a society, and who possess similar amounts of power over the allocation of wealth, privilege, resources, and technology.

**classical archaeology:** The study of the high civilizations of Greece and Rome.

**classification:** The ordering of archaeological data into discrete classes, using various ordering methods.

**cognitive archaeology:** A theoretical approach concerned with mental patterns that exist behind material culture.

**commodity:** An object specifically created for trade.

**community:** In archaeology, the tangible remains of the activities of the maximum number of people who together occupy a settlement during any one period.

**component:** An association of all the artifacts from one occupation level or chronological period at a site.

**conservation archaeology:** Another name for cultural resource management.

**context:** The position of an archaeological find in time and space, established by measuring and assessing its associations, matrix, and provenience; includes the study of what has happened to the find since it was buried in the soil.

**core borer:** A hollow tubelike instrument used to collect samples of soil, pollen, and other materials from below the ground surface.

**critical theory:** A theoretical approach to archaeology that assumes that archaeologists have an active impact on their society; includes the idea that today's interpretations are never truly value-free.

**crop marks:** Differential growth in crops and other vegetation that reveals the outlines of archaeological sites beneath the ground surface; not crop circles!

**cross-dating:** Dating of sites by objects of known age or with textual records of known age.

**cultural anthropology:** anthropology focused on the customs and traditions of human societies throughout the world; mostly used in the United States.

**cultural evolution:** A theory similar to that of biological evolution, which argues that human cultures change gradually throughout time as a result of a number of historical processes.

**cultural materialism:** A combination of critical theory and materialism in historical archaeology.

**cultural process:** An approach to archaeological research that studies the changes and interactions in cultural systems and the processes by which human cultures change throughout time.

**cultural resource management:** The conservation and management of archaeological sites and historic properties as a means of protecting them from destruction; abbreviated as CRM.

**cultural system:** A view that perceives culture and its environment as composed of a number of linked subsystems; change occurs through a series of minor, linked variations in one or more of the subsystems.

**culture:** A set of designs for living that help to mold a people's response to different situations; culture is our pri-

mary means of adapting to our environment; a "culture" in archaeology is a term referring to similar assemblages of artifacts found at several sites, defined in a precise context of time and space.

**culture area:** A geographic or research area in which general cultural homogeneity is found.

**culture history:** An approach that assumes that artifacts can be used to create a generalized picture of human culture through long temporal periods and across great spatial distances.

**datum point:** A location from which all measurements at a site are made; usually tied to local survey maps.

**deduction:** A process of reasoning that involves testing generalizations by generating hypotheses and testing them with data; deductive research is cumulative and involves constant refining of hypotheses; contrasts with inductive approaches where one proceeds from specific observations to general conclusions.

**demography:** The study of population.

**dendrochronology:** A dating method using tree rings.

**descriptive types:** Categories based on the physical or external properties of an artifact.

**direct historical analogy:** Analogy using historical records or historical ethnographic data.

**direct historical approach:** Archaeological technique of working backward in time from historic-period sites of known age to earlier times; usually only used in places where little migration has occurred, like the American Southwest.

**domestic site:** A place where people lived and conducted household activities.

**ethnic group:** A collection of people who share enough common physical and cultural characteristics to define themselves as a group; they perceive their group as distinct from all others.

**ethnicity:** The characteristics an ethnic group accepts as pertinent to them.

**ethnoarchaeology:** A form of ethnography that mostly concerns material remains; archaeologists use it to document the relationships between human behavior and the patterns of artifacts and food remains in the archaeological record; also called living archaeology.

**ethnobotany:** The study of the cultural use of plant remains.

**ethnography:** A descriptive, normally in-depth examination of a specific culture.

**ethnohistory:** The study of the past using both indigenous oral traditions and more traditional textual sources.

**ethnology:** A comparative study of several cultures.

**excavation:** The digging of archaeological sites, removal of the soil matrix, observance of the provenience and context of the finds therein, and the recording of all information in a three-dimensional manner.

**exchange system:** A network for trading goods and services between individuals and communities.

**experimental archaeology:** The use of carefully controlled experiments to provide data to aid in interpreting the archaeological record.

**feature:** An artifact, such as a house or storage pit, that can be excavated but not removed from an archaeological site.

**form:** The physical characteristics—size and shape or composition—of any archaeological find; an essential part of attribute analysis.

**form analysis:** Analysis of artifacts based on the assumption that shape directly reflects function.

**formation processes:** Humanly caused or natural processes by which an archaeological site is modified during and after occupation and abandonment.

**foot (or pedestrian) survey:** Archaeological reconnaissance on foot, often with a set interval between members of the survey team.

**formula dating:** Absolute dating using artifact attributes, especially applied to pipe stems and glazed European ceramics.

**functionalism:** The idea that an institution within a society can fulfil all the needs of the people and the entire organization.

**functional type:** A category based on cultural use or function rather than on outward form or chronological position.

**geographic information systems:** Computer-generated mapping systems that allow archaeologists to plot and analyze site distributions against environmental and other background data derived from remote sensing, digitized maps, and other sources; abbreviated as GIS.

**ground-penetrating radar:** A sophisticated scientific tool that helps archaeologists to locate sites underground without excavation; the radar transmits a pulse into the earth and calculates its findings based on the returned pulse.

**HABS/HAER survey:** Historic American Buildings Survey/Historic American Engineering Record; historic surveys of buildings in the United States.

**Harris matrix:** A method of graphically representing the relationships of soil layers and features at an archaeological site; invented by Edward Harris.

**historical archaeology:** The study of archaeological sites in conjunction with text-based records and other kinds of information; sometimes called historic sites archaeology and in Europe, Post-Medieval Archaeology.

**historical structuralism:** An approach to historical archaeology that tries to discover the hidden themes of a culture.

**historiography:** The study of how history is written.

**history:** Two senses: The study of the past with written records and other sources, often excluding archaeology. What happened in the past.

**horizon:** A widely distributed set of cultural traits and artifact assemblages whose distribution and chronology allow one to assume they spread rapidly; often indicated by artifacts associated with widespread, distinctive beliefs.

**horizontal (area) excavation:** Archaeological investigation designed to uncover large areas of a site, especially settlement layouts and entire buildings and yards.

**household:** A group of people who lived together. In archaeology, a unit defined by artifact patterns reflecting the activities around a former dwelling.

**humanistic historical archaeology:** Archaeological research intended to complement the humanistic understanding of cultural history.

**ideology:** Two definitions: Beliefs intended to hide the reality of daily life by using slogans, expressions, and attitudes that appeal to people on a visceral level. A people's knowledge or beliefs developed as part of their culture.

**induction:** Reasoning by which one proceeds from specific observations to general conclusions.

**industrial archaeology:** The study of sites that show some evidence of industrial production; sometimes used to refer specifically to the Industrial Revolution and later.

**industrial site:** In historical archaeology, a location where manufacturing of commodities takes place; any place where some production has occurred.

**inorganic materials:** Objects that are not part of the animal or vegetable kingdom.

**interpretation:** The stage in research during which the results of archaeological analyses are synthesized and explained.

**kinship:** Relationships between people based on real or imagined descent or marriage; imposes mutual obligations on all members of a related group; such ties are at the core of most societies.

**lineage:** A kinship group that traces descent through either male or female members; direct ancestry to a lineage founder is known.

**magnetometer:** A subsurface detection device that measures minor variations in the earth's magnetic field and locates archaeological features before excavation.

**maritime archaeology:** Archaeology conducted at locales that were related to shipping, seaside activities, or coastal settlement; can encompass underwater archaeology.

**markers' marks:** Manufacturing marks drawn, etched, or stamped onto mass-produced ceramics, glassware, and metals; also called hallmarks.

**material culture:** All the objects with which people surround themselves; can range from the kitchen stove to the patterns produced by a marching band on a football field.

**materialism:** Theoretical perspectives where the reality of physical matter takes precedence over ideas and thought processes.

**mean ceramic dating formula:** A formula used for assigning the temporal association of a collection of glazed ceramics by the cumulative ranges of their manufacture; abbreviated as MCD.

**military site:** An archaeological site where military activities took place; campsites, battlefields, and fortifications.

**mitigation:** In archaeology, measures taken to minimize destruction of archaeological sites.

**model:** A theoretical construction of a set of phenomena, devised for better understanding; archaeological examples can be descriptive or explanatory.

**multipurpose site:** An archaeological locale where numerous activities took place.

**natural transformations:** Changes in the archaeological record resulting from natural phenomena that occur after the artifacts were deposited in the ground.

**neighborhood:** A group of households within a well-defined area.

**oral tradition:** Beliefs, customs, and ideas passed from generation to generation by word of mouth; can include genealogies.

**ordering:** In archaeology, the arranging of artifacts in logical categories; often chronological.

**organic materials:** Materials such as bone, wood, horn, or hide that were once living organisms.

**palynology:** Pollen analysis.

**physical anthropology:** The study of humanity's physical nature; includes fossil humans, genetics, primates, and blood groups; sometimes called biological anthropology.

**pontil scar:** The characteristic mark left on the base of glass vessels by breaking off the glass blower's rod.

**Post-Medieval Archaeology:** The name of historical archaeology in places, like Europe, where a long tradition of literacy exists; the post-medieval period immediately follows the medieval period, however defined.

**post-processual archaeology:** Theoretical approaches that are critical of processual archaeology and that emphasize social factors in human societies.

**POTS:** Potomac Typological System, a system for classifying ceramics used in the Chesapeake Bay area of Virginia and Maryland.

**potsherd:** A fragment of a fired-clay vessel.

**pottery:** Generally used by historical archaeologists to refer to fired-clay objects that are unglazed.

**prehistory:** The millennia of human history preceding written records; studied by prehistorians.

**primary context:** An undisturbed association, matrix, and provenience.

**primary source:** An original historical source, like a letter written by a direct observer.

**privy:** A toilet; usually a building outdoors.

**probate records:** A list of a dead individual's estate; an important source of historical information.

**process:** In archaeology, the cultural changes that occur over time as people find new ways of doing things and different ways of interacting with their environment.

**protohistory:** See **secondary prehistory**.

**provenience:** The position of an archaeological find in time and space, recorded three-dimensionally.

**radiocarbon dating:** An absolute dating method based on measuring the decay rate of the carbon isotope, carbon 14, to stable nitrogen; the resulting dates are calibrated with tree-ring chronologies from radiocarbon ages into dates in calendar years; seldom used in historical archaeology.

**region:** A geographically defined area in which cultural patterns are basically similar.

**relative chronology:** Time scale developed by the law of superposition or artifact ordering.

**remote sensing:** Reconnaissance and site survey methods using such devices as aerial photography to detect subsurface features and sites.

**research design:** A carefully formulated and systematic plan for executing archaeological research.

**resistivity survey:** The measurement of differences in electrical conductivity in soils; used in archaeology to detect buried features such as walls and ditches.

**Sanborn maps:** Maps produced by the D. A. Sanborn National Insurance Diagram Bureau (later, the Sanborn Map and Publishing Company) beginning in the mid-nineteenth century; show the location and construction type of buildings in cities and towns.

**secondary context:** An archaeological find that has been disturbed by subsequent human activity or natural phenomena.

**secondary prehistory:** The time when literate people came in contact with and wrote about nonliterate peoples; also called protohistory.

**secondary source:** A historical source that draws on primary sources.

**selective excavation:** Archaeological excavation of parts of a site using sampling methods or carefully placed trenches; does not uncover an entire site.

**settlement archaeology:** The investigation of residential, industrial, and other patterns of building design and placement.

**settlement pattern:** Distribution of human location on a landscape and within archaeological communities.

**significance:** In cultural resource management, the assessed importance of an archaeological site or historic property to provide important information about history, people, and events.

**site:** Any place where objects, features, or other finds manufactured or modified by human beings are found; can range from a house to a quarry.

**site plans:** Specially prepared maps for recording the horizontal provenience of artifacts, food remains, and features; usually keyed to topographic maps.

**site survey:** The collection of surface data and the evaluation of a site's archaeological significance.

**slip:** A fine, wet clay finish applied to the surface of a clay vessel before firing and decoration.

**social anthropology:** The British equivalent of cultural anthropology, with emphasis on sociological factors.

**society:** A group of people who share the same basic beliefs, attitudes, customs, and traditions and who regularly interact.

**sociocultural:** A term meant to show the close relationship between social and cultural factors in a culture.

**soil phosphate analysis:** Measuring phosphate levels in the soil to detect the presence of human settlement beneath the ground; does not require excavation.

**sonar:** Underwater detection using sound waves.

**stratification:** Two definitions. The formation by natural processes of geological layers. The hierarchical formation of social classes in human societies.

**stratigraphy:** Analysis of the superimposed layers in an archaeological site.

**stratum:** Two definitions. A single layer of soil. A social level in a hierarchical society.

**structuralism:** A perspective that attempts to discover the hidden themes in a culture.

**stylistic analysis:** Artifact analysis that concentrates not only on form and function, but on the decorative styles used by the makers; a much-used approach in ceramic analysis.

**subassemblage:** Association of artifacts denoting a particular form of activity practiced by a society or culture.

**subsurface testing:** Any small-scale archaeological excavation.

**surface survey:** The collection of archaeological finds from sites, with the objective of gathering representative samples of artifacts from the surface; establishes the types of activities at the site, locates major structures, and gathers information on the most densely occupied areas of the site that may be productive for excavation.

**synthesis:** The assemblage and analysis of data preparatory to interpretation.

**taxonomy:** An ordered set of operations that results in the subdividing of objects into ordered categories.

**technological analysis:** Study of technological methods used to make an artifact.

**temper:** Coarse material such as sand or shell added to fine pot clay to make it bond during firing.

**tempering:** A process for hardening iron blades, involving heating and rapid cooling; also, material added to potters' clay.

**test pit:** An excavation unit used to sample a site before large-scale excavation or to check surface surveys.

**text-aided archaeology:** Another name for historical archaeology.

**three-age system:** A subdivision of the prehistoric past developed for Old World prehistory in 1806; includes Stone Age, Bronze Age, and Iron Age.

**topographic maps:** Maps showing the features of a natural landscape; extensively used to plot archaeological sites.

**total excavation:** Complete investigation of an archaeological site; usually confined to small sites such as cellars, cabins, and privies.

**tradition:** A persistent technological or cultural pattern identified by characteristic artifact forms; the persistent forms can occur over a wide area.

**transformational processes:** Processes that transform an abandoned settlement into an archaeological site through the passage of time; can be initiated by natural phenomena or human activity.

**type:** In archaeology, a collection of artifacts created for comparison with other collections; may not coincide with the actual categories used by the original manufacturers.

**underwater archaeology:** Study of archaeological sites and shipwrecks beneath the surface of the water.

**unit:** In archaeology, an artificial grouping used to describe artifacts.

**use–wear analysis:** Microscopic analysis of artifacts to detect signs of wear through use; in historical archaeology, used in the analysis of cut marks on ceramico and bones.

**vertical excavation:** Investigation to establish a chronological sequence, normally covering a limited area.

**zooarchaeology:** The study of animal remains in archaeology that provides information about subsistence practices and past environments

# CREDITS

## Chapter 1

2      Gilbert Stuart, "Portrait of Thomas Jefferson", 1805–1807, oil on canvas, 48 3/8 in. × 39 3/4 in (122.9 cm. 101 cm). Bowdoin College Museum of Art, Brunswick, Maine, Bequest of the Honorable James Bowdoin III.

3      Charles E. Orser, Jr.

8      Charles E. Orser, Jr.

10      Charles E. Orser, Jr.

15      Page 140 (figure 5), *Before European Hegemony: The World System A. D. 1250–1350*, by Janet Abu-Lughod. © 1989, Oxford University Press.

17      *Some Years Travel into Africa and Asia*, by Thomas Herbert, 1677. Special Collections Library, University of Tennessee.

18      Charles E. Orser, Jr.

23      Commonwealth of Virginia

24      CORBIS BETTMANN

25      From *The Old Village and the Great House: An Archaeological and Historical Examination of Drax Hall Plantation, St. Ann's Bay, Jamaica*, by Douglas V. Armstrong, © 1990 by the Board of Trustees of the University of Illinois Press.

## Chapter 2

29      Kenneth Kidd, excavation of Ste Marie I (Toronto: University of Toronto Press, 1949).

32      Woolworth, Alan, and Wood, Raymond. *The Archaeology of a Small Trading Post, River Basin Survey Papers*, Bulletin 176, Wash. D.C. Government Printing Service, 1960.

34      Artist's reconstruction of the Black Lucy's Garden site from "Historical Archaeology at Black Lucy's Garden, Andover, Massachusetts: Ceramics from the Site of a Nineteenth Century Afro-American" by Vernon G. Baker. Papers of the Robert S. Peabody Foundation.

37      Map of Fort Necessity or the Battle of Great Meadows, July 3, 1754. From Jared Sparks, "The Writings of George Washington", 1837. Negative 1217-35. From a rare book in the Albert and Shirley Small Special Collections Library, The University of Virginia.

40      Mackinac State Historical Society

42      Drawn by Cary Carson and Benjamin Hellier. From *The Transformation of Virginia, 1740–1790*, by Rhys Isaac. Copyright © 1982 by the University of North Carolina Press. Published for the Omohundro Institute of Early American History and Culture. Used by permission.

45      Reproduced by permission from *The Archaeology of Slavery and Plantation Life* (Orlando: Academic Press, 1985). © 1985 by Elsevier Science Ltd. Image courtesy of Singleton Theresa.

46      Nevada Historical Society

48      Historic Annapolis Society

50      Photograph by Mary C. Beaudry, Department of Archaeology, Boston University.

52      Shackel Paul A. And Barbara J. Little, eds., *Historical Archaeology of the Chesapeake*. Smithsonian Institution Press, Washington. Figure 1.1, page 2.

## Chapter 3

58      The Granger Collection, New York.

61      Charles E. Orser, Jr.

63        Dozier, Edward, *The Pueblo Indians of North America* (New York: Holt, Rinehart and Winston, Inc., 1970).
65        The Granger Collection, New York.
71        From the Collections of Henry Ford Museum and Greenfield Village.
74        Ruins of Middleton place's Main House and North Flanker. From stereoptic by B.W. Kilburn before 1886. Courtesy Middleton Place Foundation.
75        Curtis Brown Ltd.
76        Courtesy of the Library of Congress.
78        Heite Consulting
81        National Park Service Midwest Archaeological Center
85        Reproduced by Hillingdon Borough Council. Reproduced in Jacqueline Pearce, *Post-Medieval Archaeology*, 334(2000), p. 176.

## Chapter 4

91        Special Collections, National Agricultural Library.
95        Image by courtesy of the Wedgwood Museum Trust Limited, Barlaston, Staffordshire, England.
97        The Coca-Cola Company
99        Godden, Geoffrey. *Encyclopedia of British Pottery and Porcelain Marks*, (New York: Bonanza, 1964).
99        Godden, Geoffrey. *Encyclopedia of British Pottery and Porcelain Marks*, (New York: Bonanza, 1964).
102       U. S. Patent Office
106       Philippe, Joseph: The drake site: Subsistence and Status at a Rural Illinois Farmstead (Normal IL, Midwestern Archaeological Research Center, Illinois State University, 1990).
108       From David Hurst Thomas, "Saints and Soldiers at Santa Catalina: Hispanic Designs for Colonial America" in *The Recovery of Meaning: Historical Archaeology in the Eastern United States*, edited by M. P. Leone and P. B. Potter, Jr., Washington, D.C., Small Institution Press.
113       Courtesy, Winterthur Museum.
114       Shackel, Paul: *Personal Discipline and Material Culture: An Archaeology of Annapolis MD, 1696–1870*, (Knoxville: University of Tennessee Press, 1993).

## Chapter 5

120       Courtesy of the Museum of London.
122       Colonial Williamsburg Foundation, Williamsburg, VA.
123       Edward C. Harris, *Principles of Archaeological Stratigraphy*, New York/London: Academic Press 1979, pg. 87.
125       Charles E. Orser, Jr.
126       Graphic by Adrian Praetzellis and Nelson Thompson. Praetzellis, Mary and Adrian: *For a Good Boy: Victorians on Sacramento's J. Street*, (Rohnert Park, CA: Anthropological Studies Center, Sonoma State University, 1990).
128       John D. Rockefeller Library
129       Curtis Brown Ltd.
130       Archaeological Society of Virginia Press
133       CORBIS-NY (Lowell Georgia)
136       Stanley Smith: Evolution and Horizon as revealed in ceramic analysis History Archaeology. Conference on Historic Site Archaeology Papers, 6, 1972: 71–116.
137       Kent, Susan. *Analyzing Activity Areas: An Ethnoarchaeological Study of the Use of Space*, (Albuquerque: UNM, 1984).
139       Atwater Kent Museum of Philadelphia

142      Robert B. Honeyman, Jr. Collection. Brancroft Library.
143      From Mary Praetzellis and Adrian Pratzellis, *The Mary Collins Assemblage: Mass Market-ing and the Archaeology of Sacramento Family*, (Rohnert Park, California: Sonoma State University, 1990, p. 143).
146      Charles E. Orser, Jr.

### Chapter 6

150      Guardian Newspapers Limited
151      Colonial Williamsburg Foundation, Williamsburg, VA.
156      Minute Man National Historic Park
157      Bibliotheque Service Hydrographic
158      Illinois Historic Preservation Agency
159      John G. Franzen's article "Northern Michigan Logging Camps: Material Culture and Worker Adaptation on the Industrial Frontier," *Historical Archaeology* 26 (2): 77, reprinted by permission of The Society for Historical Archaeology.
161      E. B. Banning, Archaeological Survey, New York, NY: Kluwer Academic/Plenum 2002, p. 91.
167      J. W. Weymouth, W. I. Woods, "Combined Magnetic & Chemical Surveys of Forts Kaskaskia & de Chartres #1, Illinois," from *Historical Archaeology*, vol. 18, number 2, 1984.

### Chapter 7

177      Panhandle-Plains Historical Museum
178      University of Florida, George Smathers Library
180      CORBIS-NY
182      Kansas State Historical Society
183      Kenneth Spencer Research Library, University of Kansas Libraries.
185      Courtesy of the Library of Congress.
186      Courtesy of the Library of Congress.

### Chapter 8

195      Grace Ziesing, The San Francisco Central Freeway Replacement project: Arch. Research Design and Treatment Plan, Rohnert Park, CA, Sonoma State University, 1998, p. 04.
198      Quarterly Bulletin of the Archaeological Society of Virginia 46(1) 1911.
203      Tennessee, Division of Archaeology
204      Tennessee, Division of Archaeology
206      Tennessee, Division of Archaeology
207      Tennessee, Division of Archaeology
208      Tennessee, Division of Archaeology
214      Mary Beaudry, Janet Long, et al. *A Vessel Typology for Early Chesapeake Ceramics: The Potomac Typological System*, (Historical Archaeology 17:1, 1983).

### Chapter 9

221      Virginia Department of Historic Resources
222      Virginia Department of Historic Resources
223      Reproduced by permission from South, Stanley: *Method and Theory in Historical Archaeology* (New York: Academic Press, 1977).
225      Courtesy of the South Carolina Institute of Archaeology and Anthropology, University of South Carolina, Columbia.
226      Courtesy of the South Carolina Institute of Archaeology and Anthropology, University of South Carolina, Columbia.

229          CORBIS-NY (Philippa Lewis; Ediface)

231          © National Maritime Museum Picture Library, London, England.

232          Hall Martin, Antonia and Amann Sharon: The South African Achaeological Society, Goodwin Series: Historical Archaeology in the Western Cape, volume 7, June, 1993, p. 49. fig. 16.

**Chapter 10**

241          Atwater, W. O., Food Consumption: Qualities, Costs, and Nutrients of Food Materials, Massachusetts Bureau of Statistics of Labor 17: 237–326, 1886

253          Wylie, Jerry, Fike, Richard: "Chinese Opium Smoking Techniques and Paraphernalia," reproduced in *Hidden Heritage: Historical Archaeology of the Overseas Chinese*, Priscilla Wegars, ed. (Amityville, NY: Baywood Publishing Company, 1993) fig. 55.

260          J. S. Otton. *Cannon's Point Plantation 1794–1860: Living Conditions and Status Patterns in the Old South*, (Orland: Academic Press, 1984).

**Chapter 11**

268          Algemeen Rijksarchief Afdeling Kaarten en Tekeningen VELH 619-77. Reproduced in C. R. DeCorse, *An Archaeology of Elmira*, Smithsonian Institution Press.

271          From "The Historical Archaeology of the Impact of Colonialism in Seventeenth-Century South Africa" by Carmel Schrire From Historical Archaeology in Global Perspective, edited by Lisa Falk, (Washington, DC: Smithsonian Institution Press). © 1991 by the Smithsonian Institution Press.

273          From "The Historical Archaeology of the Impact of Colonialism in Seventeenth-Century South Africa" by Carmel Schrire From Historical Archaeology in Global Perspective, edited by Lisa Falk, (Washington, DC: Smithsonian Institution Press). © 1991 by the Smithsonian Institution Press.

276          New York State Office of Parks, Recreation and Historic Preservation, Peebles Island

278          Courtesy of the New York State Museum, Albany. Photograph by Joseph McEvoy. Image of 6 wampum beads from the Key Corp site, Albany, NY; NYSM catalog nos. A-87.5.405.1, A-87.5.404.12, A-87.5.190.11 (3 beads), and A-87.5.260.8.

281          C. E. Orser, "Toward a Global Historical Archaeology", *Historical Archaeology* 28, 1 (1994) p. 17.

282          From: C. J. A. Jorg, *The Geldrmalsen: History and Porcelain*, Groningen: Kemper, 1986, p. 50.

**Chapter 12**

286          From: Jill-Karen Yakubik and Rosalinda Mendez, Beyond the Great House: Archaeology at Ashland-Belle Helene Plantation, Baton Rouge: Division of Archaeology, n.d., p. 20.

288          Courtesy of the Massachusetts Historical Commission, Office of Secretary of the Commonwealth, Paddy's Alley Site, Central Artery Project, Boston

291          From Mary Praetzellis and Adrian Pratzellis, *Historical Archaeology of an Overseas Chinese Community in Sacramento, California, Volume 1: Archaeological Excavations*, (Rohnert Park, California: Sonoma State University, 1997, p. 143).

296          Anthropological Studies Center Sonoma State University

**Chapter 13**

302          Colonial Williamsburg Foundation, Williamsburg, VA.

# INDEX